WRIGLEY FIELD

WRIGLEY FIELD

THE LONG LIFE AND CONTENTIOUS TIMES OF THE FRIENDLY CONFINES

STUART SHEA

THE UNIVERSITY OF CHICAGO PRESS

Chicago and London

STUART SHEA

is an editor and contributor to *The Baseball Encyclopedia: The Complete and Definitive Record of Major League Baseball*, *The Emerald Guide to Baseball*, *Who's Who in Baseball*, and SABR's *Baseball Research Journal* as well as a former baseball columnist for AOL and Total Sports. He is the author of numerous books, including the forthcoming *Calling the Game: Baseball Teams and Their Broadcasting*, and coauthor of *Big League Ballparks: The Complete Illustrated History*. A terrible hitter but decent fielder, he lives in Chicago, twenty-four blocks from Wrigley Field.

The University of Chicago Press, Chicago 60637
The University of Chicago Press, Ltd., London
© 2014 by The University of Chicago
All rights reserved. Published 2014.
Printed in the United States of America
23 22 21 20 19 18 17 16 15 14 1 2 3 4 5
ISBN-13: 978-0-226-13427-7 (paper)
ISBN-13: 978-0-226-13430-7 (e-book)
DOI: 10.7208/chicago/9780226134307.001.0001

Library of Congress Cataloging-in-Publication Data

Shea, Stuart, author.
Wrigley Field : the long life and contentious times of the
friendly confines / Stuart Shea.
pages ; cm
Includes bibliographical references and index.
ISBN 978-0-226-13427-7 (pbk. : alk. paper)—ISBN 978-0-226-13430-7
(e-book) 1. Wrigley Field (Chicago, Ill.)—History. 2. Baseball fields—
Illinois—Chicago—History. 3. Chicago Cubs (Baseball team)—History.
I. Title.
GV417.W75S54 2014
796.357'640977311—dc23
2013040565

♾ This paper meets the requirements of ANSI/NISO Z39.48–1992
(Permanence of Paper).

This book is for all baseball fans,

but most of all for those who have

waited their entire lives for the

Chicago Cubs to justify their faith

and win a championship.

CONTENTS

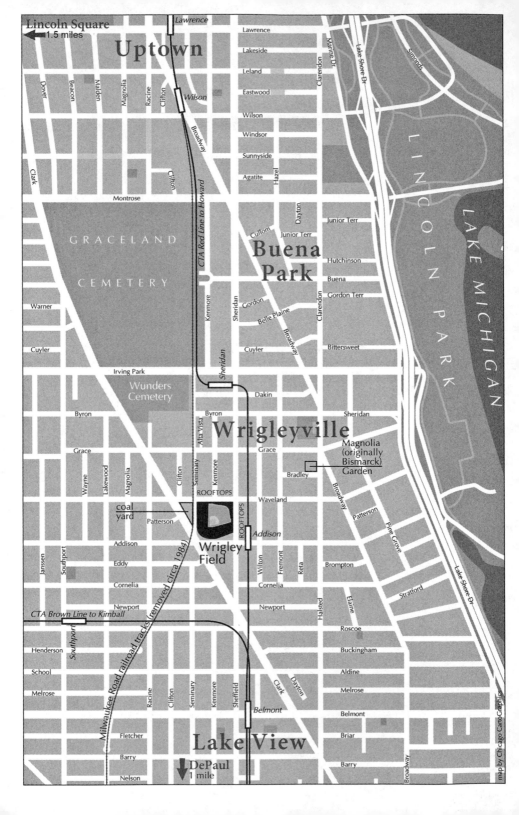

PREFACE

May 22, 1971, I saw my first baseball game.

On a cool Saturday morning, my dad loaded my two brothers and me into the purple Volkswagen Squareback and set sail for the ballyard. My brothers and I were beyond excited. Sports fans all, we couldn't wait to actually go to a game. I was eight. My middle brother, John, was seven; he never liked the Cubs and was happy to see the Dodgers—the team my dad grew up watching in New York City—battle the home team. Tom, my youngest brother, was a four-year-old Cubs fan.

Not only had we never been to a game before, we'd never even *seen* Wrigley Field since moving to Chicago less than two years before. We were, however, already familiar with the Cubs, who were telecast nearly every day on WGN. In first grade at Saint Jerome's School, I sprinted three blocks home every weekday afternoon the Cubs were at home, hoping to catch the last few innings. I would rush into the apartment of our landlords, the Sheffields (who graciously agreed to let us hang out after school), and sit on a big couch in front of a large color TV in the living room, watching the action and listening to Jack Brickhouse hold court from a small perch above Wrigley Field's lower deck.

Each Cubs win was a shot of adrenaline; each loss, an anchor painfully dragging down the soul. Even at age eight, I understood the emotional ramifications of every Cubs game. Later, victories and defeats would be replayed over the dinner table or ruminated about over a stack of baseball cards and magazines in the bedroom I shared with John. Some nights, my dad would use a cassette recorder to tape highlights off the radio after we'd gone to bed and replay them for us the next morning. At no time had we kids ever entertained the notion of actually *going* to a game; Wrigley Field, though just a few minutes from our third-floor walkup in Rogers Park, might as well have been a million miles away.

On that day in May, when we finally got to the corner of Clark and Addison, we walked into the park and gave our small stubs to the usher, getting half of them back. At that time, most lower-deck seats were general admission. I don't think I sat anywhere other than general admission, in fact, until I was at least eighteen. For me as for so many other young fans, walking up the concrete stairs into an actual baseball stadium was like stepping into a film—or a dream. Suddenly the scoreboard came into view, its olive paint contrasting with the sunny sky. Then, there were the enveloping double-deck stands, the net running up from behind the home plate wall to the upper deck, the foul poles, and, finally, the lush green of the outfield and the caramel-colored infield dirt.

The sights, sounds, and smells remain with me today. While fairly drab even by 1971 standards, Wrigley looked like a ballpark; I instantly knew that this is where a baseball fan *belonged*. Maybe adults would have picked up on its dinginess—by this time, it was nearly sixty years old—but to me this was paradise, someplace I wanted to spend a huge portion of my life.

The huge hand-operated scoreboard, with its line scores of games from all over the major leagues, was a wonder. And if you had a scorecard, you could tell who the umpires were, what teams were coming to town next, how much concessions cost, and—most important—the numbers and names of each player and coach on both teams. It was almost too much.

But even with all these sights, I couldn't fall too deeply into a trance; other fans were streaming in from behind. Everyone wanted to get to their seats and experience the sounds of batting practice—ball against glove, ball against bat, players shouting and joking among themselves, fans screaming for autographs, and, most prominently, Frank Pellico's organ playing, underscoring the thought that this was different; this was special.

Once we took our seats, which I believe were behind the Cubs dugout in the back part of the lower deck, we were also able to focus on how Wrigley Field *smelled*. Back then, most of what you could eat there was dispensed by vendors rather than purchased at food courts. Oscar Mayer hot dogs and Smokie Links, peanuts, and Borden's Frosty Malt were the top choices, with an occasional respite provided by Cracker Jack or a Ron Santo pizza, which tasted a bit like third base itself.

We strained to see our heroes at batting practice. Was that Kessinger? There's Billy, right? But soon it was over, and the grounds crew began touching up the field for the game. Wrigley's playing surface then was almost unbelievably ragtag. The infield dirt was thin in places, the grass untrimmed and at times asymmetrical, but I thought it was the most beautiful land I'd ever seen. Groundskeepers dragged big wheels onto the field, unspooling long hoses that sprayed water on the entire infield. I always worried that they'd get the dirt too soggy, but the crew seemed to know just when to stop.

When the foul lines had been laid, it was almost 1:15 PM. Pat Pieper, the Cubs' public address announcer, read the lineups, and we—with help from our dad—filled in the lineups for the home team and the visitors on our scorecards. The prospect of filling out the scorecard for each inning posed both an unbearable challenge and a joyful revelation for an attention-challenged youngster. That day at Wrigley began my love of keeping score. I picked up the lexicon from my dad fairly quickly, eventually developing my own and, as the years went on, adding some of it to a system devised by Project Scoresheet. Since that day in 1971, I'm sure I have scored a few thousand games in various systems, and each time I do, it's like going down a rabbit hole somewhere amid mathematics, art, science fiction, and history.

Most of our favorites played that day. Kessinger, Beckert, Williams, Hickman, and Santo batted first through fifth in the lineup, and Milt Pappas took the mound. There were absences, of course;

Ernie Banks's career was just about over, and Randy Hundley was on the shelf with the first of several catastrophic knee injuries that destroyed his career. Chris Cannizzaro, acquired just days before, flashed the signals from behind the plate.

The game went by in a whir. Down 2–1 in the fifth to Don Sutton, the Cubs exploded for four runs. Four straight hits, two of them bunt singles, tied the game and left the bases loaded. Glenn Beckert and Jim Hickman delivered sacrifice flies, and Santo singled in the fifth Chicago run. Pappas went all the way, scattering ten hits and picking up the 5–2 victory. We saw no home runs, and in fact just one Cub—Brock Davis—even picked up an extra-base hit, but who cared? The Cubs won, and we saw it!

Going to Wrigley Field that day changed my life. I have returned many dozens of times afterward, with friends and family, in April and October, in snow and rain and blazing sunshine, and I still revel in that feeling of discovery, that joy of the game, that peace and contentment I find at the greatest ballpark in the world.

So thanks, Dad, for taking my brothers and me to the ballgame. And thanks, Cubs, for all the memories.

different park and a different world around it. Wrigley Field has seen an endlessly passing parade of people, events, changes, comedies, and tragedies.

This most perfect of ballparks has a history as colorful and dramatic as that of any other sports arena in this country, including Yankee Stadium, Churchill Downs, Fenway Park, the Rose Bowl, Ebbets Field, or the Boston Garden. Wrigley Field has seen a lot of sports and various other events, but mostly baseball, good and bad, glorious and embarrassing. Come watch the show.

anything, except for a chewing gum company. Until 1916, Major League Baseball was never played north of downtown in Chicago, and the beloved "North Siders" actually played on the near West Side.

There are plenty of tales to tell about the evolution of the seemingly ageless ballpark, the teams that have inhabited it, and the neighborhood that has supported, tolerated, profited from, complained about, and—most of all—grown up with it. A century of ball at Wrigley Field has given birth to thick and murky legends that overrun the truth. Are the following statements truth or urban legend?

- Wrigley Field was built for the Cubs.
- Wrigley Field's walls never had advertising until the late 2000s.
- Wrigley Field has always been nothing but an open-air bar.
- William Wrigley invented Ladies Day in the 1920s.
- Philip K. Wrigley never would have permitted lights in his park.
- P. K. Wrigley never came to see the Cubs play.
- P. K. Wrigley hated artificial turf.
- Wrigley Field never hosted a night game until 1988.
- Fans have always sat on the rooftops across from Wrigley Field.
- Bill Veeck planted the ivy at Wrigley Field overnight.
- Wrigley Field has long stood alone against the grim forces of modern baseball, resisting money-driven changes.

Myths, every one of them, demonstrably wrong. And, in each case, the myth masks a far more interesting reality.

This book lays bare the myths. It outlines how the ballpark was built, why it was constructed at Clark and Addison, and who built it. More broadly, it shows what the park was like and how it was constantly changing, inside and out, as the park and the neighborhood have influenced each other over the decades. Every Opening Day saw a slightly—and sometimes not so slightly—

INTRODUCTION
MYTHS IN CONCRETE

It's a hazy, hot summer Saturday afternoon. The Chicago Cubs have just finished off an opponent—or, more likely, been finished off by one. As the sun's beams slant down Addison Street, fans spill out of the venerable ballpark on the city's North Side. Those sticking around Wrigleyville have plenty of options: bars, restaurants, theater, shopping.

Some fans simply head home. Others board a crowded Chicago Transit Authority elevated train a block away to head north toward Evanston or south toward downtown. Some take the Clark Street bus north or south. Others hop the Addison bus going west. Still others head to their cars, docked all around the park, both legally and illegally, for $30 here and $40 there, in a yard, in a lot, or at a metered space.

Many fans, especially kids from schools or Chicago Park District programs, congregate outside the left field wall on Waveland Avenue, playing in groups or looking cool just standing there, waiting to board yellow buses. Other groups of fans wait near the Cubs' parking lot on Waveland, carrying pictures, programs, baseballs, and baseball cards, hoping to snare autographs. Others hang around the gate near the right field corner, near Addison and Sheffield, hoping to get a signature and a word from a visiting player heading for the team bus.

It's an almost perfect scene—the local baseball park serving as a meeting place for fans of all stripes, for locals and visitors from far-flung towns. But Lake View has only in the past three decades become a swinging area and tourist haven, and the area around the park has been called "Wrigleyville" only since the 1970s. One hundred years ago, there were no ballpark, no nightlife, no trains or buses, no ball club, and no fans. No Wrigleyville. No Wrigley

A NEW PLACE, A NEW PARK

LAKE VIEW

Before there was Wrigleyville, there was Lake View.

When Joseph Sheffield, founder of the Chicago, Rock Island, and Pacific Railroad, founded Lake View in 1837, he envisioned it as a quiet community removed from the city in which he made much of his money. He was, essentially, a proto-suburbanite who didn't want to live near his customers and could afford not to.

The town of Lake View sat north of the city of Chicago, which was far smaller in area and population than it is now. It stretched from Fullerton Avenue (twenty-four blocks north of downtown Chicago) up to Devon Avenue (sixty-four blocks north) and from Lake Michigan to what is now Western Avenue, 2400 West.

The area had been home to mostly Illinois and Pottawatomie Indians, although Sac, Algonquin, Fox, and Kickapoo also were resident. The first white resident of Lake View was Conrad Sulzer, who purchased a hundred acres of land in 1837. The Lake View Town Hall and Courthouse, built at Addison and Halsted Streets in 1872, would be converted into the Town Hall police station in 1907; this site has figured into Wrigley lore a number of times in the years following its conversion. In the 1850s, Wunder's and Graceland cemeteries opened along Clark Street several blocks north of where Wrigley Field now stands. At the time, a trip to Lake View from downtown Chicago took half a day by wagon, and by 1853 the Lake View House hotel and several restaurants had opened to serve cemetery visitors and others.

Following the Civil War, some of Chicago's richest citizens began following Joseph Sheffield's lead and built homes in the area. Lake View grew after the great 1871 fire, as dispossessed citizens headed north. Enough families came to the area to warrant construction, in 1874, of Lake View High School, the first township high school in the state, at Irving Park Road and Ashland Avenue.

Lake View became a freewheeling, growing, exciting place where families, businessmen, fun seekers, and rich folks building summer homes on the lake gathered cheek by jowl. Prime shopping areas developed at Lincoln and Belmont Avenues as well as at Clark Street and Diversey Avenue, and these intersections remain among the busiest in the city.

And the new area's denizens didn't shy from a drink. One important gathering spot was the Bismarck Gardens at Halsted and Grace Streets. According to nineteenth-century resident Edward Walsh, John Berringer ("Beer John") opened a beer garden at Clark and Diversey in the 1860s. Foremost among the imbibers were the Germans settling in the neighborhood, although other ethnic groups liked their alcohol as well. Although it has decreased somewhat, a German presence survives in the businesses of Lake View and nearby Lincoln Square.

THE LEARNING ANNEX

During the 1880s, Chicago sought to annex the town. "It is a locality peculiarly fitted for the homes of the working classes. Cable cars and steam roads, and fresh clean property at low prices invite such people here," said David Goodwillie, an advocate for the annexation. Polish Catholics and others of that faith had begun to settle there, as had Belgians.

Annexation increases a city's population and, therefore, its tax base. With more revenue, a city can provide more extensive services for its citizens, such as sewers—something Lake View citizens demanded in the wake of a cholera epidemic in the 1880s. (Lake View's own revenue came from sources such as tollgates on several street corners, including Clark at Waveland Avenue, where pedestrians and drivers of horse carriages had to pay to get through.) By 1900, Chicago was the second-largest city in the country in population and the largest in area, due in no small part to aggressive annexation of surrounding communities.

Members of the Lake View government—who knew that their power would disappear if Chicago swallowed their town—didn't submit to the 1889 annexation without a fight. Lake View mayor William Boldenweck got permission from his board of advisers to seize $3,200 of the town's assets to legally fight the annexation order. And yet, "about the only people who were against annexation were public officials," said Richard C. Bjorklund, onetime president of the Ravenswood–Lake View Historical Association. Eventually, Judge John Peter Altgeld (later governor of Illinois) ruled that the City of Chicago had the right to take over the community.

GETTING AROUND

By 1913, Lake View was less remote than it had been, as new forms of public transportation were by then serving the North Side of the city. There had, earlier, been cable cars to the area, but those had stopped running in 1906, replaced by much faster streetcars. In addition, commuter train lines, which had run downtown and on the South and West Sides since 1893, were joined by elevated tracks built all the way up the North Side close to Lake Michigan. By 1908, these tracks reached Evanston, a prosperous northern lakefront suburb. What would later become the Chicago Transit Authority built a series of train lines, some aboveground, some beneath, and some down alleyways.

In the late 1800s and early 1900s, the power of the city lay on the South Side, and some North Siders felt like second-class citizens. An article in the *Chicago Daily Tribune* on December 1, 1913, stated: "Complaints had been made to the *Tribune* that while the south side trains are making better time than before through routing, the Northwestern [service toward Evanston] service is slower. This was denied by Mr. [Bratten] Budd [of the Chicago Elevated Railways system], who insisted the same running time from terminus to loop of each line is being made today, although more trains are run." The North Side, though, was beginning to feel its oats. People were moving north to build homes on inexpensive land, and companies were constructing factories on this unplowed and undeveloped real estate. In addition, the lakeside area around Wilson Avenue, the Uptown neighborhood, had become a hopping entertainment district.

Chicago historians Harold Mayer and Richard Wade note that "the preeminence of the South Side began to diminish after the [1893 World's] Fair. The supremacy of that area had stemmed largely from the excellence of its transit facilities. But the completion of elevated transit lines into other sections of the city, coupled with the electrification and expansion of street railways, substantially reduced this advantage in the decades after 1893. The North and West sides now enjoyed the stimulus of good connections with downtown, and both witnessed spectacular growth."

PEACEFUL CONTEMPLATION

And yet, Lake View remained in many ways a quiet retreat. One hundred and thirty years ago, the land on which Wrigley Field now sits hosted a seminary.

William Alfred Passavant (1821–94) was among the most famous and successful American Lutheran missionaries. Born in Zelienople, Pennsylvania, Passavant was interested in the spiritual from a very young age. He directed his efforts toward public service and spent much of his life founding benevolent institutions, including the Pittsburgh Infirmary, the first Protestant hospital in the country. In 1865, he founded Passavant Hospital of Chicago, which was destroyed six years later in the Great Fire. Passavant Hospital reopened in 1884 and immediately became one of the city's top hospitals due to its excellent staff and facilities. Eventually, it merged with Wesley Hospital and became

Northwestern Memorial, still as one of the area's premier health centers.

Passavant also edited religious journals and established orphanages. When he inherited a parcel of land in Lake View, he envisioned the bucolic, tree-lined area as a seminary for young men to study and contemplate. Passavant began to develop the grounds in 1868, although the Theological Seminary of the Evangelical Lutheran Church did not open until 1891. Four seminary buildings occupied the site: a dormitory, two homes for professors, and a home for the seminary president. These buildings all stood on the outer perimeter of the property, two on Waveland Avenue, one on Addison Street, and one on Sheffield Avenue.

Even in the 1890s, however, the land was not exactly quiet. The Peter Connors coal yard stood north of Addison on Clark Street, separated from the seminary only by tracks for the Chicago/Evanston Rail Road, which ran up what is now Seminary Avenue. The railroad, used both for freight and commuter travel, crossed Clark Street near Addison. The railway transported gravel, coal, and sand to local builders, while ice and milk were brought in for local residents. Streetcars and elevated trains raised the noise level.

Within only a few years after the seminary opened, everyone concerned decided that the area had become too busy for contemplative study. As noted at the time by Marjory R. Wing, representing the school, students were constantly bothered by "smoke, dust, grime, soot, dirt, [and] foul gases; railroading by night and day; whistles, ding-donging of bells late and early and in between times, and the ceaselessness of undesirable traffic incidental thereto that is growing more unbearable every week." The 1908 opening of the Ravenswood elevated line only increased the number of people and trains in the area.

The next year, the Lutheran church finally got an opportunity to address the problem. Charles Havenor of Milwaukee, a baseball man, offered to buy the land, and the church accepted in a heartbeat. The July 8, 1909, issue of *Leslie's Weekly* gives the details.

Charles S. Havenor, of the Milwaukee Baseball Club of the American Association, has bought for $175,000 the eight-acre tract in North Clark Street, Chicago. This property is considered the best vacant location in Chicago for a baseball park, and the purchase on its face appears to portend the entrance of an American Association club into that city, with a big baseball war as the result. It has been known that the American Association at various times in the last few years has cast covetous eyes on Chicago territory, and at one time last fall plans were all set for an invasion, but later abandoned. It looks as if the sports pages will be full of "baseball war" talk again this winter as in the past.

The seminary moved to west suburban Maywood, though it returned to Chicago (this time on the South Side) in 1967. Though the seminary moved, many Lutherans stayed in Lake View, as evidenced by the Holy Trinity Lutheran Church, which moved to the area in 1914 and stands just two blocks west of Wrigley Field.

Some sources erroneously report that the land went directly from the church to the Chicago Cubs. Others opine that the land wasn't sold to the Cubs but to the Federal League's Chicago club, which first inhabited the park. In fact, however, a three-year period passed between when the Lutheran Church sold the land and when a man named Charley Weeghman purchased it.

What happened between 1910 and 1913? Who was Charley Weeghman? Who was Charles Havenor? Who owned the land, and why did they want it? Here is where the story of Lake View and baseball really begins.

THE FREE MINORS AND CHICAGO

In 1909, baseball's biggest leagues were the "majors," the American League (AL) and National League (NL), each of which had ten clubs. Below them on the food chain were the so-called minor leagues, associations of independently owned clubs that could

sell their players to the major leagues if they wished but were not required to. The "organized" major and minor leagues had territorial agreements but no direct links.

The American Association (AA), at the time baseball's top minor league, represented eight Midwestern cities: Columbus, Indianapolis, Kansas City, Louisville, Milwaukee, Minneapolis, Saint Paul, and Toledo. The AA was no scrub league; the Milwaukee, Minneapolis, and Indianapolis teams all drew more fans in 1909 than the American League's Washington Senators or the National League's Boston Rustlers. Unlike today, minor league teams were not affiliated with big league organizations, so there was more direct competition among them.

Chicago already had American League and National League teams, but the AA's more ambitious owners thought that the time was right to expand and that the Windy City could support three professional clubs. Chicago in 1910 was the second-largest city in the country, having grown nearly 30 percent in the previous decade. A few enterprising businessmen began exploring. The White Sox owned the South Side, playing at Thirty-Ninth and Wentworth while readying a new park at Thirty-fifth and Shields. The Cubs played at the West Side Grounds, located at Polk and Wolcott Streets on the near Southwest. The burgeoning North Side—with Lake View's single-family homes and taste for beer and song, Uptown's swinging night life, and a new public transportation system—seemed a potentially excellent location.

On January 23, 1914, the *Tribune*'s Harvey Woodruff related the history of the Clark and Addison site: "The property which figured in the lease was bought several years ago from a Lutheran Evangelical college by the late Charles Havenor of Milwaukee, the Cantillons, and [Edmund] Archibault, at a time when the American Association was considering placing a third club in Chicago." Archambault was a relative by marriage of the Cantillons, while Charles Havenor's first wife, Agnes, owned the AA's Milwaukee Brewers. The Havenors and the Cantillons, Joe and Mike—owners of the rival Minneapolis Millers—worked together to scope out the location and hoped to sell the land to a new franchise. But in order to break into Chicago, the league was required to get approval from 60 percent of the teams in the leagues already present in the market, and the Cubs and Sox worked in concert, lobbying the other clubs to block the AA's efforts. Frustrated, Havenor gradually divested himself of his share of the land, selling out to Archambault and the Cantillon brothers before passing away in April 1912. But this was only the beginning of the story that led to the creation of Wrigley Field.

BIRTH OF THE FEDS

The American Association was not the only rival of the major leagues. Between 1910 and 1912, several entrepreneurs founded new associations. These "outlaw" leagues, which did not fall under the control of organized baseball, often came and went in the blink of an eye.

One of these, the United States League, had in 1912 a Chicago franchise, the Green Sox. The team played at Gunther Park at Clark Street and Leland Avenue, eleven blocks north of where Wrigley Field is now located. Between 1906 and 1913, local clubs, under the unswerving guidance of well-known semipro gadfly Billy Niesen (also involved in the United States League), also played at Gunther Park, a nice-looking if small field with a well-built grandstand. Burt Keeley, a native of Wilmington, Illinois, who had pitched for the Washington Senators in 1908 and 1909, signed on as skipper of the Green Sox (which, within a few weeks, were being called the "Uncle Sams" in the local papers). Despite high hopes, some former major-league players, and decent media coverage, overall attendance was low and the league disbanded on June 24, 1912. The United States League's Chicago franchise ended its brief tenure with a 17–15 record. Gunther Park, now known as Chase Park, has several baseball diamonds, but no marker indicates that a professional baseball team ever played there. Despite their heavy losses, however, United States League

owners' dreams died hard. Several of them, led by John T. Powers, tried again in 1913 with another "outlaw" organization they initially named the Columbian League before settling on the Federal League. They opened for business in six cities, including Cleveland, Indianapolis, Pittsburgh, Saint Louis, Chicago, and Covington, Kentucky, though this last team quickly relocated to Kansas City. The Chifeds, as the Chicago team was named (short for the Chicago Federals), played their 1913 games at the athletic fields of DePaul University, twelve blocks south of Addison street. With Keeley again at the helm, the Chifeds finished fourth in the six-club loop at 57–62. Though attendance records for the 1913 Feds are not available, the league did survive.

(A reorganized United States League also debuted in 1913, this time with eight East Coast clubs: Baltimore, Brooklyn, Lynchburg, Newark, New York, Philadelphia, Reading, and Washington. Just three days later, once again amid financial ruin, with players striking after not having been paid guaranteed Opening Day salaries of $75 per game, the league capitulated. The May 31, 1913, *Sporting Life* noted its passing in an article headlined "WORST FAILURE in the History of Base Ball Now Recorded," deriding the league as "the quickest and most ridiculous failure in the long history of base ball, a history teeming with ill-advised club and league ventures and with failures of small and great degree.")

During the 1913 season, Powers—who harbored dreams of elevating the quality of play in the Federal League to that of the American Association, which was about at what we would today call the double-A level—was pushed out of both club ownership and the league presidency after he attempted a markedly small-time stunt. He tried to get a Pittsburgh-Chicago game transferred from DePaul's field to his hometown of Sheffield, Illinois, about 130 miles west-southwest of Chicago, but the players refused to travel. The other owners soon saw to it that Powers was eased out of his command. *Sporting Life* reported on August 30, 1913, that

Powers "had much to do with the launching of the new league, but with the infusion of new life he was not the man to carry it along."

Tall, wealthy Chicago coal baron James Gilmore, one of two new principals of the Chicago franchise, was eager for the opportunity that Powers's departure presented. An article titled "The Genius of the Federal League," in the February 7, 1914, edition of *Literary Digest*, noted that "the real growth of the Federal League began last July, when James A. Gilmore assumed charge. . . . The Chicago team was in financial difficulties. The club owners in desperation called on their friend, Jimmy Gilmore, president of a Chicago iron company, and who already had a big reputation as an organizer, for advice. . . . Gilmore startled his callers by saying he would take charge of their club and league. . . . He first mapped out a campaign against organized ball, the supreme body in baseball."

That March 14, a writer using the pseudonym Igoe wrote in the *Chicago Evening Post*: "One glance at James A. Gilmore, big chief of the Federal League, and you are immediately stuck with the idea that he is quite a busy cup of tea . . . three minutes' talk with him made the old dyed-in-the-wool, blown-in-the-bottle baseball scribes rub their eyes and wonder how a yelping baseball public ever got along without a third big league."

Besotted with the idea of expanding the league and competing with the major leagues, Gilmore transferred the Federal League into ritzy new offices at Chicago's Old Colony Building. Powers saw this ambition as folly, telling the *Sporting News* on October 13, 1913, "I can't see where the Federal League has a chance as constituted at present. . . . They can't hope to buck the major leagues and get away with it. . . . They have a hopeless cause, as I see it, and I don't think they will start next season."

THE GILMORE GUY

Gilmore was more than ready for the challenge. Born in 1876, he grew up playing sandlot ball on the near southwest side of

Chicago. While fighting in the war against Spain, he took ill and spent thirteen months recovering. He achieved financial success in his thirties, rising from coal salesman to iron mogul in just two years. What did Gilmore see in the Federal League? A chance to exercise his ambition and achieve power, certainly, and maybe to increase his fortune. The Chicago *Inter-Ocean* reported on March 25, 1914, that the president's salary for the season would be $15,000, which today would be around $350,000.

The colorful Gilmore was also well known around Chicago as a billiards player. At some point in the early 1910s, he came to know Charles Weeghman, a local restaurateur who had turned a failed pool hall into a growing concern. The two became friends.

Despite Gilmore's verve and ambition, some weren't sure the Feds would be ready to start play in 1914. George "White Wings" Tebeau, a former outfielder who by 1913 was president of Kansas City's American Association club, noted in the November 13 *Sporting News*, "The [Federal League] clubs lost something like $15,000 each during the 1913 season and I suppose for this reason people are chary about investing in the league. . . . If I were to offer $100,000 for the league—lock, stock, and barrel—my money would be gobbled up in an instant."

But Gilmore, who had not only big plans but ways to finance them as well, brought new money into the league. The wealthy, somewhat raffish figures he enticed into investing fancied the dough to be made in baseball and enjoyed the idea of battling with established club owners. Not all the prospective owners were legitimate; some were cast aside when their talk proved thicker than their wallets. The Federal League did expand to eight clubs for 1914, though, with new ownership running most of the franchises.

The Federal League owners certainly were ambitious. Saint Louis and Chicago were already served by two major league franchises, while the Pittsburgh and Brooklyn teams would compete with National League clubs. The other four Federal League cities—Indianapolis, Baltimore, Buffalo, and Kansas City—already

had successful minor league franchises, three from the International League and one from the American Association. Unlike the American Association, however, the Federal League did not concern itself with securing approval from organized baseball, major or minor, before moving into these markets. These, after all, were hard-core capitalists at work.

On December 1, 1913, the *Tribune* printed a rumor that the Chifeds would move to Milwaukee for 1914. Edward C. Racey, team treasurer and president of the Illinois Athletic Club, denied this scurrilous hearsay. But considering the tall tales Gilmore and his Federal League associates were spreading to throw organized baseball and the press off their trail, they may well have planted this rumor themselves. The league's Brooklyn franchise, for instance, was said to be headed toward Toronto until the day the agreement was put in place to house them in Flatbush; Gilmore's spirited disinformation campaign kept the press in the dark.

"President Gilmore threw local reporters clear off the trail," the February 7, 1914, *Literary Digest* noted, "and he introduced a very apt tongue for telling fibs about his Toronto club." He had gone so far as to tell the press that Bernard Hepburn, a member of the Canadian parliament, would run that club. To convincingly carry off the deception, Gilmore almost certainly led Hepburn and his Toronto cohorts to believe the franchise was indeed theirs.

The Feds' campaign of deceit infuriated the *Sporting News*, the self-proclaimed "Bible of Baseball" and the virtual house organ for organized baseball. On April 2, 1914, the paper railed: "The Federals have played the hypocrite in their declarations that they were not seeking players and would not sign players already under contract. . . . *The Sporting News* is still honestly of the opinion that there is no demand for the Federal League in the territory it expects to occupy." *Of course* the Feds weren't always telling the truth; it was, after all, an outlaw league. The paper seemed not to notice, however, when the American and National leagues prevaricated about their own internal matters. The *Sporting News*'s

disdain for the Federal League was also apparent in its issue of January 8, 1914, when it ran an atypically unattributed story claiming that Gilmore was about to be deposed from the league presidency. No Chicago paper bothered to comment on the rumor, and the story quickly shriveled up and blew away.

The major challenge of the Federal League came not from its locational strategy but from its disregard of the reserve clause common to all major-league player contracts of the time. Under the clause, a player was bound to his team in perpetuity at the whim of the club—a proposition that was not invalidated till more than sixty years later. Gilmore and his lawyers believed that the reserve clause was invalid, and his aggressive plans included stealing the best established players in the American and National leagues by brazenly offering them far better deals than they could get from their current clubs. Noted the correspondent for *Literary Digest* on February 7, 1914, "I talked with a player who had been approached, and the proposition put up to him, he says, was that half of the three years' salary was to be paid in advance in cash and the rest was to be put in escrow. . . . To do that, the promoters of the Federal League, necessarily, must have a standing in the banks." While this strategy seems to have garnered the league some players, the advances eventually put the Feds in tough financial straits. Meanwhile, again showing his gift for fibbing, Gilmore stated to John Seys of the *Chicago Daily News* on the December 22, 1913, issue, presumably with a straight face, "The players signed for 1914 have all made application upon their initiative, without the slightest solicitation from any club in the new league."

Gilmore was more forthright in an interview with "Igoe" in the March 14 *Post*:

I want to say that *no* man should respect that [reserve] clause. I don't think it is equitable to the ball player, because it is a clause that binds him practically for life without stipulating any salary after the first year. Personally, I think baseball players, with regard in their box-office worth, are the most miserably paid performers in the world . . . we intend that the men who bring fame to our fold shall be paid accordingly. We realize before we start that it is up to the players whether we shall draw the "gates" or not. When we see that it is one player or a set of players, we won't crawl behind the safe and tighten the strings on the "dough bag," as the boys affectionately term it, but rather will we share with them.

Brooklyn team owner Robert Ward also iterated in late March that Fed players would share in the team's profits. "The plan is unique in baseball annals," reported the *Post*, "and seems to indicate that the Brooklyn Feds have a wealth of financial backing."

Gilmore and Ward's strategy of positive player/club relations was certainly slanted toward tempting talent from other clubs. The *New York Times* noted on April 6, 1914, that "President Ward of the Brooklyn Club stated yesterday that he believed his scheme of profit sharing with the ball players would be the means of attracting many players to his team."

But there was more to the establishment of the Federal League than financial incentive alone. One of the most uproarious chapters in Chicago sports history was about to begin. And the Feds got a critical boost from a rival.

MURPHY'S LAW

Chicago Cubs owner Charles W. Murphy was, by all accounts, an odd duck with a big mouth. Along with Charles Taft (half-brother of future president William Howard Taft), Murphy bought the franchise prior to the 1906 season. He annoyed Cubs fans, his players, other owners, and the press with his constant name calling, chest thumping, rule breaking, bullying, and self-promotion.

To give an idea of just how unpopular Murphy was, consider the *Chicago American*'s sports column, Dav's Day Dreams, from February 13, 1914, which observed, "Charles Webb Murphy's latest interview, written by himself, will be given to the public next week. Charles Webb, who has become his own best little interviewer, has chosen for his subject, 'Popularizing Baseball,' a subject concerning which he knows little but will say much."

Aided by the benign neglect of the National League office, which Murphy had cowed with bluster and threats, Murphy and Taft also served as "background owners" of the Philadelphia Phillies, with Horace Fogel putting his name on the front door to serve as a cover for the carpetbaggers. During the 1912 campaign, Fogel did Murphy's bidding, once complaining about umpiring in order to nettle the league's leadership, and once accusing the league of dirty dealing. In the subsequent fallout that November, Fogel—not Murphy, the man behind it all—was bounced from the league for his muckraking, which was proving a public relations disaster. Fogel became seen as so questionable and impecunious a character that even the Federal League would not consider him as an owner.

The *Chicago Post* had aided Murphy in his earlier publicity campaigns, but it now turned against the Cubs owner. It became a booster of the Feds, serving almost as a press liaison for the fledgling league. This was not unusual for the 1910s, just as it not unusual today for newspapers to ally themselves with a corporation or sports franchise for political purposes. According to W. S. Forman's piece in the February 28, 1914, *Chicago Evening Post*, major league owners were almost entirely to blame for the growth of the Feds. Their tolerance of such a cad as Murphy, and their machinations allowing him to stay in the game, were to Forman the reasons that a rival league could steal so much attention. Forman went on to say that such shenanigans undermined the public's confidence in the majors and allowed the Feds to grab the public's imagination: "The Federal League is founded on the stupidity shown by the board of directors of the National league when they broke faith with the fans in November of 1912."

What kind of guy was Murphy? In 1912, he fired Cubs manager Frank Chance *during a game* as the cross-town White Sox were thrashing his club in the annual postseason city series. Paying his players poorly, failing to keep West Side Grounds in good shape, and deriding his team to whoever would listen, Murphy tore apart the club before the 1913 season by ridding himself of players Joe Tinker, Ed Reulbach, and Mordecai Brown. He dumped new manager Johnny Evers the next season after another poor showing in the postseason Cubs-Sox series. Peter Golenbock notes in *Wrigleyville* that "Murphy always viewed the intercity series with the White Sox as having the importance of the World Series. To the players, the series was merely an exhibition." Murphy's impulsive behavior began to draw fire from other owners, and the last straw was his cavalier mistreatment of Tinker the previous year.

TINKER, TAILOR . . .

Star shortstop Joe Tinker was an early resister of the reserve clause, frequently demanding more money and better terms from his employers than they were inclined to grant. Traded by Cincinnati to Brooklyn after the 1913 season, Tinker went for broke, refusing to report to Brooklyn. Desiring a salary of more than $10,000 (rather than the $7,000 the Dodgers wanted to pay), he lashed out. As reported by John Seys in the December 22, 1913, *Daily News*, Tinker said, "I will not sign unless my demands are met. [Dodgers president Charles] Ebbets can trade me to some other club which will give me what I want, or he can keep me out of organized ball. My mind is made up, the same as Ebbets,' regarding salary."

Tinker's threat to leave organized baseball resonated with the Federal League's attempts to lure established players with better money. Knowing that the Chicago Federal club needed and wanted a marquee player with hometown connections, Tinker let it be known that he could be had for a price, perhaps $40,000. Not that Charlie Murphy took the threat seriously. Showing both remarkable spleen and bad judgment, he railed to Oscar Reichow in the December 24, 1913, *Daily News*: "This Federal League is a joke from start to finish. . . . I do not think Tinker will sign with the Federal League. All this talk of offering him $40,000 is nothing but a bluff. . . . There is no one in the league who knows anything about baseball. Besides, they have no money and it takes money to be in the game to-day."

On December 27, 1913, the star shortstop became the first big name to sign with the Federal League, garnering $36,000 as player/manager for the Chifeds in a three-year deal with at least $10,000 advanced up front. The *Literary Digest* wrote on February 7, "I am reliably informed that Tinker received $15,000 in cash before he put his name to a contract."

The same day that Tinker signed, Charles Weeghman took over the presidency of the Chicago Federal League club.

The arrogance of organized baseball, personified by Charlie Murphy, had come back to bite it. Murphy's big mouth and contract dumping helped get the Federal League's foot in the door. And it forced the AL and NL to raise salaries to keep their biggest stars, such as Ty Cobb and Walter Johnson, from defecting.

The *Post* noted on April 13, 1914, that "the real turning point in the fortunes of the Federals was the signing of Joe Tinker . . . as a result of [Charles Ebbets's] decision to refuse Joe a few hundred dollars more a season, the Feds grabbed him and made baseball a war which has cost the American and National leagues more than half a million dollars. Baseball salaries have been boosted to unheard-of levels as a result of the Fed invasion."

Star second baseman Johnny Evers considered an astounding offer from the Feds of $40,000 for three seasons. To keep him in the fold, the NL itself paid him $25,000 not to defect. It was money well spent; in the 1914 season, Evers led the "Miracle" Boston Braves to a stunning NL pennant and an even more amazing World Series win over Connie Mack's Philadelphia A's.

The Feds also wanted Walter Johnson. Sportswriter Bill Veeck Sr., working under the pen name of Bill Bailey, wrote in the April 3, 1914, *American*, "The Federal Leaguers figure that Walter Johnson, the Washington twirler, is the most valuable man in organized baseball." He asked Joe Tinker what he would have paid Johnson to pitch for the Chifeds. "'I think Mr. Weeghman would have told him to insert his own figures in the contract,' answered Tinker." Persisting for a figure, Veeck was told, "Well, I think Mr. Weeghman would have given him between $25,000 and $30,000 a year." That wrangling would wait another season.

Just six weeks later, the National League forced Charlie Murphy out from his perch as owner of the Cubs, his shares transferred to Charles Taft. Ring Lardner waxed poetic for the departed Murphy in the *Tribune* on February 24, 1914:

> Charlie, my darling, your sweet voice is hushed,
> And pale is the cheek that excitement once flushed.
> And silent the tongue that once uttered so much,
> The tongue that so frequently got you in Dutch.
> I'll miss you down here at the desk where I write,
> For you were the column conductor's delight;
> I'm wondering now wotinell I will do
> When I can no longer spring stuff about you.

In another short poem published the same day, "A reporter" penned,

> Fare thee well! And if forever,
> then forever, FARE THEE WELL!
> In my hopelessness, I never
> Dreamed that they could make thee sell.
> Would the boss would let me write it,
> All I really think of thee;
> Did I 'gainst his will indite it,
> He would tie a can to me.

CHARLEY WEEGHMAN

If one man could represent the big dreams, glorious successes, and hard falls that have characterized Chicago throughout its history, Charley Weeghman (fig. 1) could be that man. Born in

FIGURE 1. Charles Weeghman, the man who built Wrigley Field, awkwardly grips a bat. His hat appears at least two sizes too small for his head. (Credit: National Baseball Hall of Fame and Museum)

tiny Richmond, Indiana, on March 7, 1874, Weeghman—one of six children of a blacksmith and a housewife—came to Chicago in 1892, following his graduation from high school, to chase dreams engendered by the upcoming World's Fair.

Arriving in Chicago, as Theodore Dreiser wrote of Caroline Meeber in *Sister Carrie*, "full of the illusions of ignorance and youth," Weeghman had little but his dreams and, he later said, a $5 gold piece. He soon got a job pouring coffee at a restaurant south of the Loop called Charlie King's on Fifth Avenue (now Wells Street) making $10 a week. Good at his job, officious, and blessed with the gift of gab, Weeghman rose quickly in the ranks. His motto was, "I aim to please." After being appointed headwaiter, Weeghman was soon made night manager, then floor manager. He learned the ins and outs of the restaurant racket and developed his own theories of successful customer service and how to increase traffic, but even then earned just $25 a week. Still, as head man, Weeghman found himself in the catbird seat. Charlie King's was frequented by the politicians, mob figures, actors, singers, high-flying tourists, gamblers, and sports personalities of the day—and, perhaps most important, by the newspapermen. Fifth Avenue was for many years one of Chicago's seedier areas, dotted by beer halls and brothels. Originally named Wells Street, it had been renamed by city fathers in the 1870s in an attempt to improve the street's character, but the new title had little effect. (In 1918, it became Wells Street once more.) This was a heady environment for an ambitious, cagey, yet still wet-behind-the-ears rube. But Weeghman learned quickly, and he had a dream—a polished-tile dream.

EATING ON THE RUN

One could get almost anything for a price in Chicago. Always on the go, on the make, and on the take, Chicago seemingly never slept, and its inhabitants were always seeking the next score, the next big deal. Both petty grifters and top-hatted bankers flocked to the city in the early 1900s due to its seemingly unlimited potential for financial growth.

The 1893 World's Fair led more businesses to Chicago. Banks, the livestock trade, manufacturers, and wholesalers needed qualified help, and hundreds of thousands came to fill positions. Entire industries grew to serve ever larger numbers of working- and middle-class people, an increasing number of whom were living outside of the city and traveling downtown to work. Since these working people needed somewhere to eat, local entrepreneurs pushed a new phenomenon: fast food. Many working men, notes Perry Duis, ate in bars, where the "free lunch," a longtime inducement to business, was in style. Women, meanwhile, traveled to such membership restaurants as the Woman's Exchange, on Wabash Avenue near Madison Street, and the Ogontz Club of Printer's Row, later cited as the nation's first self-serve cafeteria. Duis says that the motives for the invention of the cafeteria were both financial and political: "Its dining members decided to reduce the overhead and eliminate what they regarded as a demeaning task of waitressing by lining up to serve themselves as they passed a table laden with platters and dishes."

The success of the Ogontz did not go unnoticed, and commercial versions of the self-serve format followed. In 1909, Mary Dutton began the Ontra Cafeteria chain. She had two stores downtown as well as a huge one in Uptown, then bustling with late-night entertainment and nouveau riche lakefront residents.

Yet by 1910, the "free lunch" had fallen under attack from religious groups because of its tendency to encourage men to spend time in saloons. In 1933, the *Tribune* published a fond remembrance of the free lunch: "Every beer emporium furnished iced radishes, green onions, pickled beets, sliced tomatoes—and where could one go without having a pretzel bowl within reach? Caviar sandwiches abounded in the more pretentious places. Piping hot fried oysters were ready in season in many places. Crisp potato pancakes that melted in the mouth were free with a glass of beer. Cheese straws and French fried potatoes were munched between beer sips." The public flaying of the free lunch led to the increased popularity of mobile "sandwich wagons" (which did not serve alcohol) and, eventually, lunch counters. The most successful lunch counter restaurateur was John R. Thompson, on the ball by the mid-1890s. In Duis's words, "Using one-arm chairs for easy access to counters, standard menus, and large-scale supply purchases to maximize profit, his chain grew to eight outlets in 1900 and thirty-nine in Chicago by 1914, all but seven of them in the loop." A competing chain, Raklios, had nineteen locations, and another chain, Messenger's, was also very popular.

Charley Weeghman dreamed of opening *his* own restaurant. He left Charlie King's sometime in 1899 and worked for two years managing a baking powder operation, learning the ins and outs of food production.

CHARLEY'S WORLD

By the turn of the century, Weeghman had saved some $2,800. In 1901, Weeghman and his wife, Bessie (a former King's cashier) opened their own place at Fifth and Adams Street, not far from King's. Charley was successful and popular, but Bessie was said to provide the gravity in the operation, the keen business sense and attention to detail that her husband—a big talker and a dreamer—lacked. One clear reason for Charlie King's popularity was its proximity to the high life, cheap beer, and cheaper women of Fifth Street. But Charley Weeghman's restaurant was classier than the typical joint. Says Perry Duis, "The Weeghman chain featured a white tile décor to emphasize cleanliness, a punched-check bill to minimize confusion, and coffee served in special mugs to reduce both spilling and the number of dishes to wash."

These innovative touches certainly made things smoother for personnel and gave diners a more predictable experience. But eating at your local fast-food joint, or "dairy-lunch counter" (indicating that alcohol wasn't on offer), was often far from pleasant. "You sit on a low stool, hat on, people waiting for your seat, no napkin, but quick service," groused a local guidebook of the time. Serving rows and rows of customers eating quickly off tables that looked very much like old-style school desks, these lunch chains did plenty of business in the Chicago of the 1890s and early 1900s. Weeghman, years later, claimed to have made $400 in profits in the first month running the restaurant. Eventually he purchased back all the shares in the restaurant. He opened a second restaurant at 218 South Wabash, then a third, and then a fourth and a fifth.

Weeghman's restaurants struck a chord. At the peak, the Weeghmans owned fifteen of them, serving some thirty-five thousand patrons a day. Charley was called Chicago's "first fast-food tycoon." The *Indianapolis Star* ran a profile of him written by "Casey" on January 31, 1914: "He's a clean-cut man, as lively as a cricket. He's not tall, but medium, and he's slim. His hair and features are dark. His eyes and mouth are the most noticeable features. His eyes are blue and of the gleamy variety . . . his mouth is firm. He has a stern expression. Today Charley wore an English suit of dark green. Holding a split collar together was a rakish-looking bow tie. He had on black kid button shoes and a black soft hat. The very essence of pep emulated from his makeup." Weeghman, whose mottoes included "Nerve is a big factor in everything," also ran several busy bakeries, using his own baking powder. He was known for the size and quality of his sandwiches, doughnuts ("Weeghman's Sinkers"), and rolls. One of his nicknames was Doughnut Charley, although most called him Lucky Charley for his seemingly instant rise to success.

But Weeghman had put in a lot of time and elbow grease to get his chance. For years, he had worked up to eighteen hours a day, and he was determined to be successful. And if that meant he had to follow the money down dark alleys, he would. Weeghman befriended characters best referred to as shady. He made himself available to gamblers, showbiz types, writers, and politicians and soaked up what he could of the high life.

At the time, politicians may have been the least honorable

people in the group. During the early 1900s, mobsters helped buy the election of Mayor "Big Bill" Thompson, possibly the Windy City's most corrupt leader and one of the most mercenary mayors in American history. The mob had its hands in gambling, drugs, and prostitution, the three vices that never seem to go out of style. We don't know whether Charley Weeghman got working capital from this population, but he did have a well-known ability to give his customers whatever they wanted.

During this time Chicago was a land of horrifying filth and spectacular beauty. It was the desolation of the trapped factory girls in *Sister Carrie* and the hard-fought optimism of Carl Sandburg. It was the beautiful architecture and design work of Louis Sullivan and Frank Lloyd Wright as well as the exploitation of the meatpacking industry, heartbreakingly exposed by Upton Sinclair's *The Jungle*. It was the scarcely believable poverty of the South Side and West Side slums, the quick-as-a-wink rebuilding of a city scorched by the terrible 1871 fire, and the corruption of many of its policemen and elected officials. Chicago's press was staffed by an often scurrilous but amazingly talented group of writers. Rudyard Kipling expressed his desire to see Chicago wiped off the face of the earth. Kaiser Wilhelm announced, "I should very much like to see Chicago."

H. L. Mencken wrote in the October 28, 1917, *Tribune*: "In Chicago, there is the mysterious *something*. In Chicago, a spirit broods upon the face of the water. Find me a writer who is American and who has something new to say, and nine times out of ten I will show that he has some sort of connection with the abattoir by the lake—that he was bred there, got his start there, or passed through there during the days when he was tender."

In order for Weeghman to make his dreams come true, he needed money, notoriety, and a reputation for quality. He obtained all three. In 1907, he sold his interest in his restaurants for $50,000 and, with that cash, opened a new downtown eatery near Madison Street and Dearborn Avenue and expanded his new chain, simply called Weeghman's, as quickly as the first. "His restaurants, which offered food at low prices with rapid service, thrived and he became a millionaire," recorded the *Daily News* in 1938. "Weeghman was going to town in a big way," wrote Harry Neily, "but still was big-hearted Charley to all who knew him."

Charley Weeghman was at the rise of fast food, and it is impossible to imagine any part of America—whether a big city, a suburban strip mall, or a country roadside exit—surviving without it. Weeghman's restaurant chain, marked by innovation, standardization, and predictable product amid the chaos of the workday of the early twentieth century, is a delightful metaphor for hot, swinging, innovative Chicago.

What Charley really wanted, apparently, was to continue his move up the social ladder and become a gentleman of society, a sportsman. Handsome, raffish, and sporting dandified outfits, gardenias in his lapel, and bowler hats, Weeghman began to diversify. He owned a theater at 58 West Madison Street and invested in a high-class pool hall, real estate, a coal company, motion picture houses, and even film production. Baseball would be next.

WHEN JIMMY MET CHARLEY

When James Gilmore began business discussions with Lucky Charley, he got at least as much as he bargained for. Weeghman was ambitious, calculating, hard working, friendly, proud, and fit for battle. As *Literary Digest* noted in its February 7, 1914, issue, "Mr. Weeghman for some time had wanted to buy a baseball club. In 1911 he tried to purchase the St. Louis Nationals." Rebuffed in those efforts, Weeghman grew a chip on his shoulder the size of one of his sandwiches. "He takes some pride in saying that he made his wealth in his business," noted Sam Weller in the January 4, 1914, *Tribune*.

On December 27, 1913, as part of a league-wide reorganization, Weeghman became president of the Chicago Federal League club and, according to Sam Weller in the next day's *Tribune*, its "principal backer"—the league now had serious money. For many years thereafter, Weeghman was known as the "angel" of the Federal League. Given his public persona and his huge bankroll, no other title would have fit. On December 29, 1913, John Seys of the *Daily News* summed him up. "Mr. Weeghman, immensely popular among the sporting element of Chicago, says he will make the Federal League just as important a cog in the baseball machine as the National or American league."

Weeghman was joined in the executive suite by William Walker, a successful fishmonger. While both Weeghman and Walker threw in buckets of money, the latter seemed content to remain a silent partner. Weeghman, whom Sox owner Charlie Comiskey described as "a live wire willing to risk his money in the fight," made better copy. Enthusiastic about any coverage, positive or mocking, Weeghman was one of the most well known names and well liked people in the city during the early part of the century. And he worked his buddies at the newspapers to get the coverage he needed.

THE NAME GAME

In those less formal days, before the existence of marketing firms or public relations consultancies, the Chicago Feds (much like the other clubs in the upstart league) didn't even have an official name. The local sportswriters, therefore, took matters into their own ink-stained hands. While the *American* referred to Chicago's upstart nine as the Feds, or the local Feds, and at least once as the "tots," the *Post*—bald-faced supporters of the club—dubbed them, in a none-too-obtuse reference to Charley Weeghman's restaurants, the Buns. Fans and the press liked this name, which stuck, unofficially, through the 1914 season. The *Post* also referred to them punningly as the "Feeds," while the fame of their player-manager, Joe Tinker, led to them also being called the Tinx.

Ring Lardner of the *Tribune* proposed a reader contest to name the new club. He noted sadly on April 23, 1914, that "though more than a hundred fans have entered the competition and suggested nicknames for Joe Tinker's new club, not one has come across with an appellation that hit us right between the eyes." Lardner reported suggestions of food-oriented names such as the Sinkers, Doughnuts, Buns, Chefs, Feeds, Pies, Figs, and Bakers but commented that "none of these can be called convincing."

Weeghman and his Buns certainly had all the publicity and attention they could handle in those heady days of winter 1913–14. In the aftermath of Joe Tinker's signing, more players defected to the upstart Federal League. Otto Knabe, Mordecai Brown, Howie Camnitz, Cy Falkenberg, Russ Ford, Solly Hofman, and Al Bridwell, among others, joined up. The addition of known players to each league's team—a clause that Weeghman insisted each owner agree to—afforded the new league respectability and led a few dissenters closer to the Feds' corner.

The extent to which the Chicago club dominated the Federal League is clear from the reporting from the winter of 1913–14. As Charlie Comiskey noted about Weeghman and his squad, "One club cannot make a league, and I don't believe his associates are in the same class with him as a sportsman." Harvey Woodruff, in the February 15, 1914, *Tribune*, noted that Weeghman and Walker were in the hole for at least $125,000 each before the season was to open and that "Chicago probably will have the heaviest single investment of any club in the league."

WHY LAKE VIEW?

As part of raising the profile of the league, the Chicago team needed its own field, rather than continuing to share DePaul University's athletic fields. Weeghman, Walker, and Gilmore saw themselves as forward-thinking, groundbreaking fellows, dedicated to creating a new order outside of a stodgy and irrelevant establishment. Putting a new park on the North Side of town made sense. They wanted to be far enough away from the White Sox and Cubs to build their own identity and not suffer in comparison to the existing parks. In addition, it made plenty of sense to claim this expanding part of the city.

They needed a large plot of land that could be prepared quickly. Theoretically, they had little to do but buy off the businesses and homes currently occupying the lot, clear the land, and build. Later, however, the outlaws found plenty of costly obstacles to their goal. Tearing down some of the houses on the lot, getting required signatures from several hundred area residents, whistling past the objections of community groups, and fighting off the dogged efforts of organized ball to keep them out of the game took big bites from their wallets.

In December, stories made the rounds that the Feds would acquire the site on what *Sporting Life* called, on February 27, "the famous open lot at Addison and Clark Streets." Gilmore refused to confirm or deny the reports. Several years later, in its January 10, 1918, issue, the *Sporting News'* George Robbins gave his opinion as to why the park had been built in Lake View: "The millionaires who own the Cubs love [the] scenery of the North Shore, where their homes are located. They are eager to build up a baseball following there. The game, for them, is a hobby and a diversion. They care little for a few paltry hundred thousand dollars. They want to satisfy their pride and win glory for their section. They are not in the game for money alone." Still later, Bill Veeck Jr. raised two other possible reasons for the park's location, opining that Weeghman wanted the land at Clark and Addison "to get a piece of land he could afford. Bear in mind, one wouldn't put up a ballpark next to a coal yard by choice." He also noted that since motorcars were not yet affordable by most, the park needed to be close to public transportation. "Clark and Addison was an ideal location because the streetcar and elevated lines were nearby."

ELSIE DABEL'S DIARY

Word of a new ballpark in Lake View was even noteworthy to a teenage girl living there. Among the documents from the Lake View Historical Society archived at the Chicago Public Library is the 1914 diary of Elsie Dabel. Amid her comments about going to Lake View High School, dusting the family's dining room, and heading to a local theater to see Mary Pickford in a new moving picture show, she writes on January 30: "We are going to have a grand new ball park right here on Sheffield and Addison. The Federal League ball park. It's going to be a *pippin*. Oh, you Johnnies!"

SEALING THE DEAL

Intrigue and skullduggery shrouded the Feds' early 1914 attempts to lease the land at Clark and Addison. The Feds were under a time crunch to build a ballpark, but the deal to turn over the property went down to the wire. Reported the *Tribune*'s Irv Sanborn on December 30, 1913: "Negotiations for the location, which at one time was to have housed an American Association team, have been on for a quite a spell and the deal was not consummated until the Federal people brought considerable pressure to bear on the owners of the North Side property."

What kind of pressure? And why wouldn't current owners of the property, the Cantillon brothers, presumably no longer having any other plans for the land, just sign the lease agreement? In his *Tribune* story, Sanborn revealed that "the forces of organized baseball are said to have been working to block the scheme to locate a Federal League club on the Addison street site with some prospect of success." This was what the big boys did: threaten, plead, cajole, and, finally, try to buy out the upstarts. But Weeghman, Walker, and Gilmore, who on December 2, 1913, acquired a one-month, $500 option to lease the property, were more than ready with their own brand of hardball. Sanborn continues: "As a countermove, the Federal backers obtained an option on the old White Sox park at Thirty-ninth Street and Wentworth Avenue, occupied by the [Negro League] American Giants since the erection of Comiskey Park."

Faced with the resolve of Weeghman, Walker, and Gilmore, and contemplating the frightening possibility of the new Federal

League club intending to compete just four blocks from the White Sox's current location, the major leagues gave in. The Feds would be able to lease their desired North Side property.

In a sharp last piece of strategy, Weeghman said he was holding on to his option on the Thirty-Ninth Street ballyard in case of "emergency." While the American Giants' owner, J. M. Schorling, denied that he and Weeghman even *had* an agreement, the point soon became moot. The *Tribune* reported the very next day, December 31, 1913, that Mike Cantillon was traveling from Saint Paul to sign the papers leasing the property to the Chicago Federal League club.

The complete lease terms were $16,000 for the first ten years, $18,000 for the second ten, and $20,000 for each of the remaining seventy-nine years of the lease. Weeghman told the local papers in January 1914 that he had already obtained consent of local property owners to obtain a building permit and construct the park.

Weeghman immediately violated two pieces of the agreement with the Cantillons. The first was a stipulation that the renters spend no more than $70,000 on upkeep and construction on the grounds; the second was that they tamper with no members of the Minneapolis Millers. Weeghman nevertheless announced that his new stadium would cost $250,000, more than three times the amount allowed. Rumors began to swirl that the Chifeds had offered Joe Cantillon himself a $15,000 contract to come south. Cantillon stayed put, but remained a confidant as well as a landlord for Weeghman through the Federal League's lifetime.

Building a new ballpark for a team just getting around to declaring itself major league was certainly an act of faith. Committing to doing so less than four months before opening the season was both brave and foolhardy. But Weeghman was ready, even before getting the lease. On December 28, he told John Seys of the *Tribune*, "I propose to build a grand stand of steel or concrete to cost about $100,000 or $125,000 if necessary. I have asked for bids and within the next forty-eight hours the contract will be let."

A CITY OF BASEBALL

As exciting as these developments were, did the core proposition even make sense? How could Chicago have been expected to support more than the two major league teams? Easy: it was baseball crazy. Not only were two major league teams already in existence at the time—the Sox and Cubs—but the Negro Chicago American Giants and semipro teams of various sorts and affiliations were also located in Chicago. In 1910, a winter indoor league began and prospered through the decade. Independent clubs, park teams, and church clubs formed leagues. Other local semipro leagues also worked their way into Chicago's consciousness. The March 27, 1914, *Post* reported, "The Craftsman Baseball league clubs expect to play at the Washington Park field this season. The board of directors of the league have petitioned the board of park commissioners, asking the privilege of using the park grounds and no trouble is anticipated."

On February 9, 1914, the *American* had noted the birth of yet another league. In early April, the *Post* gave its readers all the dope.

Another baseball league has blossomed forth, which is expected to prove a hummer. The new organization will be composed of teams residing back of the yards [on the south side] and will be called the Stock Yards league. There are so many boys anxious to join the new league that [organizer J.] Sokol was obliged to make it an eight-club circuit. Each club will be allowed to carry but eighteen players, and each player will have to sign a contract to play throughout the whole year—major league stuff. The clubs entered in this new organization are Jolly Boys, Woods, Silvery Bells, Willows, Waunettas, Seeley Colts, Starlights, and Deltas.

In the most general sense, as Robert G. Spinney has written, baseball was a critical factor in the "Americanization" of immigrants, and Chicago has always been a city of immigrants: "In Chicago and other large cities, baseball became the first popular professional sport. It is especially important to consider baseball's social impact on ethnically diverse cities like Chicago. The baseball park was a place (and perhaps the only place) where all Chicagoans—Anglo-Americans, Germans, the Irish, Italians, Jews, the wealthy and the poor, the educated and the illiterate—met on equal terms. Chicagoans who had little in common shared a common experience: they could root for the home team."

Another reason that all these clubs could support themselves is that each club identified with a very specific neighborhood. In those days before radio or television allowed fans to "follow" the game on a minute-by-minute basis, physical proximity was far more important to being a rooter than it is now. And despite rapidly improving public transportation, Chicago in 1914 was a sprawling mix of diverse, self-contained neighborhoods, each with its own personality. To this day, it still means something locally to say that you hail from Bridgeport, Logan Square, Bronzeville, Hegewisch, Edgebrook, Beverly, Cragin, Pullman, or Rogers Park.

The idea of the North Side getting its own team was a big deal in 1914. It showed many in the town that the power base of Chicago was indeed moving north; with a sparkling new park opening at Clark and Addison, the dirty old West Side Grounds became even less attractive and fabled Comiskey seemed that much farther away. Having a team close to one's own neighborhood—just a good walk or a trolley or a bicycle ride from home—could now be a source of pride for residents of the North Side just as it was for South and West Siders.

NUTS (AND BOLTS) TO YOU

Weeghman and his cohorts had, as of January 1914, leased the land bordered on the south by Addison Street, on the east by

Sheffield Avenue, on the north by Waveland Avenue, and on the west by Clark Street. The property's official address at the time was 1052 West Addison Street.

Weeghman noted in late December 1913 that the lot he would build on was 600 feet by 598, but city hall measured it at 532.4 feet by 540 feet. The difference was due to Weeghman's belief that he would easily be able to acquire a small piece of land "connecting the property at Addison and North Clark streets," according to the *Daily News* of January 19. "[Weeghman] said it is owned by a friend of his who was offered $25,000 by an unknown party."

The over-the-top, last-minute offer was, of course, another attempt to throw the Feds off course. "I knew that organized ball was behind that offer," Weeghman told the *Tribune*'s Sam Weller on January 18. That option to sell the land to the third party expired, though; nobody showed up to buy the land on the agreed-upon date, and Weeghman eventually acquired the extra real estate.

As Sam Weller noted in the *Tribune* on January 20, 1914, "Organized ball made another effort yesterday morning to grab that little strip of ground on the Federal's site, thus blocking the chance to put a ball park there, but when the agent of the majors appeared he was informed that Charles Weeghman . . . had been ahead of him and had obtained the property. In desperation organized ball offered $40,000, but the much-coveted piece of real estate was already in the hands of the independent body and the agent retired crestfallen."

The episode shows just how desperate organized ball was to keep the Federal League out of the picture by thwarting its strongest franchise. Organized ball tried once more to hamstring the Feds in late January, putting up money to have local residents file an injunction to stop Weeghman and his men from building on the Clark and Addison property. The protest did not work, but the story did get into the papers.

By this time, the small strip of real estate was among the Feds' smallest worries—in fact, it wasn't even the principal tool with which the major leagues were trying to disrupt the rise of the Federal League. They were trying to buy out Charley Weeghman himself.

On Saturday, January 17, Federal League magnates had held a raucous and tense meeting at a hotel in Chicago; the new amalgamation was in something resembling deep trouble. Several writers voiced doubts in the papers for which they wrote that the league would even stay alive through the weekend.

Among the areas of contention at the meeting was financial commitment. Weeghman, apparently tired of pulling the train himself, had demanded that other club owners follow his lead and fork over the dough to make their clubs competitive—and quickly.

"At four o'clock in the afternoon, it looked as if the Federal League was in great distress," penned the *Tribune*'s Sam Weller on January 18. "There was an air of nervous disorder about the meeting room in the Hotel LaSalle that seemed to forecast a collapse." *Sporting Life*'s April 4, 1914, issue subsequently quoted Weeghman's friend H. J. Murphy of Hyde Park saying that Charley "quit the fold at that meeting only to be brought in again by Otto Stifel, of Saint Louis, who put up the necessary argument in the form of hard cash, and who, it is said, saved the Federal ship." Stifel committed a huge sum to player acquisition, urging other league magnates to follow, and the league—for the moment—was saved.

It turns out that behind Weeghman's complaint lay a real threat: organized baseball had apparently offered him an in. The *New York Times* on January 18 reported that "[Weeghman] admitted after the meeting that he had been offered a chance to buy the St. Louis Browns if he would drop new league interest." In the previous day's *Daily News*, a reporter had asked Weeghman, "Would you buy the St. Louis Browns?"

"How much do they want?" he had responded. (Later, American League representatives denied involvement, though several newspaper stories said league president Ban Johnson was behind the offer.) Murphy, Lucky Charley's South Side pal, further told *Sporting Life* in its April 4 issue that, just before the January 17 meeting, Weeghman had been offered $500,000—in cash—to quit the Feds immediately. No go. According to Murphy, "I know that he is wrapped up body and soul in the new organization, and he has told me repeatedly that he fully expected the initial season to pay 100 cents on every dollar's worth of stock."

Weeghman was contrite and gracious in the January 19, 1914, *Tribune*, telling Sam Weller, "I wanted the other fellows who were going into this thing with me to show me some money and players," he noted, "and they showed me so much money right up in that meeting room Saturday afternoon that I felt ashamed for having asked it of them."

THE MAJORS DON'T GIVE UP

Even after Weeghman had signed the lease, farmed out plans for his ballpark, and stated publicly that he was behind the Feds 100 percent, the American League and National League bigwigs continued their efforts to snuff out the new league. The majors wanted badly to fend off what they saw as the strongest organization in the new league, a well-publicized and well-financed club that would cut into White Sox and Cubs attendance.

Around the time of the fateful league meeting and the failed buyout offer, someone in organized baseball came up with the idea of merging two of the top minor leagues, the International and the American Association, to freeze out the Feds, with the Saint Paul AA club moving to Chicago. This idea went nowhere, but a variant of it persisted. At one point, according to Bill Bailey (i.e., Veeck) of the *American*, organized baseball tried to buy Weeghman out of the Feds and into the American Association itself. On February 10, 1914, Bailey reported:

Charles W. Murphy, president of the Cubs, to-day was on his way to New York, and he was hopping mad . . . the thing which has riled him is the fact that they [AL & NL] are trying to place a third league team in Chicago without his consent. This third league team is to be of the organized brand. Here is the scheme which the West Side magnate is of the opinion that they are trying to put through: They would tempt Charles Weeghman to ditch the Federals and grab the St. Paul franchise of the American Association. This team would be placed on the North Side.

The defiant Murphy raged that "there isn't a chance for the American Association to place a team in Chicago. They have been trying to do it for years. They won't succeed." Agreements were already in place to keep minor league organizations out of big league cities, but these agreements were clearly not worth the parchment they were scratched on, because escape clauses were built in. And in this case, the AL and NL would try anything to peel Weeghman and his dollars away from Gilmore and the Feds.

As Bailey further explained, "In order to [allow a new organized ball league into a major league territory], it is necessary for five of the National League club owners and five of the American League fellows to vote their consent. It's a rule in organized baseball that the territory of the majors is sacred unless a majority of the club owners of both leagues vote their consent."

On February 17, 1914, the *Chicago Daily Journal* reported that Ban Johnson shot down the plan to allow Lucky Charley to take any AA club to Chicago, most likely, according to author Daniel Levitt, because some owners realized that what could be done to Charlie Murphy in his territory could be done to them in theirs.

But at this point, would Weeghman even have wanted an AA team? He had his own self-proclaimed major league franchise riding a wave of popular press and about to open its own new ballpark. Why would he defect? Indeed, Bailey noted, "Mr. Weeghman says that he will do nothing of the sort. He declares that he is in the Federal League to stick."

But then Charlie Murphy was dumped from his throne atop the Cubs empire. On March 5, 1914, the *Post* ran a story noting that fans might get "a chance to see (possibly) Charley Weegh-man become owner of the Cubs." He went to New York that week to meet with officials from the AL and NL, but it is not clear whether he was actually offered a chance to buy in. Whatever the case, Weeghman kept his lot with the Feds, and the leagues finally had to swallow the idea that this merry band of rebels was determined to see this crazy thing through.

GETTING IN TUNE

With property in hand and assurance that theirs wasn't the only franchise laying out the bucks, Weeghman and Walker went ahead with the next step: building the ballpark. While plans were laid out quickly, the process was hardly haphazard.

The Federals did not plan to bulldoze the entire existing property. "Some of the buildings on the north end of the lot will be allowed to stand, as they bring in a rental of $6,000 a year," Weeghman noted. The park's left-field fence would creep close to the rental properties but, for now, would not force their destruction. Weeghman was at all times concerned about his image in the community. M. J. Wathey of the *Herald* reported on March 5 that "Weeghman promises that it will be an edifice of beauty, which will benefit the property around it rather than be a detriment."

Some businesses and homes were marked for bulldozing, however. Most homeowners settled quickly with the Chifeds, but one business, American Sand and Gravel, liked its location and had to be "convinced" to leave. "We would like to accommodate the baseball men," said the company's manager, a Mr. Lewis, but he added, "Our lease still has a year and a half to run. It is not a question of money with us, but a question of whether we want to desert that location, which is one of the best we have."

Eventually, Mr. Lewis took the money.

PLANS

On January 7, 1914, architect Zachary T. Davis, who had built Comiskey Park—"The Base Ball Palace of the World"—just four years earlier on the south side of town, submitted plans to Weeghman for the Federal League ballpark—or "plant," as it was referred to at the time. Weeghman enthusiastically accepted Davis's design, which made room for retail stores in addition to the stadium. Irv Sanborn, in the January 8, 1914, *Tribune*, wrote that the lot would have "space enough outside the stands on the corner of Addison and Clark streets for stores which would bring good rents." When Ring Lardner heard of this, he quipped, "Space is to be left on the Addison-Clark corner for several stores. What will you bet us that one of them won't be a restaurant?"

Weeghman told Harvey Woodruff of the *Tribune*, "The terms of our lease require an outlay of $125,000 in improvements, of which $75,000 must be within the first two years. This latter amount will be more than covered by the grand stand. When we place store buildings on part of the property and rent ground which we do not need, we figure that the revenue received will pay the rental and taxes on the whole tract and give us the space occupied by the park without one cent of expense."

Davis's original plan called for 125 feet of sidewalk space at the corner of Clark and Addison, but eventually only 75 feet was earmarked. The extra room was added to the dimensions of the playing field. The *Tribune* article noted that the field would be "more spacious than the average major league park."

Weeghman said that he wanted the park to emulate the Polo Grounds, but the eventual result bore little obvious resemblance to the quadrilateral New York stadium. It was actually more like Davis's diamond-shaped Comiskey Park, save for the skeleton of the grandstand, which was very much like that of the Polo Grounds.

With the plans for Chicago's newest stadium finished, Davis—a native of Aurora, Illinois—went on to aid C. B. Comstock in designing Washington Park, new home of the Brooklyn Feds. Davis and his brother Charles designed several other important buildings in Chicago, including the Naval Armory on Lake Shore Drive, Quigley Preparatory Seminary in Streeterville, and Saint Ambrose Church on Forty-Seventh Street.

Davis's economical but attractive design was prescient. The park was planned to include a large single grandstand, rather than the double-decked park Davis had built on the South Side. Expansion was in Weeghman's mind from the beginning, however. He said at the time, "It will be so constructed that we can add wings to it at any time when patronage demands it." Irv Sanborn corroborated in the January 8, 1914, *Tribune*, "The structure will have foundations and uprights designed to permit a second deck if desired at some future time." In 1989, Kurt Rim of Osborn Engineering, which had just helped renovate Wrigley Field, observed, "Certainly Davis knew about baseball sight lines and the layout of a ballpark. From the steel work and column structure that was designed to hold an upper deck to the way he sized the ramps that can now hold 38,000 people, his knowledge of building a ballpark was more than adequate."

The initial seating plan called for a total capacity of twenty thousand, including thirteen thousand in the grandstand (with eight thousand box seats), four thousand in pavilion seats at each end of the grandstand, and approximately three thousand ten-cent bleacher seats for the hardiest of baseball fans or, as they were called back then, "bugs." In order to facilitate fan use of the Addison Street elevated station, Davis designed an exit at Addison and Sheffield near the right-field corner. The corner of Clark and Addison was earmarked for the park's main entrance and for access to the ballpark's proposed shopping complex.

Weeghman sorted through several bids before hiring Blome-Sinek, which specialized in cement paving, asphalt floors, and concrete construction, to build the new park. The contractor estimated construction and labor costs at $250,000. When Weeghman Park was finished, both Blome-Sinek and Zachary and Charles Davis were allowed, as part of the deal, to post signs advertising their services on the ballpark wall facing Addison Street.

Building a park was a huge expense, but Weeghman pressed on. "When this thing started," Weeghman said in February, "we sat down and figured it out where we could sign a ball team and have a nice, modest little park for an expenditure of $50,000. We're in $125,000 and haven't started work on our grand stand."

TURN INTO EARTH

On February 23, the actual work began. The *Tribune* reported that "the first work fell to a wrecking crew, which began to tear down the frame buildings at the corner of Clark and Addison . . . until the weather moderates it will be hardly possible to start the construction of the grand stand."

Workers ripped down four buildings on the seminary grounds on February 24, but most observers still did not believe that the park could be up in time. "It looks like a matter of difficulty to secure anything like a suitable plant by the time the season opens," noted the *Daily Journal* on February 28. Weeghman, however, remained confident, telling the papers that he expected everything to be ready for the club's first game in late April.

Weeghman and his men hastily arranged a flashy ground-breaking ceremony for the new park. The photo opportunity was originally scheduled for March 3, with Mayor Carter Harrison to turn the first shovelful of dirt into a gaping hole at the corner of Sheffield and Addison (not, curiously, at Clark and Addison, where the main entrance was built). Sam Weller from the *Tribune* noted that day that "the moving picture camera man, officials of the local club, and the mayor are to be present, and all the fans are invited."

Mayor Harrison was ill, however, and, despite thirty-five hundred fans having gathered at the site on March 3, the ceremony was rescheduled for March 4 at 10:00 A.M. Two thousand Fed followers showed up on that frosty morning. In between speeches from city and club officials, a band performed patriotic songs (although the *Herald* had promised a tango orchestra). Harrison was still unable to attend, but Chicago's building commissioner, Henry Ericsson, turned the first spade of dirt. The young son of William Walker (part owner, with Weeghman, of the Chifeds),

J. W.—nicknamed Buster—smashed a bottle of bubbly over the shovel, which led to a huge cry from the assembled throng. Ring Lardner in the March 6 *Tribune* opined that "those present at the festivities at Addison and Clark Wednesday morning think it was foolish to waste a bottle of champagne by breaking it over the spade." Referring to Weeghman's menu, Lardner continued, "A cup of coffee, [a] Boston [doughnut], or a pint of oysters would have been less expensive and more appropriate."

The energetic Weeghman, ever the ham, took hold of the shovel at one point for the benefit of the photogs. As still cameras clicked and film cameras whirred, he furiously dug into the frigid ground "as if he would build his entire stand himself," the *Tribune* noted on March 5. When the pomp and circumstance were completed, police and workmen "assisted the crowd off the field," reported the March 5 *Herald*. William Sinek, the chief contractor on the project, immediately began to direct one hundred workmen in preliminary construction of the grandstand.

Oddly enough, former Cubs owner Charlie Murphy was in the news on this day as well—though for nothing baseball related. He and his wife were involved in a three-car crash at North Avenue and Lake Shore Drive, with Mrs. Murphy thrown from the car and suffering a broken arm.

OILED

On March 5, the Chifeds held a banquet at the downtown restaurant States for four hundred fans and club officials. The room was festooned with baseballs and bats; manager Joe Tinker and his wife showed up; and Weeghman was at his usual crowd-pleasing best. Around midnight, the well-oiled guests began taking matches to souvenir balloons, which produced flashes of flame and, according to Lambert Sullivan in the next day's *Daily News*, an auditory blast that "sounded like an attack at Fort Sumter."

Before everyone got drunk, Weeghman had told the press that he was planning to install potted plants atop the brick right-field wall along Sheffield Avenue and that he intended the new park to be one of the prettiest in the nation. It does not appear that the potted plants ever showed up, but Charley had already proven that he was serious about such details; in January, he hired Mike Murphy, a former Tigers' groundskeeper with twenty years' experience, to tend his new park.

GIVE THE PEOPLE WHAT THEY WANT

The Chifeds' public spokesman was smart enough to know that baseball alone would not differentiate his club from the Cubs or Sox, or even the American Giants or semipro clubs. As a man whose entire business model was predicated on getting bodies through his doors amid fierce competition, Weeghman saw—as few other baseball men did at the time—that a pampered customer would, more likely than not, return.

At that time, owners of baseball clubs often didn't feel that they had to spend money on their fans because baseball was the top spectator sport in town; the bugs were already turning out in great numbers. And they came out despite filthy conditions.

How bad was it at the park? Back then, ballparks had no concession stands and usually only spartan (and often disgusting) rest rooms. Aisles and walkways at the park were rarely swept, and vendors crowded everyone's view to hawk their wares. And it was noisy. Opined the March 5, 1914, edition of the *Post*, "Let's express a deep-seated hope that the new president of the Cubs . . . does something to stop the noise nuisance at the West Side park this season. The fans will greatly appreciate it if the popcorn, pop, program, and perfecto [cigar] purveyors are silenced."

Weeghman was full of ideas to modernize, streamline, and decorate in order to satisfy his customers and add new ones. He would do anything to differentiate himself from the competition. As he had done in his restaurants, Lucky Charley mandated that his park be kept clean and shiny and that every possible care be taken to show the customer that he or, significantly, she was boss. "It is my belief that in order to draw and keep the fans, a club management must show plainly that the first thought is for the fan's comfort," Weeghman told a reporter from the *Post*, which ran a lengthy story on the Fed owner's plans on March 23, 1914. "'I have been a baseball fan for years,' said President Weeghman in talking over his plans today, 'and many a time have I gone to a park all dolled up in my very best regalia, only to find that in order to occupy my seat, I must either buy a cushion or ruin my clothes.'" While most fans at the time were probably not as dapper or dandified in their choice of garb as the stick-pinned, bowler-hatted, bow-tied Weeghman, the point was well-taken: ballparks were filthy.

"The dusty and generally dirty condition of several of the parks is not the only undesirable feature that the fan has been forced to tolerate," he noted. "The retiring rooms for men and women are generally a disgrace to a park . . . we will have the very best that is to be had in all branches, and will spare nothing in making the park one of solid comfort. There will be no abusive ushers to insult fans and there will be no dusty and dirty seats and filthy aisles for the fans to complain about. Every morning will find a corps of men at work dusting and cleaning the stands."

Sporting Life's April 4, 1914, issue reported Weeghman averring that "we intend to have our plant in a condition that would be a credit to Spotless Town." The phrase "Spotless Town" referred to an antigerms marketing campaign by a popular soap manufacturer, Sapolio, which pitted its hygienically minded citizens against those dirty folks living in neighboring "Dingeytown."

REFRESHER COURSE

Food, of course, was a major topic in any conversation with Weeghman. He outlined his plan briefly in that issue of *Sporting Life*: "We are considering the installation of a system for supplying our patrons with refreshments, which will lessen the annoyance caused by noisy peddlers."

In the March 23 *Post*, he discussed his plans with the same relish as one would if tucking into one of his huge dinner rolls.

> We are thinking seriously of adopting a system of passing refreshments around the crowd. This will do away with the old time-honored curse by which one is forced to do a Hercules stunt in holding up some obnoxious peanut vendor.
>
> The new system provides long rods, which are fitted with hooks for bags, and in which there is a lot running the entire length. The prospective purchaser makes known his desire, and whether it be popcorn, peanuts, or an ice cream cone, the stuff is attached to the end of the rod by the vendor and is extended out several feet. In return the purchaser drops his coin or coins in the slot and the money rolls into a cup at the receiving end of the rod.

This collection system didn't quite work out, but Weeghman soon came upon another idea to deal with the crush of leaning vendors. Weeghman's idea involved setting up small kiosks in the rear portion of the seating bowl. At these kiosks, customers could buy food unmolested and return to their seats. Thus was born the permanent concession stand.

THIS IS FOR THE GIRLS

During March 1914, Weeghman announced that he would institute Ladies Days at his new park. This was just another salvo in Weeghman's fight to draw fans away from the other two clubs—especially the Cubs, who were prohibited by National League rules from engaging in such a promotion. On March 31, the Cubs announced that they would petition the league to renounce its five-year-old ban on Ladies Day. Although the American League had no such prohibition, and the White Sox used the practice regularly, the Cubs were not successful in getting the NL to change its collective mind.

FIGURE 2. Weeghman Park during its spring 1914 construction.
Note the chain-link right-field fence, the left-field bleacher seats, and
the lower deck, which remains in use today. The left-field back wall
(between the bleachers and the grandstand) is also still standing.
(Credit: National Baseball Hall of Fame and Museum)

MYSTERY ACHIEVEMENT

Beginning late in the morning of March 4, 1914, hundreds of construction workers began building what we now know as Wrigley Field. The men dug holes, poured foundations, and began molding steel, concrete, and wood into a structure. In just seven weeks, the park was constructed. What is especially amazing is that anyone transported from 1914 to the present day would recognize Wrigley (fig. 2).

Both February and March 1914 were cold and blustery. Between March 4 and March 16, the construction men excavated the area and brought in materials despite lousy weather. Herman Hettler's Lumber Company at 2601 North Elston Avenue supplied the wood that provided the foundation for much of the bleachers as well as the scoreboard. On March 16, workers began erecting the grandstand, which was steel with a concrete foundation.

Three days later, workers were laying brick for the right-field bleachers. By March 23, the more than four hundred workers had laid a complete foundation. Five days after that, all the rivets had been placed in the steel structure. Nobody from the league (or even in the Chifeds organization) expected that the work would be done so fast.

On March 29, the *Tribune* carried a large, revealing photograph of the construction, taken from center field. The first-base-side grandstand was nearly completed, while the bleachers appeared about halfway done. The field, at this point nothing but a mass of dirt, was covered with wheelbarrows, large cranes, and woodpiles.

WHILE YOU WERE OUT

With work under way, Weeghman, his wife, other club owners, and about thirty pals traveled to the club's training camp in Shreveport, Louisiana. Weeghman rented a huge train for the trip. Once in Louisiana, he donned a uniform and took batting practice with his charges. A rumor, presumably started by rogues from organized baseball, stated that Weeghman was broke. The amount of money he was spending for himself and his friends in Shreveport should have put the lie to that.

Around this time, Lake View residents Herman and Margaretha Croon filed suit, noting that the Chifeds had failed to obtain necessary consent from owners of property bordering the new ballpark. James Gilmore told the press, however, that the club had already obtained the necessary documentation. Work continued on the park.

FINISHING THE JOB

On April 3 at 10:00 A.M., union Teamsters at the park went on strike. Union bricklayers walked off the site, and the concrete reinforcement process was halted. The work had already proceeded at such a furious pace, however, that the park was actually ahead of schedule. When the striking workers returned, they completed construction of the right-field bleachers and the grandstand roof. Weeghman hired four hundred more men to make up for lost time.

On April 6, trucks pulled up to the site holding the chairs for the seating bowl. The seats were not immediately installed, however, because it took until April 9 for the concrete runways and seat slabs to set. It wasn't until April 20—three days before the park opened to the public—that workers put in the seats.

The day the strike was called, Weeghman and Gilmore brought local reporters and officials to the site for a tour of the mostly finished park. According to reporter Handy Andy in the April 4, 1914, *Tribune*, "all that remains to be done is to erect a stone wall, roll the diamond, and install some plumbing." He declared that once the just-arrived seats were installed, "the stands, as far as the spectator is concerned, will be as fit as any in these parts."

Bill Brennan, the Federal League's chief umpire, was part of the tour contingent. He gave the *Inter-Ocean*'s Walter Roderick a glowing review of the edifice in the April 4 issue. "It seems like a dream . . . and believe me, it is some park. Here's where the fellows sit that know the game," he continued, climbing up on the bleacher seats. "Here's where they call you 'robber.' It doesn't make any difference if you're up there at the plate and they're away out here, they know, and you can't tell 'em anything about the game they don't know."

The new park had a left-field distance of 310 feet (a bit shorter than planned, perhaps because of the house still standing there) and a right-field fence of 345 feet; at West Side Grounds it was 329 feet to straightaway right. The left-field and right-field corners at the rectangular West Side park were far closer—around fifty feet closer in left and sixty to seventy feet in right—than at Weeghman. The playing surface looked small to the reporters, but that may have been due in part to building materials lying on the field and several trees in left field that had yet to be removed.

Roderick noted in the April 4 *Inter-Ocean*, "The structure sweeps around in an elliptical curve so that none of the seats are very far from fair territory. The stand is very wide and slopes at such an incline that there are oceans of room and yet every one can get as good a view as the next fellow. There are no obstructions to cut off the line of vision from any angle."

THE PRICE OF BASEBALL

On April 8, 1914, Harvey Woodruff reported in the *Tribune* that Weeghman planned to charge "big league" prices for tickets at his park. Tickets for the Feds' Chicago games would cost seventy-five cents for grandstand seats and a buck for boxes—the same amount as the Cubs and White Sox. These ticket prices were actually a league policy and not a club decision.

Woodruff also noted that the Feds planned to adopt the American League's strategy of each visiting club taking an equal percentage from every game's box receipts. At the time, the National League distributed pro rata receipts to each visiting team. Only a few seats were sold in advance at Chifeds games. Grandstand and bleacher seats were sold day-of-game, even for Opening Day.

SCORES FOR ALL

The *Daily Journal* of April 14 noted that "preparations for the local Federal opening are being rushed along. The North Side park is being completed in a hurry." A few days later, advertisements for Blatz beer appeared in Chicago newspapers, topped by an artist's rendering of the new stadium. Shortly after, the Feds announced that all parks in the league would post the scores of the ongoing games of their town's major league clubs (including International League contests in Buffalo and Baltimore and American Association tilts in Indianapolis and Kansas City). The Cubs and White

Sox did not reciprocate by listing Fed scores, even though Ring Lardner of the *Tribune* called for them to do so on April 18.

One last legal hurdle arose before Opening Day. As Handy Andy wrote in the April 23 *Tribune*, "The consent of nearly 1,000 more property owners of the neighborhood must be obtained before the Feds will be secure in their new park. Apparently everyone within 1,000 feet, or nearly three blocks, of the park must have his say in the matter, whereas the Feds have believed that only property owners immediately across from the four sides of the park need be consulted." The controversy, apparently unrelated to others previously raised, was defused in time for Opening Day, with club officials racing through the neighborhood to collect signatures.

On April 9, the crew began building the brick fence that would surround the park. By April 18, the field-level scoreboard in left-center was completed. The next day, workers wrapped up final work on the walls, rest rooms, and clubhouse plumbing, closely following Weeghman's directive that the facilities be top-notch.

AT LAST

Only at this point, when the construction equipment had been moved from the field area, could head groundskeeper Murphy roll the diamond, lay the sod, and map out the field. One hundred and fifty men from the George Wittbold Florist Company, located nearby at 727 West Buckingham Place, landscaped the new park. The gardeners from Wittbold brought in an excess of four thousand pounds of soil and four acres of bluegrass. According to an unattributed piece in the Washington, Indiana, *Democrat* of September 19, 1914, Weeghman had Wittbold's men string "a row of flowers around the top of the nice, clean brick wall surrounding the ball park, and the odors from the pop-corn and peanut vendors' baskets at the new park had to combat the fragrance of real posies."

Seeding of the grounds and smoothing of the field was done up to the last minute. Murphy could not install the sod until a couple of days before the first game, and the cold and damp conditions made footing a bit soggy. By Opening Day, April 23, however, the surface was, in the words of F. A. McInerney in the *Tribune*, "level as a billiard table." Pictures from the first game show that the infield was "squared off," as was the norm in 1914, rather than rounded off as it is today. As was customary at the time, a thin dirt track lay between the pitcher's mound and home plate.

The field's orientation was a bit off from what we know today. Only during the off-season of 1922–23 was the playing surface rotated southwest to its present configuration, with home plate pointing directly northeast.

And yet the park appeared very much then as it does today. The shape of the grandstand, though single decked at that time, has not changed. The outfield fences and scoreboard looked nothing like those of the current park, but the neighborhood landscape hasn't been altered significantly. The grandstands down the left- and right-field lines did not extend all the way to the foul lines. (Weeghman said in April 1914 that he planned on extending them the following year but did not.) The grandstands had two sections: one of ten rows that sat closest to the field and, behind a large aisle, another section of approximately twenty-four rows. Bleachers stretched from right field to center, but left field had no seating. The outfield bleachers went up only about ten to twelve rows, with the bottom row just five feet above field level; spectators in the third floors of nearby apartments had no problem seeing into the stadium. The bleachers were not exactly at ground level; they appear to have been built atop a riser of two to three feet. Just as they do today, Chicago bleacher fans sat on wood benches. The scoreboard, a somewhat ragtag affair, was located at field level in left field. The flagpole, located in deep center field, was in play. In addition, spectators looked straight out; the seats farther down the baselines were not angled toward the field (those adjustments came decades later). At that time, few ballparks had curved outfields, and Weeghman Park was no exception. Most outfields were square or trapezoidal, largely because the parks were built on small parcels of land, surrounded by other buildings. Only later did the organization round off the playing field. At first, the park's center field was 440 feet deep and was not shortened until the late 1930s.

The field was always intimate, however, and the stands always close to the action, although the playing surface is now slightly closer to the seats. Some of the rooftops past the right-field wall already had advertising posters, one of them a billboard for the neighborhood Bismarck Gardens tavern.

The Washington *Democrat* article also stressed that breezes from nearby Lake Michigan were a blessing to fans used to sweltering at Comiskey Park and West Side Grounds, both a fair distance from the water.

The local and visiting baseball writers would be comfortable as well. Only a few years before, they had formed the Baseball Writers Association of America (BBWAA) to protest lousy seating at many American League and National League parks. At Weeghman's park, the scribes sat in a small, covered deck atop the roof behind the plate. The club placed twenty-two American flags on poles atop the roof ranging from the press box to the end of the grandstand. These flagpoles remain today with some adjustments.

A wire screen behind home plate protected fans from foul balls. The dugouts were much smaller and a bit farther toward the left-field and right-field lines than they are today. As today, they were actually dug out into the structure down the first- and third-base lines, covered by what appears to be corrugated tin. Past the dugouts, on each base line, a stairway led from the field to the box seats—presumably to help dignitaries get on and off the field.

It wasn't Wrigley Field yet, but now there was a ballpark in Lake View.

2

OPENING DAY AT WEEGHMAN PARK
APRIL 23, 1914

PULL UP TO THE BUMPER

Suppose you're going to see the Chicago Federal League club play its first home game at the team's brand-new stadium on Clark and Addison Streets. Perhaps you're a member of the Union League Club, the Rienzi Restaurant Federal League Booster's Club, or the Bravo el Toro Club: North Side good-fellow societies of well-to-do businessmen and civic boosters who bought their tickets in blocks reserved for them by the Feds.

You might be a West Side businessman and friend of former Cubs business manager Charley Williams, who had recently been stolen away by Weeghman. As a member of the Charley Williams Booster Club, you've already purchased your seats either at the West Town State Bank at Madison Street and Western Avenue or the Garfield Park Bank, way out west at Madison and Crawford Avenue, as long as you showed your membership card.

Or maybe you're a North Side resident, a German, Swede, or Lithuanian living in or near Lake View, who has been waiting with anticipation for this day. You trekked downtown to Jack Shannon's sporting goods store at 54 East Monroe Street in order to buy reserved tickets. Then you made plans to skip work to watch the game, and maybe stop at the Bismarck Garden at Halsted and Grace for a beer.

You could be one of the utterly twentieth-century young women responding to Feds owner Charley Weeghman's push to bring respectability and comfort to baseball fans in his new palace. Women, recently granted the vote in Chicago, were feeling their power—one expression of which was to go out to the ballyard, make their presence known, and hoot and holler just like the men.

Whatever your background, it's almost certain that you had a first-class time at the new Federal League ballpark. Whether you took the el train to Weeghman Park for just a nickel or whether you walked, your admission was well spent. Even if you were a swell pulling up to the park in your black Ford Model T, Pierce-Arrow, or Studebaker, Charley Weeghman promised value for your money. Photos of the time show automobiles parked on the North Side of Addison Street as well as right next to the ballpark—where today an outdoor café and the Ron Santo statue are located.

With its clear sight lines, modern and clean facilities, and vibrant neighborhood feel, Weeghman Park made great impressions on everyone who attended. The verdict was unanimous: this was a keen new plant.

DOG AND PONY SHOW

The Chifeds' pregame ceremonies honoring the opening of the park were characteristically over-the-top in substance and style, beginning with a huge parade starting downtown and heading north. All sorts of hoopla marked important baseball games during these years, led by a dizzying patriotic whirl of elaborate flag ceremonies, marching bands, and players trooping the field with bats held over their shoulders like rifles. Nonmilitary flash and filigree were in evidence as well. Hometown players and managers received large flower horseshoes, massive trophies, and gold-plated loving cups. Some well-loved opponents were also feted.

Given the central role of Charley Weeghman, one of Chicago's bon vivants, in the opening of this new palace, celebrations greeting the park's debut could have been expected to veer dangerously toward overkill. While any owner might have thought to hire a brass band, Good-Time Charley couldn't settle for that; for April 23, 1914, he invited *ten* brass bands. As the *Inter-Ocean* remarked that morning, "Each band ought to be able to render one piece during the afternoon—that is, unless several plan to play at the same time."

South of downtown at Sixteenth Street and Michigan Avenue, dozens of cars met up to travel en masse to the new North Side ballpark. Headed by yet another brass band, the caravan drove north on Michigan to Jackson Boulevard, west to LaSalle Street, north to Madison, east to Michigan, and north to the lakefront. The convoy then jaunted north by the lake up toward Addison, then west to the park. This curious route was most likely taken to avoid the traffic jams found every weekday in downtown Chicago, then and now.

The Bravo el Toro Club's rooters—businessmen and social leaders from the emerging North Side—didn't ride from downtown in the parade, begging off to ready themselves for their activities. For many of them, preparation consisted of a few beverages at the Bismarck Gardens—known at the time as Chicago's Pride. The popular local restaurant, bar, and music hall was located at Evanston Avenue (now Broadway), Halsted, and Grace. The usual musical programs included opera, light opera, lieder (German art songs for piano and voice), military songs, and hymns, while the kitchen offered an extensive menu and huge wine and beer lists. When big-league baseball came to the neighborhood, the crowds of hale-fellows-well-met fit naturally. The bar—one of the many large beer gardens open in the city at the time—had already taken the intelligent step of advertising to its built-in audience, erecting a sign atop one of the apartments overlooking the park's right-field wall.

Once well oiled, the boosters departed the tavern and walked to the park. Eventually three thousand of them arrived from various locales during batting practice, all in full toreador regalia with gold and red sashes. The rooters then staggered to their reserved section. Meanwhile, a hundred of the organization's finest, decked out in sombreros and long linen coats, made their way onto the field. Drummers and a full German band accompanied the comic parade.

As if that wasn't enough, the high-spirited group had a live bull in tow. A proposed bullfight, much publicized in the days before the game, did not come off; the well-fed and sleepy bull was less than enthusiastic. But the resulting shenanigans were enough to interrupt batting practice, according to George Rice in the April 24 *Daily Journal*, and amused the fans to no end. How in the world did these bozos even get on the field? Easy. Charley Weeghman was a member of the Bravo el Toro Club.

THE WAR SPIRIT RAN HIGH

After several rooters' groups marched onto the newly laid field, the real ceremonies began. Twenty members of the Daughters of the Grand Army of the Republic Relief Corps, dressed in white and led by relief corps president Ida Wright, toted a thirty-foot silk American flag around the ballpark. During the procession, one or more of the brass bands struck up "The Star-Spangled Banner," which was not yet the national anthem. Weeghman and Walker accompanied the ladies on their jaunt, as did players from both teams, assorted dignitaries, and fans simply swept up by the emotion of the moment. Hundreds of people crowded onto the field as fifteen ladies ran the flag up the pole in deep center field.

Fans greeted the patriotic ceremony with great gusto. Soldiers fired off a twenty-one-gun salute, and the club set off a barrage of fireworks when the flag reached the top of the pole. The huge banner, made of an extremely thin, gauzy silk, did not last long in the Chicago winds. Local newspapers carry references to the club putting up "new" flags during the 1914 and 1915 seasons.

Following the salute, the parade of players, ladies, and musicians headed to home plate, where Joe Tinker received carts of flowers and, oddly, three dozen neckties. The usual awkward hilarity ensued as the manager "was compelled to smile amid the blooms for the benefit of the moving picture machine," according to Sam Weller in the next day's *Tribune*. Rooters gave a grinning Weeghman a gold loving cup.

A procession of a hundred cars, representing friends of Tinker from his west suburban hometown of Oak Park, also drove through the ballyard before the game began. Amazingly, wrote Weller, "the outfield was a bit soft, but the diamond looked fine" despite the pregame ruckus.

In what may have been a first, Weeghman paid to have thousands of baseball caps in different colors and decorated with the Chifeds logo passed out to ticket buyers. Small felt flags were also given out. "Thousands of spectators donned the little caps distributed by the local management, while others waved Chifed pennants," noted J. G. Davis in the April 24 *Tribune*.

This was a noted contrast to what other clubs did. For decades, the New York Yankees refused to allow replica caps with their club's logo to be manufactured. Yankees management felt that its logo, and by extension its franchise, would be cheapened if just anyone could wear a Yankees hat.

WHO WAS THERE?

The single-decked park officially seated eighteen thousand at this time, but nearly twenty-one thousand souls packed it on April 23. The right-field bleacher wall was topped with a row of spectators, and fans stood. Hundreds of others watched the game and ceremonies from windows and rooftops of buildings on Waveland and Sheffield Avenues, past the left- and right-field fences. Still more baseball bugs hung off the elevated platform at Addison. Two large blocks of temporary "circus" seats, placed down the left- and right-field foul lines and jutting into fair territory, were jammed as well. Other fans lined up around the field and ringed the outfield in orderly lines, sitting in fair territory. (Work on the new park went right up to the last minute; ladders, sawhorses, and tools leant against the left-center field wall, some 420 feet from home plate.) Some two thousand others were turned away because there was no room. Three of those were Elsie Dabel, her mom, and her sister. Elsie did notice plenty of handsome men hanging around the ballpark that day, though, as noted in her diary:

> Today was the opening of the Federal League Ball Park. . . . We didn't go in. I never saw such crowds in all my life. . . . There were *so* many nifts there. Before the game they shot some kind of thing into the air and a little parachute came out. They had two bands there which kept playing "This is the Life," a very appropriate song for the occasion. The Chifeds won. There was an awful cute pennant guy there who kept fancying us. We bought a pennant for a quarter. We certainly had a fine time but I was wishing I could have gone in.

The exclusion of the Dabel ladies from the ballpark notwithstanding, there were, J. G. Davis wrote the next day in the *Tribune*, a "large number of women present."

Local celebrities attended the opening in abundance, too, including chief contractor William Sinek, league president James Gilmore and his wife, Louis and Mrs. Comiskey, and several local judges. Umpire-in-chief Bill Brennan introduced the players from both sides to the fans, one hopes with the aid of a megaphone.

THE GAME

The weather was cold and damp, and a harsh wind roared in from the lake. After John Sexton, corporation counsel of Chicago, threw out the first ball (Mayor Carter Harrison was out of town), the Feds took the field.

The home team got off to a hot start against Kansas City pitcher Chief Johnson, who was removed before the bottom of the second inning, not by his manager but on orders from the authorities. Johnson, who had left the Cincinnati Reds to join the Federal League, was served with papers by the NL club and forbidden to pitch. By then, the Chifeds had already tagged Johnson for three runs, and they went on to add another in the third, two in the fourth, two more in the sixth, and another in the eighth. Claude Hendrix threw a five-hitter at the visitors, and Chicago won the game 9–1.

THE NORTH SIDE HAS SOMETHING

F. A. McInerny's words in the April 24 edition of the *Post* showed that the Feds had convinced at least some of the newspapermen:

> Charley Weeghman made a lot of friends yesterday.
>
> About 22,000 fans went to the Buns' North Side ball park, and they went away tickled to death with the treatment they had received . . . each was made to feel that he was welcome. Nothing in the park was too good for him. The fun was clean and amusing and the general effect was that of a huge family having a good time.
>
> This tone reflected Charley Weeghman's good fellowship, and it is significant because it indicates that those who went to the opening game will go again and again, and they will bring others with them.
>
> In other words, the North Side has good reason today to stand up and holler. It has something.

Even the *Tribune*, a paper not unconditionally in love with Charley or his Buns, weighed in on April 24 with unreserved optimism. J. G. Davis wrote: "Over 21,000 fans performed their part in making the opening one of the greatest in the history of the game. . . . A glance at the wonderful setting for yesterday's combat brought the thought that someone must have rubbed Aladdin's lamp to effect such a magical transformation." What the opening of Weeghman Park meant to the North Side of Chicago is nearly incalculable. The park's success on this day was the exclamation point to the region's new vitality. The pseudonymic Le Count, in the April 24 *Inter-Ocean* called it, with perhaps some hyperbole, "the greatest inaugural reception a baseball club ever had."

DON'T FENCE ME IN

During the first game, light-hitting Chifeds receiver Dutch Wilson had belted two homers over Weeghman Park's 310-foot left-field fence. Writers suggested that left field was perhaps a bit too inviting. On Sunday the twenty-sixth, three Kansas City hitters homered, causing umpires to improvise a new ground rule holding such over-the-fence hits to doubles. On the off day following the first series at the new park, Weeghman hired a construction crew to move the wall back some twenty to twenty-five feet and strap a wire fence over the top of it to reduce "cheap homers." To make room for the additional outfield area, the crew removed the front porch of a mammoth brick house that stood just past the left-field wall. The reconstruction also forced the club to relocate the left-field scoreboard.

Jack Ryder of the *Sporting News* sniffed in the May 7 issue that "the news that the Federal Park in Chicago, which was described by the press agents as a perfect marvel, is being enlarged, after the playing of three games on it, is amusing." Ryder went on to say that eight homers were hit over the short left-field fence in the Sunday game and that orders were given to enlarge the area. He concluded, with the typical *Sporting News* slant, "It is sad to think of the money sunk in this venture that will never come out again." It is not known whether Ryder or his colleagues covering the NL and AL felt that the Polo Grounds, which at the time sported left- and right-field foul lines of 277 feet, or the West Side Grounds, which had a 316-foot right-field line, were equally inappropriate.

After these changes were made to the left-field fence, Weeghman Park became an only slightly above-average home-run park over the rest of the season. The Chifeds led Federal League clubs in home runs in home games with thirty, but other clubs had home totals of twenty-eight, twenty-seven, and twenty-five. Visiting teams hit only nineteen homers at Weeghman in 1914, giving the park a ranking of third among all Federal League ballyards for the number of home runs hit by visiting teams. But even with batters combining for forty-nine homers in 1914, tied for the most in the league, it wasn't a good hitter's park; Weeghman was the lowest-scoring park in the league by a very wide margin. Meanwhile, the Chifeds led the league in runs during road games.

Weeghman Park had made its debut, and already it was starting to change—a process that hasn't abated and probably never will. ♦

3

HEADY DAYS
WEEGHMAN PARK, 1914–1917

KISSING HANDS AND SHAKING BABIES

As the season progressed, major league baseball was indeed hurt by the new competition. Per Irving Sanborn in the *Sporting News* of May 14, "The Cubs have fared pretty badly most of the time, because the Federals have weaned away so many of the dyed-in-the-wool Cubs supporters."

Yet the new Chicagos found it an uphill battle to bring in the bodies, too, with two other major league clubs to compete with. Even after the exciting beginning to the Chifeds' season, Charley Weeghman still had to roust fans to the park. This he did via handbills, advertising, good customer service, and, apparently, honoring every group in the city that had more than a few members. The July 7, 1914, *Sporting Life* reported that "Weeghman is working overtime with various stunts which are intended to edge into the good graces of the Chicago fandom . . . the boss of the local Federals has planned several days for the North Side park."

In one instance, Weeghman feted Otto Knabe, manager of the Baltimore Terrapins, with a German oompah band prior to a June 14 doubleheader. Plenty of locals came out to salute the popular Knabe, a longtime National League second baseman who was to finish his career with the 1916 Cubs. Similarly, June 18 was Fisk Day in honor of Chifeds hurler Max Fisk, a product of the South Side Roseland neighborhood. Several hundred of his pals from Roseland and nearby Pullman made their way north, with, of course, their own band in tow. Fisk, a spitballer, pitched a complete game, two-hit 3–2 win. When Fisk went up to hit in the third inning, several of his buddies jumped onto the field, strode up to home plate, and presented him with a new gold watch. Despite the honors, Fisk (whom the record books call "Fiske") did not pitch beyond this season, as he was jettisoned after he held out for more than a 5 percent raise.

The promotional festivities continued on Saturday, June 20, as the North Side Boosters came out in full force and, of course, brought a band. Two days later, a quarter of the two thousand fans on hand hailed from the Graeme Stewart School. The following day, Lake View High School pupils were Weeghman's guests, with, reported the *Tribune* on June 23, "more schools to be entertained later." On July 15, the club honored a contingent of Elks; both Weeghman and Tinker belonged to the fraternal organization. Buried in small print next to this report in the *Tribune* was a short paragraph concerning the Boston Red Sox's purchase, from the Baltimore Orioles minor league organization, of a young pitcher named George Ruth.

On July 11, Weeghman held a special German Day doubleheader with a boatload of pregame entertainment: a 1,500-marcher on-field parade, led by Ballman's Band, and several vaudeville routines. The parade, unsurprisingly, began at the Bismarck Garden. Once the game started, a second band of ragtime-influenced musicians in comic clothing entertained fans in the bleachers, while Ballman's group played for the more upscale grandstand patrons. Before the second game, a band played "Spanish fandangoes" to honor the five hundred or so members of the Bravo el Toro Club who showed up, decked out once again in fake bullfighters' togs, ready when the game let out to raid the local taverns.

The antics at the park continued through the summer. On August 12, the YMCA brought a group of kids, who led organized cheers in an impressive fashion. A few days later, a Meiji University baseball club, from Japan, played the Mandel Brothers nine, representing the State Street Merchants League. On August 21, three Greek-Americans, attempting a walk across the United States, were admitted free to the park by Chifeds secretary Charley Williams. The men sat in a field box and were "treated like curiosities" by the fans, according to Sam Weller in the next day's *Tribune*. September 1 was Cy Falkenberg Day. The Indianapolis "Hoo Fed" (or "Hoosier Federals") pitcher, who had served for eight years with the Indians and Senators, hailed from Chicago.

One important group had made its presence known at the park on June 10. Labor unionists, angered that the Brooklyn Tip-Tops had used nonunion workers to build their grandstand in April, made sure that all tradesmen in every Federal League city knew to boycott the Tip-Tops wherever they played. Perhaps as a result, only twelve hundred fans showed up for the game. Eager to dissociate themselves from the Tip-Tops, on August 15, the Chifeds held a National Union Day, and just a week later, the ballpark had a combined Flag Day/Masonic Day. (Tinker was also a Mason.) Weeghman had obtained a brand-new oversized American flag to raise that day, and two thousand Masons marched on the field before the game, accompanied by their own fifty-piece band.

In addition to the myriad special days, Weeghman held successful Ladies Days on Fridays when the Chifeds were in town. (When the schedule necessitated, he pushed the event to Thursdays.) The female contingent predictably became known as the "lady bugs." The Chifeds' first Ladies Day was May 1. Elsie Dabel and a friend went to the park and experienced more than a little condescension among the male rooters: "We understood it perfectly. Our fans called the girls 'fanettes' and one fellow said that the girls think it's like playing tag. It got me sore because we knew just as much about it as he did. After this, every Friday is going to be Ladies Day and Em and I will be present at every one."

Despite his hard work and marketing, Weeghman struggled to draw more than a couple thousand fans for weekday games. A good weekend turnout was six thousand, with the few crowds over ten thousand welcomed as godsends. Even on weekends, the bleachers were usually packed but grandstands were only a third to a half full.

Nevertheless, on balance the Chifeds were outpolling the major-league clubs. On May 11, 1914, the White Sox, Cubs, and Chifeds all held home games. The upstarts outdrew the other two clubs. Some eighteen thousand spectators crowded into Weeghman Park to watch the Chifeds play Saint Louis, which sent former Cubs great Mordecai "Three-Finger" Brown to the hill. With some fans rooting for the home team and others pulling for the three-fingered eventual Hall of Famer, the visiting Terriers won 5–4. The crowd on the North Side was about a thousand more than watched the White Sox entertain Ty Cobb and the Tigers at Comiskey Park. Honus Wagner and the Pirates, for their part, drew only nine thousand for their game against the Cubs at West Side Grounds.

Come August 14, Weeghman drew further attention to the rivalry by offering up a challenge to the Cubs and White Sox, who already engaged in an annual city series. The Feds wanted in on the action, and Weeghman said that he would pay $25,000 to either of the major league clubs if they defeated his Buns in a postseason tourney. Neither the Cubs nor the White Sox wanted to give Weeghman the time of day, so the proposal fell by the wayside, though a good portion of the local baseball public would have enjoyed such a spectacle. The Feds had nothing to lose by making such an offer; the majors had nothing to gain by accepting it. The war continued.

LOOKING GOOD

Weeghman's pride in his park continued to be a selling point— and to draw notice. The money Weeghman spent on upkeep was a big part of his strategy to get people to the ballpark. His restaurants weren't sloppy; why should his baseball field be? Sam Weller of the *Tribune* laid bouquets at Weeghman's and groundskeeper Murphy's feet on May 31, writing, "While the team was away, the infield was skinned, leveled up, and re-sodded. The grass in the outfield is perfect." Weller went on, "it is doubtful if there is a ball field in the country which looks any better than Weeghman Park today." Clearly the press appreciated the care Weeghman took, especially compared to the penny-wise, pound-foolish ways shown by the Cubs at sooty, dirty, rodent-infested West Side Grounds.

Weeghman did, however, indulge in some antics not found in ballparks today (which is probably for the best). For example, he had a small stable built under the third-base stands, where he kept a horse named Queen Bess. According to James Crusinberry in the June 14, 1914, *Tribune*, Bess was "an old, gentle, fat bay mare which had done service on a pie wagon in the loop for more than ten years." Weeghman kept Bess fed and had her pull the lawn mower when the ballpark grass needed to be cut. At nights, with the team out of town, Bess had the run of the diamond.

SUNSHINE AND SPEED

On May 8, it was too wet for the Whales and Brooklyn Tip-Tops to play their scheduled game, but fans were let in to watch the teams practice. Weeghman did other things to accommodate fans on inclement days. On June 15, when it was unusually chilly, he permitted the fans sitting in the grandstand to move into the box seats in order to catch some sun. Conversely, on July 13, with the Saint Louis Terriers in town, the skies opened up. Weeghman allowed the bleacher fans into the covered grandstand. (Irving Sanborn, in the next day's *Tribune*, noted that some of the fans took advantage of Weeghman's good nature and "rushed right down into the choice box seats and sat there in spite of the rain, which was not so wet apparently as it was out in center field.") He really did believe that it was important to make fans comfortable.

Weeghman was also conscious of the time it took to play a game. With July 4 falling on a Sunday, Weeghman tried to pump attendance for the team's July 5 game (when the holiday was observed that year) with ads in the local papers. With pregame entertainment featuring a fifty-piece band and singers, Weeghman wanted to make the day at the park a family affair. Conscious of selling the product as enjoyable and convenient, his ad blared that "the Federal League is playing 'faster' and 'closer' ball than any other Major League this season . . . if you enjoy good ball and want to see a fast game, be a 'Fed' fan and join us at Weeghman Park to-day!" Somewhere between five thousand and six thousand fans showed up for the 2–1 Feds victory. Two days later, the Chifeds completed a game in a snappy eighty-four minutes.

UNDISCIPLINED

As much as Weeghman catered to the fans, they were still capable of powerful unruliness, yelling at umpires and causing other ruckuses. On August 16, one umpire's lack of fortitude caused a twenty-minute rhubarb that delayed the Chifeds and Baltimore Terrapins' game. With a man on base in the eighth and Baltimore up 1–0, plate umpire Charles Van Sickle called time, at Feds' coach Jimmy Block's request, as Terrapins pitcher Bill Bailey began to deliver a pitch to Dutch Zwilling. Bailey threw the ball anyway, and the Chifed center fielder smacked the ball into the bleachers and circled the bases. Baltimore manager Otto Knabe ran onto the field to protest that time had been called. Van Sickle wavered, discussing the situation with base umpire Monte Cross and trying to get all sides to agree rather than simply imposing the correct decision.

All hell broke loose. Tinker and his players were up in arms; the fans showered the field with garbage. The band entertaining that day tried to drown out the booing by playing popular songs. For nearly twenty minutes, Tinker refused to send Zwilling back up to bat and, during the fray, Weeghman made his way down to the field and began yelling at Van Sickle as well.

Van Sickle was unable to restore order. Rather than simply threatening to forfeit the game to the visitors, he was reported to have told Tinker, "Come on Joe, get the boys out there. Be a good fellow." Weeghman and Tinker asked the local scribes, who had run down from the press box to cover the brouhaha, to explain the rules. Once the writers notified the Chifeds that they were in the wrong, the game resumed. The next day, the Federal League fired Van Sickle, who reappeared in the news in June 1915 when a player in the Western League slugged him.

AND I'M TELLING YOU I'M NOT GOING

Despite his passion for his team and his park, and even as his Feds fought for the league's first pennant, Weeghman had to fight off more rumors that he was ready to split for the majors. The September 12 *Sporting Life* carried a story in which the Chicago owner admitted that four Federal League clubs would lose money on the season and that "it is a bad year in base-ball." He denied once again, however, that he would desert the new league even if he, Otto Stifel of Saint Louis, and Robert Ward of Brooklyn were awarded franchises in the American Association.

Indeed, it was rough for most baseball men. Weeghman noted in October that he had been informed by an American League owner that only Boston and one other club in the junior circuit had actually made money in 1914. For himself, however, Weeghman claimed financial victory. The August 8 issue of *Sporting Life* reported on an August 2 dispatch that said: "Over $5,000 in paid admissions to the Chicago-Pittsburgh Federal League game today. . . . Chicago has played to good and paying crowds ever since the league started, and the receipts today were just enough to cover all the expenses for the remaining month. From now on every cent taken in will be profit for the owners." Other sources assert that the August 4 game, which brought attendance over two hundred thousand for the season, was the one to put the Chifeds into the black—but in either event, they were in the black.

DISAPPOINTED

On the field, the Chifeds appeared to be in the driver's seat for the 1914 Federal League crown, but a tough doubleheader loss to the sixth-place Kansas City Packers on October 6 turned the tide in the favor of the Indianapolis Hoosiers, who clinched the next day. Eventually, the Chifeds finished a game and a half out. The result disheartened Weeghman, who had staked much of his pocketbook on winning a title.

Still, he continued to invest in the team by raiding the major leagues for talent. All winter, he pursued Walter Johnson, the greatest pitcher in baseball, and nearly got him. At one point, Johnson agreed in principle to playing in Chicago, but the Washington Senators eventually "convinced" him to return with a new contract. White Sox owner Charlie Comiskey, fearing the gate attraction for the Feds should the "Big Train"—as Johnson was nicknamed—pitch in his hometown, agreed to the unusual step of kicking some money toward the Senators to keep Johnson in the nation's capital.

MODIFICATIONS

During the winter of 1914–15, Weeghman altered the seating of his park. He scrapped initial plans to double-deck the right-field bleachers. Instead, Weeghman had Zachary Davis design a plan to tear down the existing outfield seats and construct a much larger bleacher section in left field, seating 1,000 more customers. This project also shifted the scoreboard to straightaway center field. Since the right-field wall already abutted Sheffield Avenue and the left-field wall was well south of Waveland Avenue, this decision made sense. The project, again run by Blome-Sinek, cost the team $17,000.

The large left-field bleacher was some fifteen rows deep and ended near center field. The distance to the left-center fence was around 340 feet. In right field, no seats remained, just a large brownish-red brick wall that extended all the way to the scoreboard in deepest center. Handy Andy noted in the March 6, 1915, *Tribune* that Weeghman was holding off traveling to Shreveport for spring training until he finished working out the details of tearing down the large house occupying part of the left-field territory. As always, Weeghman presented the change in the grandest possible terms. The 1915 Whales game program maintained that "the new and larger bleachers were erected and the playing field enlarged because there is nothing too good for the patrons of the Chicago Federal League Baseball Club."

On the field, Murphy and his crew rounded off the infield dirt behind second base so that the infield was no longer a box. From where the second baseman played to where the shortstop played, the dirt behind second was changed from an angle to a straight line.

Last, Weeghman made two improvements off the field that were aimed at increasing convenience for the fans. First, he had Illinois Bell place public phone booths inside the park. Second, he developed a system by which fans could reserve game tickets by mail or phone and pick them up either downtown, at Shannon's Sporting Goods, at 54 East Monroe, until noon of game day, or at the park until 2:30 that afternoon.

There was another change for 1915 as well, when the Chicago Fire Department built a new firehouse for Engine 78's company at 1052 West Waveland. The firehouse remains an integral part of the neighborhood. Just across the street from the left-field gate, it's been a hangout for Cubs fans, locals, the press, and even the athletes and coaches.

THE NAME GAME . . . AGAIN

Early in 1915, Weeghman—always looking to keep his business in the public eye—sponsored a contest to name the Chifeds. The entries began rolling in to area newspapers, giving the local reporters plenty of guffaws. G. W. Axelson, in the February 4 *Herald*, reported that some of the suggestions included animals such as Colts, Eagles, Swans, Condors, Pelicans, Zebras, Bunnies, and Rats; food jokes such as Spuds, Beefers, Chibuns, and Pepper Pods; and topical or local references like Kaisers, I Wills (Chicago being known as the "I will" city), Navajos, Iroquois, Bismarcks, and Windy Lads. The writers had already used several of the nominated monikers—Tinx, Tots, Buns—in 1914. This contest was popular: G. W. Axelson claimed on February 4, 1915, that 500 letters with 289 different names were submitted, while the same day, the *Daily News* noted receiving 368 letters with 287 names.

The February 5 *Daily News* reported that Chix was going to be Weeghman's choice, but that a fan—having heard the rumor that this name would be chosen—wrote the club and said that he'd never return to see a team that could be mocked as Chickens. So Chix was out and Whales, Charley's second choice, was in. D. J. Eichoff of 1451 West Hood Street in the North Side Edgewater neighborhood was responsible for the name. Eichoff also sent in a logo: a whale with its large tail upturned, as if having just vanquished an opponent. "I certainly am delighted to learn that my title was adopted. I think it will become a popular name with the fans, too," he told James Crusinberry of the *Tribune* after being announced as the winner on February 4. The Eichoff family received a set of season tickets as prizes. This made Eichoff very happy, as he and his wife had been Federal League fans since the club played at DePaul in 1913.

Historians have wondered about the "whales" reference. Some thought it was a food reference; a note in the *Evening Post* in February 1915, shortly after the new name was adopted, made a joke of the name, referencing Weeghman's large sandwiches, which supposedly had to be cut "with a safety razor."

But Eichoff's inspirations were far more literal. His reasons given, as reported by H. D. Johnson in the February 5 *Herald*:

- The most commercially valuable whales are found in the frozen north, meaning that the North Side should have the best team.
- Whales lash and drub their opponents.
- Anything marked a "whaler" is large and extraordinary.

With a new name came new duds much flashier than the austere pinstripes worn the year before. The 1915 Whales boasted cream-colored jerseys and pants when in Chicago, with blue stockings and caps and cherry-red sweaters. A large blue *C* on the left breast held inside of it a blue whale. The logo looked as much like a submarine sandwich as a sea creature, perhaps on purpose. Weeghman, now being called Whale Oil Charley by the writers, certainly was happy with the size and domination that the name intimated—big and brassy was his modus operandi.

FEDS FETED

On March 4, the team began spring workouts in Shreveport. Prior to departing Chicago, Weeghman and the Whales were feted at a booster's club banquet at Rienzi's restaurant at Clark and Diversey. At least 750 diners, and possibly as many as a thousand, were served chicken. The crowd, in a jovial and most certainly drunken mood, were treated to singing, jokes, and speeches, including a very short one from Weeghman and a fiery one from James Gilmore.

The next day, Weeghman got off the best line of the year. Boston Braves hurler Bill James wanted to jump his contract and sign with the Federals, but when Weeghman saw that the pitcher's current contract did not have a ten-day escape clause (which allowed a player to void a deal within ten days of signing), he demurred. "I still have some respect for the law," Weeghman proclaimed, "Even if I *am* a baseball club owner."

OPENING UP AGAIN

The day before opening the 1915 season at home on April 10, the Whales held a public workout at Weeghman Park. Admission was free, and John O. Seys in the *Daily News* noted that "President Weeghman, who was one of the early comers, gave orders to allow everyone to enter, and the front rows of the box seats were well filled with the admirers of the new North Side team." Seys also reported that "the remodeled outfield was a revelation to the players who were on the team last year. Dutch Zwilling and

Al Wickland, who covered right and center fields last year, found they had been given a lot more room through the removal of the bleachers in right center."

Come Opening Day itself, April 10, fans and ballplayers again paraded to and around the Weeghman grounds. A trail of some four hundred cars began in the Loop and headed up to the park. Manager Joe Tinker, decked out in a long coat and a Whales cap, rode in a car festooned with flowers. Several rooters' clubs had cars swathed in Whales pennants and garlands. Some five thousand people were said to have greeted the parade, which arrived at the park around 2:30.

The commercialism of the day and of the park, which had been evident from the start, was made perfectly clear in Chicago *American* reporter Jay Davidson's April 11 description of the parade: "Most of the cars were decorated with banners and signs, and the usual number of advertising dodgers were seen in line. It was interesting to the innocent bystanders to learn that John Pumpernickel's raisins constitute the chief diet of Whales, and that the Whales nightly wallow about at William Whosit's biggestcabaretinthecity [sic], but this natural history lesson soon was forgotten."

Unfortunately, the parade's late arrival at Weeghman Park wiped out batting practice, so both clubs hastily grabbed their gloves for a quick infield toss-around. (During the 1915 season, all Federal League games were scheduled for 3:00.) The fences around the park were decked in American flags, and despite the chilly and wet conditions, the park welcomed an overflow crowd of twenty thousand. Newly elected Chicago mayor Big Bill Thompson was also running late and reached the premises just in time for the first pitch ceremony. Carter Harrison, the former mayor, was there, as was Bob Sweltzer, the Democratic candidate Thompson had vanquished just days before. Thompson walked onto the field wearing a sombrero as a band played "Illinois." The assembled crowd stood and applauded while the suddenly ubiquitous motion-picture machines recorded the event. Weeghman, knowing on which side his buns were buttered, presented Thompson with his own box seats—gratis—next to the Whales' dugout for the duration of the season. The mayor, accompanied by campaign manager Eugene Pike and some other aides, threw a perfect strike to catcher Art "Dutch" Wilson. Both Tinker and Saint Louis manager Fielder Jones received flower garlands. Finally, at 3:15, the game finally began. The Whales won 3–1.

ADVERTISING SECRETS

Want to go back to those innocent days when baseball was played for fun and not money? Let's take note of the Whales' 1915 scorebook, a forty-four-page, five-by-seven-inch, five-cent affair in which the club managed to cram in 114 advertisements. Some of the businesses featured there appealed to the well-to-do. Several car companies, steamship lines, and high-class hotels took out advertising in Weeghman's program, as did insurance companies, coal companies (including Collins and Weise, whose large lot bordered the park), tailors, haberdashers, banks, sporting goods stores, and the *Examiner*. Several types of liquor were represented, as were nearly a dozen different brands of cigars. Hollowed and O'Hara's, a restaurant and saloon downtown on Monroe near State Street, advertised "The Largest Bar in the World." The Rienzi Café, eight blocks south of Weeghman Park, was also a happy advertiser.

Everyone wanted into the inner circle. The People's Hand Laundry touted itself as the club's official laundry service; the Rittle Restaurant billed itself as "Federal League Headquarters," inviting fans to its location just a few blocks from the park. The makers of Hydrox Ice Cream, which was served at Weeghman Park, stretched credulity to the breaking point by claiming that its nutritional value was such that humans could survive on it. Arthur Feilchenfeld's Hats offered a new model for 1915. The Whale, a fairly ridiculous hat that was taller than a bowler but shorter than a topper, looked like an expensive version of the green cardboard hats given away at Saint Patrick's Day parties.

Joe Tinker's own brand of cigar was manufactured by Spector Brothers, while the G. V. Electric Truck Company claimed that its trucks were "Whales for Work." Of course, Weeghman also placed an ad for his ten downtown lunchrooms.

Several local concerns also bought ads, indicating that a hopping scene had already cropped up around the ballpark to serve the Whales' patrons. The Federal Ice Cream Parlor, located kitty-corner from the park at 959 West Addison, enticed fans to come in for a frozen treat before or after the game. In addition, the Addison Buffet, directly across the street from the park at 1059 West Addison, served hot and cold lunches and sandwiches. Just south of the park on Clark Street sat the Hemming Brewery at 3530 North Clark, and close by at 3557—the southeast corner of Clark and Addison—Reid's Buffet offered food and liquor. K & G Billiards, inside the still-standing Links Hall building at Sheffield and Newport, bid fans to come by after the game and shoot a few rounds. Even a new barbershop had opened, on Addison just east of the park. Some more prosaic local companies advertised as well—the Bernstein Painting and Decorating Company and the American Plumbing and Heating Company—though they were less likely to be patronized by fans seeking further entertainment after a game.

The ads weren't always on paper. On June 3, 1915, reported the *Daily Journal*, fans at the game were entranced by a hot-air balloon advertising a local tavern. Cubs fans familiar with the inflatable balloons installed on rooftops around Wrigley in the 1980s and 1990s know that in some respects times haven't changed that much. In one particularly enjoyable incident on a windy day in the early 1990s, Budweiser's forty-foot inflatable Spuds McKenzie slowly deflated during a game.

EVERYTHING BUT A BALLGAME

Despite his devotion to the team and its revenues, Weeghman didn't always spend his days at the ballpark. On May 27, he took a look at the skies and called off that day's scheduled game with the Newark Peppers, forcing a doubleheader two days later. He then hauled his golf clubs out of the front closet. "Immediately after calling the game," remarked the *Herald* on May 28, "Weeghman hied himself to the Exmoor Links, but returned in time to bat .300 in the entertainment at Bismarck Gardens at night."

That day turned out to be sunny. Early-season bad weather did result in a number of postponements, however, and Weeghman, needing to raise money, tried to fill the park, much as he did when his team was out of town—which was often. When a team wasn't playing league games, it was likely that they'd be on the road playing an exhibition to raise more revenue. The Whales spent many "off days" in towns like Ottumwa, Iowa, Richmond, Indiana, and Marion, Illinois, playing exhibitions against local nines and pocketing a chunk of the gate.

Early in 1915, Weeghman had gone to see the Pittsburgh Pirates play at home and was greatly impressed by a postgame exhibition of hippodroming at Forbes Field. "Hippodroming" had two meanings. One was negative—it meant to make a farce of something serious, which in baseball terms meant "players throwing games for money." The other meaning signifies entertainment—namely, singing, dancing, comedy, animal acts, and other vaudeville-type shows. Originally, a "hippodrome" was an arena used for equestrian exhibitions (the term derived from the ancient Greek term for "horse race course") but ultimately came to represent any entertainment held in open-air stadiums. When Weeghman saw Pirates owner Barney Dreyfuss raking in cash with popular entertainment, he figured that he could give the North Side another option for evening fun. Weeghman attempted to compete with downtown shows, featuring ticket prices and acts comparable to those in the chichi theaters. Certainly this was a good option for those living in Lake View.

While fireworks had been set off the previous July 3 (according to Elsie Dabel: "We couldn't get a seat because mother wouldn't go in the crowd"), the debut of Weeghman's hippodrome came on June 12, 1915, with the Whales on a lengthy road trip. Local vaudeville veteran Jake Stenard arranged the program. Turning Weeghman's baseball field into an amusement park took some doing, particularly to ensure that people could see at 9:00 at night. Many people believe that lights didn't sully Wrigley Field until 1988, but in order to run the hippodrome Weeghman found it necessary to construct an electric lighting system to illuminate the field. He even hauled in a circus-type double spotlight system. Workers also installed a large platform on wheels, used for animal acts, near the pitcher's mound, facing the third-base side.

Tickets for various seats cost ten, twenty, and thirty cents, with the program scheduled to last from 7:30 until 11:00. Festivities opened with a parade, but the star of the first night's show was Slivers, a famous comedian renowned for his apparently excellent baseball pantomime. "Everybody who ever went to a circus has had a real, genuine laugh with this baseball clown," opined the *American* on June 12. Seven other acts appeared that night, and their names seem like parodies of vaudevillians: The Six Royal Hussars, Holland and Dockroll, the Holman Brothers, the Five Juggling Normans, the Armanto Trio, the Paul Rondas Trio, and the Three Fanchon Sisters.

The hippodroming continued at least through Independence Day and probably longer. On the nights of July 4–5, Weeghman not only presented the usual acts but also blew off five-grand worth of fireworks arranged into patterns portraying the Liberty Bell, the American flag, and even President Wilson.

But singing, dancing, and comedy weren't the only things going on with the Whales out of town in June 1915. Weeghman also let the park out to various organizations, including the U.S. Army baseball team, which played the University of Chicago at least three times and also whipped the local semipro Modern Woodmen team and a squad organized by Billy Niesen, Chicago's preeminent organizer of semipro baseball; during the 1910s, Niesen ran the Ogden Grove league, which included a team sponsored by

Wrigley's gum. On June 7, Lane Tech High School, eight blocks west of the ballpark at Addison and Western, held its all-school field day at Weeghman. In addition to various track and field contests, a color guard presented the flag and a dance squad went through various routines on the infield. They were almost like cheerleaders—a harbinger of things to come.

DISASTER RELIEF

Weeghman drew on his entrepreneurial sense and on his desire to be a good neighbor in the wake of one of Chicago's most shocking disasters. On July 24, 1915, when the cruise ship *Eastland* capsized while preparing to leave Chicago, more than eight hundred drowned. Weeghman held an Eastland Sufferer's Day on July 29. (A Joe Tinker Day planned for a few days before at the ballpark was canceled to respect the victims' families.) The Whales donated all gate proceeds that day, as well as the funds from concessions, to the victims' families. Weeghman, who received some good notices in the press as well as a few barbs for exploiting the terrible event, said he hoped to raise $10,000.

Local actresses from two popular stage shows, *All Over Town* and *The Lady in Red*, walked through the stands selling programs and flowers, as did society figures and wives of some Whales players. These proceeds also went to the fund. To increase traffic, Weeghman lowered ticket prices to a quarter for the grandstand and fifty cents for box seats. "It will greatly please Weeghman," said the Chicago *American* on July 28, "if he has to stretch ropes around the playing field to keep the overflow crowds off the diamond." The pass gate, where the press, players, and club personnel entered, was closed; everyone had to pay to get into the park that day, including players, writers, telegraph operators, policemen, umpires, and Jim Gilmore. "I just want to look at the fellow who would begrudge spending 50 cents for such a cause," he sniffed to the *Evening Post* on July 28. Weeghman even offered to pay the admission out of his own pocket to anyone who couldn't afford it.

Another selling point to the game was the pitching match-up. Tinker tapped Three-Finger Brown, the former Cubs hero, to start the game, while Buffalo Feds skipper Harry Lord countered with his top pitcher, Fred Anderson. It was also noted that both player-managers would "participate in the game in some capacity," though Tinker did not play.

At one point, Jake Sternad, who handled nighttime amusements for the Whales, was set to arrange a vaudeville show before the contest, but good taste seems to have won out. The 3:00 start was not delayed by "any frills or fussing," wrote Jay Davidson of the *American* the next day, although rain kept down attendance and made playing conditions substandard. The event raised nearly $1,000 for the emergency fund, a good sum of money in those days.

Everything got back to business shortly thereafter. A few weeks later, on September 2, the Whales held Intercollegiate Day, featuring an East versus West all-star college baseball game.

WHALES WIN!

The 1915 Federal League pennant race is among the most fascinating in baseball's history. Five of the league's eight teams remained in contention in mid-September; on the final weekend, the Whales, Saint Louis Terriers, and Pittsburgh Rebels were tightly bunched. The Terriers split the four games of their final series at Kansas City to end up with eighty-seven games, more than either the Whales or the Rebels. The Terriers had played all 154 of their contests, while the Whales had suffered two rainouts and the Rebels one, and league policy was not to make them up. But Charley Weeghman, the league's most powerful owner, inveigled the league to allow him to play a season-ending makeup doubleheader to give his club a chance to win it all.

Francis McInerney of the October 4, 1915, *Evening Post* doubted that "ever a World Series crowd had anything on that roaring, crowding, screeching turnout of 34,212 fans which watched Joe

Tinker's Federal League Buns" on October 3. Nobody expected that kind of crowd, even Charley Weeghman, and he and his staff were caught flat-footed. By the time Mayor and Mrs. Thompson showed up, secretary Charley Williams was sweating bullets as he escorted the dignitaries to their seats. Two days later, J. J. Alcock noted in the *Tribune* that "Weeghman is lamenting the fact that he did not know how to distribute the fans, for he believes he would have broken the record for attendance at a ball game if he could have crowded in everybody who tried to get inside the grounds."

Four hours before game time, hundreds of fans lined up waiting to buy tickets. The trains and streetcars brought in thousands more, and tickets sold out an hour before the first pitch. Five thousand fans waited outside the stadium and added their cheers when alerted to the goings-on. Fans stood ten deep in the grandstand. The aisles were jammed, and fans formed a giant horseshoe around the field, six people deep at its narrowest around the outfield. Young men sat on the brick outfield walls. Women in full fancy dress uncomplainingly sat on cushions. Fans even went under the stands to watch through small portholes. Some three hundred rooters forced themselves into the press box, nearly crowding out the writers.

In game 1, the Whales led 4–1 with two outs in the ninth. But just one out from the championship, the team showed the hysterical crowd the kind of Chicago finish that has become almost a ritual, blowing a seemingly safe lead and losing 5–4 in eleven innings. This disheartened the crowd and made it a life-or-death concern that their pod of Whales capture the nightcap before the sun went down. A Pittsburgh victory or a tie meant a pennant for the Rebels.

Federal League umpire-in-chief Bill Brennan ran the plate this day. (Brennan always seemed to be in Chicago, possibly because Charley Weeghman would have demanded the best umpire be at his field.) Brennan signaled at the beginning of the second game that the contest would be called off after whatever half-inning was completed after 5:24 P.M., the exact minute of sundown. The Pittsburgh players tried to loaf their way through the game and produce a tie. But with the score 0–0 in the bottom of the sixth, Chicago's Max Flack rapped out an RBI double to right that set the crowd into hysterics. By the end of the inning, the Whales led 3–0.

Brennan looked at his watch and announced that the top of the seventh would be the last inning. With two out, Pittsburgh's Ed Konetchy stroked a lazy fly to center field. When Dutch Zwilling squeezed it at 5:25 P.M., the Whales had the flag. The victory awarded Chicago the crown by 0.0009 percentage points. Their 86–66 record was just that much better than Saint Louis's 87–67, while Pittsburgh finished 86–67.

The Whales' clinching triumph produced bedlam at the North Side park. J. J. Alcock of the *Tribune* reported the next day on "the deafening cheers of one of the greatest baseball crowds this city has ever seen." In the words of McInerney in the next morning's *Trib*, the fans "went Borneo," tossing their seat cushions into the air. "One of the biggest cushion fights ever staged in a Chicago ball park took place," wrote Alcock, his words suggesting that this type of event was not a rarity. "The multitude on the field rushed for the Whale bench to congratulate the winners and were met with a steady fire of cushions from the stand. The men on the grass were prompt to accept the challenge, and within a minute there were a couple of thousand cushions sailing back and forth." Mayor and Mrs. Thompson were caught in the crossfire and barely escaped being beaned by several cushions, which also came sailing from the hands of interlopers in the press box. McInerney wrote that "many were struck by the flying pads, and altho ground attendants and police got busy, it was several minutes before the frenzied fans became rational enough to seek the street and elevated cars."

Following the contest, Weeghman held court in his office, inviting in dozens of friends, sportswriters, and fans. Weeghman's parents were there as well, "smiling as pleasant a pair of Hoosier smiles as one could picture," according to the next day's *Tribune*.

IT'S ALL OVER NOW

At the same time that year, in the major leagues, the Red Sox and Phillies were about to square off in the World Series. In an October 5 telegram to both teams, Weeghman entreated the winning club to take on his Chifeds for the benefit not only of his players but also for "the many thousand fans who have been patrons of the Federal League games throughout the season."

Everyone knew the majors wouldn't respond to Weeghman. "The best the Buns can do is claim the world's title by default. Empty honor," mourned columnist Howard Mann in the October 5 *Evening Post*. So Weeghman finally had his championship, tattered as it was, but he had no luck leveraging it. "Now that you have it, Charley, whatinell are you going to do with it?" the October 4 *Tribune* asked. Even the Chicago city council weighed in, passing a resolution urging Mayor Thompson to call for a round-robin series among the Phils, Bosox, and Whales. But no go.

His calls for a true battle with the big boys unheeded, Weeghman again turned to the local city series. His team, he argued, was the only champion in town, but neither the Cubs nor the White Sox showed interest in Weeghman's offer. Mann groused about the Cubs and Sox, "The winner will claim the city championship in the face of the fact that the Buns won a league pennant. It is to laugh." Ring Lardner, as usual, had a verse for the occasion.

The Whales have copped the Federal flag,
As experts knew they'd do.
And now that they have copped the rag,
Whom can they sell it to?

This is not to say, of course, that the Whales were above playing refusenik. Rube Foster, the legend behind the American Giants

Negro League club, challenged Weeghman and the Whales to a series for the second straight season, knowing full well that neither the Cubs nor Sox would take on the Federal League champions. Weeghman's heart, however, was apparently as hard toward the Negro Leagues as the American and National Leagues' were toward the Feds. There was no Whales–American Giants series; one suspects Weeghman knew that the American Giants would have easily whipped his squad.

The greater irony is that, at the moment of their greatest triumph, the Whales had played their last game. No sports franchise ever went out with such a bang. That week, the Whales held a huge ball at the Arcadia Hall in Lake View in honor of the team and Weeghman. Dancing, dining, and drinking were all part of the package, and after the party the team disbanded for the year—and, as most of them suspected, for good. The October 5 *Tribune's* J. J. Alcock reported that the players on the club wrote up a hilarious skit for the occasion, mocking themselves and their organization's alleged financial tight spot.

THE DEATH OF THE FEDERAL LEAGUE

Despite the 1915 Federal League's exciting pennant race, it was bleeding money at a furious rate. Even lowering ticket prices didn't bring enough Fed fans out. Meanwhile, the major leagues continued to suffer decreased attendance, increased salaries, and less press coverage. Several minor leagues shut down completely, while others in less baseball-mad regions struggled to keep the gates open. Everyone involved on the management side—the majors, the minors, and the Feds—wanted relief from of the current situation.

The unexpected October 1915 death of Brooklyn Tip-Tops owner Robert Ward—who, unlike Weeghman, had a seemingly bottomless wallet—removed much of the impetus for the Feds to continue, and the FL, AL, and NL began considering a settlement to the antitrust suit filed months before by the Federal

League against organized baseball, which federal Judge Kenesaw Mountain Landis sat on all season, wishing not to have to rule on the case. Everyone wanted peace; the AL and NL hoped to be rid of competition and get salaries back under control, while the Fed owners wanted to recoup their losses and, if possible, crowbar themselves into better leagues.

To press their case, Fed president Gilmore and some of the clubs—mainly Chicago and Saint Louis—went on the offensive. In June 1915, the Fed leadership had announced plans to invade New York City for 1916. Reiterating that strategy in October had the desired effect of hauling the established leagues to the bargaining table.

On December 22, 1915, in Cincinnati, the Feds and the majors inked a pact. To rid themselves of the Feds, organized baseball paid $600,000 to be distributed among the upstart league's owners. Ward's heirs received two-thirds of that, and the Pittsburgh club took a $50,000 payout. Some teams got nothing, including Baltimore, which was the only Federal League club not to drop the lawsuit against the majors.

Weeghman and Phil Ball of Saint Louis took no large payout but sold out their former colleagues for a bigger prize: the chance to buy major league franchises. Weeghman was steered toward buying the Cubs, with Ball given the opportunity to purchase the Browns. James Gilmore's role in the game essentially came to an end; without a league to command, he went back into private business.

The big winners were Weeghman, Ball, and organized baseball. The losers were the four other Fed clubs (which received little or no money for their troubles) and the players, whose salaries sagged to pre-1914 levels.

Also among the winners were Cubs fans. Previously stuck in a decaying ballpark on the West Side, with terrible ownership and a dwindling fan base, the Cubs got a jolt of fresh money, fresh attitude, and—perhaps most important—the ballpark they still play in today. Allowing Weeghman to buy the Cubs had been discussed by those inside and outside the game since early 1914. Now, Lucky Charley would see his dream come true.

WEEGHMAN BUYS IN

On December 14, 1915, eight days before the official end of the Federal League, the majors and Weeghman hammered out an agreement at the Waldorf-Astoria in New York. Weeghman was allowed to buy controlling interest in the Cubs from Charles Taft, who had assumed full control of the club following Charlie Murphy's ouster. As an absentee owner, Charlie Taft had been viewed in Chicago as only a slight improvement on Murphy. The fans weren't too unhappy to see him go. He made a handshake deal with Weeghman for $500,000 cash, to be delivered by close of business January 20, 1916. Half a million dollars was the highest price that had been paid for a major league team up till that time. For that sum, Weeghman was to obtain 90 percent of the club, with the remainder belonging to investor Harry Ackerland of Pittsburgh.

Lucky Charley was already stretched thin, however, and rumors went around that he would not be able to make the deadline. Charles McCulloch (of the Thompson's restaurant chain, mentioned in chap. 1) and partner John Hertz made an offer of $750,000 for the ball club, but Taft kept his word to Weeghman. With about half an hour left before the close of business, Weeghman found himself unexpectedly short of the necessary cash as two expected checks had not come in. He made an emergency call to a friend who worked at the Continental Bank and borrowed $75,000 in thousand-dollar bills. He then strode over to Taft's offices and presented him a suitcase full of bills. Photos of the moment show a dapper and confident Weeghman passing an oversized $500,000 "check" to the Corn Exchange National Bank, holder of Taft's accounts.

Weeghman had now achieved one of his great dreams: to own the Chicago Cubs. Truly it was remarkable that in twenty years, this self-made man had risen from filling the coffee cups at the tables of the rich and powerful to sitting with them himself. "This is the biggest day of my life," he told reporters.

In mid-January 1916, Weeghman announced that he would sell some shares of the team to J. Ogden Armour, the meat-packing magnate who was one of the hundred richest men in the United States. Armour then convinced William Wrigley, head of the Wrigley Gum Company, to buy in. Both Armour and Wrigley paid $50,000 each for their initial shares, and both took seats on the board of directors. (This apparently was not the first time that Weeghman and Wrigley worked together. On January 27, 1932, the day after Wrigley's death, the *Tribune's* Irving Vaughan reported that the chicle executive had been one of the early backers of Weeghman's restaurant expansion plans, possibly investing as much as $100,000 in the enterprise.) In addition, advertising executive A. D. Lasker, sales magnate R. A. Cavanaugh, and C. A. McCulloch bought in and were added to the board. It is not clear whether Weeghman was struggling financially; he may have simply wanted to bring in his friends. Other pals, such as Adolph Schutter and Al Plamondon, purchased shares. The final deal on the additional investments was sealed April 7, 1916. The next day the *Daily News* reported, "The club is now a million-dollar corporation." Weeghman essentially folded the Whales into the Cubs. The Saint Louis Terriers were also allowed to transfer their talent to the Browns, but the other six Fed clubs lost their players to the open market. The best Whales players (Rollie Zeider, Max Flack, Les Mann, Dutch Zwilling, Claude Hendrix, Mike Prendergast, and George McConnell) donned Cub flannels in 1916, and Joe Tinker became the new Cubs manager, replacing Roger Bresnahan; Bresnahan still had two guaranteed years on his existing Cubs contract, and in order to get him out of town Weeghman brokered a deal in which the former Giants catcher was able to purchase the Toledo club in the American Association.

A new North Side Rooters' Club was formed in early April.

The group hoped to have five hundred members by Opening Day, and it established a club and lounge at the Hotel Morrison. The lounge was festooned with baseball photographs, books, and newspapers for the members, as well as desks for any writers who wanted to come in, have a drink, and hang around.

CUBBIES ON THE MOVE

It made all the sense in the world for the Cubs to move from the west to the North Side. West Side Grounds was older and had grown decrepit from years of poor care in the hands of Murphy and Taft. It was far from the tonier neighborhoods in which Weeghman and his friends lived. But the departure was sad for those who remembered the Cubs' glories of the early 1900s and knew what might happen to the West Side once the club departed for greener pastures.

On April 20, 1916, the day the Cubs played their first game at Weeghman Park, Ring Lardner penned a bittersweet twelve-stanza tribute to West Side Grounds, "Elegy Written in a West Side Ball Park," in the *Tribune*. It read, in part:

Now fades the glimmering landscape on the sight.
Save for the chatter of the laboring folk
Returning to their hovels for the night,
All's still at Taylor, Lincoln, Wood, and Polk.
Beneath this aged roof, this grandstand's shade,
Where peanut shucks lie in a mold'ring heap,
Where show the stains of pop and lemonade,
The Cub bugs used to cheer and groan and weep.

NEW KID IN TOWN

During their first practice at Weeghman Park on April 18, the Cubs hitters found the outfield distances much to their liking. All the club's sluggers drove batting-practice pitches well past the fences.

Legendary field announcer Pat Pieper, who served the club

until his death in 1974, accompanied the Cubs from West Side Grounds to Weeghman Park. Originally a vendor at West Side Grounds beginning in 1904, Pieper was hired as the Cubs' field announcer in early 1915 and intoned the daily lineups with a megaphone. In the 1930s, he finally got a microphone, and by the 1960s, the Cubs had seated him inside the scoreboard.

Many of the old West Side fans stayed with the team, too. New location or not, true fandom isn't that easy to give up. This was a new kind of game, though; Cubs fans were used to on-field success and much less glamorous off-field doings. The loud, somewhat obnoxious, and often filthy quality of the West Side game and ballpark gave way to a shiny, new, somewhat more polite form of baseball.

It did not, however, get rid of scalpers, who were probably much happier that the Feds were gone; the extra club had created more seats than could be filled. Now demand was going up. Weeghman told the newspapers: "It is certain there will be attempts at ticket scalping. This cannot be helped, but the fans can see to it that the scalpers lose money if they refuse to be held up." Of course, the scarcity of tickets and the buzz that the opening created didn't hurt Weeghman at all.

MORE CHANGES

Fans snapped up tickets for the Cubs-Reds opener as soon as they could, leading to expectations of a bursting-past-capacity crowd. Therefore, the team installed more seats. On April 19, "Weeghman was at the park for several hours," wrote Oscar Reichow of the *Daily News*, "superintending the construction of extra seats that have been stationed in front of the grandstand, extending from the extreme left end to the extreme right, with a break behind home plate." These seats would hold three thousand additional fans.

It didn't stop there. Just a day before the game, a group of carpenters constructed another seating section on the field, this one in the only space not previously filled: directly behind the plate. Other extra patrons were to be ringed around the outfield, as usual, this time on two rows of benches. In addition, plans were made to place other fans down the right-field line.

ONE MORE PARADE

Things began poorly for the Cubs in 1916; the club lost four of its first six games and had to return to Chicago "under cover of darkness" on April 18, according to James Crusinberry of the *Tribune*.

On April 20, 1916—the Cubs' first game in Weeghman Park—visiting Cincinnati dignitaries, including owner Garry Herrmann, paraded through the downtown streets, despite having spent the previous evening at the Bismarck Gardens—or, rather, the Marigold Gardens, as the tavern had been renamed in view of rampant anti-German sentiment in the war years.

Weeghman once more pulled out all the stops. He again arranged a parade of city officials to ride to the park from downtown, but this time around it was higher class. A ten-motorcycle police caravan provided an escort from Grant Park at 1:00 P.M., with Chief Deputy Sheriff Charles Peters serving as grand marshal. Two hours later (one hour behind schedule), the mile-long parade arrived at Clark and Addison. The procession comprised six brass bands, players from both the Cubs and the Reds, politicians including Mayor Thompson and Illinois governor Ed Dunne, and assorted flag bearers and hangers-on.

Twenty thousand cold fans waited impatiently for this illustrious group. Some spectators had been there since the gates opened at noon. Pregame festivities took place in the usual Weeghmanian (or, perhaps, Wagnerian) manner. Bombs, fireworks, and the brass bands made the noise, drowning out a speech that a local judge was making on the field. Some three hundred rooters from Cincinnati had hauled along their own German music makers as well. The Cubs Rooter's Club traveled "in tallyho" (in horse-drawn carriages) from the Hotel Morrison with their own band. And surely not the only ass on the premises was the live donkey that Chicago's Twenty-fifth Ward Democratic Organization trooped out.

As a twenty-one-gun salute greeted the raising of the flag, the press was told that local tailor George Kelly had offered a suit to any player who smacked a homer on Opening Day. Only one did: Cincinnati's John Beall. Another interesting offer came from J. Ogden Armour, who gave the Cubs a baby bear named "Joa" in honor of its giver. It cavorted in front of whirring motion-picture cameras as the players warmed up. The small bear lived in a cage at the corner of Clark and Addison, just outside the park, during the 1916 season. At various times in Cubs history, baby bears were brought around to the park for photo opportunities, fed milk out of small bottles, and the like.

As one of the Cubs' chief shareholders, Armour sat in a special field box with Continental Bank president George Reynolds. Armour had presented Weeghman with a floral bouquet grown at his Lake Forest home, just one of the many garlands and wreaths given to players, officials, and managers. Charles Comiskey and James Gilmore also made appearances.

The game finally started at around 3:30. It had rained on and off for a few days before the opener, muddying the park and giving groundskeeper Murphy quite a challenge to have the field in top shape. Stories in mid-April mention the Cubs covering the playing field during rainy times with "pieces of canvas that kept off a great deal of the water." The game ended after 6:00 P.M., with Chicago having taking a 7–6, eleven-inning decision. It included nine ground-rule doubles hit into the crowd down the right-field line. The overflow crowd caused at least one near miss. During the seventh inning, Cubs outfielder Bill Fischer, attempting to catch a foul fly, accidentally ran over a small boy. Neither party was seriously injured.

"It was another epochal day in the history of baseball," the *Tribune*'s Crusinberry wrote the next day, "and quite convincing that the Cubs have found a welcome to the North Side. There was a newness and a curiosity to things. It was the first time many of the players and doubtless many of the fans had ever seen the North Side ball park. But they seemed to have no trouble in finding it." The April 21 *Tribune* noted that several hundred fans watched the game "from the roofs and windows of flat buildings across the street from the ball park." The next game, scheduled for the following day, was canceled due to inclement weather.

HAVE A BALL

The 1916 season was less notable on the field than for the moment when Weeghman permanently altered the nature of fan/team relations by beginning to allow fans to keep fouls hit into the stands. This must have happened in midseason because an article in the August 12, 1916, *Sporting Records* was headlined, "President Weeghman of Chicago Makes Big Hit with the Fans; Permits Them to Retain Baseballs." The accompanying picture depicts a jaunty Weeghman decked out in a high-button suit and straw hat.

The season was also notable for being Mordecai Brown's last. Cubs manager Joe Tinker had called on thirty-nine-year-old Brown, a star of the Cubs a decade before who had fashioned a 17–8 season with the 1915 Whales, to fill out his pitching staff. Never a hard thrower, Brown had little left but guile and experience and pitched just twelve games in 1916. But Brown didn't depart without filling the stands one last time. On September 4, the Cubs and the visiting Reds arranged a real Weeghman special—a game started by Brown and Cincinnati manager Christy Mathewson, Hall of Fame hurlers famous for their duels in the first decade of the century. Mathewson had been dealt from the New York Giants earlier in the year.

With the Cubs and Reds both out of contention, the decision was easy. Neither pitcher was really on his game, but it hardly mattered. The memory-making special, the twenty-third and last matchup of the two immortals, drew a sellout crowd with the Reds defeating the home team, 10–8. Mathewson went all the way for the win in this, the final performance in each of the great hurlers' careers.

That season was also the end of the line for Tinker, who was relieved of his duties at the end of the campaign and replaced by Fred Mitchell.

CALIFORNIA DREAMIN'

In preparation for the 1917 season, the Cubs trained in California, which became the Cubbies' spring home because of the persuasiveness of William Wrigley, one of the team's part owners. Wrigley convinced the board of directors that the Cubs should train out west, where the Cubs would enjoy (1) clement weather, (2) enough distance from the home fans to whet the appetite for the season opener, and (3) ready-made exhibition-game opponents in clubs from the Pacific Coast League. This was the first visible evidence that the gum magnate wanted to be more involved with the club. Two years later, Wrigley bought Catalina Island, off the coast of Los Angeles, and built the scenic isle into the Cubs' training base (and, not coincidentally, a tourist destination).

When the Cubs got home, they found advertising on the left-field bleacher fence as well as rendering of a huge American flag on the center-field scoreboard. In addition, outside of the park, atop the right-field wall, a new sign read "Chicago National League Ball Club" (fig. 3).

NO NO SONG

One of the most remarkable games in baseball history took place at Weeghman Park on May 2, 1917. With dry understatement, Oscar Reichow of the *Daily News* noted the next day, "Cub fans to-day saw one of the most remarkable pitching duels they probably ever have seen"—or that anyone ever has seen. James "Hippo" Vaughn of Chicago and Fred Toney of Cincinnati each no-hit their opposition for nine innings. This feat has never been duplicated.

In the tenth, the Reds broke Vaughn's heart. Shortstop Larry Kopf singled with one out to smash the no-hitter, and scurried to

FIGURE 3. It is opening day, April 11, 1917, and the Cubs and visiting Pirates pose in right field with a battalion of soldiers. The right-field bleachers in evidence in 1914 had been torn out and replaced by a solid wall, which remains in use today. (Credit: National Baseball Hall of Fame and Museum)

third, one out later, when Cy Williams dropped Hal Chase's long fly. Chase then swiped second. Jim Thorpe bounced back to the mound. Vaughn, hoping for a play on Kopf, fired the ball toward home, but catcher Art Wilson wasn't expecting the throw and let it get by. Kopf crossed the plate, but Wilson tagged out Chase attempting to score. The play was ruled a hit.

In the last of the tenth, with one out, Cubs first baseman Fred Merkle nearly got the run back. His deep fly backed Manuel Cueto to the left-field wall, but the ball stayed in the park. Cy

Williams then whiffed to end the game, and Toney had a spectacular no-hit victory. Vaughn—who fanned ten men and walked just two—had nothing but a painful 1–0 loss on an unearned run. It was the first no-hitter thrown at Weeghman Park. Charles Weeghman collected two balls from the game, had them bronzed, and awarded them to Hippo Vaughn.

Warren Brown wrote, years later, that "350,000 wished they had been in the vicinity" when they read the papers the next day. Unfortunately, this great game, completed in just one hour and fifty minutes, was witnessed by only between twenty-five hundred and thirty-five hundred souls. The next day, horrible weather, the two teams drew just three hundred hardies.

VIVE LA FRANCE!

While players battled on the field that season, the country was actually at war, and civic leaders sought to demonstrate their patriotism whenever possible. When a group of French dignitaries announced a trip to the United States in early 1917, various civic organizations scrambled to entertain them. When the French visitors, including onetime field marshal Joseph Joffre and former premier René Viviani reached Chicago, guess who wanted to take them out to the ball game? The same day that Vaughn and Toney tossed their double no-hitter, Weeghman requested, via the newspapers, that the committee appointed to entertain the visiting Frenchmen consider bringing the party by his ballpark that Friday or Saturday to take in the national pastime. Weeghman wanted to hold France Day over the weekend and fill his park, as well as add some money to the war relief fund. "I am sure the visitors would enjoy the game, knowing it to be a national institution, and the fans undoubtedly would give them one of the greatest receptions they could get in this country." Never shy about pressing his case, Charley told the *Daily News*' Ben McCutcheon on May 2 that the presence of such impressive foreign allies and the resultant pomp and ceremony would swell the ranks of the military: "I believe such a celebration would have an impressive effect on the younger men and stimulate enlistment in the national service." Unfortunately, the visiting dignitaries never made it to the park; they already had too much on their plates. Even Weeghman's offer to donate an ambulance to the war effort couldn't draw the party to a Cubs game.

As the war spirit reached new peaks, baseball tried to climb over all other public entertainments to show its patriotism. On Friday, June 29, 1917, the Cubs held Red Cross Day and drew a big enough crowd to contribute $3,858 to that organization. The papers made note of the fact that Friday was a lousy day to fundraise at the ballparks, with most people working to finish up the week and waiting to spend their money on the weekends. On July 27, the Canadian Highlanders and their band came to Weeghman Park and were feted by the fans. The Cubs also hosted various U.S. military personnel that day. Unlike today, celebrations of military forces at sporting events were not yet routine.

PIGGYBACK

Charley Weeghman loved to hitch his wagon to whatever was passing by, meaning that the promotions and parades were nearly endless at the ballpark. On June 22, the Pirates held Honus Wagner Day at Forbes Field. Two days later, with the Pirates—or Bucs (short for Buccaneers)—and Cubs traveling back to Chicago for a series, Weeghman held his own celebration. The Cubs and Bucs drew ten thousand rooters to Weeghman Park to celebrate perhaps the game's most beloved player. Wagner received a flower garland from Weeghman. Asked to make a speech, he simply replied, "Much obliged."

HOUSE SALE

On December 24, 1917, Charles Weeghman sold his lush residence at 5627 North Sheridan in Chicago to John Collins, a coal executive who helped run the business bordering Weeghman Park. The terms of the sale were more than a tad strange. First, how many house sales are consummated the day before Christmas?

Second, the sale price was $80,000, some one-fourth of what the newspapers estimated as its potential value. Collins was said to have bought the house as a present for his new wife, Elsa, who had given up a singing career to settle down. Maybe Weeghman did a favor for his friend. But one must wonder whether Charles Weeghman simply needed some quick cash. Even for the owner of a respectable team, the baseball business was no sure thing.

1918

WEEGHMAN AND THE WAR

BAD TIME

The year 1918 was fateful for the Chicago Cubs and for Charles Weeghman. The Cubs won the National League pennant for the first time since 1910, giving Weeghman his first taste of the World Series. That crazy campaign had the potential to be Lucky Charley's biggest triumph; instead, it capped a catastrophic economic collapse.

Several factors were responsible for Weeghman's sudden financial crisis:

- *World War I's impact on the working population.* With many working men serving in the military who otherwise would have spent their days in downtown Chicago, fewer people ate in Weeghman's restaurants, sat in his movie theaters, and frequented his pool halls. Attendance at baseball games also decreased significantly.
- *The influenza epidemic,* which led local and federal governments to urge citizens to avoid crowded places, such as restaurants and ballparks.
- *Weeghman's investment strategy.* He had paid top dollar for players since breaking into baseball and gotten results, but this caused financial woe when his other businesses began to struggle. Even though overall player salaries had dropped in 1916 after the Federal League's demise, Weegh-

man was still paying his players well and taking good care of his park.

The First World War was the first truly industrial war, fought with unprecedentedly lethal technology in an era when military tactics were mired in the past. Chemical weapons, for instance, did their first major damage in this war, while officers still sat atop horses. Yet Americans, not cursed with having to fight on their own soil, enthusiastically embraced the war spirit. Newspapers of the day spread jingoism, urging aggression toward "the Jerries." For many Americans (especially businessmen who profited from the manufacture of armaments), the time couldn't come too soon for "our boys" to join the fight to "make the world safe for democracy," in the quaintly pompous phraseology of the day. Newspapers carried headlines like "Doctors, Nurses Eager to Go to War."

And yet, the economic boon of the war did not benefit most people. The international instability brought about by the destruction of Europe's economies affected the United States. Even before America joined the war, citizens of most countries were tightening their already cinched purse strings. In America, fewer people could afford discretionary spending on ballgames, movies, or restaurants—three businesses that Charles Weeghman depended on.

Most people believed that hale and hearty baseball players should be among the first to fight in the war. The game may have been a national mania, but in the absence of broadcast media, baseball was deeply rooted at the local level, a national business but far less a focus of cultural attention than organized sports in our day. Few thought the game was as important as aiding the "good fight."

Ballplayers had long been encouraged to take part in pregame military-style parades on the field, shouldering baseball bats like rifles. There was no shortage of patriotism at the nation's

1918: WEEGHMAN AND THE WAR

ballparks, just as there was no such shortage in the mid-1940s or after September 11, 2001. Patriotism even outranked piousness at this time, as the barrier against Sunday games in the nation's capital fell on May 14, 1918, largely to benefit the many war workers unable to attend weekday afternoon contests.

For the same reason, this season saw another startling innovation designed to bring fans to the park: twilight baseball. The first night game in the major leagues was held not, as often believed, on May 24, 1935, in Cincinnati but rather on July 1, 1918, when the Boston Braves began a game against the Brooklyn Superbas at 6:00 P.M. The *Sporting News* enthusiastically supported the idea in its July 11 edition, opining that "twilight baseball is what we have in mind as the game's salvation" as a way to help working stiffs come to the games that they'd otherwise miss. The Braves were a bad team that year, however, and nobody wanted to come to their games anyway. While Boston won that night 5–3, only a thousand fans showed up, albeit in part because of bad weather. Left uninspired by this, the club abandoned twilight ball after the one attempt.

THE 1918 IRREGULAR SEASON

Despite the new social and economic environment, a series against John McGraw's Giants in early June attracted record crowds to Weeghman Park, and the Cubs were looking like winners. Nevertheless, gate revenue was down, and Lucky Charley's costly player acquisition began to grate on his partners, who insisted that he tighten his belt. Following the 1917 season, Weeghman had spent $60,000 to obtain superstar pitcher Grover Cleveland Alexander and battery mate Bill Killefer from the Phillies. And that wasn't all. "The deals that brought us Alexander, Killefer, [Lefty] Tyler, and [Dode] Paskert are not the only ones we will pull this winter," the enthusiastic and somewhat imperial Weeghman told George Robbins, who filed a report for the January 10, 1918, *Sporting News*. "I want a heavy hitting, clever outfielder to add to my collection of trophies, and I'm willing to part with the price to get them. We would pay $25,000 or more for the right one. Nor have we given up the hope of landing [Rogers] Hornsby." Hornsby did not materialize, but the Cubs did deal for Fred Merkle, Phil Douglas, and Pete Kilduff. Unfortunately, Alexander wound up in the army and pitched just three games in 1918.

One thing went right financially for the Cubs in 1918. Charlie Murphy, former club president, filed a lawsuit in January to force the current management to pay rent on old West Side Grounds. The case, though, was dismissed July 11, and Weeghman and his associates were not liable for the rent. The Cubs' new park had long since made their old one irrelevant. David Rotroff of the *Daily News* noted on August 14 that "persons have seen a five-foot snake crawling around over at Des Plaines and West Madison streets. It is a relief to know that we don't have to go over on the West Side grounds any more to see the Cubs play ball."

Moreover, as grim as the finances looked to the partners, the public still loved Weeghman and saw him as a model owner. "Weeghman's success in the majors is fortunate for the game," said George Robbins in the *Sporting News* on July 4. "It proves that a good business man who loves baseball, studies the game, and has the gift of seeking the proper advice is the fellow who should and will succeed in baseball." (While Robbins, usually sharp as a tack, was wrong about this, Weeghman's profile in the game had clearly improved.)

THE SHUT DOWN

The pressures of the war were becoming more profound. In July, Washington Senators catcher Eddie Ainsmith was drafted and applied for a work-related deferment. In rejecting this claim and acting to forestall others, Secretary of War Newton Baker ruled that baseball was a nonessential industry and that its employees could be required by the government to take more critical wartime jobs instead.

Most minor leagues, as a result, wound down by the end of July, and National League president John Tener—speaking without consulting club owners—was quoted as saying that he didn't favor a World Series. With his Cubs in first place, Charley Weeghman gasped that he couldn't believe that Tener had been correctly quoted. On August 14 Oscar Reichow wrote in the *Daily News*, "It would be a blow to President Weeghman and his associates if a world's series is prohibited. They have gone to a lot of expense to give Chicago a winner in the National league and would be hard hit if the team wins and cannot get into the games."

With baseball seemingly about to shut down, the *Daily News* reported humorously on August 5, 1918, that "restoratives were being administered to Charley Weeghman" as Billy Niesen announced plans for a new semipro "city league" to meet fans' need for competitive baseball. Niesen, however, apparently never got his league off the ground. Within a few years, local leagues began to die out. Within a generation, far fewer adults would play baseball as more began to watch and listen to it.

The American and National Leagues told the press and the government that they would shorten the 1918 regular season so that everyday competition would end on September 1. After that date, all ballplayers would be required either to join the armed forces or get other "essential" war-related jobs. An unattributed item in the August 29 *Sporting News* suggested that Cubs players would have two choices of essential jobs: managing a Weeghman doughnut shop or becoming cattle herders at the Chicago stockyards with weekend ball-playing privileges.

The season that resulted was truncated and uneven. In this era, since clubs traveled by train, road series were bunched together in long trips. Teams might not play their first home games until late April or might not have home games scheduled after early September. By September 1, the 1918 Cubs had played seventy-six of their seventy-seven scheduled home games, more than any other team, but only fifty-three on the road. This meant that Weeghman's coffers were stuffed, relative to other clubs.

Some major league owners with low-drawing clubs were just as happy to close the gates of their parks and blame it on the war. But their patriotism didn't keep these owners from trying to tie up their players without paying them. As the *Sporting News* noted on August 29,

> Letters were sent to National League players last week notifying them that their services would not be needed after September 2 and that they would be paid off up to and including that date and dismissed until further notice.
>
> That "further notice" stuff is what gets the players. If they are to be "reserved" for an indefinite renewal they'd like to know why their contracts should not be carried out until the end of the season. "If they want to reserve us, they got to pay us," seems to be the player's slogan. It sounds reasonable.

The National League pennant race was not close, and much of the drama of the season was lost as a result. But after a thrilling AL race won by the Boston Red Sox and their star pitcher, Babe Ruth, fans all over the country still salivated at the thought of a competitive World Series. By agreement with President Woodrow Wilson and Secretary of War Baker, the World Series would indeed go on, but with some changes. To cut train travel and save resources, the first three games would be played in Chicago, with the next four slated for Boston. To make matters worse for Weeghman and the Cubs, the games would take place during the week, in order to allow for the players and press to travel on the weekend.

Photos from the 1918 season and World Series show Weeghman looking less chipper than a few short years before. Still nattily attired, Weeghman put up a brave front for his friends in the press and in business, but everyone connected with the club knew that Lucky Charley was in trouble.

TICKETS, GET YOUR TICKETS

The Cubs were going to get as much revenue out of the series as they could—though this time it was not Charley Weeghman who had the flash of marketing genius but his young business manager, Walter Craighead, who had replaced the popular Charley Williams. Craighead persuaded management to rent out Comiskey Park, the South Side "Baseball Palace of the World," for the postseason, because it had twice as many seats as Weeghman Park. It would be nearly impossible today imagine the Cubs playing home games at the grounds of their intercity rivals, and even then some North Side fans can't have been pleased to travel to an American League park to watch their heroes. And it is, of course, ironic that the Cubs' first World Series after the club moved into what is now Wrigley Field didn't even take place there.

Nevertheless, as one would expect, the Cubs' financial needs won out, and Comiskey agreed to rent his space. The National Commission (the governing body of the two major leagues), however, wanted to appear patriotic and forced ticket prices lower than usual. Box seats, $5 for the 1917 World Series, instead went for $3 this time around, with grandstand seats at $1.50, pavilion seats a dollar, and bleachers fifty cents. Even in a bigger park, poor Charley couldn't get his pot of gold.

He did, however, win respect for a letter he sent to Comiskey (and released to the press), thanking the White Sox magnate for his warm welcome: "The many courtesies extended to us during the Series have added to your nationwide reputation for good sportsmanship and to our admiration for you." (Comiskey had also won Weeghman's admiration by helping to convince other AL owners not to call off the World Series in the first place.)

Craighead also devised a system whereby the most loyal Cubs fans would have a chance to buy series tickets. As the *Daily News*'s Oscar Reichow reported on August 20, "[Craighead] has put a crew of girls to work at listing the names of the Cub fans who have attended the contests regularly at the North Side park and have dropped their rain checks in the boxes at the park to show they are entitled to consideration when the distribution of the tickets takes place." The *Sporting News* reported on September 5 that Craighead also invented this system in order to better handle projected postseason crowds.

Chicago played poorly in the series and lost in six games. Of the three games played in Chicago, the Cubs won just one. After game 1 was rained out on September 4, the contest went off the next day in front of only 19,274 chilled spectators. As remains the case today, fat cats bought up the reserved seats, but many of them refused to brave the cold and stayed home. "It was unfortunate that many fans could not have had access to the reserved grand stand seats, which were sold out early in the morning," George Robbins sniffed in the September 12 *Sporting News.* "Hundreds of fans waited outside trying to get general admission seats and were finally turned away. Some seats went to waste." The police were out in full force busting up dice games near Comiskey, prompting David Rotroff to joke in the *Daily News* on September 6, "If a person wanted to shake the bones, he had to buy a ticket and go inside and shake his own."

To the consternation of Cubs fans, the home team lost, 1–0, on a six-hit complete-game shutout by Babe Ruth. As part of the general patriotic atmosphere, "The Star-Spangled Banner" was played during the seventh-inning stretch—yet another baseball tradition that originated in Chicago. From this point, the song was played at all World Series contests, though it was not routinely heard before regular-season games for many more years. Even at Wrigley, the anthem was not regularly played in peacetime until the end of the Vietnam War.

Game 1's crowd was disappointing, but 20,040 fans watched the Cubs win the next contest, 3–1. The third game of the series was played in front of 27,054, but the Cubs fell 2–1. Both clubs then boarded trains for Boston, where the finish came too soon for Chicago fans. Two of the final three games went to the Red Sox, and the Crimsons were the champions of the world. Despite the Cubs' disappointment, the season was viewed as an artistic success, if not a financial one. Manager Fred Mitchell received bouquets from the press. Seen as a hardy soul who kept his club together in rough times, Mitchell soon expanded his role.

The scribes of the day believed that the Cubs were overconfident and simply fell apart in the Fall Classic. They also wrote that players from both sides were overly concerned with their share of the slim profits engendered by the games. In fact, the players were unhappy about this and worried by rumors that they would receive little—or even none—of the proceeds. Players from both clubs had nearly gone on strike prior to game 5, holding up the start of the contest for nearly an hour and bringing down a shower of press criticism. Allegations surfaced, too, that some Cubs were available to the highest bidder—an issue that would erupt much more seriously in Chicago two years later with the Black Sox scandal.

Such concern for mere money was seen as inappropriate during wartime, although nobody in the papers bothered to criticize Cubs management for their decision to move the games from the North Side to the South Side in order to jam more cheeks into the seats. Press outrage at player "greed" is unsurprising given the press's attitude toward labor-management relations at the time. Sportswriters, a comfortable and urbane crowd, were often wined and dined by the owners.

GOOD-TIME CHARLEY'S GOT THE BLUES

For his part, Charley Weeghman wasn't wining or dining too many people in 1918. He had, in fact, been raising money to support his other businesses by selling shares of Cubs stock to the one man in the ownership group who, to most at the time, appeared to have the least interest in taking over a baseball club: chewing-gum magnate William Wrigley, whose business was doing just fine during the war. He is said to have bought into the club because he personally liked Weeghman and believed that he and the other Cubs' owners had something of a civic duty to ensure the team's success.

Weeghman was what today we would call overleveraged. His businesses, even when riding high, always seemed on the edge of collapse. With rents to pay, loans to repay, and a decreasing customer base, his financial situation turned bleak. His empire was built on traffic, and the wartime economy reduced people's disposable income. His clean and shiny lunch counters were less crowded, and many breadwinners could no longer take their families to the movies, shoot pool, or go to the ballyard.

In 1915, Weeghman owned ten downtown "Weeghman's" lunch counters as well as the Casino Theater at 58 West Madison and two downtown billiard rooms. He lived at 5627 North Sheridan Road, a block from Lake Michigan in the then upscale Edgewater neighborhood. But it wasn't going to last.

To make matters worse, the influenza epidemic that blazed across America in late summer 1918 had terrible consequences for businesses at which the public gathered. The flu killed approximately 195,000 Americans in October 1918 alone, including many prominent members of society. Chicago, as a major rail center, served as a locus of sickness. By mid-October, the disease had officially been declared an epidemic in Chicago, where more than two thousand citizens had already perished.

The resulting panic led government authorities to urge citizens not to frequent places where people gathered in large numbers and where germs could be spread. The city shut down theaters, night schools, and pool halls, and inspectors often cited bars for violating capacity rules. Schoolchildren were sent home from parks and church services were shortened. Despite the city's efforts, approximately eighty-five hundred Chicagoans passed away from the "Spanish flu" before the disease ebbed during summer 1919.

Religious groups and public moralists took advantage of the crisis to inveigh against what they considered sinful behavior, such as dancing, drinking, billiards, and gambling. As David E. Ruth has written: "In closing dance halls, theaters, and cabarets, [health officials] aimed a traditional weapon of social control— enforced adherence to a middle-class moral code—at the new realm of commercial leisure. Activities that had recently shed their lower-class stigma and had gained middle-class acceptance, or at least toleration, became unacceptably pernicious during the emergency. The healthy society was austere; frivolity invited disaster." Chicago Health Commissioner John Dill Robertson was at the forefront of this movement. According to Ruth, "the primary motivation for closing the theaters, Robertson admitted, was not to control the spread of germs, but 'to discourage the late hours kept by most adults.'"

Obviously, such pressure from the city hurt Weeghman's businesses. While disease needed to be checked, the money spent hosing down streets and providing protective masks for citizens, as well as the money *not* spent in restaurants, theaters, and other public places, hurt an already struggling economy.

Late in 1918, under the influence of moralist reformers, Illinois ratified the Eighteenth Amendment, banning the sale, manufacture, and transport of liquor. This misguided effort further assisted the mob in expanding its base of illegal activity and closed more than seven thousand bars in Chicago. Some residents rebelled against what they perceived as heavy-handed, dictatorial measures and began looking for social opportunities outside the traditional venues.

CHARLEY AND THE MOB?

In the first decades of the century, Chicago was run by corrupt politicians, mobsters, and grifters. This was the time of the greased palm and the inside deal, the times and events that cemented the city's reputation of dirty politics and graft that seems to define the "City That Works" to this day.

How closely was Weeghman associated with the mob? He ran businesses in food service, entertainment, construction, and sports. It would have been difficult for him not to be in contact with the criminal element. But were any of his financial troubles of 1917–18 caused by mob connections? Weeghman made a Herculean rise in the business world and took a Herculean fall. He could have borrowed money to expand his businesses and sunk when the loans were called in; there is no record either way.

We do know that Weeghman was intimately involved with the underworld that masterminded the 1919 World Series fix, to the point that he was called to testify at the 1920 Black Sox trial. The authorities wanted to know about his friendships with New Yorker Arnold Rothstein, believed by most scholars to be the biggest financial beneficiary of the fix, and gambler Monte Tennes, the top dog in racetrack bookmaking in Chicago for many years. They also wanted to find out what Weeghman knew about his club's disappointing performance in the 1918 Fall Classic. Weeghman and Tennes (whom Steven Longstreet called "The Daniel Boone of big crime, a forgotten pioneer of the methods of the Capone mob") were old friends, as both testified.

Moreover, Weeghman spent much of the summer of 1919 vacationing at Rothstein's home in Saratoga Springs, New York, and seemed to know a lot about Rothstein's (and Tennes's) wagering habits. At the trial, Weeghman said, "[Tennes] told me that the series had been fixed. This was in August [1919], mind you. Seven White Sox players had agreed to lay down . . . but [Tennes] didn't want it because he liked baseball and didn't want to go in on such a crooked deal. I understand that in spite of the tip, he bet thirty grand on the Sox!" Tennes, for his part, denied ever having spoken to Weeghman about any rumors of a fix, and the matter was—incredibly—dropped.

It's likely that what Weeghman said about Tennes was crafted in the best possible light to make his friend appear innocent while avoiding telling an easily disprovable lie (that Tennes never bet on baseball games). At the time, sportsmen of day openly wagered on horse races, golf tournaments, and the like, and everyone in baseball knew that gambling was widespread. And in any event, with his empire in ruins Weeghman had plenty of reasons in 1920 to curry favor with any friend with money.

GOODBYE, CHARLEY

On November 18, 1918, the Cubs put an end to nearly a year's worth of speculation, announcing that Weeghman would step down as president of the Chicago Cubs. Bill Wrigley, who held the cards, engineered Weeghman's departure. In buying more and more of unlucky Charley's shares, he told him, according to Harry Neily in the *Sporting News* of November 28, "If I help you out, you must retire from baseball and devote all your time to business." Wrigley himself presented Weeghman's resignation at the club's December 1918 board meeting.

More than fifteen years later, Weeghman looked back on the entire episode with warmth and humor. From a restaurant he owned in New York City, he told the *Tribune* in the January 4, 1936, issue, "It was in fact the familiar story—I was young and cocky and took in too much territory. I suppose I should have stayed out of the Federal League which ultimately cost me $3,000,000, and should have let [others] have the Cubs."

Fred Mitchell assumed Weeghman's duties and remained the field manager. Mitchell, apparently seen as a comer, had "had to do nearly all of Weeghman's work last summer," wrote Oscar Reichow of the *Daily News* on November 19 "while the latter was looking after his restaurant interests that were in a precarious condition owing to war conditions."

The *Sporting News*'s George Robbins had a different theory, opining in the November 28 issue that Weeghman's downfall came from moving the Cubs from the West Side: "Weeghman went to the North Side, was the active force in constructing a modern baseball plant, and ran the capital stock into big money to meet expenses . . . the general opinion is that the desertion of the great West Side, hotbed of baseball, was the chief item in the financial failure." Mention of the "great West Side," deserted by the moneyed classes decades ago, may seem odd to us now, but it was once the most important part of the city. The Cubs' determination to depart the crumbling, rocky, bug- and snake-infested old West Side Grounds in favor of the newer, fresher, and greener pastures of Weeghman Park was a sensible business decision, but it was also an early nail in the West Side's coffin.

Whatever the reason, Weeghman was now gone. The papers carried tributes to the man who had brought so much vitality to the city and to its sporting scene. Most everyone in the press was sorry to see Weeghman go and lauded his good spirit, sense of fun, and general bonhomie. The *Sporting News*, never a booster, even tossed him a small, unattributed bouquet: "He was never accused of not being a splendid fellow personally and a game sportsman, and good wishes of the fan public generally go out to him . . . if he may be lacking in baseball acumen he is a master in his business, out of which he arose from a $12 a week waiter to one of the best known and most popular restaurant magnates in the country."

Weeghman remained in Chicago, intending to continue his restaurant businesses but had a difficult time making ends meet and was reportedly bankrupt. He was hauled into court as proceedings began to put the restaurant chain into receivership, and several of his friends, including Bill Wrigley, had to bail him out.

Charley and Bessie divorced in 1920. In February 1922, Charley eloped to East Saint Louis with the former Miss Carol Osmund. The Weeghmans continued to appear in the society pages, particularly with regard to horse shows, but not without controversy; in November, Charley was accused by his landlord of defaulting on rent checks and selling racehorses that were not his.

Not every potentially controversial story involving Weeghman was made hay of, however. On Tuesday, August 16, 1921, the Ku Klux Klan held a large initiation rally at a spot of farmland just south of Lake Zurich, Illinois. The land belonged to Charles Weeghman, a fact that only one newspaper—the nearby *Barrington Review*—reported in a story two days later.

Perhaps the Chicago papers kept Weeghman's name out of their stories, or perhaps they simply did not know who owned the land. By that time, Weeghman was spending much of his time at another farm in Palatine where he bred competition horses. He was rarely in the news by 1921 anyway, having given up the high-profile businesses (movie houses, restaurants, pool halls) and only sporadically appearing in the city.

That a rally was held on his property does not mean that Weeghman was a member of the Klan—as some have irresponsibly asserted—or even that he gave permission for his land to be used. It is certainly *possible* that he rented out or gave out the land or that he was a member; in the early 1920s, the KKK was presenting itself as a patriotic, anticommunist, and antilabor group, rather than simply a group of violent racists, and in doing so, suckered in some otherwise well-meaning people. The true nature of Weeghman's involvement will likely never be known.

In any case, by early December 1922, Charley had completely divested himself of restaurants in favor of horses, though the Charles Weeghman Corporation continued to run restaurants, without his involvement, until finally being put into receivership in 1926. And in 1923, the Lake Zurich mansion at which the KKK rally had been held was sold by a strapped-for-cash Charley to bootlegger Terry Druggan for some $150,000, a sum well below market value, though he continued to maintain a residence in the city, on Waveland Avenue near the lake. (Recall he had similarly sold off his Chicago home in 1917.) Lack of cash remained the story of Charley's life. More than once in the 1920s, Weeghman found himself hauled into court for nonpayment of rent, loan fraud, and check kiting.

It was a humiliating turn for a man who made himself and who was responsible for building the field that bore his name. After Weeghman died in 1938, Harry Neily wrote a lengthy eulogy in the November 10 *Sporting News* that summed him up quite well: "Baseball has settled down since the Weeghman era, but if there were more Charley Weeghmans in the sport today, the duties of the scribes would be lightened, there would be more frivolity and mirth. . . . Charley Weeghman was a showman and lived by the standards of that picturesque profession. He ran a shoestring into a million and when luck turned, nobody ever heard him complain. He really had a greater depth of character than his associates suspected, for he could take it when the going was tough." But the local press didn't waste much space honoring him, and nobody proposed naming any part of his field in his honor. In the public mind, Weeghman was soon to be only a footnote to the landmark he created.

NO DEPRESSION
CUBS PARK/WRIGLEY FIELD, 1919–1932

GUMMY BEAR

In 1874, thirteen-year-old William Wrigley dropped out of school to help run his father's soap manufacturing company in Philadelphia. That same year, the Wrigley Company also began selling baking powder—coincidentally, one of the products that Charley Weeghman had sold on his way up.

Young Bill proved an able study and popularized the idea of offering premiums with purchases, which helped revolutionize the retail industry. One of the premiums he used in order to sell baking powder was chewing gum. The elastic compound proved to be such a good sales tool that Wrigley decided to devote his time and energy to producing, advertising, and selling it. Using solid sales techniques, keeping costs low, and developing efficient distribution, Wrigley soon made his gum company (incorporated in 1910) the world's largest vendor of the stuff. By 1925, when Wrigley handed over day-to-day management to his son Philip, the Wrigley Company boasted assets of $60 million.

NOT ANY WORSE

When Charley Weeghman gave up the Cubs, William Wrigley—despite owning the biggest share of the club—seemed an unlikely caretaker for the franchise. "I'll never attend a meeting," he was reported to have said when named to the team's board of directors in 1916. But this may be so much folderol. In Forrest Crissey's article in the September 13, 1930, *Saturday Evening Post*, Wrigley claimed that owning a team had been his childhood dream. In either event, during the 1917 and 1918 seasons Bill Wrigley began to take a greater interest in the doings of the club.

In February 1914, Wrigley had bought a $175,000 mansion in Pasadena, California, joining the "Chicago Colony" of businessmen wintering in the sunnier clime of the West. The *Chicago Daily Journal* on February 24 called Wrigley's new home "one of the most pretentious in the city." (At the time, the word "pretentious" had a less pejorative meaning.) Early in 1919, Wrigley was dining at this home with a group of Chicago sportswriters. One of them, Bill Veeck Sr., made some cutting remarks relating to the fashion in which the Cubs had been run. According to Warren Brown in his 1946 book *The Chicago Cubs*, Wrigley asked Veeck, "Could you do any better?"

"I certainly couldn't do any worse," said Veeck.

Wrigley knew the Cubs needed strong management, so he put together a new team of Fred Mitchell as president and manager, Veeck as vice president, and John O. Seys, another former reporter, as secretary. For the first time in many years, the Cubs had a management group with enough baseball sense to win the respect of the writers. Bill Veeck Sr. knew baseball. According to Brown, his "acquaintance with ballplayers in major leagues and in minors was perhaps as large as anyone's."

Born in Indiana, Veeck married his childhood sweetheart, Grace, and started his newspaper career in Louisville. He came to Chicago in 1902, first to write for the *Inter-Ocean* and then for the *American*, establishing a reputation as a smart man with flair. He was, according to his son, no great writer but "a good, solid reporter," well respected in the game, and "dignified without being stuffy." Fair-minded, honest, and scrupulous, he was well suited for his new job. It must be said, though, that despite his outward appearance of rectitude, he fielded teams full of gamblers, hard drinkers, and reprobates. As did everyone else.

Veeck's influence grew quickly. The National League, not

inclined to have a team with a manager/president, forced Fred Mitchell to give up the Cubs' presidency in June 1919. Wrigley was happy to hand the position to Veeck.

HERE COME THE CHANGES

With Weeghman out of the picture, things began to change at what was now called Cubs Park. For one thing, photos from 1919 show what appears to be a hill rising toward the center-field scoreboard. It's not clear why this happened, as the ground had always been level at the park. It simply may have been a design idea.

Another big change in the park in 1919 was the increase in the amount of advertising. A sign was painted against the right-field wall, hawking sporting goods, probably for either The Fair, a huge downtown department store with a big sporting goods department, or Wilson's Sporting Goods, which had long sold Cubs tickets. More advertising dotted the center-field scoreboard, including a large mention of the *Tribune*. Two figures, one throwing a ball and one getting ready to hit, sat atop the scoreboard in 1919. They resembled the Wrigley's gum "Doublemint Twins" figures atop the board in the early 1920s and were the earliest Wrigley's advertising at the park.

The left side of the scoreboard in these years featured the data on the game at hand, while the right side listed out-of-town contests. The center of the board featured advertising. At some point in 1920, American League scores were moved to a board attached to the right-center-field brick wall (fig. 4), possibly to allow more advertising on the main scoreboard.

Other changes were made to the park. Sometime before 1921, the Cubs cut a space out of the wall down the left-field line, past the home dugout, in order to store a tarpaulin. They also decorated the ticket windows outside the ballpark with attractive art-deco awnings.

FIGURE 4. Wrigley Field between 1918 and 1922. The bunting indicates preparations for an Opening Day or holiday contest. On an apartment building past the right-field wall is an advertisement for the popular Marigold Garden, a large beer garden a few blocks northeast of the park. (Credit: National Baseball Hall of Fame and Museum)

KNOW WHEN TO FOLD 'EM

While William Wrigley was brilliant and sympathetic (at least as wealthy magnates go), he wasn't completely savvy. In fact, Wrigley walked face-first into a beehive when he took over the Cubs in 1919.

Salaries had dropped since the Federal League's demise following the 1915 season, and as a result some resentful players had started selling out their efforts. Some players had been gambling away at bats, and even games, for years, but the frequency of such activity seems to have increased after 1915. While the 1919 "Black

Sox" were obviously the most heavily tainted by corruption, the Cubs were hardly choirboys. Veeck and the rest of the management team knew that gambling was in baseball, at the deepest levels, but they seemed more interested in making the game look clean than actually having it be clean. "In the Cubs camp, as well as in New York, a number of ballplayers had been in touch with not only players but booking and betting agents," wrote Warren Wilbert. One of them was Lee Magee, a thirty-year-old infielder/outfielder the Cubs acquired from Brooklyn in 1919. After the season, he was implicated in helping fix games. The final contest of the 1919 season, a Cubs-Giants tilt, was said to be well off the level, and Magee was hurled from baseball for life.

On August 31, 1920, just a couple of weeks before the "Black Sox" story broke, the Cubs and Phillies were scheduled to play at Cubs Park. At the time, both clubs were well out of the race, but the Cubs were a better team. Oddly, the gambling odds favored the pathetic Phillies.

What seems to have happened is that, some time before, gamblers got to some Cubs, including starting pitcher Claude Hendrix, and promised money if they threw the game. Once enough Cubs agreed to cooperate, the gamblers spread the word that a fix was in. After myriad bets were then made on the Phillies to win, the intrigue really began. An hour before game time, telegrams began arriving at Cubs Park addressed to Bill Veeck, most from Detroit and signed by those who called themselves "concerned fans," informing him of rumors that the day's game was to be thrown. (The police later ascertained that the addresses given by these "concerned fans" were bogus.) A group of gamblers from Detroit—probably the original gamblers but possibly double-crossers—sent the telegrams and made phone calls to the same effect.

This news prompted Veeck and Fred Mitchell to remove Hendrix from the slab immediately in favor of Grover Cleveland Alexander. Mitchell even gave Alexander a $500 bonus to bear down. By forcing the situation, the parties responsible for the telegrams hoped to make the Cubs try extra hard to win, then bet on them at high odds and clean up. Unfortunately for them, Chicago lost anyway, 2–0, due in part to a crucial error by Buck Herzog on a sure double-play grounder. Authorities eventually implicated four Cubs in the scheme: Hendrix, Herzog, first baseman Fred Merkle, and scrub pitcher Paul Carter. As one would expect, most players involved in betting scandals were veterans with little to lose and a heap of resentment from the baseball wars. (Some were just plain corrupt.) Merkle had played in the majors since 1908; the thirty-one-year-old Hendrix was an old Chifeds pitcher. The popular Herzog, thirty-five, had even served as player/manager of the Reds for two years.

Veeck threw open the investigation, asking his former press colleagues to dig up the dirt. The Cubs left Hendrix behind when the club went east for a road trip in early September. Although everyone associated with the club said that the pitcher stayed behind because he was ineffective against Pittsburgh, Hendrix clearly was no longer trusted by management or his teammates. On September 7, Judge Charles McDonald of the Criminal Court of Chicago ordered a grand jury investigation of the incident. The court subpoenaed the entire team, as well as Veeck, Mitchell, and William Wrigley.

Veeck told the grand jury what he knew about the gambling scandal, but whatever he said didn't land him in trouble. The day after that, pitcher Rube Benton of the Giants—no angel himself—implicated Herzog, as well as the already bounced Hal Chase and Heinie Zimmerman, in hippodroming the 1919 Cubs-Giants contest. Other players, including Art Wilson and Tony Boeckel, also made affidavits.

The *Daily News* reported on September 4, 1920, that earlier in the summer, a gang of gamblers "suspected of betting in the stands and bleachers at the North Side park" had been arrested and hauled east a few blocks to the Town Hall police station.

While gambling had been going on at Cubs Park for quite some time, only with increased pressure did Veeck and Wrigley feel the need to clean things up.

On September 25, the *New York Daily News* quoted Monte Tennes asserting that he had given up betting on baseball. "I won't say I won't bet on it any more, but I made a good big bet last year and lost. I haven't made any this year." Asked if he knew anything about rumors of a fix of the 1919 World Series, he simply remarked, "I do not care to talk until I get back to Chicago and see just what the situation is there." When he got to Chicago, the situation was hot. On September 28, eight White Sox players were indicted for throwing the 1919 World Series. Tennes, with his connections to Charley Weeghman, Arnold Rothstein, and the Black Sox, became better known to the general public in the ensuing days.

While the Black Sox scandal wiped the Cubs-Phillies affair off the front page, the wheels of justice continued to grind. Merkle did not appear in the majors again until 1925, when he was a player-coach for the Yankees. Herzog and Hendrix both became unwelcome in the major leagues though not officially banned. (The eventual commissioner of baseball Kenesaw Mountain Landis, in his autobiography, insisted that he had banned Hendrix from baseball, and his is the only opinion that counted.) Herzog played in the minors after 1920, but hapless Paul Carter was simply bounced.

GOOD RIDDANCE

In retrospect, it is amazing that anyone was surprised when players started throwing games. Gambling culture was omnipresent in sports during the 1910s; wagering on all types of competitive sport was common among players, managers, fans, and writers. Even New York Giants manager John McGraw had part ownership in a gambling house—with Arnold Rothstein! Baseball players routinely gambled on other sports and said so. The other biggest spectator sports of the time were boxing, horse racing, and golf, all of which featured significant gambling subcultures.

Major league teams of the time outwardly tried to discourage gambling, occasionally asking police to bust the most obvious gambling rings and posting signs in the ballparks iterating that no wagering was allowed. But owners also knew that a significant portion of their audience came to the games expressly to bet.

As Bill James has pointed out, every big baseball story of the 1910s concerned money, from the Phillies' famous "$100,000 Infield" to the founding of the Federal League to the crash-and-burn of the nascent Players' Fraternity. Once the Federal League was bled to death and salaries decreased, some players felt betrayed.

This is one aspect of the game that has changed dramatically for the better over the last hundred years. Purists may cry foul, for instance, that the bleachers at Wrigley Field are full of rich, sun-worshipping, baseball-challenged yuppies—and, indeed, the cost of a bleacher seat is outrageous—and not everyone at the park really cares whether the Cubs win. But that's not new. Plenty of people go to the ballpark not caring who wins. Families go for sunny fun. Teenagers go to ogle one another and sneak beers.

All these annoyances don't compare with the effect on the game of money changing hands based on player performance. That environment almost ruined baseball once and it has no place at the ballpark today. Fan gambling began to be accepted again in the 1930s, once everyone figured that the games themselves were clean. This became even truer following Judge Landis's death in 1944. These days lasted, in Chicago, into the early 1980s, when Wrigley's bleachers, often only half-filled, served as open-air gambling parlors for "fans." For whatever reason, some people romanticize the 1950s, early 1960s, and mid 1970s, when a "crowd" of seven thousand was a good showing and the Cubs were awful for everyone but the gamblers. A popular late 1970s

Chicago play, *Bleacher Bums*, got it right, depicting the game as a sort of Greek tragedy, with nobody but the gambler happy when the Cubs lost. Does anyone who really cares about baseball want it to be like that?

AND TO MAKE THINGS WORSE . . .

On the morning of January 16, 1920, America went dry, a result of the Eighteenth Amendment to the constitution and the Volstead Act. The forces of moralism had inveigled the government into declaring the sale, manufacture, and drinking of alcohol illegal. The efforts of the well-meaning reformers put thousands of Americans out of jobs, increased violent crime, lowered the quality of life for millions of taxpaying citizens, and helped the Mafia gain a foothold in liquor production and distribution. So when the Black Sox scandal drove fans to drink, most of them couldn't—at least not legally.

The Black Sox scandal threw baseball into a panic. Major league owners sought someone, something, *anything*, to help restore public confidence in the game. When Cubs shareholder A. D. Lasker, a towering figure in the history of advertising, came up with an idea for some sort of tricornered group to run baseball, Bill Veeck and William Wrigley listened. But they tinkered with the idea, suggesting instead that just one man have absolute power over the game.

On Veeck's recommendation, Wrigley pushed for Judge Kenesaw Mountain Landis, a known, respected, and extremely authoritarian arbiter known for his business decisions and for his love of baseball. Landis, who lived in Chicago, became the commissioner of baseball and was often a happy visitor to Wrigley Field, resting his chin on a bar in front of his box seat. Veeck generally supported Landis, even finagling to get his salary raised, though later, the two fell out after Landis suspended Cubs second sacker Rogers Hornsby for gambling.

By 1920, the fifty-seven-year-old Wrigley (fig. 5) was one of the game's more powerful owners. He bought most of the shares of

FIGURE 5. "Jovial, well-upholstered" William Wrigley, with sunglasses, pipe, and Panama hat, at his box at Cubs Park. Note that the best seats in the house appear far from comfortable and were not even bolted in. While the park was constructed in concrete, Wrigley's seats appear to be resting on a wood surface. (Credit: National Baseball Hall of Fame and Museum)

the other owners, including Lasker and J. Ogden Armour, consolidating his power. At about this time, he also began construction of a huge office tower on Michigan Avenue, overlooking the Chicago River. The Wrigley Building remains one of the most identifiable landmarks in America.

DRAINING

Before his departure at the dawn of the Veeck era, Fred Mitchell had made one critical move. On March 1, 1919, he hired his friend Bobby Dorr as Cubs groundskeeper. During the 1922 season, Dorr helped improve the Wrigley Field draining system, installing an eight-inch tile pipe under the playing field from home plate to deepest center field, with two pipes shooting toward the foul lines. The field was configured to rise from foul line to foul line by 16 inches, allowing for improved two-way drainage.

The new drainage system couldn't stop the rain from falling, though. On May 14, 1922, rain delayed the three o'clock start, and the tarpaulins apparently provided little protection for the field, which was muddy and nearly unplayable. But with some eighteen thousand in the stands, the Cubs and Giants soldiered on. In the top of the fourth, heavy rain began to fall, causing delays between pitches, sloppy fielding, and slippery baserunning. Fans in the left-field bleachers began tossing pop bottles, popcorn boxes, and seat cushions onto the sodden outfield grass in protest.

Still the game continued. In the bottom of the fourth, Charlie Hollocher doubled past Giants third sacker Heinie Groh, who fell in the mud trying to field the ball. Left-fielder Irish Meusel also slipped into the muck retrieving the hit. Hollocher then tried for third on a short grounder; when he slid, he kept on sliding and was tagged out when he went right by the bag. Two plays later, Ray Grimes, who had doubled, was also out when *he* overslid third.

In the sixth, Jesse Barnes of the Giants hit an easy grounder, but first baseman Grimes couldn't hold the wet ball when it was thrown to him. Umpire Paul Sentelle ruled Barnes safe, which caused a huge argument as the rain became a deluge. "Fans in the bleachers started a roughhouse act," wrote Frank Schreiber in the May 15 *Tribune*, "tossing boxes and cardboards on to the field until Umpire Klem was forced to call the contest until the obstructions had been removed."

In the eighth, the rain became interminable, and many in the bleacher crowd climbed over the outfield fence, onto the field. Swells in box seats had already rushed under the roof to stay dry, and the bleacher fans stormed the field, attempting to climb into the grandstand themselves. Unfortunately for the four-bit fans, the policy of the 1910s, allowing these fans access to dry areas during deluges, had been changed. The *Tribune's* Schreiber noted that "it took the efforts of ten coppers to shoo them back."

After ten innings, this hellish game finally ended, the Giants escaping with a 5–4 win.

WEIRDNESS AFIELD

The 1922 season saw other especially dramatic moments. On August 19, fans rushed the field after the Cubs' 2–1, eleven-inning win. And on August 24, the Brooklyn Dodgers were the beneficiaries of some weird Chicago baserunning—Ray Grimes tried to steal third, forgetting that Charlie Hollocher was already there.

The very next day, things got even weirder. The Cubs have hosted some slugfests through the years, but none have yet topped the game of August 25, 1922, when the Phillies were in town. Seven thousand fans witnessed a ridiculous game that shattered all sorts of records. The 26–23 Cubs win set a still-extant major league record for most total runs scored in a game.

Trailing 3–1 in the last of the second, the Cubs piled on against pitcher Jimmy Ring, scoring ten times. Two innings later, already up 11–6, Chicago scored fourteen more. Cubs right-fielder Marty Callaghan batted three times in the inning. Ring was pulled in that inning in favor of Lefty Weinert, who absorbed the rest of the pounding. Hack Miller homered twice for Chicago, while Cliff Heathcote went five-for-five, walked twice, and crossed the dish five times. But in true Cubs style, it wasn't easy. The Phillies trailed 26–9 after seven innings but beat up Chicago relievers Uel Eubanks and Ed Morris, tallying eight runs in the eighth. In the ninth, the first four Phils reached base against Morris, leading manager Bill Killefer to bring in Tiny Osborne, who was hardly better. The Phillies, who left sixteen on base, scored six times but ran out of gas.

Before the game, the *Tribune*'s Frank Schreiber dutifully noted the next day, Cubs outfielder Jigger Statz had been presented with unique gift: a rubber-tired baby carriage. One hopes that the popular Statz was about to be a father. The gift came courtesy of eight showgirls appearing in a local production of *The Dancing Honeymoon*.

BRING ON THE BEARS

Despite their pummeling of the Phillies, the Cubs did not have a sterling 1922 season: they finished fifth in the NL. Following the close of the season, the Cubs did defeat the Sox in a rain-soaked city series then left the field to the Chicago Bears. While the football club, formerly known as the Decatur Staleys, had moved to Chicago and into Cubs Park the previous season, this was the first year that the team would be officially known as the Bears, a name chosen expressly to gain favor with Cubs fans. In fact, some newspapers at the time actually referred to the *Cubs* as "Bears."

The football Bears made their 1922 Cubs Park debut on October 15 against Rochester, winning 7–0. By October 21, a new scoreboard for football—featuring a clock—had been installed and grass laid over the baseball baselines and the mound. The next day, the Bears defeated Buffalo, again rolling up the score to 7–0.

From 1921 through 1970, the Chicago Bears played 365 home games at Wrigley, setting a record for most games at one stadium that stood until 2003. Bears games at Wrigley Field became nearly as much a part of fall as Cubs games were of summer, but the football team was always a tenant of the Wrigleys and, there-fore, a clear second on the priority list when it came to seating and facilities. This put them on a par with other tenants of the 1930s through the 1950s, including boxing and wrestling matches and basketball games, some competitive and some featuring the world-famous Harlem Globetrotters.

THE FIRST BIG RENOVATION

When the Bears completed their home schedule on December 3, the Cubs began a $300,000 renovation program designed to boost capacity in the park by twelve thousand, up to thirty-one thousand. Consistently large crowds in the late teens and early twenties had convinced management that the time was right to expand. Zachary Davis, the original architect, helped design and engineer the renovation, which was to be carried out in a way that retained the feel of the park while expanding it.

News of a possible expansion had leaked out back on May 2, when the *Daily News*'s Oscar Reichow hailed, "Cheer up, Cub fans! There may soon be room to seat 30,000 at the North Side park." Reichow noted that "the plans are to cut the main grand stand in half, move it back to Clark Street and the railroad tracks, and extend it north to the bleachers."

When the renovation got under way, the existing concrete grandstand, which at the time seated approximately fifty-five hundred in the boxes and eleven thousand in general admis-sion, was actually sliced into three parts. The right- and left-field "wings" were separated from the home plate section. The third-base grandstand was placed on rollers and pushed northwest to-ward the intersection of Waveland Avenue and Clark Street. The home plate section was moved south, about sixty feet, toward Addison Street. It is believed that the pitcher's mound is cur-rently located where home plate had been. The first-base/right-field stands stayed put. The grandstand was also lowered several feet and a new fence was installed around it from foul line to foul line. There was now no need for a stairway from the field to the stands. The retaining wall was about two feet high, with a two-foot heavy wire fence atop it.

The act of moving the stands and reattaching them created the odd curve in the grandstand near where the first-base dugout is now located. The dugouts themselves did not become much larger, but they were now covered with cement. In addition, one hundred flags were hoisted on poles around the park, and would be raised every day henceforth.

With all the new extra room, the club was able to increase its box seat capacity to ninety-three hundred and its general admission to seventeen thousand. Cubs Park now held more seats than any other single-decked ballpark in the country. According to Bill Veeck, there would be no upper deck: "Fans do not like the top seats, and we find we can get enough by splitting the main structure."

Veeck also stressed to Reichow a secondary goal in making the changes: enlarging the playing field. "It will increase our playing space to excellent proportions. Right field, which is now the shortest, will be the longest, for by moving the stands back to Clark and the railroad tracks we will get more than 100 feet additional." Dimensions in the "new" Cubs Park were 325 feet from home plate to the bleachers in left, a whopping 447 feet to deepest center, and 318 to right.

The expansion came not a year too soon. On August 17, 1922, the Cubs and Giants played "before the largest weekday crowd that had been to the North Side park in years," reported the *Daily News* the next day. "It was estimated that 22,000 were present. The jam was so big that ropes were put in the outfield to handle the overflow. . . . This is the first time in many years that the Cubs have had spectators on the field on a weekday." That the game was promoted as Ladies Day helps in part to explain the high attendance. But the next day, another twenty-five thousand fans paid to see the two clubs, and the day after some twenty-six thousand crammed the yard for the final game of the series. Fans stuffed the outfield, sat on the high right-field wall, and even perched themselves atop the scoreboard some forty feet above the ground. More than three thousand hopefuls were left outside. The crowd on that Sunday, according to the Frank Schreiber in the August 20 *Tribune*, was "probably the greatest crowd that ever witnessed a game at the Cubs' North Side park." The expansion, therefore, was welcome and well received. "The grandstand with its sweep from wall to wall looks like the finest in the big leagues in its newness, its green paint, and [its] graceful curves," huzzahed the *Daily News*'s William H. Becker on April 7, 1923, when given a tour of the nearly finished product. "From the promenade at the foot of the grandstand seats to the concrete wall about the field, the boxes are ranged twelve deep. These boxes sweep right and left to the full extent of the grandstand," he said. Noted Becker, "The old bleachers [are] looking painfully small and inadequate when one looks back a score of years and remembers when the bleachers in ball parks predominated and the grandstands were small and apologetic."

Becker also wrote that enlarging the grandstand indicated a big change in the financial standing of ballpark patrons. The Cubs increased the number of box and general admission seats because their buying public could, and would, happily pay higher prices for a rarified view. On the North Side, as in many parks across the nation, baseball had become more lucrative.

OUTSTANDING IN THEIR FIELD

The Cubs allowed fans into the park during April, while the squad was off at training camp, to watch workers fix up the field and the stands. Workmen rebuilt the twenty-five hundred bleachers in left field from all wood to steel-framed wood. The seats ranged from near the left-field line to left-center, leaving straightaway center and the scoreboard open. Twenty-five hundred new bleachers in twenty rows were also constructed from right-center to close to the right-field foul line; for the first time since 1914, there would be seating in right field. Also as in 1914, a wire fence separated the bleachers from the field.

On both foul lines, a section behind the fence did not include bleachers; photos of the time show tarpaulins stored there, and one assumes the spaces housed other groundskeeping equipment. Both foul poles, housed inside of these areas, were out of play.

On April 5, 1923, when tickets for the home opener went on sale, the *Tribune*'s Frank Schreiber reported that construction work on the stands was complete. By April 7, the infield and outfield had been resodded; steamrollers ran incessantly over the turf in order to mash it down sufficiently. Further, large figures representing the "Doublemint Twins," Wrigley gum mascots, had been installed atop each end of the scoreboard in center field. (Photos show them to be slightly different than the figures atop the scoreboard in 1919.) The pixie on the left-field side held a bat, while the other wound up to deliver a pitch. Around this season, white-coated ballpark vendors began wearing Wrigley gum hats while peddling their wares.

The plumbing was still an issue at this time. Wrigley had hired nonunion contractors to build much of the spanking-new plumbing system, and the local unions took offense. On the night of Sunday, April 15, a wrecking crew affiliated with the aggrieved union broke into the park and did $10,000 in damage to the plumbing, scattering the scabs' tools around the lot. Nobody associated with the union bothered to deny responsibility. The next day, six more angry union members attempted to break into the park and stop the nonunion workers from repairing the busted plumbing, but the ruffians were thrown out. By 5:00 P.M., most of the pipes and fixtures had been repaired.

As the April 17 home opener neared, the crew shaped and rolled new base paths filled with fine clay. All that was left to do before was to install seats and gussy up the playing field. The new green-painted seats were installed and painted by April 11, but not all of the freshly decorated chairs had dried by the first game. (In fact, newspaper stories of the time refer to the common annual inconvenience of getting green paint stains on one's clothing at Opening Day.)

That was not the only aspect of the reconstruction that went less smoothly than Cubs management would have led you to believe. On March 1, 1948, the *Tribune* ran Ed Prell's interview with groundskeeper Bobby Dorr, then entering his thirtieth year on the job. He said that lowering the playing field for Opening Day 1923 was a project fraught with difficulty and went right down to the wire:

> Dorr's biggest operation at Wrigley Field started in mid-October 1922 and was finished a few minutes before Opening Day in April 1923. This was a 6-foot-6-inch bite into the entire field, or 52,000 yards of dirt. . . . The job was complicated by strikes in the building unions and much of the material was left in nearby alleys under cover of darkness. . . . One hundred men each worked on day and night shifts in the race against time.
>
> "On the morning of Opening Day," says Dorr, "there was a hole 30 feet square around shortstop. . . . We even had to scrape up dirt out of the alley for this last fill-in, but we made it."

On April 12, the *Daily Journal* had quoted Bill Veeck as planning to give fans "fewer frills and more baseball" on Opening Day, April 17. But it would have been impossible to escape all ceremony. Jack Bramhall's band, on hand for its twenty-eighth straight Cubs opener, began playing at 1:00, and at 2:45 a battalion of blue- and red-clad U.S. Marines from Fort Sheridan headed toward center field, picking up first the Cubs from their dugout and then the Pirates from theirs—much like the scene captured in figure 6. The parade marched out to the flagpole where Old Glory was raised in front of the scoreboard. What William Becker of the *Daily News* in the late afternoon April 17 edition called "inevitable" pink roses (huge flower garlands were common on Opening Day) were laid around home plate, and the Cubs

FIGURE 6. This is Opening Day sometime between 1923 and 1925 at a packed Wrigley Field. The Wrigley Gum Doublemint Twins are visible atop the scoreboard. The white-suited gentleman with the cornet may be Jack Bramhall, whose band played many a Wrigley season opener. (Credit: National Baseball Hall of Fame and Museum)

presented floral offerings to manager Bill Killefer and outfielder Hack Miller. Newly elected mayor Bill Dever arrived at the park at 2:45 and threw out the first pitch from his box behind home plate. Given the plumbing-related vandalism a few days before, a large squadron of police was on hand; no exploding commodes were reported.

Some thirty-five thousand fans packed into the "new" ballpark for the Cubs' 3–2 loss. Thousands more were denied entry. The new bleachers built in left and right field left little room, at least this day, for extra standees in the outfield. The cold day was marked by sloppy baseball; Hugh Fullerton of the *Tribune* cracked the following day that "the frappéd crowd witnessed a fricasseed contest." Fullerton also noted that the crowd was high class: "The leaders of social, business, and political life of Chicago were there, and the proportion of women was large."

Contrast this with the foundering post–Black Sox White Sox, who were in the nether regions of the American League and were not to contend again until the 1950s. The North Side was now the place to be for winning baseball in Chicago.

SCORES IN GILEAD

There were other innovations in the Chicago sports world at the start of this season. The *Tribune*, a step ahead of the competition, opened up the first sports telephone update line in the city. Radio broadcasts had not yet begun, but fans away from the park who wanted to know lineups and current scores could call to get the information from a *Tribune* staffer.

"Telephone baseball fans began limbering up the score wires before 10 A.M. yesterday with requests for the lineup, opening hour, and other details," wrote Anna Garrow, the newspaper's chief phone operator, on April 18. "For the fans who cannot attend the games in person, there is still 'balm in Gilead,' the *Tribune* score department, State 6110." By the 1930s, twenty trunk lines were devoted to the *Tribune*'s score service, with a new number: SUperior-0220. Into the 1980s, every major newspaper had a score line, though usually these held only tape-recorded messages reporting the previous day's totals.

WHITE RIOT

The increased capacity in Cubs Park had a negative effect on September 16, 1923. A Sunday crowd of around twenty-six thousand, among them Commissioner Landis and National League president John Heydler, witnessed one of the more dangerous demonstrations of loyalty ever seen at the field.

When umpire Charlie Moran ejected Cliff Heathcote of the Cubs for arguing in the fourth inning, the shouts began for Moran's head, and some fans pitched bottles onto the field. In the eighth, Moran's close call on a force play, going against the Cubs, set the crowd alight. "Bottles came from the bleachers," wrote Irving Vaughan of the *Tribune* the following day, "and in a moment the outfield was floored [*sic*] with them. From the grand stand came others, some sailing as far as second base, whence Moran had retreated to be out of range."

The broken glass on the field caused a fifteen-minute delay, as the Cubs refused to take their positions for the ninth until the pieces were picked up. Finally, the crowd decided to let the game continue. Fans also whipped bottles toward Giants outfielders in the bottom of the ninth, but New York walked away with a 10–6 win. Not much could be said for the bugs' accuracy; the only player hit by a bottle was Cubs third baseman Barney Friberg. After the final out, the fans roared and hooted anew, to the point that Moran and John McGraw needed an escort of some one hundred policemen to leave the premises. "The scene surpassed anything ever seen on a local field," noted Vaughan. "Even after the show was over, the pop-eyed fans failed to cool off, hundreds whooping and howling like wolves outside the umpires' dressing room and thousands camping outside the main entrance waiting for something to happen."

The commissioner, Vaughan noted, "merely shook his cane at the mob and moved on."

FESTIVITIES AND BALLS

More changes to Wrigley Field came in the off-season, as the Cubs installed another new drainage system in the outfield, which measurably improved the ability of the field to dry, and purchased a new field tarpaulin. Less visibly but no less significantly, in 1924, William Wrigley purchased the land on which the ballpark sat from descendants of the family that had leased it to Charley Weeghman in 1914. Before the season, Wrigley and Bill Veeck elected—perhaps in response to fan demand—to remove advertising from the center-field scoreboard, using the extra space to post both American League and National League line scores.

The Cubs had what was becoming a typical Opening Day on April 23. An unbylined note in the *Tribune* reported that "customers will find the park as tidy as a doll house. The stand and bleachers have been given a new coat of paint, [and] the field is in perfect trim." A hundred boys from Senn High School's ROTC raised the flag at 3:00, following the customary concert from Jack Bramhall's band. The Cubs clouted Saint Louis 11–1 before twenty-seven thousand fans. For the first time, the Cubs wore red sweatshirts under their uniform tops; this was a big topic of conversation for the press.

On July 18 of this season, the city of Chicago dedicated a statue of Civil War General Philip Sheridan at the corner of Sheridan Road and Belmont Avenue, just off Lake Michigan, four blocks south and six blocks east of Wrigley Field. The statue depicts the general riding high on his steed. For reasons that remain obscure, it soon became de rigueur for out-of-town teams to command their rookies to visit the statue and paint, in luminous team colors, the testicles of General Sheridan's horse.

CHECK, PLEASE

The new drainage system got a big test on April 27—and failed it. After a morning of pouring rain, groundskeeper Bob Dorr and his crew were literally shoveling water off the field and into wheelbarrows. Most of the fans left the park before the start, thinking the contest wouldn't go on, but the Cubs and Pirates waited out the storm only to play a wet, error-filled 4–2 game.

"President Veeck, after the game, declared that any fan who held a seat check could get his money refunded," noted the *Tribune*'s Frank Schreiber on April 28. "There were less than 4,000 customers in the stands when the game started, and there had been a big advance sale. This action establishes a big league precedent." Another first for Chicago baseball?

Giving out rain checks was of a piece with William Wrigley's broader philosophy: do the right thing over the long term. This meant taking care of the stadium, treating customers well, and delivering a quality product. While he lacked Charley Weeghman's unmatched ability to get his name in the papers, Wrigley was methodical and smart and had plenty of pals in the press himself. He knew that it was critical to maintain, clean, and repair Cubs Park constantly, and for this reason he was an ideal caretaker. The amount of money the Cubs poured into the park in its first few decades is one reason it remains functional.

In Forrest Crissey's September 13, 1930, *Saturday Evening Post* article, Wrigley showed that he, like Weeghman, understood that to bring in a higher and wealthier class to the ballpark, you had to make nice: "Persons used to refined surroundings will not voluntarily go to places for entertainment which offend their sense of cleanliness, comfort, and decency. Therefore I spent $2,300,000 to make Wrigley Field clean, convenient, comfortable, and attractive to the eye—a place in which any woman accustomed to refined surroundings would feel safe, comfortable, and in a frame of mind to enjoy the game."

William Wrigley belonged to a class of businessman who felt a civic obligation to keep people employed, happy, and—not coincidentally—active in the capitalist system. As a successful civic leader and businessman, he already had his money and now wanted the esteem that public acceptance would bring. Wrigley was said to be proud of having created jobs in the gum industry and in his other businesses and in how much he gave back to his community. The 1933 edition of the *National Cyclopædia* that "he was a liberal contributor to many hospitals, charities, and organizations working for the education and welfare of boys and girls of all races and sects."

While Wrigley believed that "no man is qualified to make a genuine success of owning a big league team unless he is in the game for the love of it," he was no cream puff; he pushed his business hard and had a very hardheaded and realistic approach to baseball. Since the First World War helped spread his product throughout the world, he saw all people as potential customers of one sort or another—Bill Veeck Jr. called him "the last of the super salesmen, a man who made his name synonymous with his product." And Wrigley felt that his primary business fit quite nicely with the uniquely American phenomenon of baseball. As William Wrigley's son Philip told his own biographer, Paul Angle, in the 1970s, "The customers of the Cubs were exactly the same people that we sold most of our chewing gum to."

William Wrigley was a jovial visionary, capable of focusing on long-term results and choosing to invest in his businesses. A believer in the power of advertising, he was one of the first to embrace radio broadcasting of games in order to publicize his product, first allowing Cubs games on the air in 1925.

RADIO KILLED THE VAUDEVILLE STAR

Radio scared the hell out of a lot of people, among them the movie moguls, the theater industry, the concert hall promoters, and the baseball men. Many in baseball believed that "giving" away baseball via the new medium would kill attendance. But Wrigley, having done great business in new markets because of advertising—that is, getting the product before the public—understood that putting Cubs home games on the wireless and keeping baseball in people's minds would draw a whole new class of customers to the park.

The focus of the new broadcasting was home games. Until the 1950s, most clubs had their announcers work only home contests live because of the prohibitive costs of sending radio broadcasts across great distances. Road games were re-created in the station's studio, where the announcer would read a ticker-tape feed of the play-by-play, aided by an engineer using sound effects records to supply crowd noise and the crack of the bat.

At times in the 1920s and 1930s, long before the Cubs granted one station exclusive broadcast rights, multiple channels—WGN,

FIGURE 7. Bill Veeck Sr. (*L*), former sportswriter and president of the Cubs from 1919–33, with Irving Vaughan, a longtime *Chicago Tribune* baseball beat writer, at the WGN radio microphone. (Credit: National Baseball Hall of Fame and Museum)

WCFL, WIBO, WBBM, WIND, and WCFL—aired the contests from Wrigley Field with different announcers, among them Quin Ryan, Hal Totten, Pat Flanagan, Russ Hodges, and Bob Elson. (Only in the mid-1940s did the Cubs auction rights to the highest bidder for radio.) Instead of limiting access, the Cubs threw the gates open. Wrigley believed that the more people heard the games, the more people would be interested. And he was right. With radio spreading the word, attendance at Cubs games exploded.

The first Cubs regular season broadcast came on Opening Day of 1925, April 14, with WGN's Quin Ryan bringing the game to the listeners from Wrigley Field's roof. There wasn't anywhere else to put him; according to Irving Vaughan in the next day's *Tribune*, this was the biggest attendance to that time for an opener in Chicago: "They were in the seats and on the seats, on the field and in the aisles, and even on the fences and the iron girders—in fact, no vantage point was in need of an occupant." WGN, an innovator in baseball broadcasting, always carried a great deal of sports programming (see, e.g., fig. 7). Even before the game, the *Tribune* had predicted that the park, "newly painted and looking as neat as a Dutch bakery," would be packed. "Useless, timeworn opening ceremonies will be dispensed with," the paper continued. "The exceptions will be a couple of bands that probably will try to drown out each other."

JUBILEE

Later that season, the Cubs celebrated the NL's fiftieth anniversary on June 9, a date that had no real connection to the actual anniversary of the league's organization. Management invited approximately seventy-five former players to Cubs Park for the event, including seventy-five-year-old Deacon White, the catcher in the first game the NL Cubs ever played, on April 25, 1876. (The only other survivor of the team, crusty first baseman Cal McVey, was not in shape to travel from California, and he died about fourteen months later in San Francisco.) At the event, Jack Bramhall's music makers serenaded a parade of players aged and current, and a special pennant marking the occasion—which had first been raised on Opening Day 1925—was flown in center field. Commissioner Landis was on hand to present floral pieces to several of the players, in front of fifteen thousand fans. The Cubs promptly went out and lost to the Giants, 9–7, allowing three home runs.

Long balls at Wrigley Field had become quite common. All season, the Chicago nine had been victimized by what were called "cheap" home runs into the left-field bleachers. (Surely the Cubs hit plenty as well, but sabermetric research—that is, mathematically sophisticated statistics, developed or inspired by the work of the Society of American Baseball Research, whose initials gave birth to the term—hadn't yet come into vogue. Even weekly averages in the papers were a luxury.) The left-field corner was a cozy 319 feet from home plate, with straightaway left just 325.

Things reached a head on July 28 when the New York Giants slugged five home runs in a 10–3 shellacking of the Cubs. Irish Meusel's second homer of the game bounced off the back wall in left field and landed on Waveland Avenue. In the seventh inning, while the Giants were busting the game open, William Wrigley looked at his watch, rose from his seat, and hurriedly departed the park. In the next morning's paper, James Crusinberry of the *Tribune* wrote the following day that "one rumor was that Mr. Wrigley had rushed to city hall with the hope of closing a couple of streets and enlarging the field before the game today."

On August 2, Brooklyn's Elmer "Dick" Cox smashed a three-run homer to left to beat the Cubs 3–2. Crusinberry lamented in the following day's *Tribune* that, "if that left field bleacher could just be lifted up and put over the right field one as a double deck, there would be the same space for the four-bits guys and there would be some room out in left for the Cub outfielders to go and catch about two-thirds of the homers that are hit there."

Talk about power of the press! That very day, the Cubs' board of directors heeded the growing cries and voted to rip out fifteen hundred left-field seats, and workmen did the construction while the Cubs took an eastern road trip in early August. Only a small, sixteen-row-deep section of fifty-cent bleachers—soon known as the "jury box"—remained in left-center field. Suddenly, the distance down the left-field line was 370 feet rather than 319. The distance to the jury box was 353 feet. As a result, far fewer cheap homers traveled to left field.

The changes decreased capacity in the outfield for sitters but increased the space for standees. On big-crowd days, the Cubs still allowed fans to stand in the deeper parts of the outfield, which brought "ground rules" into effect for balls hit into the humanity; the effect of moving the seats out to help the pitchers was lost on well-attended days. In a remembrance published in 1980, an old fan named Papa Carl Leone, who spent much of his time from the 1920s through the 1980s in the right-field bleachers, recalled, "When the Cubs were up, we'd all step forward and pull the rope up. When the other team was up and hit one deep, we'd pull it back and let the guy catch it."

Nevertheless, a large number of balls were lost to the crowd. Pat Pieper, the Cubs' field announcer, was responsible for counting the number of baseballs used in each game. "It costs the front office no little money to keep the two teams supplied with throwing material for 77 contests," wrote William Becker in the *Daily News* of November 1, 1926. During that season, Pieper reported, 3,004 balls had been used—nearly forty per contest. Just a few years earlier, such a number would have been unheard of. Dirty, scuffed baseballs had been kept in games as long as possible to save money until Cleveland Indians shortstop Ray Chapman was fatally beaned by a pitch he couldn't see in 1920. Following that tragedy, the press pushed for clean balls and the banning of illegal pitches to increase batter safety.

But differences still existed from day to day in how balls were distributed. Becker noted that "On July 2, when [Ernie] Quigley was behind the bat, only 17 balls were taken out of the boxes and handled by the players. But on May 9, when [Bill] Klem was calling strikes, 60 balls were given the once-over with the batters."

The standard of what constitutes a clean ball hadn't yet been fully established, but clearly a great umpire like Klem had a lower tolerance for dirty baseballs.

GROWTH SPURT

The next major change in Cubs Park came after the following season. On December 3, 1926, the Cubs announced that their home would now be known as Wrigley Field—a reasonably appropriate act, since William Wrigley was pouring another vat of money into the premises, having recently announced a plan to build an upper deck.

"Several times during the season just closed," ran an unbylined item in the October 15 *Evening Post*, "Cubs Park was filled to capacity and thousands were turned away." Huge crowds during the fall's city series between the Sox and Cubs (fig. 8) also convinced Wrigley and Veeck that more seats were necessary. In addition, the White Sox were expanding Comiskey Park.

The Lanquist Construction Company handled the building work, and Graham, Anderson, Probst & White designed the expansion. The Cubs hoped to have the entire project, projected to cost $600,000, completed in time for the 1927 season. The fifteen thousand new upper-deck seats would raise the park's capacity to forty-five thousand. The new upper tier would feature box seats in the lower half and general admission in the back.

The first step in the process was to remove the current roof support and replace it with stronger steel that would support an upper deck. This work began during the football season, and the heavy building commenced after the Bears' home season ended with a 3–3 tie against Green Bay on December 12.

Unlike the speedy initial construction of Weeghman Park, however, this expansion hit some snags. The team announced that a "delay in materials" caused the slowdown and that completion would have to wait till 1928. There may have been more to the story, however. On November 9, 1926, the *Daily News* reported that "there is not the progress [at Wrigley Field] as evi-

FIGURE 8. Players warm up prior to a Cubs-Sox postseason city-series game, sometime in the late 1920s or early 1930s. Fans are ringing the outfield. Note the exit deep in center field under the scoreboard. (Credit: National Baseball Hall of Fame and Museum)

dent at the domicile of the White Sox." The paper went on to note that Bill Veeck had returned to the city from a vacation and that "there will be action, and more of it, on the North Side." Did the mice play while the cats were away?

When the snow melted, and springtime rolled around, the Cubs invited in the writers, who saw that only the third-base-side stands had been doubled. The Chicago *American*'s Jimmy Corcoran, reporting on April 7, 1927, wasn't especially impressed by the half-done job, although he did cut the Cubs a little slack:

"An expert in design, symmetry, or equilibrium likely would walk into Wrigley Field next Tuesday when the Cubs pop open the season against the Cardinals and comment on the fact that the Cub officials had lost their sense of what constitutes beauty in a ballpark. Such a comment, however, would be extremely moist [i.e., 'all wet']."

The new almost-half-deck, which ranged from the left-field corner of the grandstand to close to home plate, did raise the capacity of the park to forty thousand. The chairs in the park were not especially wide, in fact smaller than the old ones, which allowed for a larger crowd (albeit one with, on average, smaller tushes). The ramps built to take spectators to the upper deck were attractive in their simplicity, and they still stand. Though the deck is by modern standards relatively low, it was seen at the time as being almost unbearably high. Corcoran again: "It will be well for those who use the upper deck at the Bruin orchard to maintain their balance at all times. When you start to climb you can't get away from the feeling that you are going up in the air—and no fooling." The upper deck at Wrigley—which can be seen in figure 9—has been added to, reconstructed, repainted, and reconfigured, but it is essentially the same deck built more than eighty years ago.

Some final cosmetic touches were still being done before the season opened. Cubs' secretary John Seys supervised the painting, building, and adjustment of various aspects of the park. Corcoran noted that this was being done "with the avowed purpose of fulfilling owner Bill Wrigley's intention, and that is to make the park the prettiest in the major leagues." The beautification effort, which eventually became an annual ritual, included repainting the bleachers and reserved seats in their typical Irish green and touching up the trim around the park in cream and red. Pictures taken in early April 1927 show that the field was not in the best of shape, and the Cubs blamed this on its use by Bears for their season just past.

FIGURE 9. This spectacular aerial view of Wrigley Field, complete with plane, likely dates from the early or mid-1930s. Note the coal plant and train tracks directly west of the ballpark. Both are now gone. (Credit: National Baseball Hall of Fame and Museum)

On a cold Opening Day, April 12, 1927, Mayor Thompson joined the forty-two thousand fans crammed into every available space. The new deck was jammed and the outfield full of standees. Uniformed policemen stood in the outfield to try to maintain order. Photographers and movie cameras set up on the first-base-side roof. "Other thousands were clamoring at the gates for admittance," Wayne Otto wrote in that afternoon's *Daily News*. A band from Senn High School played during the flag raising. In addition, Jack Bramhall's combo tootled away.

The 1927 season was good on the field for the Cubs, who finished 85–68, albeit in fourth place. It was an even greater fiscal success. The new half-deck allowed 1,159,168 paying fans to enter the gates, an all-time league record and the first time that a club had busted the million mark.

Radio broadcasting of games continued to boom, too. With most games starting at 3:00, most broadcasts began with pre-game announcements and hot gossip at 2:45. Hal Totten, the city's top baseball broadcaster of the time, aired all Cubs and Sox home games on WMAQ. The *Tribune*'s radio station, WGN, assigned Quin Ryan to full-time baseball duties to challenge WMAQ's dominance, and other stations followed suit.

DECKED
Workers finished the first-base-side upper deck at Wrigley Field in time for the first game of 1928, on April 18, and interest ran high in the "new" yard. All 15,300 box seats for Opening Day sold out well in advance. The thirty thousand grandstand and bleacher tickets, put on sale at 11:00 on the morning of the game, went quickly. The crowd was, at that point, the largest ever to watch a baseball game in Chicago. "Paid admission was approximately 44,000," noted the *Tribune* the next day. "Another couple of thousand seeped through the pass gate, which from 2 to 3 o'clock P.M. was the busiest spot in the park."

Opening ceremonies used to take two hours or more with Charley Weeghman at the helm, but the 1928 lid-lifter (opening game of the season) began at 3:00 after a reasonable fifteen minutes of ceremony. A squadron of ROTC cadets from Senn High provided the pomp and circumstance; Bramhall's band again provided the light entertainment. "Prof. Bramhall promises to have a corps of sterling tooters out," opined the *Tribune*'s Frank Schreiber on April 18, "and threatens to play his two cornet solos— he's played the same pieces for the past thirty-five years—as an added feature." Cubs manager Joe McCarthy and fan favorites Grover Cleveland Alexander of Saint Louis and Gabby Hartnett of Chicago received flowers. According to the April 19 *Tribune*, "Alex also drew a traveling bag and a large gourd that was the exact shape of a bat," a gift from a barbershop quartet from Grand Island, Nebraska. What Alexander was supposed to do with that, was anyone's guess.

The *Tribune*'s Wake of the News column waxed romantic about the Cubs and their fans on April 19: "There are some owners who attach more importance to the making of money than they do to winning. The Cub management is not in that category. We venture to say that Bill Wrigley, whose fortune is not dependent on baseball earnings, would rather see his team in a world's series than see a ledger profit of $250,000." It's hard to believe that anyone could write that with a straight face, but then again Veeck was friends with the newsboys, and Wrigley did go to a lot of trouble to make the park beautiful and satisfy the fans with good baseball. The Cubs had developed a good-faith pact with their fans.

The fans loved their Cubs, and at times they expressed their devotion with what might be seen as excessive emotion. On June 20, 1928, the Cubs hosted the Cardinals in a doubleheader. The Cubs won the first 2–1, but were losing the second game 4–1 in the ninth. Despite having drawn two walks and hit a single, hard-hitting, hard-partying Cubs slugger Hack Wilson was getting the business from some of the fans. One particular rooter, seated in a box behind the Cubs' dugout, made Wilson so angry that after making the second out in the inning, he rushed into the stands to attack the fan. After landing a few punches, Wilson was pulled away, but a riot had already begun. Fans, policemen, and players all joined the fray, and it was several minutes before order was restored and the Cardinals recorded the third out.

Under these circumstances, it was perhaps for the best that patrons were unable to purchase a beer at Wrigley Field—or, indeed, anywhere, since Prohibition was still the law of the land. Any number of intrepid citizens procured their pick of poisons in any event, and the neighborhood around Wrigley Field was a hotbed of arrests and crackdowns on illegal purveyors, who saw their products seized or spilled into sewers by the authorities. The Mob's local influence could be seen across the North Side, as evident from the police logs from the time.

Whatever their character, 1,143,740 rooters paid their way into Wrigley Field in 1928 to see a club that went 91–63 and finished just four games behind pennant-winning Saint Louis.

A BIG SEASON

The start of the 1929 season saw not only the now requisite fresh coat of paint on the seats—Hal Totten wrote in the April 6 *Daily News* that "the entire plant is dressed in new coats of green and cream-colored paint"—but the debut of new peanut roaster that could handle two hundred pounds of nuts at a time. Fans ate around two hundred fifty thousand bags of peanuts at the park per season, and they sucked down about three hundred thousand bottles of soda, while filling out some six hundred thousand scorecards.

While Totten remarked that little about the park had been altered for 1929, he did point out that a fifteen-foot-high corrugated steel wall had been built from the end of the left-field bleachers to the right-field open seats. This new wall replaced a wood fence. Certainly the change was critical for any outfielders who had the misfortune of running into the new wall. In addition, two new flagpoles, each close to ninety feet tall, graced the end of the foul lines, and a brand new 110-foot pole was placed in a newly lain eight-foot square and twelve-foot-deep concrete slab in deep center field.

Photos from April 1929 show that box seats at the park provided no contemporary standard of comfort. The removable chairs, featuring four slats of wood on the seat and just one supporting slat up the back, are far narrower than today's chairs—seven chairs sit where five or six would now be used. The Cubs did not actually bolt down all of their box seats until the late 1960s.

Reports put more than fifty thousand fans at Wrigley Field on Opening Day 1929 when the Cubs fell 4–3 to the Pirates. Some twenty-two thousand general admission seats went up for sale the morning of the game, while the box seats and the first twelve rows of the grandstand sold out well in advance. The crowd surged on the field, noted the *Tribune*'s Ed Burns the following day, "making ground rules necessary an hour and a half before game time." According to contemporary reports, the ubiquitous Jack Bramhall Band played the popular song "Avalon" incessantly before the contest. It must have been hard to mouth the brass instruments, as the temperatures reached a high of only forty-seven degrees with winds whipping in from the north.

During the game, Town Hall police arrested two men—one from Lake View, one from the Northwest Side—for betting in the park. One of the arrested, a well-known gambler, inadvertently tipped off the cops by leaving his seat and going underneath the grandstand to place a wager.

PENNANT FEVER

The Cubs' 1929 pennant push started when they got the man they'd been chasing for years: second baseman Rogers Hornsby, who had batted .387 for the Boston Braves in 1928. Eventually the Cubs pried him loose in exchange for four players and $250,000. Hornsby, a great hitter but an irascible, cranky man, combined with outfielders Hack Wilson, Kiki Cuyler, and Riggs Stephenson to give the Cubs a fearsome attack that battered opponents at home and on the road.

The 1929 team is among the most storied in Cubs history. Several of its players, including Charlie Grimm, Gabby Hartnett, Zack Taylor, and Hornsby, later managed in the majors. Others, like Charlie Root, Woody English, Pat Malone, and Guy Bush, remained local heroes for decades. The club went 24–9 in July, and after July 24 they had first place to themselves. And the fans came out. Wrigley Field welcomed 1,485,166 paying customers in

1929, a record that stood until 1946. After an ugly road trip in late August, the Cubs came home (still well in front) and were greeted by a huge crowd at Union Station.

As exciting as this season was, it wasn't so dramatic that Bill Veeck jumped onto the field screaming at the end of a taut game against the Giants; this legendary story seems to have originated with Bill Veeck Jr.'s *Veeck as in Wreck*:

> We were playing the Giants to break a tie for first place, a game of such importance that we found Judge Landis sitting with my father. The Giants seemed to have the game sewed up right into the ninth inning when the Cubs scored four runs to tie it up. The Giants bounced right back with four runs in their half of the tenth.
>
> In our half, the first two batters went out. Mark Koenig kept us alive with a home run. The next three batters got on to load the bases. Up came Kiki Cuyler, representing the winning run. And Cuyler belted one. The ball was still climbing over the fence when William Veeck Sr. let out a rebel yell and vaulted over the railing. . . . By the time we got onto the field, my father was in the very center of a mob scene, grabbing for Cuyler's hand.

Veeck seems to be conflating two, or maybe more, separate events. First off, Mark Koenig wasn't even with the Cubs in 1929. In addition, Kiki Cuyler's only Cubs grand slam came on September 17, 1929, against the sixth-place Dodgers, in the fifth inning. The game Veeck may be referring to occurred on August 31, 1932, in which Cuyler's *three*-run homer in the last of the ninth beat the Giants 10–9. But that year the Giants were in seventh place and the Cubs comfortably in first.

But even without the conflations and exaggeration, the 1929 season was a corker. On September 1, forty-three thousand bugs attended the first game of a home stand. "Every player was given a tremendous ovation on his first appearance," wrote Ed Burns of the *Tribune*. "In the course of all of this, a ton or so of straw hats was cast upon the playing acreage." The following day, eighty-one thousand attended a morning/afternoon separate-admission Labor Day doubleheader sweep of the Cardinals. The game 1 crowd of thirty-eight thousand was said to have broken all records for morning contests. More straw hats rained from the stands in the afternoon following Hornsby's three-run homer.

While the team's excellent play contributed to the high attendance, the big crowds could not have been attained without a structural adjustment. The Cubs chose during the season to squeeze eight—rather than the customary six—chairs into each box-seat section, again increasing capacity at the expense of comfort.

And even that wasn't enough seating. With the Cubs far enough in front to make early World Series plans, the club wanted more ducats and therefore applied for (and on September 11 received) permission to build temporary bleachers outside the park, on Sheffield Avenue, past the right-field wall, and on Waveland Avenue, past the left-field wall. The Patent Scaffolding Company began construction on September 15. The project completely shut down the two streets along the borders of the ballpark. The temporary bleachers stretched from the back of the ballpark wall approximately forty feet, reaching halfway deep into each thoroughfare. On both the left-field and right-field sides, the bleachers ranged from the scoreboard out well past the foul poles. These interim stands seated eight thousand and rose high above and behind the already existing bleacher seats in right field and left-center field, nearly to the level of the Atlas Special Brew sign on the roof beyond right field that had replaced the longtime billboard promoting the Bismarck Garden.

These "circus seats" ran for $1 each. The Cubs sold them all out, making $16,000 for two games, a rate well below cost, which Bill Wrigley later put at $40,000. The bleachers clearly were more profitable than that, however; Bill Veeck Sr. claimed at the time that the seats would cost "90 percent of the greatest amount the club possibly could derive from it," indicating that the Cubs were counting on selling a lot of concessions. No record exists of any owners of buildings past the outfield walls filing lawsuits against the Cubs for blocking their view.

FOR THE LOVE OF MONEY

The first two games of the series were held in Chicago on October 8 and 9, both starting at 1:30. Box seats were $6.60 each, with the sixty cents going to Uncle Sam. Reserved grandstands went for $5.50, including a fifty-cent tax. Fans could buy only box and grandstand seats by mail, in advance, in a three-game package (1, 2, and, if necessary, 6), making the outlay for a box seat $19.80, which in 1929 was a lot of money. If you were driving to the game, protected parking for your car cost another dollar. Tens of thousands of applications for box and grandstand seats arrived at Cubs Park. In order to be fair, the team's ticket office employees simply picked envelopes from a huge grab bag and filled orders.

In addition, ten thousand bleachers went on sale the day of the game, and the Cubs made twenty-five hundred standing-room tickets available at $2 and $3 apiece, depending on location. The rush to get bleacher tickets, which sold for a buck apiece (equal to about $13 today), began early. According to John Keys in the October 8 *Chicago Daily News*, one enterprising fellow, "James Macek, of 2459 Washtenaw Avenue, parked himself on a cracker box beneath the ticket window just after yesterday's final ball game of the regular season." By the afternoon of October 7, approximately thirty people had camped out in the ticket line, "passing the time by playing rummy over a box, passing remarks with the wisecracking bystanders, and trying to place small wagers on the outcome of the big event." Hot dog merchants descended on the area to feed the crowd, which had swelled to the thousands by evening. Macek, who spent thirty-six sleepless hours in line, did enter the bleachers before anyone else.

Arch Ward, in the *Tribune*'s Wake of the News column on September 12, noted that while the ticket prices probably felt like a productive of mass turnouts of women as were these Ladies Days at Wrigley Field." During the late 1920s, ladies would show up on Friday afternoons, causing an unpredictable (and often huge) crowd. At one time, the Cubs tried having the "fanettes" come to Wrigley Field on Wednesdays to claim tickets for that Friday. In 1930, three downtown stores took over the duties, serving free passes to the female fans.

William Wrigley was making his park appealing for women, just as Charley Weeghman had done. But at the same time, Wrigley noticed that not all the ladies who came to the park were proper. "It is easier to control a crowd of 100,000 men than of 10,000 women," he told Forrest Crissey in the September 13, 1930, *Saturday Evening Post*. Wrigley found that no matter what he did, the ladies who crashed the gates for free on selected Fridays were surprisingly rough: "The ladies listen to a speech urging them to take their time and assuring them that each applicant will be accommodated; then they storm the wickets, sweeping aside policemen and guards in a way to make men gasp and wonder how the phrase 'the gentler sex' ever originated. What they do to one another in the process of crashing the gate is astounding to male spectators." Ladies, who were supposed to make things more genteel, were among the rowdiest and uncontrollable crowds Wrigley Field saw. As P. K. Wrigley told Paul Angle years later, "We couldn't get a policeman to work up there. We couldn't get an usher. We had to *drive* them up, because if a man talks back to a policeman or an usher, they are liable to get punched in the nose, but women can say anything with impunity, and they abuse these fellows something terrible."

Half of the thirty-five thousand at the June 20, 1930, game were women. Before the game, the Cubs debuted a new silver flagpole, which was to hold the 1929 NL pennant flag. The following day, some forty-two thousand rooters watched Cubs players, led by a military procession, troop around the unfurled championship pennant. Once everyone had marched out to center field,

skinning to most fans, "Wrigley Field would be a sellout if admissions were $10 or even $15 per game." Ward's article, however, argued that postseason ball wasn't such a financial windfall, claiming that "[owners'] profit in victory is increased drawing power the following season." Ward posited, therefore, that prices for World Series tickets should be reduced. "To the regular fan of all season, who must take seats for three games to get any, they are too high . . . perhaps they already have passed the limit fair to regular customers."

The teams weren't doing this for love. The cost of the tickets for game 6 would be refunded if the game wasn't played, but the money would have sat in the bank for a week gathering interest. And you thought that such ticket policies began recently?

WRIGLEY'S FIRST SERIES

Little modesty was evident as both women and men waited out the eve of the first World Series game ever played at Wrigley Field. Ladies with smudged makeup and wrinkled clothes and hats did their best to stay dignified. Men talked, smoked, and played cards. One assumes that the bathrooms of any surrounding bars and stores were perpetually filled. A cold wind blew, and John Keys of the *Daily News* noted October 8 that it "bestirred a ragtag carpet of torn newspapers that littered the streets and sent a shivering chill through the huddled forms of at least 10,000 red-eyed, sleep-hungry but hard souls" hoping to enter the park.

In order to clear the streets, the Cubs threw open the bleacher gates at 7:00 A.M. October 8, sending twelve thousand "sleepy-eyed individuals," in John Keys' words, into the park. "The action brought a sudden splurge of wild activity among the waiting thousands. Boxes, chairs, cushions, and other paraphernalia were joyfully kicked aside as the waiters jumped into place to begin the happy scamper through the gates."

Once inside Wrigley Field, Keys noted, the fans "sat jammed in a towering wall of drab-colored humanity," completely filling the bleachers by 11:00 A.M. Before the game, Bramhall's band played as famous baseball clowns Nick Altrock and Al Schacht did their crowd-pleasing routines. Fans waved pennants, stomped up and down, and did cheers to stay warm. Policemen lingered on the field to deter anyone jumping onto the green, while vendors distributed peanuts, soda, and popcorn. Blankets and heavy fall coats were in evidence, especially in the grandstand where the sun was barely evident. It was cold enough that "firemen patrolled the wooden seats to see that none of the fans there built fires to keep warm."

Temperatures rose to the fifties by game time. Approximately fifty-one thousand saw the contest, though not everyone was present by the time Charlie Root threw the first pitch; plenty of grandstand ticket holders were still in line outside the park. Eight men trying to scalp tickets were arrested outside the park, while another group of men hustled tickets downtown to be made available at the last minute to well-to-do, under-the-table buyers.

At least one man saw the game for free. A fellow named One-Eyed Connolly, "the country's best-known gate-crasher" according to the October 8 *Daily News*, "Houdinied himself in with the crowd" at the Addison Street entrance. "How did I get in?" he was asked. "Oh, just walked in. Me, a ticket? I should say not."

DISASTER

The 1929 World Series was a crusher for Chicago. Favored to win over Connie Mack's Athletics, the Cubs were instead vanquished in five painful games. In the opener, thirty-five-year-old Howard Ehmke's slow-slower-slowest deliveries baffled Chicago hitters. Ehmke, whose 3–1 win was his last in the majors, whiffed a baker's dozen Cubs to set a record. Chicago also dumped the second game, 9–3, when starter Pat Malone couldn't get out of the fourth. Thirteen Cubs hitters fanned in this contest as well.

Once in Philadelphia, the Cubs took game 3, 3–1, and appeared to have turned the momentum around. In the fourth contest, Chicago led 8–0 in the last of the seventh, looking to

knot the series. But the Athletics staged a rally for the ages, posting a spectacular ten-run comeback in the seventh, and won the game. They took the series the next day, coming back from a 2–0 bottom-of-the-ninth deficit and winning 3–2.

Hack Wilson hit .471 in the series but fielded poorly, especially in game 4's ten-run inning. In 1930, Wrigley Field fans began to roll lemons at him when he came to bat. A tremendous hitter who had already paced the league in home runs in 1926–28, Wilson went on to smash fifty-six homers in 1930 and drive in 191 runs—a record that still stands. By 1931, however, falling prey to the sauce, he wore out his welcome with manager Joe McCarthy.

KEEPING THE CUSTOMER HAPPY

Nevertheless, the 1929 season had been a triumph, if only in the ledger books. Wrigley admitted to having sold 694,954 score cards, 539,938 bottles of soda, 482,364 rolls, 425,820 hot dogs, 388,410 ice creams, 266,900 bags of peanuts, and 132,650 sacks of popcorn. The Cubs ran their own in-house concession operation to guarantee quality of the goods and to manage expenses more efficiently. The Cubs' sales income from concessions in 1929 was $233,450.

The following year, after the stock market crash in November, Wrigley employed 499 people, most of them on a part-time basis. Thirty-one were uniformed personnel; twenty-three were members of the grounds crew; seventeen were on the executive level. The remaining 438 were game-day workers such as ushers, ticket sellers, and concessionaires.

A good number of the concessions were sold to women who got into the park for free. As Warren Brown wrote in 1946, "This gesture of setting aside an afternoon each week in which the gentler sex might watch a ball game as guests of the club had been tried by the Chicago National league club as far back as the days of Pop Anson . . . [but] Wrigley not only invited 'em out, he practically insisted on it. . . . Not even a sale of nylons in early 1946 was as

the pennant was run up the new flagpole and the Cubs went out and whipped the Boston Braves twice.

The next Friday, June 27, the largest crowd in the history of Wrigley Field—51,556, a record that seems unlikely to be broken—attended a game between the Cubs and the Brooklyn Dodgers. Of that more-than-capacity crowd, 30,476 were women who entered free. Several thousand more ladies were unable to get into the park, and at least ten thousand male customers with tickets were left holding the bag. Today, fire regulations wouldn't permit such a crowd.

"Mothers standing in the deep extremities of center field with babies in their arms. Little tots purring, scrambling on the green in right, center, and left fields, where the jam pack ran twenty deep. All aisles packed to a point where navigation from one end of the stand to the other was impossible," commented Jimmy Corcoran in the late afternoon edition of the *American*. Proper ladies, some bouncing children on their knees, sat in wool skirts on the concrete slabs at the fronts of seating sections. Families picnicked on the grass in deep left field. Gentlemen sat in the pasture, or hunched in their seats and removed their hats in order to provide ladies with a better view. For the first time in the history of the park, according to Corcoran, the aisles were so full that paying patrons in the first six rows of the grandstand were forced to stand up in order to watch the game.

Despite cloudy skies, the crowd had begun to descend on the park by noon, three full hours before game time. Management began herding the excess fans onto the outfield grass at 2:00, and the ladies and kids kept coming. During the game, which ended 7–5 in the Cubs' favor, several hard-hit balls ricocheted into the outfield standees for ground-rule doubles.

To ease such a crush and panic in the future, and to ensure that paying fans weren't locked out, the Cubs again altered the Ladies Day policy for 1931. Fans looking for comps now had to send the club a request, along with a self-addressed stamped envelope, for the game in question. Only one pass was available per customer, and the previously unlimited free supply was brought down to a more reasonable twenty thousand.

The Ladies Day custom continued into the 1970s, though the day of the week fluctuated. In 1940, the Cubs held Ladies Days on Fridays. During the 1941 season, they were held on Tuesdays. By 1957, it was back to Friday. During 1961, ladies were allowed in free on Saturdays. By 1963, they were again on Fridays. In 1969, the day was changed to Thursday.

The generous Ladies Day policy created a ground swell of female support for the Cubs, one that continues to this day. Much of the team's fan base is built around teenage girls who grow up, continue to go to Cubs games, and, later, bring their children, grandchildren, or nieces and nephews.

Ladies Day was seen as such a successful innovation in this era that William Wrigley was soon taking credit for Charley Weeghman's innovation. "When I entered upon my experience as a ball-club owner back in 1916," he said in the September 13, 1930, *Saturday Evening Post* article, "the typical ball crowd was generally considered rather rough stuff. . . . The socially elect of our city did not then crowd the ticket lines. A Ladies Day at that time would have been a joke—a target for the gibes of sports writers and columnists."

This is demonstrably incorrect, and Wrigley surely knew better. Weeghman had worked as hard as anyone during the teens to make baseball cleaner and safer, especially for women, and Ladies Days at the time were far from a joke. In addition, Wrigley's comments about the social order are inaccurate—Weeghman had brought all sorts of good fellows, nouveaux riches, and gadflies to the park, and Wrigley knew this, too.

In truth, the movement to attract women to baseball predated Weeghman. For instance, Jack Norworth's smash hit "Take Me Out to the Ball Game," featuring its female protagonist, was written in 1908, six years before the advent of the Federal League. Team owners had courted women customers since at least 1886, when Cincinnati's Tony Mullane, "The Apollo of the Box," set hearts fluttering when he assumed the mound. Not all owners wanted women at the park, and Weeghman's innovations were groundbreaking for the time. But the idea that both halves of the population might be good audiences for the sport had many fathers, as it were.

One Cubs marketing promotion that Wrigley could and did rightly take credit for was the policy of admitting four thousand children under the age of sixteen to the park free every day except Friday, "through the cooperation of the school board and the athletic committee of the city council." Not only did Wrigley help kids cut school, but he also created future Cubs fans. No wonder people thought he was a genius!

HACK'S EXIT—AND BILL'S

Hack Wilson, formerly a fan and club favorite, was increasingly helpless in the field, difficult to live with, dependent on alcohol, and less effective as a hitter. By the summer of 1931, the Cubs tired of his act. Already skidding at the plate, Wilson did not help himself by repeatedly breaking curfew. The final straws came on a train ride from Cincinnati to Chicago in early September where he encouraged pitcher Pat Malone to punch out two sportswriters, then informed teammates that club management could go to hell. Once informed of Wilson's transgressions, the Cubs—indeed, Wrigley himself—suspended him for the balance of the season.

Nevertheless, Wilson showed up at Wrigley Field on September 7 and sat in the stands to watch the Cubs and Cardinals. The *Tribune* reported, however, the following day that management didn't welcome him. "The club is definitely through with the home-run hero of 1930. He has been told to remove his belongings from the clubhouse."

Wilson wasn't only the icon that departed Wrigley Field as the 1931 season gave way to 1932. William Wrigley suffered a stroke on January 18, 1932. A heart seizure soon followed, and

NO DEPRESSION

157

he passed away, at age seventy-one, in Phoenix, on January 26. At his death, William Wrigley owned about 70 percent of the club's stock. William Walker, the heirs of Adolph Spielman, and William's son Philip K. Wrigley—widely known as P. K.—owned most of the rest.

Asked about his feelings concerning Wrigley, Bill Veeck Sr. simply stated, "It's a terrible shock. It's like losing a parent. Mr. Wrigley was the finest man that ever lived." The magnate's passing surprised and saddened the baseball community and threw those associated with the club into panic about whether P. K. was ready to take over.

P. K. was the logical heir. As Irving Vaughan wrote in the January 27 *Tribune*, "It was [William Wrigley's] wish, often expressed, that after his death, his son, Philip K. Wrigley, should conduct the club on the same high plane. That the son will do so, for several years at least, seems certain." William Wrigley, it is said, begged his son on his deathbed never to sell the team, to keep it forever in the family. While it is not crystal clear that this is true, it may explain why P. K., in the face of many challenges on and off the field, held onto the club for decades to come.

6

LAST HURRAHS
WRIGLEY FIELD, 1932-1945

P. K. FAQ

Philip Knight "P. K." Wrigley was born on December 5, 1894, in Chicago. He and his sister, Dorothy, were the two children of William and Ada Wrigley. P. K. was born at the southeast corner of Clark Street and North Avenue, about twenty blocks south of the ballpark, in the Plaza Hotel.

While William Wrigley loved his son enough to name a brand of gum after him, he also let it be known early on that the son was expected to work for his position. Father and son were not alike. Bill Veeck Jr., who knew and worked for them both, wrote, "It is hard to understand how a father and son can be as completely different as William and Phil Wrigley." (We will put aside the question of whether Veeck Jr. was a carbon copy of *his* father.)

Quiet young Philip lacked the smiling bonhomie and the love of the social ramble that characterized his father. He was interested in the mechanical—engines, machines, cars, and airplanes. It has been written that P. K.'s favorite activity in life was to strip down a car, upgrade it, and put it back together. He would not hesitate to whip out a screwdriver and repair the malfunctioning watches of visitors.

P. K. graduated from Phillips Academy in Andover, Massachusetts, in 1914 and then joined the Navy. During World War I, he served at Great Lakes Naval Station in the northern suburbs of Chicago. In 1918, he married Helen Atwater, who gave birth to three children. Seven years later, Philip succeeded his father as head of the Wrigley Gum Company. Another piece of William Wrigley's empire, the baseball club, was heretofore of little interest to P. K. But this changed out of necessity when the elder Wrigley passed; at age thirty-eight, P. K. assumed control of the Cubs. Bill Veeck Jr. felt that "Phil Wrigley assumed the burden out of his sense of loyalty and duty. If he has any particular feeling for baseball, any real liking for it, he has disguised it magnificently." Along similar lines, Stanley Frank wrote in the September 11, 1943, *Saturday Evening Post* that "the chewing-gum magnate is astonishingly naïve in baseball matters and is given to impulsive decisions which seem to be splendid ideas at the moment, but never quite work out."

Veeck's judgment, however, may be more than a little unfair. Veeck and Wrigley fils were fish from different oceans (maybe a fish and a bird). But P. K. did care whether his team won or lost, although it seemed like more of a personal quest to burnish his father's image than a need to win based on competitive zeal. "The club and the park stand as memorials to my father," P. K. told the *Daily News* in 1933, according to P. K.'s biographer, Paul Angle. "They represent all the sincere and unselfish ideals that actuated him in all his public contacts. . . . I will never dispose of my holdings in the club as long as the chewing gum business remains profitable enough for me to retain them." He also told Warren Brown, "We aim to have the Cubs pay their own way, just as if they were my only interest. In this the Cubs are no different from any other major league club whose owners have no outside interests. Actually, the Cubs do make their way on their own, too; but it is hard to get anyone to believe that this is so."

Philip Wrigley could afford to think this way because the Cubs and Wrigley Field were actually two separate business entities. The Chicago Cubs were a Delaware-based corporation under the

Wrigley family's ownership. P. K. Wrigley was the controlling but not the only stockholder. In contrast, P. K. privately owned Wrigley Field; William had willed the ballpark and property directly to his son. This meant that the club itself actually paid rent to the Wrigleys.

This hints at why P. K. Wrigley paid so much loving attention to the ballpark at the expense of the team for forty-five years. The ballpark, not the club, was his personal inheritance, and Wrigley was its thorough—even fussy—caretaker. One of his first acts, according to Paul Angle, was to cut the number of seats in a box from eight back to six. P. K. figured, correctly, that it wasn't good business to annoy the highest-paying customers just to achieve the short-term financial benefit of jamming them in too tightly.

GOOD TIMES

April 20, 1932, was Opening Day at Wrigley Field (fig. 10). A Senn High School ROTC unit trooped onto the field, and players from both sides, as usual, marched to center field for the flag-raising, where the banner was lowered to half-mast in honor of the late William Wrigley.

Despite the death of Wrigley and the departure of Hack Wilson, this was another fun year at the park. The Cubs played great ball, remaining near the top of the league all season long.

One fun day came on August 16, when Cubs first baseman and manager Charlie Grimm received a testimonial day. "Jolly Cholly," a popular, banjo-playing jokester, received flowers, a platinum watch, and a set of silverware (a common ballpark gift of the time). The Cubs trailed Boston 3–0 in the ninth but jumped off the mat with one out. Three straight doubles made the score 3–2, and Riggs Stephenson's single knotted the game. A hit and an error later, Billy Jurges rapped out a hit to deep center that brought in Stephenson and gave the thirty-two thousand fans a thrill. The win kept Chicago a game ahead of hard-charging Pittsburgh. Hundreds of straw hats sailed out of the stands, according

FIGURE 10. Opening Day 1932 drew an overflow crowd in the right-field bleachers. Bobby Dorr and his grounds crew kept the tarpaulin near the foul pole in the corner prior to the outfield conversion in 1938. (Credit: National Baseball Hall of Fame and Museum)

to Ed Burns in the August 17 *Tribune*, but "the owners of more expensive Panamas are going to wait a while to see how times proceed before they let enthusiasm carry them away."

The following day, the Cubs and Braves played nineteen innings at Wrigley Field, with the home team finally prevailing 3–2 on Frank Demaree's run-scoring fly ball. (At this time, the "sacrifice fly" was not a recognized statistic.) On August 18, the two teams played fifteen *more* innings, this time with the Cubs taking a 4–3 decision.

The pennant tangle continued on August 20, when a three-run homer by newly acquired Mark Koenig with two out in the ninth capped a four-run rally that topped the Phillies 6–5. Koenig's homer deep in the right-field bleachers sent sixteen thousand crazed fans into hysterics. As Koenig reached home, "the ushers had to drive back several hundred fans," each of whom wanted a piece of him to take home, according to the *Tribune*'s Ed Burns.

As the Cubs moved closer to the flag, Wrigley again had temporary bleachers built on Waveland and Sheffield Avenues. This time, the work, estimated again at $40,000, began long before the team actually nailed down the pennant. The temporary bleachers killed the view for the men at Company 78, the firehouse just past Wrigley Field's left-field wall. The men had been able to watch games from the station's rooftop, but now they couldn't see much more than the pitcher's mound and home plate.

In an eighteen-game string between August 16 and September 3, Chicago went 17–1 with an amazing eight wins garnered in the bottom of the last inning—what are now called "walk-off" wins. On August 31, in perhaps the wildest of those games, fan favorite Kiki Cuyler's three-run homer off New York's Sam Gibson in the last of the tenth secured a 10–9 battle for the Cubs and caused more hysteria at Wrigley Field.

The Cubs were in position to clinch the flag at home on September 20; all they had to do was win half of a doubleheader against the second-place Pirates. Even though both Sheffield and Waveland Avenues were blocked by bleacher construction, thirty-eight thousand rooters jammed the park on a misty, warm day. As game time drew near, it became clear that the Cubs could cram thousands of extra fans onto the field if they wished, but Bill Veeck, according to the *Tribune*'s Ed Burns on September 21, said, "No customers on the field today." Unfortunately, the overflow crowd caused a ruckus. Some fifteen thousand, denied the chance to stand in the outfield, began to agitate. Several hundred fans stormed the pass gate, and it took scores of policemen to quell the near-riot.

The decision to keep the fans off the field was a break of sorts for the Cubs. Kiki Cuyler spurred the Cubs' eventual 5–2 win with a three-run triple in the seventh. Had there been an overflow crowd in the outfield, Cuyler's triple would have been just a ground-rule double. When second baseman Billy Herman threw out Pirates pinch hitter Gus Dugas to end the game, fans threw hats onto the field, and the Chicago dugout emptied. Photos taken at the time show groundskeepers immediately heading toward the infield to get the park ready for game 2 of the twin bill (so much for celebration). More than half of the fans remained at the park for the second game despite heavy rainfall. "They must have thought that maybe Charlie Grimm would rush across the field with the pennant and climb the flagpole with it," cracked Ed Burns. Most of the Cubs regulars, spared having to play the nightcap, chose to fill up on ice cream in the clubhouse.

THE LOVE PARADE

Mayor Anton Cermak and the City Council arranged a parade for September 22. Fans with motorcars were encouraged to join the fun; the parade was reportedly several miles long. The party began at 9:00 A.M. at Wrigley Field, where Jack Bramhall's band clambered to the top of a bus and played. Several popular old ballplayers, including Jimmy Archer, Jimmy Callahan, and Jimmy Slagle, also showed up. Taking Addison to Sheridan Road, then Sheridan south toward downtown, the team was showered with tickertape on LaSalle Street, home of the brokerage houses.

The love was felt inside those houses as well, as the 10 percent of Cubs shares on the market gained in value. (At this time, the Wrigley family owned 60 percent of the Cubs; presumably P. K. had sold off a small part of the family's share during his first year.) From an in-season low of 125, Cubs stock opened September 20 at 265 and closed at 350. Five shares were being sold at 400. During the clinching game, prices fluctuated, rising fifty points to 350 immediately following Cuyler's three-run triple. (Day trading clearly didn't begin with the Internet.)

Following the Cubs victory, a Cincinnati gambler named Frankie Moore walked into a Chicago establishment and offered $7,000 against $5,000 that the American League champion Yankees would beat the Cubs in the World Series. Moore, reported the papers, had sued former Chicago manager Rogers Hornsby several years before to collect unpaid wagering debts!

An uncredited piece in the September 23 *Tribune* estimated that the ballplayers, fans, and media traveling to Chicago for the series would bring $10,000 a day to the city's hotels and restaurants. In addition, local telegraph companies could earn some $15,000 per game laying down lines to transfer the 1.5 million or so words sent back to newspaper offices from the ballpark. The Cubs assigned three hundred press credentials at Wrigley for the series.

TICKET MASTERS

The Cubs began selling World Series tickets before the pennant was clinched. This time around, fans could reserve tickets at the ballpark and then have them mailed to their homes. Owing most likely to the poor economy, seats didn't begin to sell until the flag was won. As in 1929, grandstand and box tickets were available in three-game packages only. Meanwhile, the Chicago Department of Revenue announced plans to tax any fans trying to watch the games by sitting on the roofs or in the windows of local buildings. This was no high-income operation, apparently pulling in just enough money to pay the collectors. The revenue department's chief collector, Gregory Van Meter, also told his deputies to collect a 10 percent tax on all ticket brokers charging more than list price.

Two fans camped at the bleacher window more than three days before game 3 was played at Wrigley Field. They took turns sleeping on a cot, with the other guarding their place in line. Later on, two young ladies who were fourth and fifth in line reaped the benefits of belonging to the fairer sex, as the Cubs gave them a spot sheltered from the cold while allowing them to keep their places in line. The $1.10 bleacher tickets went on sale at 6:30 A.M. the day of game 3, as did twenty-five hundred standing-room tickets at $2.50. The cheaper bleacher seats didn't sell out until around 12:30, less than an hour before game time.

ANOTHER SERIES, ANOTHER DISAPPOINTMENT

The overpowering Yankees, who had taken the AL title by thirteen games, won the first two contests in New York, 12–6 and 5–2, before coming west to Wrigley Field. The fans, to say nothing of the Cubs, were already deflated by Lou Gehrig's and Babe Ruth's bats, and few thought that Chicago had a chance.

Skies were cloudy but the temperatures were warm for game 3 on October 1. The wind blew out to right field, and 49,986 were on hand. The Board of Trade American Legion band entertained the faithful before the first pitch. The Yankees jumped ahead 3–0 in the first inning off Charlie Root, and the rally included a home run by Babe Ruth. Many fans missed it. Arch Ward of the *Tribune* noted October 2 that "hundreds of fans who arrived after 1:15 o'clock yesterday were unable to get to their seats until after Babe Ruth had knocked his first home run." Ward blamed the congestion on poor entrance facilities, which "forced many to stand in line for 20 minutes." Bill Veeck denied that the Cubs did anything wrong. He said that all turnstiles were in use, but that "it is impossible to eliminate congestion when thousands attempt to enter at game time. There is no way we can provide more entrances."

FIGURE 11. Fans leave the stands for the center-field exit following a World Series game in 1929. The tradition of fans traversing the grounds to the exits had mostly died out by the 1930s and was brought to a crashing halt at Wrigley by the 1937 outfield renovation. (Credit: National Baseball Hall of Fame and Museum)

While entry to the park was difficult on days with large crowds, exiting was not as much so. Following the custom of the time, fans were allowed, after a game concluded, to walk across Wrigley's playing field to the exit under the center field scoreboard (fig. 11).

The Cubs drew into a 4–4 tie against George Pipgras in the fourth, which set the stage for one of baseball's most famous home runs. In the Yankees fifth, Babe Ruth clubbed a monstrous laser beam to center field off Root.

This was Ruth's supposed "called" shot. What is known is that Ruth raised his finger and pointed during the at bat. What is not clear is whether he was simply saying, after taking two strikes, that all he needed was one swing, or whether he was truly predicting that he would sock the ball toward the bleachers. When radio announcer Quin Ryan described the play, he was unequivocal in his belief that Ruth had pointed to where he eventually hit the ball; Root, in contrast, said that if he'd believed Ruth was predicting a home run, he'd have knocked him down with the next pitch. Ruth's prodigious drive, which came after some vicious bench jockeying by the Cubs, sailed past the flagpole on the right-field side of the center-field scoreboard and smashed into the box office at the corner of Waveland and Sheffield. Ruth yelled, cursed, and pointed at the Cubs bench as he rounded the bases. Sportswriter Warren Brown later wrote that following the game, seven different people on the streets claimed to have the ball.

Following the Yankees' 7–5 win, the AL champs hosted popular dancer Bill "Bojangles" Robinson in their locker room. Robinson tapped on top of a trunk while the New York players yelled and clapped their hands.

SWEPT AWAY

Fans arrived earlier for game 4 than on the previous day, leading to lessened crowding. This time, 49,844 stuffed Wrigley Field hoping for a miracle.

Prior to the game, Ruth—who had, in his way, won over the crowd with his two homers in game 3—went out to the left-field jury-box bleachers and had some fun with the fans. Cranky sportswriter turned right-wing screed writer Westbrook Pegler, who took great pains to criticize the Babe's fielding as well as his tonnage, was mortally offended and said so the next day in the *Tribune*: "[Ruth] had the naïve effrontery to take a stand before the left field bleachers, whose occupants pelted him with lemons on Saturday afternoon, leading them in rousing cheers for Babe Ruth."

After the Cubs took a 4–1 first inning lead, knocking out Johnny Allen, their pitching fell apart. Before the third inning, a huge cloud of gnats descended on the box seats, causing several minutes of consternation. The Yankees battered Chicago's Jakie May and Burleigh Grimes for four in the seventh and four more in the ninth to break open what had been a close game. The final was 13–6, and by the last inning the Cubs were being booed loudly by their own fans.

BACK TO THE BARS

The Cubs had lost two World Series in a row, and there was a Depression on. But the news wasn't all bad. One of Franklin D. Roosevelt's first initiatives following his election in 1932 was to repeal Prohibition. Everyone concerned now realized that the moralist movement had failed in practical terms.

The first step in ending prohibition was the Beer Revenue Act of March 22, 1933, which legalized beer and wine with alcohol content up to 3.2 percent. The government planned to tax liquor sales in order to refill depressed federal coffers. Beer and wine became legal again across the nation at 12:01 A.M., April 6, 1933, and that night some saloons sold alcohol for as little as a nickel a glass. Restaurants and hotels planned all-night parties to sell the beer now being bottled in Chicago by seven breweries: Prima, Atlas, Schoenhofen, Bosworth, McDermott, Monarch, and United States Brewing.

Oddly enough, prior to Prohibition, nobody had ever bought a glass of alcohol at a Cubs game, even back in the hazy, good-time Charley Weeghman era. John Carmichael noted in the March 24, 1933, *Daily News*, "In the old days at the west side park, and even in the present spot, beer was never sold."

Why was this? It's not as if the Lake View neighborhood was dry or even faintly squeamish about drinking—witness the nightly debauchery at the Bismarck Garden. There are several possible explanations. Some in the neighborhood might have protested the sale of beer. The Whales and then the Cubs might have been magnanimous in protecting local bars. Beer sales might have been seen as unprofitable, or there might have been a lack of suppliers. Finally, antiselling laws might have been on the books.

Most of these possibilities hold no water (or liquor). Few in Lake View opposed drinking. There is also no evidence that the Whales or Cubs held back sales to protect local businesses. Selling beer has always been good business, and there was certainly no lack of breweries before Prohibition. It is possible that a city ordinance prohibited ballpark beer sales. The White Sox had never sold alcohol at Comiskey Park, which opened in 1911. The Pale Hose (a.k.a. the White Sox) had last vended beer at the Thirty-ninth Street Grounds, where they played from 1900 through 1910. The city might have been working on a form of protectionism for local businesses by prohibiting beer sales at the ballparks and racetracks. But by 1933, everyone had had enough of over-regulation, and the gates were thrown open with force.

During the latter part of prohibition, the Cubs had sold watery beer substitutes, such as Prager, from taps at the concession stands under the grandstand seats. Wrigley opted to have those taps outfitted for the 1933 season to serve 3.2 beer. "We are going ahead with beer for the ballpark," Wrigley told Carmichael. "But as far as I know it will be draft beer only, served down at the bars along there under the grandstand. I think most fans like a sandwich or two with their beer. So, for the present, at least, there will be no bottle beer sold at the ballpark." Wrigley was probably worried that fans would drain their beer bottles and drunkenly pitch them onto the field, as some unruly fans had done with soda bottles when protesting unpopular calls.

The sale of beer at Wrigley made an immediate impact on Opening Day 1933 (fig. 12). "The volume of business in beer alone far surpassed the soft drink sales under the stands on Opening

FIGURE 12. It is May 18, 1933, and the Cubs are raising the 1932 pennant on the flagpole in center field, in full view of the Doublemint Twins. (Credit: National Baseball Hall of Fame and Museum)

Day last year, according to attendants," reported Arch Ward of the *Tribune* on April 13. "The bar on the third base side was crowded even while the game was in progress."

That same year, on July 4, the Cubs added another drinking-related fixture, dedicating a new marble and bronze drinking fountain behind home plate to the memory of William Wrigley. The fountain remained in operation at this location until the 1980s, when the Tribune Company put a souvenir shop at the spot and moved the fountain to a spot down the first-base line.

Prohibition was fully repealed on December 5, 1933. New businesses, including bars and restaurants, opened (and reopened) around Wrigley Field. The southeast corner of Waveland and Sheffield became home to Ernie's Bleachers, a hot dog stand that also sold beer in pails. During World War II, Ernie's was built into an actual tavern. Ernie sold it 1945, and the bar was known as JB's for a couple of years before Ernie repurchased it. In 1965, Ray Meyers acquired the bar and renamed it Ray's Bleachers, which it remained until 1980. That year, Jim Murphy bought it and renamed it Murphy's, the name it carries today.

. . . AND OTHER ATTRACTIONS
Another Wrigley Field innovation for 1933 was even more attractive to some men than the pleasure of drinking a beer. Arch Ward, in the April 13 *Tribune*, pointed out that "a comely young woman attired in white dress and bonnet dispensed cigarettes to the box-seat patrons. This is the first time the Cubs have had a girl vender. Her high French heels gave her the appearance of walking on stilts."

ALL-STAR SQUADRON
Also in 1933, the first All-Star Game was played at Comiskey Park. The game was the brainchild of *Tribune* sportswriter Arch Ward, who thought that such a spectacle would be a great addition to the World's Fair held in Chicago that summer. Ward also saw the

contest as a benevolent event for indigent former players. Ward convinced Judge Landis that a gala midseason exhibition, with its attendant fan balloting and extra publicity, was good for the game. The All-Star classic was so well received that the previously reticent owners were forced to make it an annual event. What is not generally known is that a simple coin toss decided the location of the first contest: Comiskey Park or Wrigley Field.

GOODBYE, MR. VEECK

The Cubs lost another of their formative leaders when Bill Veeck fell ill in September 1933 after catching a chill in poor weather at Wrigley Field. He was home in bed for a week. When he didn't improve, Veeck entered the hospital, where an exam led to a diagnosis of leukemia, a relatively newly diagnosed disease for which there was no known treatment. The fifty-five-year-old Veeck went quickly downhill and passed away October 5 at Saint Luke's Hospital, with the Giants-Senators World Series and the Cubs-Sox city series in progress.

Bill Veeck Jr. wrote that, in order to help ease the misery of his father's last days, he went to an unimpeachable source to get the best bootleg liquor in town. "The last nourishment that passed between my daddy's lips on this earth," he wrote, "was Al Capone's champagne."

The flags at Wrigley Field and at Griffith Stadium in Washington, D.C., were lowered to half-mast on Veeck's account. The following day's city series game was canceled, and the tributes flowed in as everyone wondered who in the world would run the Cubs. The press had admired Veeck, who had been one of them and therefore understood that the flow of information was important. He rarely stonewalled on a story. An Associated Press report written on his passing noted that "Veeck was a firm believer in taking the public into his confidence in all baseball affairs of general interest, despite the protests of many of his associates." The *Tribune* noted, in its eulogy in the late edition of

October 5, that "the doors were never closed against any baseball writers seeking news. . . . [Veeck] never was known to complain to a writer about any unfavorable comment published about the Cubs."

Baseball history features several cases of famous and talented sons outrunning their fathers: Ken Griffey Jr., Barry Bonds, Cal Ripken Jr., and Buddy Bell come to mind. Bill Veeck Jr. is another such figure. Few people today know how much Bill Veeck Sr. helped the Cubs become a great team in the late 1920s and 1930s, even as his son continues to be lauded for his decades of fan-pleasing stunts as a club owner.

Will Harridge, the AL's president, best summed up the senior Veeck's impact: "He was forceful. He made friends. Baseball is a tremendous loser in his passing."

THE LONG DOWNWARD SLOPE

P. K. Wrigley was completely unprepared to deal with life after Veeck. In desperation, he hired former Cubs owner William Walker as president. Walker, however, stood intractably against marketing ideas that Wrigley wanted to implement; on the field, an ill-advised trade of Dolph Camilli to Philadelphia brought down a hailstorm of criticism. In 1934, according to Paul Angle, P. K. eased Walker out and bought his 1,274 shares of the club for $150 each.

Wrigley ultimately chose to man the posts of president and general manager himself. Warren Brown recalled in the March 17, 1938, *Sporting News* that when Wrigley called the press together in 1934 to announce the news, he told the writers that "I don't know much about baseball, and I don't care much about it, either." Wrigley was convinced—by the writers—not to allow that comment out for publication. Though Wrigley took the job of team president reluctantly, he eventually grew so attached to it that he refused to hire anyone else. Once in control, Wrigley was able to work on his own marketing projects, one of which was to let children in for half price. Other clubs in the league thought this was a terrible precedent, but eventually they all followed. By 1938, Brown conceded that Wrigley "seldom misses a game any more, if his many other duties permit," and that he, indeed, truly had gained knowledge of and passion for the game.

On the field, the Cubs remained solid through 1938, as they had a good talent base and hadn't been afraid to spend on players. But as Wrigley became more and more entrenched in his position, he relied more and more on yes-men, hangers-on, and loyalists, few of whom had the ability to run a club.

All the same, while P. K. Wrigley was no baseball man, he was smart and innovative marketer and understood the value of advertising. His goal was to make Wrigley Field not just a place to watch winning baseball, or a destination for a guys' day out, but a place for families to spend a healthy, happy afternoon in the sunshine. "Our idea in advertising the game, and the fun, and the healthfulness of it, the sunshine and the relaxation, is to get the public to go to see ball games, win or lose," he said.

Key to understanding Wrigley's achievement is to realize that this goal was, at the time, extremely radical. Despite the prevalence and success of Ladies' Days (fig. 13), many still viewed baseball as the property of hard men, louts, ruffians, bettors, and the working class. People gambled, smoked, cussed, and drank at games. Baseball parks were one of many places where women and children weren't especially welcome in the 1930s, and many male fans viewed ballparks as sacred territory. For many of its early years, in fact, the NL had refused to allow Ladies Days, even though their decision was probably less about sexism than about wanting to attract paying visitors rather than free ones.

Charles Drake, at one time an assistant to the president of the Cubs, told Paul Angle that "Wrigley had looked out of his office window onto Michigan Avenue and asserted: 'See those people going by. They are all consumers of chewing gum. They are all baseball customers if we can convince them they ought to see the Cubs play. We are going to sell them baseball.'" During the winter following the 1934 season, the Cubs took out advertising in the

FIGURE 13. Beginning in Charley Weeghman's time, the park at Clark and Addison hosted hundreds of Ladies Days. This gathering, from 1934, is diverse in age and race but united in its unbridled love for the Cubs. (Credit: National Baseball Hall of Fame and Museum)

Chicago papers urging fans to spend time at Wrigley Field next summer. It had been several years since the club had taken out ads in the papers, although Charley Weeghman had done so often.

Wrigley was controlling what he could. He understood that baseball was hard, but upkeep was easy. Even if you couldn't guarantee the fans a winner, you could make their experience at your ballpark positive if the place was clean, the food good, the facilities first-rate, and the attendants friendly. He had inherited—and was expanding on—his father's mandate to make Wrigley Field the nicest-looking plant in baseball. As George Castle wrote, "Wrigley did one important thing right as owner. He kept a regular schedule of ballpark upkeep that preserved Wrigley Field for decades to come." Nearly every season, the park was repainted in its trademark green, red, and cream. Seats were regularly replaced. The entire place was swept, rinsed, and mopped. Overall fan comfort—including clean rest rooms, polite ushers, and well-stocked and clean concession stands—became the first priority. In his devotion to comfort and cleanliness, P. K. Wrigley was a more evolved incarnation of Charley Weeghman, although advances in technology, increased space, and extra capital helped Wrigley make his vision possible in a way that Lucky Charley's never could have been.

"In the general area of promotion, Wrigley and I agreed on only one thing: keeping the park clean," wrote Bill Veeck Jr. "Phil Wrigley carried it even further; he made the park itself his best promotion. Wrigley kept the park freshly painted. He threw out the sidewalk vendors, newspaper boys, and panhandlers. He stationed ushers out front to guide people to their sections. He insisted that ticket sellers be polite and courteous. We sold 'Beautiful Wrigley Field.' We advertised 'Beautiful Wrigley Field.' The announcers were instructed to use the phrase 'Beautiful Wrigley Field' as often as possible."

Even when the Cubs were lousy, from the 1940s through the middle 1960s, they usually drew better than their performance merited. The early 1940s, Warren Brown noted, "proved beyond any reasonable doubt that P. K. Wrigley's plan of selling baseball amid pleasant surroundings was a happy thought and a profitable one."

THE VACANT CHAIR

Arch Ward of the *Tribune* noted that all the regulars came to Opening Day 1934, on April 24, except one: "The seat between the screen and the Cubs dugout, which for 16 years had been occupied by the late president of the Wrigley baseball forces, was vacant." The other usual customs were followed. Jack Bramhall's band showed up for its forty-first or so straight opening; the Senn High School ROTC presented the flag; and Cubs manager

Charlie Grimm received a huge floral horseshoe. There was a new public-address system this year, though when it was first used—in the first of two preseason exhibitions against the defending AL champion Washington Senators—it had exploded.

Two particularly silly things happened on Opening Day before the Cubs beat the Reds 3–2. Prior to the game, Cubs hurler Lon Warneke tried to catch a fungo and inadvertently swallowed his chaw of tobacco. Around the same time, a bass drummer of Bramhall's band was nearly brained by a foul ball. In response, the band struck up a song entitled "Was That the Human Thing to Do?" Arch Ward wrote, "The answer was in the affirmative."

The rest of the season was human, too—the Cubs finished in third at 86–65—but nothing more than that.

TRAINING

Since organized baseball sprung up mostly on the East Coast, most teams originally held their spring training in Florida. As baseball moved west, so did spring training. Beginning in the 1980s, a number of teams began deserting their spring training homes in Florida for ones in the southwest. The Cubs, of course, had to be an exception. Back in March 1935, the Cubs—training in Catalina Island all these years—considered leaving the west for the south.

The reason given for considering a move was that Pacific Coast League clubs—whose seasons started much earlier than the majors—no longer wanted to take the bloom off their own rose by scheduling so many preseason exhibitions with high-drawing major league clubs. In addition, Pacific Coast League owners were said to be unhappy with the mediocre level of intensity shown by the big leaguers in the games.

But the Cubs remained on Catalina. It would take World War II and restrictions on travel to force a move to French Lick, Indiana, in 1942. They returned to Catalina for 1946–47 and 1950–51. During 1948–49, the Cubs trained in Los Angeles. They then went to Arizona, and except for 1966 (when they trained in

Long Beach, California, while new facilities were bring prepared at Scottsdale), the Cubs have been there since.

BEST OF TIMES, MOSTLY

April 16, 1935, Opening Day at Wrigley Field, was once again, according to the *Tribune*'s Arch Ward, "the most unusual in Chicago's history . . . not a single floral tribute was presented at home plate before the game." Perhaps all the flowers had died; the weather was chilly and snow sat in the upper reaches of the stands. While advance sales for the game were brisk, many fans stayed home due to the chill.

Mayor Ed Kelly was there to toss out the first ball, which he did from the stands rather than on the field. Bramhall's band was again involved in a silly episode. This time, when Dizzy Dean of the Cardinals was injured by a line drive, the band rather insensitively struck up "Happy Days Are Here Again."

And they were, as the Cubs had another championship season. This year, however, also saw the Cubs' lowest-paid date in at least a decade, when a mere 1,229 fans paid for tickets on June 5. Depression-era fans weren't initially ready to drop their dimes on this Chicago squad, but an August 6 game that began a home stand brought out six thousand payees, forty-five hundred school-age kids who were let in free, and ninety-five hundred women given special passes because they hadn't been accommodated the previous Friday, a ladies' day.

The Cubs hung around the top of the NL standings all summer in what eventually became a four-team race. Chicago found itself in a scramble with the world champion Cardinals, the Giants, and the hard-charging Pirates. As late as September 4, the Cubs trailed Saint Louis and New York, but a long home stand proved to be the tonic. Augie Galan's bat, a series of strong pitching performances, and a schedule packed with below-par opponents carried the team. On September 5, the Cubs defeated the Phillies 3–2 at Wrigley in front of just 4,780 fans for their second straight win.

Two days later, before another victory over the Phils, eighteen-year-old first baseman Phil Cavarretta was honored by local friends, who gave him a new car, a basket of flowers, and a guitar, which came from a fellow Lane Tech High School alumnus. Prior to the game, the Cubs had the grounds crew place a piece of canvas on the left-field side of the hitting background near the center-field fence. (According to manager Charlie Grimm, the canvas was installed to give left-handed hitters a better look at deliveries from right-handed pitchers; it's not clear when this piece of canvas was taken down, but it didn't last long.) That day, before 8,642 paid admissions and another three thousand school kids, the Phillies fell 4–0, protesting plate umpire George Barr's ball-strike calls by tossing bats from the visiting dugout and eventually suffering three ejections.

Three days later, the Cubs won their seventh in a row, shutting out the visiting Braves 4–0. The streak went to nine, with two more wins over the last-place Bostons, but crowds remained small. The Cubs finally started to capture the city's imagination in the next few days. On September 14, 13,328 paid to see the Cubs take over first place from the struggling Cardinals with a loony 18–14 win over the Dodgers. The following afternoon, nearly twenty-nine thousand paid to see the Bums, as sportswriters then referred to the Dodgers, fall again, 6–3. Chicago's winning streak stood at twelve.

The Giants, coming off a three-of-four series win against Saint Louis, were next, and they suffered four straight pastings by a combined score of 34–10. The fourth game, the Cubs' sixteenth consecutive win, was a 6–1 decision over Carl Hubbell. On September 18, when the Cubs stomped the Giants 15–3, P. K. Wrigley himself was photographed at the park, sipping lemonade.

Crowds verging around thirty thousand saw the games, and more tried to enter through the pass gate; the Cubs were suddenly the hottest ticket in town. On Saturday, September 21, the Pirates invaded and were vanquished 4–3 before 38,624 (including more than twelve thousand women admitted free because

Friday, usually Ladies Day, had been an off day). On Sunday, 40,558 edged in to see the Cubs close out their home season with a 2–0 decision, their eighteenth consecutive win.

While the Cubs probably could have sold fifty thousand tickets for the last game, P. K. Wrigley, according to the September 23 *Tribune*, "ordered that general admission ticket sales be stopped as soon as the grandstand was loaded to capacity. The ticket windows shut down more than an hour before starting time, leaving thousands on the outside with money in their hands, but no place to spend it." Scalpers were out in force that day and did a raging business before the men in blue swept in and nailed every speculator they could find. Keepers of local parking lots also made big money, charging a buck per car.

Chicago, accompanied by Wrigley, journeyed to Saint Louis and won three more to clinch the NL before finally dropping the last two games of the season. WGN radio, which had been broadcasting only Cubs home games during the year, arranged to have announcer Bob Elson travel to Saint Louis to bring those contests live to listeners in Chicago despite the cost.

REGULARLY TEMPORARY

For the third time, the Cubs decided to build temporary bleachers in case of a World Series. This $29,000 project, undertaken by the R. C. Weiboldt Company, began immediately following the Cubs' last home game on September 22. The next day's *Tribune* reported that "cranes, lumber, and tools were moved onto the scene last night, and actual construction will begin this morning. The seats will begin at the top of the walls in left field and right field and extend more than halfway across Waveland and Sheffield avenues. They will be nearly 800 feet long and will accommodate 12,000."

P. K.'S FIRST BLUNDER

These days, plans for the World Series—dates, broadcasting arrangements, and, until 2003, home cities—are mapped out months or even years in advance. But back in the 1930s, such arrangements were not finalized until late in the season.

On September 17, representatives of the four National League and two American League clubs still in contention met with Commissioner Kenesaw Mountain Landis in Chicago to iron out arrangements. The NL was putatively scheduled to host the first two and last two games of the Fall Classic, but Landis saw a problem. Saint Louis was already hosting a large convention on October 2, the date of game 1, and the city couldn't promise enough hotel rooms for visiting press and baseball people. Landis decreed that, as a result, the AL would host the first two contests. This seems a bit ridiculous now—by September 16, the Cubs were two games up and rising—but for Landis, whether something actually made sense was not always relevant; the appearance of fairness and logic was paramount.

Meanwhile, Cubs manager Charlie Grimm was furious, according to the September 18 *Tribune*, "because Cubs representatives at the meeting for the purpose of making World Series arrangements did not hold out for opening the series in a National League park." Representing the Cubs at the meeting were P. K. Wrigley and his operations manager, John Seys.

P. K.'S SECOND BLUNDER

When it came time to sell World Series tickets, P. K. Wrigley wanted something better than the labor-intensive mailing process. So he decided on a public sale of tickets for the battle between the Cubs and the AL champion Detroit Tigers. This clearly was a recipe for trouble, but, as Irving Vaughan noted in the *Sporting News* of October 10, "as he is the club owner, none of the other officials questioned it."

Prices remained at 1932 levels: $16.50 for a one-ticket, three-game block of grandstand seats and $19.80 for box seats. As always, the twelve thousand $1.10 bleacher tickets and the standing-room tickets were sold only on the day of the game. The sale was scheduled to start October 1 at 8:00 in the morning. Ten thousand or so fans lined up at Wrigley Field the day before. An uncredited piece in the October 1 *Tribune* reported that industrious local carpenters "did a thriving business in makeshift shelters—wooden screens that could be attached to the walls of the ballpark in case of rain." Furthermore, "Many of the men in the crowd brought along shaving equipment. One had a portable gasoline stove and kept himself and friends supplied with hot coffee." Some of the crowd simply sacked out on the sidewalk near Clark and Addison, wrapping themselves in blankets, while others stayed awake. "Card games were numerous and plenty of bottles were sighted, although few contained milk."

The *Tribune*'s story also carried a note of foreboding: "Many boys and young men who were well up toward the windows last night frankly admitted that they had no intention of seeing the series themselves, but were holding places in the line at anything from ten cents to a dollar an hour. Not so talkative were representatives of ticket speculators, who hoped to carry away enough tickets to make their employers a substantial profit."

THE CORRUPT ONES

At the scheduled time, the sale commenced—and it was a shambles. The Cubs, and Wrigley, apparently did not factor in the shameless avarice of their fellow man. As a result, the team failed to set up even the most rudimentary precautions against cheaters and bullies. "No effort was made to ferret out suspicious-looking characters," reported Irving Vaughan. "Twenty-four hours before the ticket booths opened, there were about 200 in line. About 75 per cent was made up of seedy-looking youths, who obviously couldn't have been shaken loose from a dime if turned upside down. They were merely fronting, in most cases, for scalpers. These were the fellows who could have been spotted if the club had properly safeguarded itself."

A crowd approximated at twenty thousand had lined up when

the ticket windows opened. Thousands hoping to get tickets had shivered all night in line but were cut out of the process by scalpers, their representatives, and some dirty cops. Police presence was light, and the finest of Chicago's finest apparently stayed at home. Noted the *Tribune* on October 2, "Two or three dollars in the hands of a policeman or an usher enabled all of the young men to return to the front portion of the line and repeat the business of buying another set [of tickets], and from there it was just a matter of going to head of the class again and again."

Abuses of the process were rampant. Two sellers were fired for allotting a hundred tickets to a known scalper. Those with ready money and no scruples bribed cops and ushers to get to the front of the line. The *Tribune* piece reported that "through the morning hours, the patient legions who were a block away from the front office in many cases continued to stand and amuse themselves, unaware that they were being rooked in the matter of preferred position by the speculators' stooges, who must have numbered nearly 300." Perhaps happiest were the downtown ticket brokerages, which almost immediately began fetching prices of $50 or more for each three-game block—this despite a new antiscalping law that had been on the books for just a few months.

To make matters worse, the club never announced how many tickets would be sold to the public, leading to suspicion that the more moneyed were given first crack. Public outcry was swift and intense as the press and fans excoriated the Cubs. In Vaughan's words, "Wrigley, who was sincere in his belief he was doing the right thing by ordering a public sale, was greatly agitated over the repercussions."

The controversy affected the box office. Only 45,532 of a hoped-for game 3 crowd of fifty thousand showed up despite good weather. Several thousand bleacher tickets went unsold. In addition, according to Arch Ward in the October 7 *Tribune*, at game time, "there were plenty of empty box seats. Most of them were occupied before the first inning was over, but it appeared the scalpers had been hooked slightly, at least." Perhaps chastened by the debacle, the police were out in full force to shut down some of the more heinous scalpers. The cops arrested Harry Cohen, who through his ticket agency at 63 West Randolph was selling two sets of box-seat tickets at $70. Cohen was holding forty-three more sets of tickets. Just a few doors from Cohen's agency, a hapless Northwest Sider named Philip Schwartz was nailed for trying to scalp two sets of tickets to visitors from Kansas and Missouri. Schwartz had eight sets of tickets on his person. Even as early as October 5, the day before the series reached Wrigley, some brokerages were unloading their seats at box-office prices or less. Ward noted that before the game, one fan bought two box seats just before the first pitch for the grand total of twenty-five cents.

Even with the slightly smaller crowd, car traffic was heavy. The police had decided previously to deactivate all traffic lights in Lincoln Park and on Sheridan Road, before and after each series game in Chicago. Uniformed policemen served as traffic controllers at the streets without lights. The city dreamed up a series of complex northbound and southbound traffic routes to help alleviate the congestion, but the multitude of cars and the closing of Waveland and Sheffield to accommodate the temporary bleachers jammed up the roads.

Police were also on the lookout for anyone climbing to the top of the roofs of local buildings in order to see the series. It was still illegal to be on a rooftop—even one's own—due to concerns about the safety of buildings under the pressure of extra weight, and Police Commissioner James Allman ordered any violators arrested.

THE EDGEWATER BEACH HOTEL

The opposing Detroit Tigers were staying at the Edgewater Beach hotel, about twenty blocks north of Wrigley Field. The choice of hotel was no accident. The 1929 Athletics and the 1932 Yankees had found the lodgings comfortable. Tigers manager Mickey Cochrane, an alumnus of the 1929 A's, was said to be quite superstitious. Ed Burns of the *Tribune* commented on September 22, however, that the New York Giants bunked at the Edgewater Beach during their trips to Chicago in 1935, and they had lost their last eight games at Wrigley.

HERE WE GO AGAIN

Prior to game 3, the series tied 1–1, the American Legion Band of the Chicago Board of Trade, led by Armin Hand, entertained the fans. The musicians wore dark jackets, white pants, and white helmets and brought their own like-outfitted flag guard. The band walked on sod laid by groundskeeper Bob Dorr and his crew when the Cubs were on the road at the end of the regular season, and played "The Star-Spangled Banner." Meanwhile, P. K. Wrigley, in clear flouting of tradition, had the Cubs' NL pennant raised before the game. (Usually this was not done until early the following season.)

After the ceremony and controversy, the game was outstanding. The clubs traded leads, with the Cubs up 3–1 after seven. In the eighth, the Tigers used a walk, four hits, and a steal to score four runs, but the Cubs knotted it in the bottom of the ninth. In the eleventh, the Tigers tallied an unearned run off Larry French for a 6–5 win.

Game 4 was equally riveting. Nearly fifty thousand witnessed an outstanding pitching duel between General Crowder of Detroit and the Cubs' Tex Carleton. Both hurlers went the distance, and a sixth-inning unearned run gave Detroit a 2–1 decision.

The traffic jams, patrols of rooftops, and arrests of scalpers continued before game 5, as four more unauthorized ticket speculators were nailed, and the Cubs won 3–1 behind the pitching of Lon Warneke and Big Bill Lee as 49,237 onlookers held their breaths. Chuck Klein's two-run homer provided the difference.

Both teams then trained it back to Detroit, where the Tigers'

Goose Goslin singled in the last of the ninth to plate Mickey Cochrane with the series-clinching run, winning 4–3. Chicago hadn't played badly; the club led at one point in five of six contests and was only blown out once. And yet, the Cubs had dropped their third series in seven years.

DEMANDING FANS

The Cubs, expected to repeat as National League champions, sagged in 1936. The club fell back into the pack in August and finished five games out. The low point of the season may have been May 30, when the Pirates whipped the Cubs 7–5 and 11–7 at Wrigley. The 43,332 fans overflowing the park were cantankerous, and the crowding caused tempers to rise.

"The crowd became pretty peevish," reported the *Sporting News* in its June 4 issue, "and manager Charley [*sic*] Grimm was treated to the noisiest booing ever heard at the Cubs' park. He couldn't make a move without precipitating a choice round of razzberries." The *Sporting News* continued, "Maybe some of the fans were sore because, after spending their money to get in, there was no place to sit and in many cases not even room for a glimpse of what was going on, so they took it out on the boss."

In part because of the continued high demand for tickets, P. K. Wrigley worked with Western Union to design an innovative ticketing process. Each of the 102 Western Union offices in Chicago had operators with blocks of blank Cubs tickets and Wrigley Field seating diagrams. Customers could visit the nearest office and inform the operator where they wished to sit. The operator would then phone the Cubs' box office at Wrigley Field and, if seats were available, fill out the details on the ticket, validate them with a signature, collect the customers' money, and send them along. Western Union turned over the ticket revenues— less their cut, presumably—to the Cubs at regular intervals. The Cubs installed fifteen operators and a twenty-line switchboard at Wrigley Field to handle the demand.

There wasn't much to celebrate on the field in 1936, but to mark the National League's sixtieth anniversary, the Cubs held an 1876-style baseball exhibition at Wrigley Field on Saturday, August 22, 1936. Boston's Braves had already held their 1876 celebration, as the *Tribune* reported on August 19: "The feature of that [early August] event for the Cubs was a gentleman on an old high-wheel bike, who as he pedaled past the dugout yelled, 'How do you get off this thing?' The Cubs couldn't answer. The gentleman afterward fell off and his problem was solved."

The *Tribune* reported that the 1870s exhibition players entered Wrigley "in barouches, buggies, and victorias, the horse-drawn equipage of the nation's centennial year." The parade began at 1:15, led by Jack Bramhall's band. A huge cardboard cake was rolled out to center field. Mordecai Brown cut it, and, said the *Tribune*, "out sprang the 1876 athletes in the full glory of mustachios and padded uniforms," referring to the young men who then played a three-inning exhibition before the scheduled Cubs-Reds contest. The players wore the uniforms of the times: "thickly-padded pants, high-collared blouses, and flapping neckties." The exhibition contest commenced at 1:30, with the Cubs vanquishing Cincinnati 3–1. Relevant rules differences and customs in vogue in 1876 were explained to the fans via the public address system.

Prior to the affair, P. K. Wrigley had honored a group of old-time players with a luncheon at the Congress Hotel then invited them to watch the exhibition from box seats. Some of the players from the past on hand included Jack Pfiester, Jimmy Slagle, Jimmy Archer, and Mordecai Brown of the Cubs, Ginger Beaumont of the Pirates, and Fred Luderus, onetime first baseman for the Phillies. The one surviving member of the 1876 Chicagos, ninety-year-old catcher Deacon White, was ill and could not attend.

While the regularly scheduled game was delayed by the ceremonies and the heat was stifling, the *Tribune* reported that "the time was well put in by the customers and there was no impatience manifest in the stands." The fans may have been less sanguine after the Cubs fell to the Reds 6–4.

INCIDENT AT WRIGLEY

The Cubs did rally a bit in late August of that year, but on August 30, they met a buzz saw at Wrigley Field in the form of the Giants. The doubleheader that day was a sellout; 45,401 paid to get in, another two thousand pass holders entered free, and more wanted in. According to the next day's *Tribune* Cubs news-and-notes column, "At 11:50 o'clock yesterday the thousands around the portals of Wrigley Field were advised that all boxes, general admission, and bleacher tickets had been sold. The locked out crowd was orderly until almost 1 o'clock. Then a group tried to batter down the gate at Waveland and Sheffield avenues." Fans were once again strung around the outfield, roped off from play. On this day, the ropes were forty-three feet from the wall in left field, thirty-five feet from the scoreboard in center, and twenty-five feet from the right-field screen. This made the dimensions for the day a very cozy 325 to left, 405 to center, and 331 to right. Unfortunately, New York took greater advantage of this than did the Cubs, and the Giants' two-game 6–1/8–6 sweep knocked Chicago from the National League flag race for good. The two wins raised the Giants' August record to 24–2.

THE DORR WAY

Win or lose, the field had to be kept up. The November 19, 1936, *Sporting News* published Ed Burns's profile of head groundskeeper and park superintendent Bob Dorr, on the job since 1919. Burns notes the effort to keep the field in shape for both baseball and football: "After the close of the baseball season, Dorr levels off and sods his infield so that there is no trace of the skinned area, the base lines, the pitcher's box, or the batter's box. The transition this year will cost $4,000 before the place is returned to its baseball status. Dorr and his crew take one and one-half inches of soil off the skinned portion of the diamond, ten inches of clay from the area around home plate, and 18 inches of clay from the pitcher's box. Some 1,500 yards of sod were laid [in October 1936]."

To prepare the field for baseball, Dorr laid between five thousand and 6,500 feet of bluegrass and red sod every December. (In later years, perhaps either because he learned that laying sod in midwinter didn't work or because the Bears played more games at Wrigley and the field needed more time to recover [see, e.g., fig. 14], he did not lay the new baseball sod until March or April.) A distinguishing characteristic of the time was the mixing of the infield dirt with clay to create an attractive reddish-brown variety rather than the more common gravel-like brown-gray. The infield dirt fit the park's cream, buff, and green color scheme.

At the time, Dorr had a staff of sixteen, all of whom were part of the Theatrical Janitors' local union. They were each paid six dollars a day. Of the crew, five were retained for seven months at full-time status. Eight were ten-month employees and three worked year-round. During the baseball season, the crew began work at 8:00 A.M. on game days. They also worked when the club was on the road, though for only a few hours a day. Dorr wasn't crazy about using a tarp to cover the field, preferring instead to keep the grass as wet as possible most of the time. Moreover, Dorr felt the drainage was better at Wrigley Field than at any other park because "there are 85,000 feet of land tile [a type of subterranean draining tile still used in agriculture] under the field." He "will lay the canvas, 3,150 feet of it, only when ordered to do so by Cub officials," said Burns.

As park superintendent, Dorr was also responsible for repairing the nonplaying areas of the park and keeping the stands clean. He had 135 tools stored at Wrigley for his and his crew's use. Burns noted that Dorr was a fanatic about keeping the park painted and "probably would run about the place with a paint brush in his hand but for the rigid union policy of the Cubs." Burns wrote later that year in another article that "there's always

Figure 14. Note Chicago's less prominent skyline in this picture taken sometime in the 1930s from the upper deck. This may be an early-season photo due to the quality of the outfield grass, which features indentations most likely caused by the portable bleachers used to hold fans for Bears games.
(Credit: National Baseball Hall of Fame and Museum)

some painting being done at Wrigley Field. The paint is so extensive, in fact, that the groundskeepers after each game have to eject Ira Hartnett, a paint salesman, who lives in constant terror that someone will chisel the account."

Dorr's devotion to Wrigley Field was remarkable, yet all the more understandable since, as Burns noted, Dorr and his family lived in a six-room house, designed by William Wrigley in the early 1920s, that was built into the left-field corner of Wrigley Field. (The home, which longtime Cubs employee Bob Lewis lived in following Dorr's death, is now used by the Cubs' concession department.) When Dorr lived there, the front door of the house let out onto Waveland Avenue.

1937: CHANGES IN THE MAKING

The year 1937 was to be a better one for the Cubs than the previous year, but Opening Day drew just 18,940, well below the club's forecast of forty-two thousand. The weather wasn't great—nobody tried to climb to the rooftops, due to a chilling wind from the east—but it wasn't miserable, either. Mayor Kelly showed up to toss out the first ball, and once again Bramhall's band entertained, and Senn High School sent over its ROTC corps to lend the flag raising the required dignity. In addition, there were two other less than dignified ceremonies. First, the Cubs presented a large bouquet of flowers to Paul Dominick, the team's official mascot. (In this era, "mascot" meant full-grown, uniformed, nonplaying adult around four feet tall.) Second, manager Charlie Grimm posed near the Cubs dugout with two small bear cubs and fed them from baby bottles. According to Harvey Woodruff in the April 21 *Tribune*, the little bears, a gift from American Airlines pilot A. D. Ator, were hauled in from Sonora, Mexico.

This was to be the last Opening Day before Wrigley Field underwent the changes that would make it recognizable to today's fans—though even throughout the 1930s, the ballpark would be unmistakeable (see, e.g., figs. 15 and 16). On Opening Day 1937, the dimensions were 354 feet to the left-field line, 364 to the jury-box bleachers in left center, 440 feet to center, 356 to right center, and 321 to the line in right. The scoreboard was still in deep center with the Cubs' game data on the left, NL line scores in the middle, and AL line scores on the right. The building on Sheffield just off the right-field foul line that once had boasted advertisements for the Bismarck Garden now carried a sign hawking Prager Beer, a local brand lost to history.

Figure 15. A wet day at Wrigley Field in the 1930s. The upper deck is
closed (note the unbolted seats). While the seats down the line are
filled, the more expensive ones behind the plate are not.
(Credit: National Baseball Hall of Fame and Museum)

For 1937, the Cubs unveiled new uniforms, the first in many
years to use the large "C," little "ubs" logo that adorns Chicago
players' chests to this day. Otis Shepard, the art director of the
Wrigley Company, designed the new suits in collaboration with
Wrigley. Shepard, an outstanding graphic artist, was also responsible for the spectacular game program designs the Cubs used
from the 1940s through 1971.

There were other uniformed personnel in the park this year—
1937 saw the debut of formal outfits for the ushers (known as

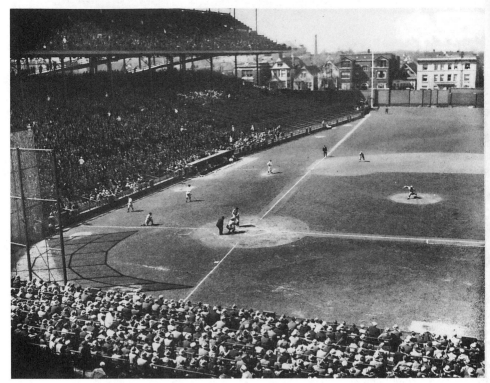

Figure 16. It is either an early- or late-season game at Wrigley Field sometime in the 1930s, as the men are wearing felt and silk hats rather than the more summery straw hats.
(Credit: National Baseball Hall of Fame and Museum)

"Andy Frain's Stylists," as they technically worked for the Andy Frain Company), who flipped the turnstiles at the ballpark. Andy Frain ushers and security served at the ballpark until the early 1980s, when the Cubs opted to hire and train their own security force. The ushers had an additional responsibility by 1937 as well: encircling the playing field at game's end to keep fans off of it, a practice that caught on around both leagues. This practice, which eventually ended the long-standing custom of allowing fans to exit the park via center field, kept fans under control and protected the playing surface.

The changes to the stadium began in June 1937, first with something small: on the sixteenth, the Cubs introduced a bat rack in their home dugout. No more would the team's bats lie in front of the dugout, in foul territory, where fielders chasing pop flies could trip over them. A bigger change came to light when the Cubs announced plans to ring the outfield, from foul pole to foul pole, with seats. Management estimated the cost of the project at between $150,000 and $200,000. This decision, which would increase bleacher capacity from thirty-five hundred to approximately eighty-five hundred, was motivated in part by the fact that the Cubs were once again involved in a pennant fight—Irving Vaughan reported in the July 1, 1937, *Sporting News* that "the bleachers are being enlarged sufficiently to add seating space for 5,000, which space will come in handy if a World's Series is played here." It seemed that P. K. Wrigley was growing tired of building temporary bleachers, though Ed Burns wrote in the December 9, 1937, *Sporting News* that money wasn't Wrigley's chief motivation for expansion. "The desire for scenic distinction probably was more of an incentive than the desire to spring the capacity of the field." It is amazing to think that sportswriters once wrote so glowingly of team owners, but Wrigley did have a strong belief in the importance of aesthetics.

P. K. Wrigley signed off on the idea to expand the bleachers and turned the project over to Bill Veeck Jr., who had been working at the park since 1934. When Veeck fils began making his name in Chicago, some in the press refused to take him seriously. But despite his goofy demeanor, overblown presence, and sometimes scene-stealing antics, he did good things for Wrigley Field, and his presence is still felt there.

Veeck loved baseball and loved nightlife. After some of his frequent nights on the town, he slept at the firehouse near the left-field gate. Marketing and promotion were his areas of interest; he constantly argued with Wrigley on behalf of new ways to bring people to the park. Customer chasing was undignified, Wrigley felt, and Veeck fumed. Nevertheless, he trusted him with this major expansion project, beginning in the spring of 1937, when Wrigley had asked Veeck to negotiate with various architectural designers on the project.

Eventually Holabird & Root signed to handle the expansion, assisted in the project design by Otis Shepard, although Wrigley and Veeck were also involved. The new outfield seating, according to an unbylined story in the July 10, 1937, *Tribune*, was to be made of "reinforced concrete construction supported by an open steel framework. Smooth pipe railing and woven wire fences will afford protection where required." The new bleachers were, like the old bleachers, to be constructed from slats of wood, this time made of a longer-lasting cypress.

On June 24, workers began the renovation by constructing a temporary left-field wall (fig. 17). The old Wrigley was beginning to change, but at the same time the Cubs were conscious of their history. The day before, the team had unveiled a plaque of former first baseman and manager Frank Chance. This was to be the first exhibit in a planned Cubs Hall of Fame. Both Johnny Evers and Joe Tinker, the late Chance's double-play partners, were on hand for the ceremony, along with Three-Finger Brown and Jimmy Archer.

The temporary left-field wall was actually a nine-and-a-half-foot-tall fence some nineteen feet in front of the current wall. It was put in so that the Cubs could evaluate how the shorter dimensions created by the new bleachers would affect the game. Under the original plan, left field was going to shrink considerably, with the new wall just 335 feet away from home plate at its closest point. The new wall would slant backward before reaching the foul poles so that each foul pole would be 341 feet from the plate.

This plan was altered just two weeks later, apparently based on some feedback from players and perhaps the press. A story in the July 4 *Tribune* reported that "the new plan calls for stands built on the bias so as not to shorten the left foul line as much as had been intended when the scenic fence was erected." Irving

Figure 17. During the 1937 season, the Cubs began their outfield renovation, installing a temporary wall in left field. The seats down the left-field line were only turned toward the infield years later. (Credit: National Baseball Hall of Fame and Museum)

Vaughan, in the July 15 *Sporting News*, suggested that "the revamping plans . . . have been altered, either because the officials didn't like the criticism of the short fences which would be created or because somebody erred in figuring the distances from home plate." As a result, straightaway left (and right) would be farther from the hitters, and the new bleachers would curve toward the foul poles, meaning that the distance to the poles would be deeper as well. In addition, the outfield wall's height was raised to twelve feet. The final foul line measurements of 355 and 353 feet, which remain today, gave the Cubs the deepest foul lines in the major leagues. One assumes that pitchers everywhere breathed a sigh of relief.

The shortening of left field was to be balanced by an increase in the size of right field. The removal of the old right-field bleachers, and the installation of new ones, would give "the pasture" (i.e., the outfield) some extra playing room. Center field, long a Death Valley in Wrigley, would be chopped to a more hitter-friendly four hundred feet.

On July 5, Wrigley Field hosted its last games in its old configuration. Thirty-nine thousand watched the Cubs sweep Saint Louis in a doubleheader, 13–12 and 9–7. The first game went fourteen innings, which meant that the second game didn't even begin until after 6:00 P.M. On July 9, the John Griffiths & Son Company began work, ripping the center-field scoreboard and the Doublemint Twins in half. They disposed of the portion showing the American League line scores and reinstalled what was left some fifty feet off the left-field line, where it remained in operation until the end of the 1937 campaign. As a result of this surgery, instead of "Wrigley Field, Home of Chicago Cubs," fans beyond the ballpark fences saw the back of the scoreboard reading, "ey Field, ome of go Cubs."

The left-field bleachers were built first. For the first time, bleacher fans were no longer at ground level; all the new seats were located above the wall. This was a significant change; since its opening, the park had always featured some field-level bleacher seats. The Cubs then tore out the right-field seats and installed new ones.

Perhaps unsurprisingly, Bob Dorr's needs played a role in the design of the bleachers. Prior to 1937, Dorr had no shielded area to keep his gear, so it sat, uncovered, down both foul lines and suffered whenever rain fell. Dorr's state-of-the-art lawn mower, capable of the unprecedented speed of thirty miles per hour, was in constant danger of rusting. The raised bleachers would provide covered space in which to store all the mowing, rolling, chalking, and planting equipment and the tarpaulin, as well as player equipment such as batting cages and pitching machines. The space under the bleachers near the corner of Waveland and Sheffield also provided necessary space for rest rooms, kitchens, and ticket windows. The new brick outfield wall featured six embedded metal doors, which allowed the grounds crew to move all the equipment on and off the field. The doors, reddish-brown for years, were painted green in the 1980s.

In addition to all the logistical improvements afforded by the new outfield configuration, aesthetics were in play. In accordance with Wrigley's standards of upkeep and unified design, the Cubs wanted to present an outfield more modern, slick, and consistent than the charming but frankly slapdash look that Wrigley Field had sported for its twenty-four years. So out went the field-level bleachers, the ramshackle corrugated metal center-field fence, the old-style scoreboard, and the left-field jury box.

In came a smooth, tailored, generally symmetrical outfield. P. K. Wrigley, though something of a maverick concerning how organizations and machines should operate, believed in uniformity in selling his products—in step, perhaps, with the conservatism and caution of America in the late 1930s.

Distances to the outfield walls were displayed on white-painted plywood numbers screwed into the wall. In the late 1940s, the numbers were at ballplayers' waist level but were moved higher in the 1960s. By the 1980s, the Cubs had painted the dimensions directly on the brick, this time in yellow.

The new bleachers changed the game for the players, who now had to deal with a hard brick wall everywhere, rather than just in left field. The addition of ivy later in the year didn't make the wall any less painful to run into. The new bleachers also changed the game considerably for fans, who no longer would be as close to the game. The tradition of rushing the field after big wins began to die out at this time because of the addition of ushers. But the view from the new bleachers was beautiful.

The three thousand–seat center-field section of the new bleachers opened on September 5, 1937, as the Cubs, still fighting for first place, hosted a doubleheader against the Pirates. The Cubs lost both games, 7–0 and 4–1, and the new layout immediately proved to be a problem. With a huge crowd packing the new outfield benches, hitters immediately noticed that they couldn't see the ball coming from the pitcher's hand. The old dark-hued center-field fence had proved to be a helpful hitting background. Ed Burns wrote in the September 8 *Tribune*, "The Cubs are worried about the new bleachers. . . . The Cubs figured [they] would have a depressing effect on their hitting when any except a sidearm or underhand pitcher was facing them. After Monday's experience trying to hit into the shirtsleeve background against Paul Derringer and Lee Grissom, both of whom are more overhand than otherwise, the Cubs are convinced their early fears are justified."

Players were upset at having to adjust to an entirely new hitting background during the season. But few in the press bothered to analyze the issue—players' complaints didn't warrant much ink in those days. But it wasn't just strugglers complaining. In September, Ed Burns noted both that Cubs and Cardinals regulars were concerned that the bleacher fans' white shirts were too close to the color of the baseball. Little of consequence was done to address the hitters' concerns for nearly four years; the new bleachers were too lucrative to shut down.

BREAKDOWN

The Cubs led the National League by six and a half games on August 12, but poor performance against second-division teams and a disastrous road trip allowed the Giants to catch and pass them in September. Yet the Cubs still clung to hopes of winning, and on September 18 they began accepting applications by mail for World Series tickets. Chastened by the nightmare of the abortive "public sale" of 1935, Wrigley went back to the old by-mail plan. With games 3–5 scheduled for play in the NL winner's park, the Cubs vended tickets, two to a customer, through the post. Available in strips of three games, they cost $19.80 for boxes and $16.50 for reserved seats for the trio of contests.

The Giants came to town on September 21 up two and a half games. After the Cubs won and sliced the lead to one and a half, 41,875 fans crammed into the "new" Wrigley on September 22, filling the entire outfield bleacher section, which had opened a full three days prior. Fans lined the catwalks down the left- and right-field line and even sat on the fences overlooking the catwalks. The next day's *Daily News* reported that the warm weather meant that the bleacherites were "in their shirtsleeves, making it look like a mid-July afternoon. And, incidentally, making the hitters moan a bit more about 'them white shirts.'" All seats in the bleachers cost fifty cents. P. K. Wrigley had special ticket windows designed for the bleacher section—"cupolas so elegant," wrote Ed Burns in the December 9, 1937, *Sporting News*, "that the boys in the $1.65 end of the park, the main entrance guys, are jealous."

Unfortunately for Cubs fans, the Giants won 6–0 on September 22 and took the home team again the next day to wrap up the flag.

DAWN OF THE IVY

The Cubs' season was over, but the renovations to the outfield weren't. P. K. Wrigley decided late in 1937 that he wanted ivy to cover the entire outfield wall. Once again, he asked Bill Veeck Jr. to implement the project.

"I had planned on planting it at the end of the season, after the bleachers had been completely rebuilt," Veeck wrote in his autobiography.

By the time the new season came around, the ivy would have caught and Mr. Wrigley would have his outdoor atmosphere.

The Cubs were ending the season with a long road trip, returning home only in the final week for one last series. The day before the team was to return, Mr. Wrigley called me in to tell me he had invited some people to the park to watch the game and gaze upon his ivy.

So, according to Veeck, he and several assistants planted the ivy overnight, expressly for the last Cubs series of the year, against the Cardinals, which began on October 1—another terrific Veeck story. But not quite true.

Either Veeck's memory was off when he wrote his autobiography, or he was exaggerating for dramatic effect. The initial planting, at least, was done well before the last series of the year. Cubs historian Ed Hartig has found, in the September 14, 1937, *Chicago Cubs News*, a photo of scraggly looking vines already planted on the outfield walls. Newspaper photos from the Cubs-Giants series of September 21–23 also show the vegetation, which is in the same pattern as existed on the outfield walls on Opening Day 1938. Even more to the point, the *Tribune* printed an Ed Burns article in its September 12 edition noting: "Bittersweet is now climbing the buff brick circular wall, and when planting time is right Boston ivy will thicken the foliage."

It is nevertheless not clear when exactly the landscaping was done, but Hartig estimates that it might have been planted September 3. Since the official team publication of the time ran a story about it, this was certainly no secret. All the same, there was an overnight planting session, since what had already been planted clearly wasn't enough for Wrigley, who asked Veeck to make it greener and lusher. Still, as both Veeck and Burns noted, it wasn't even ivy that Veeck and his crew used to line the walls. When Veeck and Bob Dorr learned, after calling the Elmer Clavey Nursery in northwest suburban Woodstock, that that ivy could not simply be planted overnight, they instead turned to the fairly hardy and quick-growing vine called bittersweet. Under a string of light bulbs attached to the top of the outfield wall, Veeck, Dorr, and a few others covered the wall with the newly purchased foliage. The 350 Japanese bittersweet vines gave the bleachers some color for the short term—although the immediate result was far from the lush growth we see today. Two hundred strands of ivy were also planted in between the bittersweet, and eventually the ivy, which grows slowly but more thickly, became the dominant plant.

The ivy became a defining feature of Wrigley Field, but sometimes P. K. Wrigley didn't know when enough was enough. One of his less brilliant schemes to beautify Wrigley was to install Chinese elm trees on the concrete "steps" leading up to the scoreboard on the upper center-field bleacher level. And he didn't want to plant saplings and let them grow; he wanted full-grown Chinese elms, yesterday. Bill Veeck was put in charge of this project, too, but it repeatedly foundered; high winds would continually blow the leaves off the newly planted trees. "It took about ten sets of trees before Mr. Wrigley began to spot a trend," Veeck wrote later. "The trees were quite inexpensive; the footings cost about $200,000." As a result, this part of the beautification process was abandoned in the early 1940s.

BACK OF THE HOUSE

The Cubs had more immediate success with the off-field aspects of the 1937 renovation. By the late 1930s, Wrigley Field's concession stands were believed to be the best in the business. This was no accident; Wrigley had given Veeck the freedom and funds to design the right kind of concession stands, and according to Veeck (who, as we have seen, at times, exaggerated), it took more than one try:

> Concessions are a whole little world in themselves, a world that has continued to fascinate me. You would be amazed how much sheer psychology is involved in selling a hot dog and beer. In designing the new concession stands at Wrigley Field, I wanted to install fluorescent lighting. I was told that fluorescent lighting could not be used outdoors because, as everyone knew, the lights wouldn't work in the cold. Well, baseball isn't exactly a winter sport. I told them to put in the fluorescents

anyway and we'd see what happened. What happened was that the lights worked fine. . . .

What also happened was that our business immediately fell off drastically. I had made the mistake—in the luck of the draw—of choosing a hard blue-white fluorescent, a lighting particularly cruel to women. Women seem to be born with some tribal instinct about these things; they would not come to the stands no matter how hungry they were. We changed to a soft rose-white, which is flattering to women, and quickly picked up the old business and more besides.

By 1938, the grandstand concessions had been updated and decorated with attractive red and orange awnings.

In addition, the new $100,000 scoreboard, completed late in 1937 and installed atop the new upper center-field bleachers, was, and still is, a marvel. Combining slick late art-deco design with a smart layout of vital game information, the seventy-five-foot-wide, twenty-seven-foot-high structure remains one of the best boards in sports. The pitch and out information is located in the center of the board, with eyelets conveying the ball and strike count, the outs, and the batter's uniform number. Line scores from both leagues fill both sides of the board. The man who designed the scoreboard for the Cubs, however, didn't follow through to complete the project. He skipped out on Veeck and the team, forcing Veeck to do much of the work himself.

A helpful innovation, especially for the sportswriters of the time, was the use of yellow numbers on the line scores to indicate innings in progress. This tradition began in 1938. When an inning was finished, the run total was reposted in white.

The scoreboard operators were sufficiently busy that they were required to stay up inside the scoreboard all through the game. *Sports Illustrated*'s E. M. Swift, for his July 7, 1980, article, inquired—with no little decorum—where the operators relieved themselves during a game. The scoreboard chief at the time, Ray

"Cotton" Bogren, pointed at an old copper funnel and said, "Same one that's been there since 1937. Shows you how good copper is."

In 1938, a clock intended for football was strapped to the bottom of the scoreboard. It wasn't until 1941 that the clock, still in use today, was moved atop the board. A ton of steel was needed to keep the clock secure at that height. This clock initially sported a white face with dark numbers and hands, but eventually was changed to the familiar green-faced, white-numbered, white-handed model. At around the same time the clock was altered, the club painted the entire board—originally reddish-brown—the green that defines it to this day.

The new scoreboard was used for the first time on Friday, October 1, 1937, with a Ladies Day crowd of 15,667 on hand. The Cubs lost 4–1. While the press was effusive in its praise of the scoreboard's design, it was equally disappointed with the board's utility; the inning-by-inning numbers were too small for anyone to see clearly. By Opening Day 1938, this problem had been addressed. Also by that time, an auxiliary scoreboard—this one electronic—had been installed in the middle of the upper deck grandstand. This was done so the folks in the upper deck wouldn't have to strain their necks and eyes toward center field if they had lost track of what was going on.

The scoreboard is sufficiently amazing that it can convey a game's results even to people who didn't attend. White and blue flags fly above it after the game's completion to tell who came out on top. Back in the 1940s, when the practice got under way, the winning flag was blue; now the winning flag is white with a large blue "W." In addition, light bulbs outside the scoreboard note who won. Unsurprisingly, this innovation came courtesy of Bill Veeck. As he wrote:

There was only one promotional gimmick I ever got away with. Mr. Wrigley permitted me to install lights on top of the flagpole to let homeward-bound Elevated passengers know whether we had won or lost that day. The flagpole was on top of the new scoreboard, and at its summit I put a crossbar with a green light on one side and a red light on the other. The green light told the El passengers we had won, the red that we had lost. . . .

It wasn't much, but it was all I had and I was proud of it.

Since the 1980s, the two lights' colors had been changed to match the flags. A blue light now means the Cubs have lost, while a white one indicates victory.

And there were yet more innovations. In a November 4, 1937, *Sporting News* profile of Margaret Donahue written by Ed Burns, the Cubs' bookkeeper, she noted that P. K. Wrigley had made several recent changes to make going to the ballpark easier for most fans: "After a three-year fight, he has been successful in introducing special tickets for children under 12 years of age, something which never before had been permitted. He has continued the idea of a beautiful park and always has before him the fans' comfort. In striving to provide comfort for them, he has replaced all the box seat chairs with larger and more comfortable ones, and has installed the more modern legless chairs in the grandstand."

Note the Cubs' philosophy concerning ballpark seating: fans paying more money for box seats were put in portable chairs and could be crammed more closely to one another during a World Series. Meanwhile, grandstand patrons were in bolted seats that didn't move around. One would assume the "legless" chairs to be more comfortable. The Cubs apparently believed that their box-seat fans valued proximity to the action rather than seating comfort. While in most new parks, the highest-priced tickets get you a plush seat, Wrigley Field still adheres to a more democratic process; chairs in the different sections are nearly identical.

The comfort of fans was further addressed in January 1938, as the Cubs began a project to help them avoid painful neck strain. As Irving Vaughan wrote in the *Sporting News* of January 27,

Approximately $125,000 will be spent rearranging some of the [left-field] seats so that the occupants thereof will be able to see the game without having to look over their right shoulders. Next year, the right field end will be curved in similar fashion.

The plan provides that the last couple of sections of the left field extremity, involving about 5,000 seats, be curved toward the bleacher, thus turning the chairs in the direction of home plate by about 30 degrees. As it is now, the fans in the ends of the stand see only the left and center fielders if they look straight out from where they are sitting. Visibility also will be improved by slanting the boxes in the regular section up to a point level with the left field wall.

Warren Brown also commented that "the size of the chairs was increased, with a resultant drop in the park's seating capacity, but a tremendous increase in the comfort of patrons who had been jammed together on big days." Box-seat capacity was reduced to 14,097, and grandstand seating to 19,343. While the Cubs fully intended to turn the right-field-line seats in 1939, the project was delayed and then the war came. The project wasn't completed until after the 1951 season.

Fans weren't the only ones benefiting from physical improvements to the stadium. The dressing rooms for the players and umpires were also fixed up, with new facilities and improved plumbing. The shower-room tiles were rendered in a striking shade of orchid. Brown noted that, in addition, "More attention was given to sound equipment and other details connected with the proper presentation of a ball game." (This must have relieved field announcer Pat Pieper, who on August 13, 1937, had to communicate lineup changes by megaphone after the public address system went down.) Players also received new and better places to expectorate, noted Vaughan: "It is possible that even brass cuspidors will be provided in place of the Bowery-like gobboons which now serve as targets." These days, of course, players just spit tobacco juice and sunflower seed husks onto the dugout floor.

ANOTHER BRICK IN THE WALL, PART 2

Having built a new outfield wall in 1937, prior to the 1938 season the Cubs constructed an attractive brick wall around the inside of the park, from foul line to foul line, replacing the earlier stone and wire fence. This wall remains today and is such an identifier of the "good old days" that the Baltimore Orioles and Houston Astros, among others, installed similar walls when they opened new parks in 1992 and 2000.

Gone in the new setup was the foot-high barrier rising above the dugouts; fans now had a better view of the field from the box seats. When seats had been turned toward home plate down the left-field line, they had to be raised somewhat from ground level. As a result, the brick wall, four feet high at most parts, rises sharply as it moves down the left-field line toward the foul pole.

Further, before the 1938 season started, the entire park was repainted in gray and reddish-brown, the last color matching the scoreboard. All of the park's chairs were also changed to an attractive Kelly green. In addition to the cosmetic changes, the park received a structural boost. The Cubs replaced the original 1914 building materials with brand-new steel and concrete.

TURNING COAL INTO PARKING

A month before the 1938 season began, the vacant Wright & Company coal yard—across the street from Wrigley Field on Clark (where a McDonald's restaurant now sits)—received a new lease on life. On March 12, the land, owned by a Flora Talbot, was leased by Downtown Parking Stations, which had eighteen lots in the Loop. Downtown Parking took out a ten-year lease on the forty thousand square-foot tract, which could store three hundred cars. As more people were driving to the ballpark—evinced by the filling stations that had opened around Wrigley—the move made sense.

Figure 18. A full house checks out the renovation early in the 1938 season. The ivy has barely begun its crawl up the outfield walls, but the Chinese elms in the center-field upper tier have not yet blown away. (Credit: National Baseball Hall of Fame and Museum)

PERFECT NIRVANA

P. K. Wrigley had spent $350,000 in repairs between fall 1937 to spring 1938, and he reaped plenty of benefits from the enthusiastic local press, who agreed that the Cubs indeed were in Nirvana (fig. 18). John Carmichael of the *Daily News* waxed on April 16, 1938, that "the Cub park glistened like a newly turned out streamlined train. A new seat arrangement, fresh paint everywhere, and refurnished dressing rooms caught the eye. There isn't a layout in either league to touch it for class at the moment." *Herald-Examiner* columnist Wayne Otto dubbed Wrigley "the ultra in outdoor sports palaces" on April 18. Warren Brown, in 1946, made these notes: "Here was now the most beautiful of all the country's ballparks. It possessed a distinct type of bleacher, skirting the outfield. In dead center, high above the top row of the stands, was a mammoth scoreboard, perhaps the outstanding feature of the face-lifting job . . . in this streamlined setting, every wish of the patrons for comfort was satisfied. Concession stands and rest rooms for the bleacherites were above what was considered standard in other ballparks for grandstand and box-seat patrons. There was a blending of colors within the field which enhance the beauty of the place."

The idea that Wrigley's spartan, at best, bleacher facilities were better than those in box-seat sections at other parks says much about the conditions of ballparks in 1938. During the first preseason exhibition of 1938, on April 15 against the White Sox, the new bleachers were "filled almost to capacity," noted Carmichael, despite a total crowd of just over six thousand on a cold and wet day. The new bleacher design notwithstanding, the crowd wasn't any better behaved than usual. "Customers had fights over two home run balls by Rip Collins and 'Bozey' Berger before the game was halfway along."

THE ARRIVAL OF DEAN

The Cubs had made investments in the team as well. Over the winter, they had acquired sore-armed, wily, and phenomenally popular right-hander Dizzy Dean from the Cardinals for $185,000 and three players. Dean couldn't pitch often, having developed arm problems by adjusting his motion to deal with the pain inflicted by a broken toe. P. K. Wrigley knew, however, that the extra customers Dean brought in would more than compensate for the money spent acquiring him.

Longtime Chicago radio man Martin "Red" Mottlow remembered, "I saw Dean in the home opener in 1938. They played it up pretty big. Fortunately my father, Harry, got box seats behind first base. It was a wonderful day, the place was packed. It was an exciting home-opener crowd." As happens so often with distant recollections, Mottlow's memory failed just a bit. Dean pitched the third home game, against the Cardinals on Sunday, April 24, and shut out his former teammates 5–0 in front of 34,520.

Friday, April 22, was Wrigley Field's official 1938 NL opening. Wrigley was noticeably absent, having traveled to Los Angeles to look over the Angels' ballpark (also named Wrigley Field). "He is going to miss Jack Bramhall's band today," joked Warren Brown in that day's *Herald and Examiner*, "when it blares forth those dulcet notes that make conversation within a range of a quarter of a mile impossible." Bramhall's band was, as usual, seated behind home plate deep in the lower grandstand, which bothered the press corps, situated just above, to no end.

A more congenial sonic innovation this season came from Pat Pieper, who began broadcasting every player's name and position the first time that the player came to bat.

Perhaps the Cubs should have innovated enough to hire a press box attendant. In the June 2, 1938, edition of the *Sporting News*, a correspondent reported that a *Daily News* writer's new portable typewriter had been stolen, along with the press box's coffee urn.

DULL AND UNINTERESTING IN COMPARISON

The Cubs were a hot ticket at this time. The *Sporting News's* November 1937 profile of Margaret Donahue gives an idea of what a big crowd at Wrigley Field was like in those days.

There is plenty of excitement in handling capacity crowds as well as heartaches when you have to close the gates and turn down thousands who are waiting to get in, some of whom had stood in line for hours. The pleading for tickets, standing room or anything, is pathetic, as there is nothing you can do once the capacity is reached. With thousands of people milling around, shoving, and crowding, there is always danger of accidents, as frequently gates are crashed and people pushed and shoved and almost walked upon. It is queer how throngs of people little realize the danger at a time like this.

I remember a woman and small child narrowly escaping injury when the gate fell as the crowds crashed one of our main entrances. The big days are the ones I enjoy most, however, the others being dull and uninteresting in comparison.

It must not have been much fun to work for the team at that point; everyone wanted a favor, a ticket, or something. Donahue remembered, "In the 1929 series we turned down enough ticket requests to sell out the park a second time. After it is all over you will find you haven't a friend left in the world, no matter how many you may have taken care of."

PENNANT RACE?

Every Cubs fan believed that the 1938 National League pennant was a cinch even before Dean was brought on board. But the Pittsburgh Pirates started the season hot and held the league lead through the summer. The Cubs were three and a half games back of the Bucs on September 18. But the Cubs began to win and the Pirates to lose. At one point, the Cubs amassed seventeen wins in a twenty-game stretch.

On September 26, eight photographers on the field got in the way of a possible run-scoring wild pitch. According to the *Tribune*'s Ed Burns the following day, "The hypo squad was banked solid a few feet from the right of the plate . . . when Davis caromed a wild pitch off Owen's glove. Owen plunged into the huddle and got the ball. Hack could have scored easily had he been able to see just where the ball was." Burns went on to note that "the umpires, however, scattered the photogs, but with sympathetic appreciation that the lads simply were earning an honest dollar."

(Interestingly, while photographers no longer are found on the playing field—most of them are in specially constructed "photo wells" past the dugouts—they are not officially banned from the field. Major League rule 3.15 states: "No person shall be allowed on the playing field during a game except players and coaches in uniform, managers, news photographers authorized by the home team, umpires, officers of the law in uniform, and watchmen or other employees of the home club.")

Pittsburgh came to town on September 27 just a game and a half ahead. As the *Tribune*'s Ed Burns wrote the next day, "42,238 giddy guests" were at Wrigley Field for the Cubs' 2–1 win that day. Among the giddy were league presidents Will Harridge and Ford Frick. Dizzy Dean, who missed most of the year with various miseries, went eight and two-thirds innings for the win. Bill Lee entered to strike out Woody Jensen to end the game and send the fans into a tizzy, leaving Al Todd, the tying run, standing on third base. The Pirates' lead was now the slimmest of margins—just a half-game.

The game of September 28 would go down as one of the greatest in Cubs history—and, if not for a decision made the previous day, things might have turned out differently. The morning papers announced that the starting time had been moved up a half hour to 2:30 in order to ensure that extra innings wouldn't result in the game being called on account of darkness. Other critical late-season games at Wrigley—for instance, the Cubs-Giants showdowns of the previous September—had also been started early.

Under dark and threatening skies, 34,465 tense fans filed into the park. The Cubs went up 1–0 in the second, but the Pirates scored three in the sixth to take the lead. The Cubs knotted things 3–3 in the bottom of the sixth, but the Bucs went ahead 5–3 in the top of the eighth before three Chicago pitchers stemmed the tide. Darkness was beginning to fall at Wrigley Field, literally and figuratively, but the Cubs came back in the eighth. With two men on, old pro Tony Lazzeri doubled home Rip Collins, and Stan Hack knocked in Billy Jurges for the tie. At this point, as Ed Burns wrote in the following day's *Tribune*, "Mob ecstasy was choked by bitter disappointment, only to be supplanted by more ecstasy."

Prior to the bottom of the ninth, the score still 5–5, the

umpires, looking at the sky, realized that this would have to be the last inning. The Cubs, having used six pitchers already, very much wanted to avoid having to play a doubleheader the next day. Pittsburgh's Mace Brown retired Phil Cavarretta on a fly to center field and Carl Reynolds on a ground out. He then got two strikes on Gabby Hartnett, and some of the fans began to gather up their belongings.

Next, Brown threw his signature curve, and Hartnett swung. Years later, Hartnett told Jim Enright of the *American* for an April 19, 1964, story, "I've read and heard it said that I closed my eyes and swung the bat with everything I possessed. That is only half true. I was swinging for the downs, but my eyes were never more wide open because I had a good look at the curve ball Mace served up." Hartnett belted the ball deep to left field, where it disappeared in the growing darkness. Plate umpire George Barr watched the ball soar and eventually raised his right arm: home run.

"You have seen them rush out to greet a hero after he touched the plate to terminate a great contest," Burns wrote. "Well, you never saw nothin.' The mob started to gather around Gabby before he had reached first base. By the time he had rounded second, he couldn't have been recognized in the mass of Cub players, frenzied fans, and excited ushers but for that red face, which shone out even in the gray shadows." Despite the twelve-foot wall in the outfield, thousands of delirious fans helped usher Hartnett around the bases, with dozens of blue-suited Andy Frain ushers doing their best to protect the Cub hero, pushing rooters out of the way and giving Hartnett some sort of path to each bag. Years later, public address announcer Pat Pieper recalled, "That was the only time I ever lost my head. I ran to third base, carrying my ball bag, and escorted Gabby across the plate."

"There was new hysteria," according to Burns, "after Gabby reached the catwalk [behind the third-base dugout] that leads to the clubhouse. But this time the gendarmes were organized.

Gabby got to the bath house without being stripped by souvenir maniacs."

Meanwhile, Mace Brown, the league's best relief pitcher, sat in the Pirate clubhouse and sobbed.

Hartnett, a six-time All-Star and Hall of Famer, is still the greatest catcher ever to wear a Cubs uniform. In 1969, retired nearly thirty years, he ranked second in an all-time Cubs popularity poll, finishing a little behind Ernie Banks. And on September 28, 1938, he probably could have been elected prime minister of Ireland, mayor of Chicago, and pope all at the same time— thanks, perhaps, to the 2:30 start time.

The Cubs whipped the demoralized Pirates 10–1 the next day and clinched the flag in Saint Louis. The party was on. On October 3, the Cubs were beneficiaries of a huge late-morning parade that began at Wrigley Field and picked up steam as it headed down Addison to Lake Shore Drive, then south on Michigan Avenue toward city hall. Somewhere around a million people watched. Once downtown, the accumulated throng listened to music from the Chicago Police Band and cheered the players, who were individually introduced to the crowd from a platform as Mayor Ed Kelly looked on.

Meanwhile, the grounds crew quickly readied the mashed-up field (still damaged by the Hartnett riot) for the first two games of the World Series against the powerful Yankees. To prepare for the onslaught of out-of-town writers, the Cubs strung up a special intercom system from the main press box to the overflow press box in the upper deck (as well as the radio booths) to ensure that everyone knew the official scorer's decisions. According to Arch Ward in the October 5 *Tribune*, more than a hundred wire connections were installed in the press areas to allow newsmen covering the games to file their stories. There were other critical preparations as well; Ward reported that Ray Kniepp, the concessions manager, had ordered "72,000 redhots, 1,600 pounds of baked ham, 1,600 pounds of roast beef, 6,000 dozen rolls, 800 two-pound loaves of bread, 42,000 bags of popcorn, 3,000 cases of pop, and 400 pounds of coffee" for the first two contests.

DOLLARS

In the ticket department, the typical "pay for three games, maybe get two" setup of tickets-by-mail was in effect, with costs remaining $6.50 for box seats and $5.50 for reserved grandstand per contest. (Regular season prices in 1938: $1.65 for boxes, $1.10 for reserved grandstands, and fifty-five cents for bleachers.) Reversing his regular policy of box-seat comfort, Wrigley crammed more and smaller chairs into the swell sections. Seating capacity for the series was more than forty thousand, rather than the usual 37,500. Fans snapped up all 32,660 presale tickets almost immediately. According to Ed Burns in the October 4 *Tribune*, the Cubs raked in $659,000 in advance sales.

The eight thousand bleacher seats were sold for $1.10 starting at 9:00 A.M. the day of each game. The Cubs also vended three thousand standing-room-only slips at $3.30 apiece, which went on sale an hour later. Some fans stood in line for several days in order to get a good seat in the bleachers for game 1. By the evening of October 4, the night before the first contest, some two thousand fans were in line, and ten thousand others strolled or drove their cars around the neighborhood, just wanting to be in on the fun and excitement. Bleacher seats sold out in ninety minutes, and the standing-room tickets were gone by noon.

GAME 1

A complete sell-out—43,660 fans—stuffed Wrigley Field on October 5 for the first game, which began at 1:30. The American Legion's Board of Trade Band supplied the music (where was Jack Bramhall?), and pleasant weather greeted everyone—including dozens of fans who sat on curbs around the ballpark and looked up at the scoreboard. Some fans tried to perch in the trees around the park to get a good view, but the cops flushed the climbers to the ground.

With no temporary bleachers to block the view, the buildings on Waveland and Sheffield avenues became private businesses offering a near-ballpark view. Marcia Winn penned a piece for the October 6 *Tribune* in which she sorted out this underground economy: "Peanut galleries, known also as window boxes or observatories, are what has become of windows space in homes fronting on the park. In these the right of gazing is rented out at scalpers' prices, usually to latecomers or fans from out of town. For an ordinary ballgame, a window sells for 50 cents. Yesterday standing room ten feet behind a crowded window—where you could manage to see if you could find a ladder to stand on—sold for a minimum of $2. A box seat, one directly in front of the window, sold for $4.40 and up." According to Winn, Mrs. Fred Nelson of 3625 North Sheffield fit forty-three souls into two front rooms. Another housewife on Waveland stuffed fifty-seven paying customers into her front rooms. The same humanitarian spirit that led Wrigley to place more chairs in the box sections also led this woman to open her doors to visitors with money in hand. "I'd hate," the woman said, "for anyone not to see the game. It makes me so excited, baseball, that I almost jump out the window."

Winn went on to note that fans also were seated on table leaves propped in tiers in front of windows, on ledges, and on fire escapes. Police, however, remained vigilant in their efforts to keep fans from watching the games from rooftops—even their own home's dome. Lieutenant Michael Ahern of the Town Hall Police Station told Winn that the practice of standing on the roof to watch is "illegal and it is dangerous."

Arch Ward of the *Tribune* reported on October 6 that Andy Frain hired 737 ushers, including six captains each from his Los Angeles and Brooklyn operations, to come to Chicago and handle the crowds. Additionally, the Chicago policemen assigned 656 men to traffic duty around the park. Frain's men appear to have done their jobs quite well, at least in one documented instance. One-Eyed Connolly, the nonpaying Houdini from 1929, did not get inside the gates this time—Ward noted that the gate-crashing legend "was still on the outside when [Frankie] Crosetti stepped to the plate to start the series."

The ticket brokers, however, did just fine. Before game 1, a set of one ticket for each of the three games was going for as much as $80. But, as always, if you hung around for a while, you might do better. An hour before game time, the agencies at the downtown hotels were selling tickets for only a little more than list price. At least one well-known local politician was a beneficiary of this tactic. "At 1 o'clock Assistant State's Attorney Richard Devine paid $7.70 for a choice box seat at the Sherman hotel office," noted the October 6 *Tribune*. "The elevated railroad then transported him to the baseball park just in time for the beginning of the game."

Despite this fanatical level of interest, in the end it seemed that Andy Frain should have brought in a few new players as well. The Cubs, perhaps worn out from their tight pennant race, lost 3–1 to Red Ruffing.

Interest remained high for game 2, though. According to the aforementioned *Tribune* story, "the highest price asked last night for a $6.60 box seat for the Cubs-Yankees baseball game at Wrigley Field today was $20 and the lowest was $11."

DIZZY

The Cubs' backs were against the wall in game 2 as sore-armed Dizzy Dean took the mound before 42,108 fans. In the second inning, with the Cubs up 1–0 and two men on, Yankees second sacker Joe Gordon grounded a hit through the left side. Shortstop Billy Jurges and third baseman Stan Hack collided chasing the ball. As Joe DiMaggio and Lou Gehrig crossed the dish, Dean himself had to track the ball down.

The Cubs came back to score twice in the third and led 3–2 in the eighth. With Dean wearing down, New York shortstop Frank Crosetti homered for two runs. The exhausted Diz also allowed DiMaggio's towering two-run bomb onto Waveland in the ninth before exiting the mound. Close to the scoreboard and past the right center-field wall was a large sign, put up some time in the mid-1930s, advertising Baby Ruth chocolate bars. Some believe that it was put up there because of its proximity to the path of Babe Ruth's 1932 "called shot." It's not clear whether this inspired Crosetti and DiMaggio, or whether Diz simply had nothing left.

The 6–3 loss effectively broke the Cubs' spirit; they went to New York and lost 5–2 and 8–3, suffering their fourth series loss, and second sweep, since 1929.

GREAT EXPECTATIONS

The Cubs' success in 1938 meant that 1939's Opening Day, set for April 18, had the biggest advance sale for a lid-lifter in many years. Unfortunately, rain kept the Cubs from beginning the season at Wrigley until April 24. When Chicago finally did play its first home game, there were no ceremonies and no band. The Cubs did install a microphone for the official scorer for the first time during a regular season game, and a brand-new bar under the stands behind home plate, decorated with action photographs of infielder Billy Jurges, won the admiration of fans.

During the year, Addison Street between Clark and Sheffield was widened. A Standard Oil service station stood on the southwest corner of Clark and Sheffield, a site currently rented to a convenience store. Several service stations now dotted the area, and a parking lot was opened just west of Clark on the south side of Addison, where the Cubby Bear tavern is currently situated.

The Cubs, never serious contenders in 1939, finished fourth, 13 games out. Nobody knew it at the time, but the franchise's golden age had ended (fig. 19).

The neighborhood seemed to be changing, too. Lake View had long been Germanic yet also patriotically American. In the wake of the Depression and with the rise of German militarism in Europe, some locals seemed to be growing less interested in the United States' idea of freedom and democracy. In October 1938, some local Nazis had celebrated the annexation of the Sudetenland at Lincoln Turner Hall at Diversey and Halsted, though other German and Bohemian Americans had protested. Steven

Figure 19. The bleachers are open and the game is about to start, but where are the fans? The Cubs did not win often after 1938, beginning a nearly thirty-year slide into mediocrity. (Credit: National Baseball Hall of Fame and Museum)

Bedell Clark notes that "members of neo-fascist groups like the German-American Bund openly paraded down *Lincolnstrasse* [Lincoln Avenue], and even staged a Nuremburg-style extravaganza one evening at [local fairground] Riverview Park. Lake View's traditionally easygoing German community seemed for a time bitterly divided over whether Hitler deserved their active support, cool neutrality or vigorous opposition."

AFTER THE GOLDEN AGE

Many fans expected the Cubs to win the pennant in 1941, if only because they had won it every three years from 1929 to 1938. But by now, the rot was beginning to set in. After capturing the 1938

National League pennant, the Cubs were to suffer through nearly five decades of frustration, winning again only in 1945 when the war-depleted NL was especially weak. Between 1939 and 1966, the Cubs enjoyed only three winning seasons.

On Opening Day 1941, April 15, Al Balder took over as scoreboard operator, replacing Charles Taubman, who had manned the board since the nineteenth century but had passed away over the winter. In addition, reported Arch Ward the following day in the *Tribune*, "For the first time since memory of man runneth not to the contrary, Jack Bramhall's band was missing from the Opening Day exercises." (Ward had forgotten about the rainy start to 1939.) Instead of the old-time favorites Bramhall's assembly provided, a swing band parked in the upper portion of the center-field bleachers provided the pregame entertainment. Ward noted sarcastically that Bramhall's band would still have been employed by the Cubs "if someone in other years had been so thoughtful as to remove them as far as possible from the customers."

That day, only 17,008 turned out to see the Cubs beat the Pirates 7–4. Of course, the ivy was not yet in bloom on the outfield wall, "which is a tough break for the hitters," according to Ward, "who will have to wait until the leaves come out to enjoy a good background for the pitchers' slants." The first batter of the game, Pirates second baseman Frankie Gustine, whistled a line drive off Cubs pitcher Claude Passeau's left shin. The hurler went down like he'd been shot, and players from both teams rushed to the mound. Remarkably, Passeau remained in to pitch a complete game.

KNIGHTS OF THE KEYBOARDS

At least Wrigley continued to improve the scenery. On April 26, 1941, the Cubs instituted yet another innovation by installing the first ballpark organ. Roy Nelson was the first man at the keys. According to the editorial page of the May 1 *Sporting News*, Nelson "played a varied program of classic and soulful compositions at the premiere." The innovation was so popular that other clubs rushed to copy it.

The *Tribune* reported on April 28 that in addition to Nelson's regular repertoire, "in prospect is a Cub theme song titled, 'When the Midnight Choo Choo Leaves for T-U-L-S-A.'" Fans were invited to submit other titles for possible Cubs themes as well, but none of these compositions has survived the ages.

Since Nelson, Wrigley Field has featured several talented organists. In the late 1960s, Jack Kearney sat at the keys. During the 1970s, Frank Pellico, Vance Fothergill, and John Henzel entertained the fans. Ed Vodicka came aboard in 1982, and then Bruce Miles in 1984. Gary Pressy has been in service at Wrigley since 1987, both playing the keyboard and providing prerecorded music before and during the game.

Another innovation for 1941 was an anteroom that the Cubs built off the press box overhang, a press and management hangout that for some reason soon came to be known as the Pink Poodle. A May 22, 1941, article in the *Sporting News*, credited to "La Petite Gourmet" but probably written by the portly Ed Burns, laid out the benefits of such a "recreation parlor": "General manager James Gallagher and Manager Jimmie Wilson are available there after every game, thus removing the necessity of clubhouse ferreting. Visiting managers have also been dropping in, especially if they win. . . . Matt Mack, a talented chef, is in charge of the snack department and in addition to fixing routine victuals can bake a charming pie or cup cake." Interestingly, while writers were happy to talk to the managers after games, they generally didn't think it important to talk to the players; the postgame interview didn't become routine until legendary reporter Dick Young made it a staple in the 1960s.

WHITE SHIRTS NO MORE

The problem with the white shirts in the bleachers hadn't gone away.

Former Cub Dolph Camilli came up with a novel solution for it in the May 19, 1941, edition of the *Daily News*, telling Howard Roberts, "Why not reserve the three middle sections of the bleachers for fellows wearing blue shirts? Make a blue shirt a requirement for admission to that portion of the bleachers." Roberts continued, with tongue firmly in cheek, "the Cubs could carry the idea farther, of course, by inaugurating a sort of Cub cheering section that would wear blue shirts while the Cubs were batting and then do a rhythmic change into white shirts to confound the enemy batsmen."

Joking aside, there had been years of protest from hitters on both the Cubs and opposing teams. Finally, with the moribund Cubs in the middle of a terrible slump in July 1941, General Manager (GM) Jim Gallagher closed off a section of the center-field seats in order to provide a consistent dark background for the batters. On July 3, as the Cubs and Cardinals began a three-game series, three sections had been roped off, and the gray stonework on the aisles and steps had been painted a shade of brown.

And did the papers ever have a ball. Much was made in the press of the Cubs drawing a crowd of forty thousand on July 4 and having to turn away fans who otherwise would have sat in the roped-off sections. The July 17, *Sporting News* ran a smarmy editorial titled "Laundering the Cubs' White Shirt Excuse."

By the next Opening Day, the policy was already beginning to slip from the club's control. According to the April 18, 1942, *Tribune*, bleacher fans "swarmed into the space in the first inning and no attempt was made to dislodge them."

Nevertheless, the problem was real. Ed Burns wrote in the September 22, 1943, *Tribune*, "Somebody ought to do something about that background, most of the Cubs believe. The bleachers can't be remodeled this season, however, because of priorities, and it can't be torn down, because of the labor shortage." By then, after all, there was a war on.

The looming prospect of war and the lingering effects of the Depression put a big bite into people's wallets and cut down the amount of money they could spend on diversions. Moreover, the Cubs were terrible in those years. They and the other teams engaged in all sorts of promotional activities to bring fans out: war bond drive days, recycling days, GI days, military all-star games, and the like. May 18, 1941, for instance, was "I Am an American" day, showing that the patriotic spirit was strong even before America joined the war. July 22, 1941, similarly, was Aluminum Day at Wrigley Field. The *Tribune*'s Irving Vaughan noted on July 22 that "women fans bringing aluminumware would be admitted to today's game on the payment only of the tax. The material collected will be turned over to the government for defense purposes." Some teams experimented with starting times to entice different populations to the park.

Contrary to P. K. Wrigley's reputation as a rugged traditionalist, the Cubs were trying just as hard as anyone else to raise attendance. And yet, until a few years ago, it was widely accepted that Phillip K. Wrigley never considered one major change: night baseball. Conventional wisdom long held that P. K., standing alone against the rising tide, would not soil the hallowed roof of Wrigley Field with light towers. Bill Veeck put it this way. "Old men, playing dominoes around the hearth, like to say that Phil Wrigley is the last of the true baseball men because he is the only owner who still holds, in the simple faith of his ancestors, that baseball was meant to be played under God's own sunlight."

Wrigley himself said many times over the years that he didn't want night baseball. He believed, for one thing, that the effects of daylight and sunshine were good, healthy habits. Second, he said that he didn't want to disturb the neighborhood. But concern for the neighbors didn't keep Wrigley from renting the ballpark out during the 1940s and 1950s for boxing and wrestling matches, basketball games, and other night events. For his part, Veeck thought that Wrigley didn't go for night baseball for more egotistical reasons: "Having blown the chance to be first with lights, Mr. Wrigley just wasn't going to do it at all."

Since the first official major league game under the lights, which took place in Cincinnati in 1935, other teams had embraced night baseball as a way to attract more fans. The minor leagues and Negro leagues had cavorted under artificial light for years. The Depression certainly kick-started the major league movement toward night baseball—almost anything that got people to the park was considered—and high attendance under the stars proved a windfall.

By early December 1941, the Cubs were ready to join the party. Management had secretly ordered the steel, electric cable, and lighting equipment to install towers for the next season. General Manager Jim Gallagher—like Bill Veeck Sr., a former sportswriter—was a fervent supporter of the project and ready to give construction workers the nod. Gallagher, interviewed by Jerome Holtzman in 1984, affirmed that "Mr. Wrigley didn't like the idea. He had his quirks. But he had authorized me to go ahead. This was in 1941, right after the season. It was a bad year. We were going over the books, suffering, wondering what the hell we were going to do and so he said, 'All right, we'll put in lights.'"

Unfortunately, on December 7, 1941, a Japanese squadron bombed Pearl Harbor, and the United States was suddenly at war.

Gallagher recalled, "I called Mr. Wrigley. He said, 'Call the War Department the first thing tomorrow morning and ask them if they want the material' . . . he was delighted to have an excuse to call the whole thing off." The Cubs gave their steel to the War Department, intending it to go to a defense plant, though Gallagher suspected that it wound up as part of a local racetrack, where night horse racing was being instituted.

THE WAR YEARS

Once the war was on, baseball's patriotism hardly abated. Opening Day 1942 at Wrigley Field, on April 17, began with nearly two hours of pregame ceremonies. Bob Strong's orchestra played patriotic airs, and nearly five hundred marines and sailors marched around the field to the accompaniment of a forty-piece band from Navy Pier. The marines held a bayonet drill. The *Tribune*'s Cubs notes column of the next day reported that the Cubs were presented a Minute Man flag by the Department of Defense "for the club's 100 per cent cooperation in the purchase of defense bonds."

Ominously, however, the Opening Day crowd numbered just 10,149.

GAMES WITH BENEFITS

Among the many promotions the Cubs tried in the war years were games involving Negro Leaguers, a shocking innovation to some. With the Cubs out of town on May 24, two All-Star teams held a special benefit. Retired hurler Dizzy Dean fronted a team of players currently serving in the army that took on Satchel Paige and the Kansas City Monarchs, reigning three-time champions of the Negro American League.

For some reason, the game was billed as a tribute to "Banana Nose" Zeke Bonura, a popular former White Sox player then based as a soldier in Louisiana, but the money from the 29,775 paid admissions went to military relief. The Monarchs, with Paige on the mound for six innings and Buck O'Neil at first base, tamed the all-white army all-stars 3–1.

Three days later, on Wednesday, May 27, the Cubs hosted the Reds in a doubleheader consisting of one regular game and a benefit for the army and navy; prior to the regularly scheduled contest, the baseball team of the northern Illinois Navy boot camp Great Lakes Naval Air Station played Camp Grant, an army facility just outside of Rockford, Illinois. (The two clubs had enjoyed a fierce rivalry during World War I.) Ninety-three sailors stationed at Navy Pier went door to door delivering tickets that had been ordered in advance for the event. The tickets were also available at regular season prices at Wrigley Field, the *Tribune*'s offices, and at the usual Western Union outlets.

Yet another benefit was scheduled, on July 28, with the Dodgers in town for a doubleheader. "The entire receipts will go to the Red Cross and the War Relief Fund," wrote Edgar Munzel in that day's *Sun*. "Everyone who enters the ball park, including players, newspaper, and radio men, will have to buy a ticket." The crowd of 25,735 poured $29,733.55 into the fund. Before the game, a guard from the Glenview Naval Air Station presented the colors, and the Glenview Station band played. Field announcer Pat Pieper himself sold seven hundred tickets to the contest.

DAY FOR NIGHT

With industrial employment suddenly skyrocketing and many more people working night shifts, the Cubs decided to start a pair of games in the morning. Chicago hosted Cincinnati on June 11, 1943, at 10:00 A.M., but the novel start time drew only fifty-three hundred spectators. On June 22, another morning contest attracted but thirty-seven hundred, and the Cubs ended the experiment.

The franchise tried another innovation, the "twilight" game, at Wrigley Field on Friday, June 25. The 6:00 P.M. start was a first for Wrigley, and by today's standards it would be considered a night game; this, therefore, was arguably the first major league night game played at Wrigley Field. Hi Bithorn pitched the Cubs to a 6–0 win over the Saint Louis Cardinals, allowing just two hits—the game took just two hours and seventeen minutes. Though it was a warm summer night, only 10,070 fans came to the park, with nearly thirty-five hundred of them Ladies Day freebies. As a result, the experiment was not repeated. Stories in the papers the next day barely mentioned the odd start time.

INDIGNATION

Two days later, Sunday, June 27, Wrigley fans revolted as the club lost both ends of a twin bill against the Cardinals. The Cubs had led both contests in the late innings. The outcry was significant enough that the *Saturday Evening Post* led off its September 11, 1943, issue with a story titled "The Decline and Fall of the Cubs." One section noted that "a crowd of 37,792 reared back on its hind legs and howled its indignation at the floundering Cubs on the field and the blundering in the front office . . . old inhabitants of Wrigley Field say it was the most violent demonstration against the Cub management since the wolves attacked Rogers Hornsby in 1932." The author of the piece, Stanley Frank, declaimed: "Wrigley gave his product a resplendent wrapper, only to make a rather discouraging discovery. The customers weren't buying the inferior product, the slipping ball club, he was selling."

NOBODY HOME

Attendance at Wrigley Field continued to lag, as it did all over baseball in 1943, the nadir of the wartime economy. On September 24, just 314 fans kept the faith at Wrigley for a rain-shortened Cubs victory, in which Chicago's young outfielder Andy Pafko made his major league debut. The Cubs' final 1943 attendance was just 508,224, their lowest total since 1921 and worst to date. Even with this poor showing, the Cubs still ranked third in the NL in attendance. Some teams played in front of fewer than four thousand fans per game in 1943. The Boston Braves drew just 271,289 fans, while only 214,392 watched the Saint Louis Browns.

Phil Wrigley believed that the war would be long, and, knowing that Cubs receipts would be down, he sought to keep his ballpark occupied. No one wanted to consider the idea of shutting down the major leagues, but Wrigley wanted to be ready just in case. Therefore, he decided to professionalize a popular local activity: girls' softball. "In 1942," Paul Angle wrote, "it was estimated that more than a hundred million spectators watched softball games each year." According to Lois Browne, during that year one Chicago women's softball league drew 250,000 fans.

Wrigley formed a corporation in order to back the plan. Members of the group included GM Jim Gallagher, public relations man Art Meyerhoff, and Cubs employee Ken Sells. Baseball executive Branch Rickey also agreed to be a trustee.

While the concept itself proved sound, Wrigley soon realized that softball was, compared to baseball, perhaps too slow to retain large-scale interest. Therefore, the new league would play with a hard ball a bit larger than a regulation baseball. "By insisting that the women play baseball, not softball, Wrigley hoped to sustain interest in baseball as a spectator sport," wrote Susan Cahn. The All-American Girls Professional Baseball League (AAGPBL) debuted in 1943.

Wrigley set about raiding the amateur leagues for the best players—at least those who fit his narrow criteria. The game was to be played by feminine girls, not the so-called mannish Amazons derided by the less-than-enlightened. Yet the game was expected to be fast and competitive. Laughably, the players wore short skirts. While these outfits certainly afforded spectators marvelous views of the players' legs, the skirts did nothing to protect the ladies from injury, as they dove and hustled all over the field. "Sliding strawberries" were a common problem.

On May 17, 1943, the league held tryouts at Wrigley. (Decades later, this scene was reenacted at Wrigley for the film *A League of Their Own*.) Photographers clicked away as the young ladies pitched, hit, and fielded in hopes of landing jobs. Six weeks later, on the evening of July 1, the Women's Army Air Corps held a rally at Wrigley Field in order to boost recruitment. The rally included two exhibits of ladies' baseball, one featuring the women of local bases Fort Sheridan and Camp Grant, the other pitting AAGPBL All-Stars from Wisconsin against those from Illinois and Indiana. In the 6:00 P.M. game, Fort Sheridan whomped Camp Grant by a ridiculous 33–5, while in the second game the Wisconsin AAGPBL All-Stars mangled their opponents 11–0. Approximately seven thousand curious onlookers watched the games as well as calisthenics, precision drills, and the twenty-eight-piece Fort Sheridan band.

The contest was, Lois Browne wrote, "notable for several reasons. For one thing, it was the first [baseball game] ever played at Wrigley Field under lights," with a temporary bank of floodlights strapped to the top of the grandstands, P. K. Wrigley's care for the community's sleeping habits be damned. Visibility was nonetheless poor; player Dorothy Hunter recalled to Browne that "you were lucky if you could see who was sitting next to you. The outfielders were dead ducks."

Unfortunately, girls' league games weren't popular. They weren't major league baseball, and they suffered in comparison when played in Wrigley Field. Professional parks tended to remove the neighborhood-style intimacy perhaps necessary for the game to succeed. Tickets were a dollar each for the games, a relatively steep price.

Following the 1944 season, Wrigley, who now felt that the war would end soon, sold the AAGPBL to Art Meyerhoff for a reported $10,000. Wrigley had sunk some $135,000 on the league. Paul Angle wrote that "the venture had been costly for [Wrigley] personally, and from his point of view, nothing was to be gained by further expenditures." The league continued on through 1954, though no more games were played at Wrigley Field.

FOLLOWING THE FLAG

For the opening of the 1944 season at Wrigley Field (an exhibition on April 13) against the White Sox, the Cubs sought to demonstrate their patriotism and do something about the white-shirt bleacher problem. The outfield bleachers had been painted a kale-like shade of green to better match the color of the scoreboard and, Jim Gallagher noted, to help improve the hitting background—at least on days when the bleachers weren't full. Lyall Smith, in the April 13 *Daily News*, compared the new color to that from "a left-over can of paint from a General Grant tank."

On April 17, the Cubs held a day to honor twenty-five thousand teenagers who had sold war bonds. Selling $25 worth of bonds admitted the kids to bleacher seats, and fifty bucks got them into the grandstand. The big sellers—anyone shifting more than $100 worth of war bonds—netted box seats. By all accounts, no adult spectators were present. Army and navy bands were on hand to entertain.

That was about it for excitement that year, as the Cubs finished fourth in 1944.

THE LAST PENNANT

While few expected the Cubs to contend in 1945, the defending world champion Saint Louis Cardinals exited the gate poorly. After a hot start by the New York Giants, the Cubs came alive; Chicago's 26–4 stretch during June and early July catapulted them into first. On July 15, the Cubs swept a doubleheader from the visiting Giants, 5–3 and 7–2, to move four games up in the NL race. Wrigley hosted an overflow crowd of 48,803, the biggest of the season; usual crowds that year had been more like twenty thousand, but they began turning up in bigger numbers down the stretch.

Chicago slumped in late August and was on and off through most of September. On September 23, with the Pirates in town, the Cubs held Andy Pafko Day for their popular young centerfielder, and 43,755 packed the ballpark. All of the box seats had been sold since the middle of the month. Before the game, Pafko received two large suitcases and a watch from the Chicago Slovak Good Will Club. The fan favorite responded in kind; his third inning grand-slam homer gave the Cubs a 4–3 lead in a game they went on to take, 7–3. The win kept the Cubs one and a half games ahead of the Cardinals.

With just seven games to play, the Cubs entertained the Cardinals on September 25. The weather was still gloomy after a few days of rain, so only 20,438 came out to see a game on which the NL pennant race would surely turn. Down 3–2 in the seventh, Chicago broke through for four runs. After Don Johnson's single tied the score, Phil Cavarretta's bases-loaded hit scored Stan Hack to put the Cubs up 4–3. Pafko then doubled in two more. After Chicago held on for a 6–5 win, the players quickly proceeded up the ramp to their clubhouse, cheered by hundreds of raucous fans. As Lon Warneke and Roy Johnson broke into the team's victory song of the time, "John the Baptist," the Cubs made for the beer tub.

CLINCH

The next day, World Series tickets, which had gone on sale the previous morning, were already sold out. (Indeed, a hundred workers had been hired to return extra applications.) The weather was better, and 42,289 Cub crazies came out, but the Cardinals won a zany 11–6 game to trim the lead to just one and a half games with five contests left.

Chicago went to Cincinnati and swept a twin bill from the Reds, 3–1 and 7–4. On the year, the Cubs won twenty-one of twenty-two from the hapless Reds—and in general the Cubs cleaned up against weaker teams. While they were just 6–16 against the second-place Redbirds, and 11–11 versus third-place New York, the Cubs finished an almost incredible 81–29 against the remainder of the National League.

Two days later, the Cubs made up a rain-canceled double-header in Pittsburgh that had been originally scheduled for Chicago. Sweeping their twentieth doubleheader of the season (an all-time NL record), 4–3 and 5–0, Chicago wrapped up the NL crown.

While the Cubs were not particularly good—no wartime aggregation was—they were relatively deep, especially in starting pitchers. Five Cubs hurlers finished in double figures in wins, including Hank Wyse, who paced the NL with twenty-two wins, and Ray "Pop" Prim, whose 2.40 earned-run average led the league. Midseason acquisition Hank Borowy, brought over from the Yankees in a waiver-wire deal, was 11–2 for Chicago and won the hearts of thousands of Illinois women with his good looks.

COME GO WITH ME

Unfortunately, wartime travel restrictions worked against the Cubs as they had in 1918. The first three games of the series were played in Detroit, with the remainder held in Chicago. This meant that the Cubs might theoretically have as few as one home date. Fans were sold tickets in strips for games 4–6, with game 7 tickets to be sold only if the game was necessary.

Prior to game 4, Andy Frain—who was in charge of 525 ushers, one hundred of them women—gave the press a series of suggestions to help fans avoid problems at the park: (1) go to the gate specified on the ticket; (2) bring only the ticket for game 4; and (3) leave home early. Frain noted that in 1938, several people bringing their tickets for all three games either had lost them or had ushers tear off the wrong ticket. In addition, fans always ran a risk of theft. To help with the crowding, the city had once again closed down some streets and planned to open express lanes for Wrigley-bound cars at 11:00 A.M. each game day. In the park itself, some of Frain's ushers would for the first time be equipped with walkie-talkies. In the words of Ed Prell in the October 4 *Tribune*, "Girls with the radio gadgets will be posted at strategic points in the park in contact at all times with Frain, who will station himself at a vantage point. . . . This will lessen the strain on Frain, whose practice in the past has been to dash all over a park or stadium in his capacity as supervisor." These young ladies were hard to miss, kitted out as they were in navy blue skirts with gold stripes down each side, powder blue blouses, and capes of blue and gold (the Frain service's signature colors).

Less ostentatiously dressed but notable nonetheless was Frain's least traditional usher, One-Eyed Connolly, who had snuck into Wrigley during the 1929 World Series. Apparently believing that someone who knows the tricks of getting in free makes the most efficient gatekeeper, Frain hired Connolly to mind the front gate before game 4 and told him to keep out the riffraff. Unfortunately, before game 6, according to Arch Ward in the *Tribune* on October 9 Connolly refused to allow in P. K. Wrigley, whom he did not recognize. Connolly submitted his (forced) resignation after the game.

TAKE ME HOME

After winning games 1 and 3 with scores of, respectively, 9–0 and 3–0 in Detroit for a 2–1 advantage in the series, the Cubs arrived home on a special train on Friday night, October 5, to a cheering crowd at Union Station. They had left Detroit on a high as right-hander Claude Passeau threw one of the great games in World Series history at the Tigers—a one-hit, one-walk shutout.

The Cubs decided, for the 1:30 starts to games 4–6, and (if needed) game 7, to begin selling five thousand bleacher seats (at $1.20 apiece) at 7:00 in the morning and open box and grandstand gates at 10:30. (Two hundred bleacher seats had been reserved for wounded servicemen from local Vaughan Hospital. The soldiers, who arrived in five buses, ate box lunches supplied by the Cubs.) When all bleacher tickets were sold, twenty-five hundred standing-room tickets were to be vended at $3.60 apiece. (The idea of charging three times as much for standing room as for bleachers boggles the mind.)

Fans gathered in line for bleacher seats early in the morning of October 4, two days before game 4. Art Felsch of Milwaukee, a factory worker, was first in line at 8:00 A.M. He survived on cans of cold chili and slept on an army-style cot. Two army vets from the Italian and North Africa campaigns, on three-day passes from Kentucky, told a *Tribune* reporter in the October 6 issue that waiting for bleacher seats was "no worse than being in a chow line." By Friday night, five thousand Cub supporters surrounded the park, five hundred in line for bleacher seats and the others enjoying the atmosphere. Some of the kids in line were just holding places to sell to the highest bidder; one wanted $15 for his place. Some men sold wooden boxes to tired standees for a quarter or two. To deal with the crowds, three hundred of Chicago's finest walked the area, along with forty-three navy patrolmen and twenty-five army military police.

It took only one hour for the bleacher seats to sell out, but not all of the standing-room tickets went. Attendance for game 4 was 42,923, some fifteen hundred under capacity. (All the standing-room seats sold for game 5, but game 6 again was less than a sellout.)

Despite the city's road management, newspapermen and broadcasters covering the game still had trouble getting to the park. The press bus, leaving from the Palmer House Hotel, broke down on Lake Shore Drive near Belmont Harbor, forcing the reporters to grab their typewriters and notebooks and catch taxicabs to the park. When they arrived, they found P. K. Wrigley— who often wouldn't even show up for critical games—in an atypically jolly mood, entertaining NL owners at the Pink Poodle.

In July 1972, David Condon wrote that getting to Wrigley Field at all in 1945 was an adventure. "I rode the Clark Street surface cars, an experience likened to Russian Roulette with a carbine." The neighborhood was modernizing; more cars, more people, more businesses—and, apparently, more fun. By 1945, laws against sitting atop one's roof to watch a game had either been changed or simply forgotten. One fan perched on a slanted roof on a Kenmore Avenue house to take in the World Series in his overcoat and hat. As always, a few local residents decided to cash in on the Cubs' success. City inspectors, following up on complaints, sued thirteen parking lot operators for asking more than they were licensed to charge. Some lots were demanding $2 per car, more than twice the limit.

KISSED BY A GOAT

Though most of game 4 was played under rainy gray skies— groundskeepers did not remove the tarpaulin until 1:25, eliminating batting practice—it got off to an unexpected start when, before the first pitch, actress June Haver ran onto the field and kissed manager Charlie Grimm and pitcher Hank Borowy. According to Arch Ward, "It was good clean fun and all that, but we wonder what would happen if Grimm and Borowy dashed onto a set at the 20th Century-Fox studio and reversed the procedure."

But a stranger event near game time had a bigger impact on Cubs lore. Fans have often heard about the "Billy Goat" curse, but its origins are not too well known. David Condon of the *Tribune* wrote on May 23, 1972, of what happened just before game 4.

> One of the merriest fans was William (Billy Goat) Sianis, keeper of the [Billy Goat] saloon and a prominent herd of goats. Billy had unique intentions.
>
> Governor Dwight Green was in Wrigley Field [that] afternoon. Mayor Ed Kelly was present, too. Mr. Billy Goat Sianis and his blue-ribbon goat, Sonovia, also appeared.
>
> Mr. Sianis presented a pair of box-seat tickets and escorted Sonovia to choice pews. The Frain ushers started squawking on those newfangled handy-talkies and very quickly both goats, Billy and Sonovia, were being rushed exit-wise. Sonovia's ticket was retrieved. Presently it is mounted in the Billy Goat Inn.

Sianis, a huge Cubs fan, had adorned Sonovia with a blanket reading, "We Got Detroit's Goat." But apparently, the Cubs weren't humored. Condon continues, "When the Tigers surged ahead by winning both the fourth and fifth games, Billy Goat placed an eternal hex on the Cubs. As an afterthought, he telegraphed Owner Philip K. Wrigley: 'Who smells now?'" Thus was born the Curse of the Billy Goat.

Sianis visited Wrigley on July 4, 1973, again with goat in tow, and was turned away. But in 1981, William Sianis's son, Sam, was allowed to bring his goat to the park. He again came in 1984 and 1986, and in a cringe-worthy pregame ceremony in 1994, the team invited Sianis and a goat onto the field in order to end the hex "officially." It doesn't seem to have worked.

BURNED

Wrigley had his issues to deal with besides being hexed by a goat. Realizing that ticket scalping made many fans angry, Wrigley took out an ad in the papers headlined "We're burned up too, Cub fans, about scalping of World Series tickets." The ad read: "The Cubs went to a lot of trouble and extra expense to engage outside office space and a large force of bank tellers and clerks to try and do an extra good job of distributing evenly and fairly the comparatively limited supply of World Series tickets . . . once the tickets are in the hands of the public, there is nothing to prevent individuals from selling their seats at a neat profit through scalpers . . . we all know this to be true, but as we said to start with—we do not like it." Wrigley realized that the whole process reflected badly on him, the Cubs, and baseball. (Times change: in 2002, it was revealed that the Cubs themselves were running a scalping agency.)

Perhaps pressured by Wrigley's public stance, bluecoats were busy nailing scalpers. The day before the series started in Chicago, twenty city detectives and twenty-five revenue department deputies began canvassing the streets. Six speculators were arrested near Wrigley Field before games 4–6 for selling above the printed price. Some were trying to move $1.20 bleacher seats for as much as ten bucks, although most of the hapless capitalists were bottom-feeders on the scalping food chain. No arrests of downtown ticket agency employees were reported. One scalper, Louis Pike, owned Pike's Texaco, kitty-corner from Wrigley Field. Another man arrested for scalping said that Pike rented him a space in his gas station from which to operate his ticket-reselling operation.

After game 7 was made necessary and more tickets came on the market, the authorities made more busts. On the morning of that game, several young men were caught scalping in the lobbies of the Sherman and Morrison hotels. Judge J. M. Braude ordered the tickets sold, in an impromptu fashion, to locals. The original ticket value was then given back to the scalpers, who were also forced to donate money to the Red Cross or the Victory Loan drive. (Proceeds from tickets sold to locals also went to war relief efforts.)

GAME 7

When the Cubs, who had lost games 4 and 5 to fall behind three games to two, forced a game 7 with a wild twelve-inning 8–7 win in game 6, Wrigley sprang into action. Somewhat worried about a riot over seats for the deciding game, Wrigley used the off day before the deciding contest to contact as many as possible of the fans left out of the previous ticket sales and offered them tickets for game 7. He explained it to Ed Prell in the October 9 *Tribune* as "attending to the wants of his own 'personal customers and rooters.'" Thirty-six thousand tickets, less those marked for previous lottery losers, went on sale October 9 at normal series prices: $7.20 for boxes and $6.00 for grandstand.

When asked which team would take the series, *Chicago Sun* editor Warren Brown is said to have replied, "I don't think either of them can win it." Cubs rooters, however, believed in their team. Fans began lining up by the ticket windows on Addison Street almost immediately after game 6, and by midnight two hundred fans were in line, burning paper and wood in garbage cans to keep warm. Members of this well-behaved crowd could hardly have suspected that this was the last World Series game the Cubs play in at least sixty-eight years, but apparently they were somewhat solemn. Few, if any, rooters drank liquor, and the standees agreed to have club employees mark their places in line with chalk numbers on the backs of their coats.

While many kids tried to stake out places in line, some saw their chance to view a World Series game dashed. According to Ed Prell:

At 11 P.M. there was an appreciable dwindling of the bleacher population when the police ordered all school boys and girls to leave for home. There were some murmurings of disapproval. One disappointed lad said, "That's a pretty dirty trick—the World Series happens once here every seven years and we can't see it."

A philosophic policeman [said] . . . "Look at 'em," pointing to dozens of youngsters lying on blankets or quilts. "Those kids are running a risk of getting sick. I was a boy once—but I wouldn't want one of my kids out in this chilly weather."

The cops let those youngsters remain who were occupied by their parents. It may be reasonably assumed that there were more than a few on-the-spot adoptions last night.

Wrigley and several members of the Cubs' staff were up all night preparing for the mass sale. Andy Frain was also on hand, having called as many staffers as he could to the park. Frain himself was the recipient of several bribe offers for a good place in line, including, according to Prell, a freshly caught six-pound fish.

The sale began at 8:00 in the morning of October 9, and all the tickets were gone by 11:30. The next morning, all five thousand bleachers tickets were snapped up in an hour. On the whole, the series was a great financial success, breaking all sorts of records for box-office receipts despite what most felt to be low-quality baseball. Before game 4 alone, 180 vendors had sold fifty-four thousand sandwiches. During the four games at Wrigley, fans bought ninety-one thousand programs.

But the result on the field was less salubrious. Unfortunately for Chicago's fans, Detroit scored five runs off Hank Borowy and Paul Derringer in the first inning. The game was never close, and the Tigers cruised to a 9–3 win and a World Championship.

The Cubs have not returned to the Fall Classic since.

7

POSTWAR BLUES
WRIGLEY FIELD, 1946–1965

CHANGES

The Cubs had been in the World Series more often than contemporary fans can dream of—four times in seventeen seasons. But they hadn't won in decades, and a long, agonizing drought was about to begin. The Cubs were not just going to fall short, they were going to fall far. The decades after 1945 saw a succession of underperforming, underwhelming, underattended teams—and Wrigley Field would not be the better for them.

In truth the whole city was changing, not always for the better, and Lake View was no exception. Mostly a residential neighborhood, it also had important commercial hubs. Beginning in the 1940s, however, some of its outstanding businesses began to close down. The legendary Bendel Bakery at Lincoln and Belmont, which had been in operation for fifty-seven years, was shuttered in 1949. The Best Brewing Company, at 1301 West Fletcher Street, which had been delivering beer to homes and businesses since 1891, did not survive long past the war.

The biggest change was residential. Citywide after the war, young whites flocked to the suburbs to build their families as more African Americans and Latinos moved into the city. In Lake View, while the population went up, the rate of home ownership declined steadily, according to a 1957 University of Chicago study. Long-term residents were aging and dying, and younger ones were moving away. Some of this was white flight. While few blacks have ever lived in Lake View, lower-income whites and Latinos began to move in during the 1950s. The ethnic shift meant that, in the opinion of the press and much of the public, Lake View's profile was declining.

In an article about the history of Lake View in the September 1, 1957, *Tribune*, Erwin Bach obliquely referred to "problems [that] also plague this neighborhood of Wrigley field, famed ball park and home of the Chicago Cubs." This seems to have been an allusion to the shifting population and its effect on home values, businesses, and perceived safety.

At the same time, in the years after World War II, the national entertainment industry exploded with the growth of television. By the 1950s, with entertainment options coming out of every wormhole, prospective fans needed more than sunshine. The conditions were all aligning for a serious decline in baseball attendance all over the country—and in Chicago, the poor performance of the Cubs was only to make this downward spiral more profound.

YEAR ONE

The Cubs were expected to slump in 1946, when the Cardinals and other clubs got back plenty of good players from the military. And they did.

On a very cold April 20, 40,887 fans flocked to Wrigley Field to watch the defending NL champions inaugurate their season. Cubs manager Charlie Grimm received the NL pennant from league president Ford Frick as well as—to commemorate the victory in World War II—a small jar of Japanese soil from twenty-one-year-old Chicagoan Warren Jungwirth, who had spent thirty-eight months overseas. The crowd was the largest for an Opening Day at the park since 1929. Armin Hand's band, dressed in spanking new blue uniforms, were "further decorated by the presence of six slightly frostbitten drum majorettes," according to the *Tribune's* Ed Prell on April 21.

At close to 1:00, half an hour before game time—most major

league contests now started around that time—Grimm pressed a buzzer mounted in the dugout that called the Cubs' players out of the clubhouse and onto the field for their pregame drill. With the players on the field, a small tractor drove the pennant to the right-field corner, where it was raised on the foul pole. The band, Prell wrote, "perhaps in the spirit of peace time, substituted 'God Bless America' for 'The Star-Spangled Banner.'"

WBKB television was on hand, hoping to air the game to the few thousand Chicago-area owners of television sets. This was to be the first telecast of a baseball game in the Windy City. Interference interfered, however. An item in the April 21 *Tribune* noted that things didn't come off as planned: "The station's mobile unit televised the game successfully at the field, but electrical interference in the State-Lake building, where the transmitter is located, resulted in such poor images after the relay that William C. Eddy, director, declined to put them on the air. Eddy blamed the interference on elevator operations in the building where the studios and the transmitter are located."

WBKB tried again on July 13. This time, everything went swimmingly. Larry Wolters of the *Tribune* reported the next day that "televiewers saw the game from an upper tier position looking across home plate down the first-base line, with the pitcher in view on the mound. Except when the camera was swung to follow action, they missed the activity at second, third, and in most of the outfield." The game, won by the Dodgers 4–3, featured a ninth-inning Cubs rally that fell just short, as well as an argument involving Dodgers manager Leo Durocher. The commentator for the WBKB telecast was Jack Gibney, who, Wolters judged, "judiciously let the pictures speak for themselves." Despite the use of just one camera, the telecast was a clear success; viewers as far away as Michigan City, Indiana, picked it up. WBKB broadcast another game two days later and several more home contests that summer.

CHANGING COLORS

When Jackie Robinson made his first visit to Wrigley Field, on May 18, 1947, a crowd of 46,572 paid to get in. At the time, this was believed to be the largest paid regular-season crowd in park history, and certainly the largest gathering since 1936, which is when the ban on fans standing on the field went into effect. Ed Burns wrote that the fans "jammed all available spaces to see Jackie Robinson" in the May 19 *Tribune*. Oddly, though, no accounts in the white papers of the time note what portion of the fans were black. Even the *New York Times's* Roscoe McGowen did not mention in his May 19 piece on the game that Robinson was a center of attention. Perhaps everyone knew how momentous each game with Jackie was. Or perhaps the Chicago papers did not want to alarm local fans by painting a picture of crowds of black people streaming from trains and streetcars and invading what had mostly been an all-white playground. In its May 17 issue, the weekly Chicago *Defender* implored its African American readers who were journeying to Wrigley Field to be respectful and leave the liquor at home. This plea to leave a good impression on the press and on white fans was made by black newspapers in most National League cities that year. At this time, most of Chicago's blacks lived on the South Side. Those who did attend big league games usually patronized the White Sox, whose home park, Comiskey, hosted many a Negro League All-Star game. It's likely that this trip to Wrigley was the first that most African American fans had ever made.

While white papers didn't make mention of black fans, Mike Royko did, noting in the *Daily News* on October 25, 1972, the day after Robinson died, that he was among African Americans "by the thousands, pouring off the northbound els and out of their cars." Royko sat next to a middle-aged black man who, when Robinson batted, was "beating his palms together so hard they must have hurt."

For many years, the Cubs were among baseball's least-integrated clubs. From 1947 through 1952, the Cubs had no blacks and only one Latino: Sal Madrid, who played eight games in 1948. It was a white club in a white neighborhood, and Phil Wrigley (fig. 20) seemed in no mood to change things.

"We aren't going out and hire a Negro ball player just because it is popular to have a Negro ball player," he said at the time. "When we have a Negro ball player, he will be an outstanding ball player. He has to be outstanding . . . he has to be better than any white boy because he will be under the microscope." (This, of course, raises the question of just how good any Negro would have to be to outplay the "white boys" composing the execrable Cubs teams of the era.) Some felt that Wrigley was tacitly admitting that he felt that his customers were racists. Or was he just stonewalling on account of his own prejudices? Several historians have claimed that Wrigley, like many in the establishment, simply believed in slow progress: nothing too radical, nothing too shocking, everything in its proper place and time.

He doesn't seem to have put the success of the team first. Concerned more about marketing than about baseball per se, Wrigley probably felt it was more important not to risk offending the fan base by bringing in too many black players. If so, Wrigley seems to have overestimated his club's ability to succeed, even as others had improved by taking advantage of an expanded market for talent by beginning to sign blacks and Latinos in the late 1940s and early 1950s. The White Sox, for example, integrated much more quickly than did the Cubs, and it corresponded with their rise out of the AL's doldrums. Even if Cubs fans were as racist as Wrigley seems to have believed, they probably would have preferred a winning team over anything else.

The organization's historical record on race was poor throughout Wrigley's regime. The Cubs did not sign Ernie Banks or bring up Gene Baker from the minors until 1953, and from that point gingerly embraced the concept of integration. In the early 1960s,

the Cubs had a significant black presence, but soon began trading some blacks for whites. For most of the 1960s and 1970s, the Cubs were considered a bad place for black players, unless they were quiet like Billy Williams or jolly like Ernie Banks (whose signature phrase was, "Let's Play Two") and Willie Smith. Batting champion Bill Madlock was disposed of when he had the temerity to ask for more money. Over the years, the Cubs dumped Oscar Gamble, Bill North, Lou Brock, Fergie Jenkins, and Andre Thornton, often for little in return, presumably to be rid of players that they considered "trouble." Most of them weren't stars when they were traded; they only became stars for other teams. And while the Cubs occasionally employed Latino players during World War II, it wasn't until the mid-1970s that the team had a serious Latino presence.

Were the Cubs afraid that they'd lose their audience by playing more blacks? Well, by the late 1950s and early 1960s, they didn't have blacks or Latinos, and they stunk, and they had lost a big chunk of their audience anyway.

WHY WERE THEY SO AWFUL?

The Cubs were bad for many reasons besides being well behind the curve on black and Latin players. One was Wrigley's belief that minor league teams should not be owned by big league teams. Bill Veeck Jr., who in the 1940s owned a Milwaukee club directly subsidized by Wrigley, noted admiringly that Wrigley "did not believe in farm systems. It was his belief—and he was right— that baseball could only remain healthy if the minor league clubs were free to develop their own players and sell them to the highest bidder. He put his money where his mouth was. He subsidized Milwaukee, through a direct cash grant, and renounced all rights to their players." But as a result of this magnanimity, the Cubs had far less talent in their system than other clubs, even those that had far less money to play with—the Cardinals, for example.

By the early 1940s, the press was pointing out the Cubs' substandard minor-league system. Irving Vaughan in the July 27, 1941, *Tribune* wrote an article entitled, "Backward Cubs Begin to Learn about Farming—Crop Is Poor." He made this point: "The Cubs' officials were sustained, first off, by the fact that a few pennants had been won. Maybe they thought this would go on indefinitely, completely oblivious to the patent fact that men grow old whether they are playing baseball or sitting in a rocking chair. . . . Nothing had been done about making minor league connections, either through purchase or agreement." Vaughan concluded by noting that, for the purposes of owning a major league club, Wrigley's argument was silly: teams need to do whatever they can to compete. Only players, who could be trapped in deep systems, could possibly have a beef.

The general trend was for major league teams to own their affiliates. This didn't please all the minor league owners, of course; their ability to run a business as they desired was being destroyed. But the major leagues' greed and the rise of television eventually squashed the free minors. The Cubs, late to the party, suffered for years.

SPRUCING UP FOR THE STARS

The Cubs hosted the 1947 All-Star Game on July 8. The game had not returned to Chicago since the initial contest in 1933. Wrigley Field was well positioned at the time to house the fans, baseball people, and media. There were new ticket windows on Clark Street, down the third-base line, as well as on Addison Street down the first-base line. With six ladies' rooms, which had been doubled in size the previous year, and five men's rooms, as well as adequate concession facilities in several locations and even a first-aid station, it was as well-appointed as any major league facility.

Wrigley Field in 1947, of course, wasn't much like Wrigley Field today. At that point, both teams' clubhouses were on the mezzanine level. (The current visitors' clubhouse, the smallest and smelliest in the game, remains in the same spot.) Clubhouses were not built adjacent to, or accessible from, dugouts until much later. When games were finished, clubs left their tiny dugouts (which were, indeed, small shelters simply "dug out" of the dirt) and walked down the foul lines to access their clubhouses—the Cubs' down the left-field line and their opponents' down the right. The very small umpires' room was located right next to the visitors' clubhouse. (The arbiters got a new space in 1955.)

Partially due to the war, attendance at the midsummer classic had flagged somewhat since the event's initial novelty wore off; the 1942, 1943, and 1944 contests had meager crowds of 33,694,

31,938, and 29,589, respectively, and the 1945 contest was canceled outright. A heartening gathering of 41,123 came out to see the 1947 All-Stars, however. Phil Cavarretta and Andy Pafko represented the Cubs.

More cosmetic changes came to Wrigley Field after the All-Star Game. In late July, the Cubs announced a pair of improvements. First, the photos overlooking the main concession stand, which dated back to the 1930s, were removed in favor of baseball action pictures from the current season. Second, the Cubs once again tried to address the problem of the distracting hitting background in the bleachers without actually closing seats off. This time, head groundskeeper Bobby Dorr installed, in time for a July 22 doubleheader, a large piece of blue plastic near the top of the outfield wall in dead center field. The plastic screen was intended to cut down on glare from the white shirts worn by bleacher patrons, but the "innovation" was removed without ceremony on July 29. During the nine games the screen was used, the Cubs plated thirty-one runs and the visitors forty-eight.

HACKING MASS

On the suggestion of a loyal fan, Mrs. Margaret Barnard of Chicago, the Cubs honored veteran third baseman Stan Hack, who had announced plans to retire, on August 30, 1947. Hack, one of the most popular Cubs ever, received a carload of gifts—and a car. In addition to a shiny new gray sedan, Hack was presented a $1,000 TV set, which had a screen the size of an Etch a Sketch. He also got a freezer, two radios, fishing tackle, two pen and pencil sets, a traveling bag, a cigarette box, a crate of fruit, a humidor full of cigars, a wristwatch (from the Cubs), and presentations from five Chicago florists.

More than twenty-seven thousand turned out for the game between the fifth-place Cubs and sixth-place Pirates, which Pittsburgh won 8–5. One spectator, Mike Devore from McHenry, Illinois, who checked in at ninety-eight years of age, was definitely old enough to remember when the Cubs had last won the World Series. Hack went hitless in three at bats and walked. When asked to speak, Hack said, "As far as I am concerned, there is no greater city in the world than Chicago, no finer team to play for than the Cubs, and no greater fans in the country. Cub friends, I love you all."

Irving Vaughan wrote in his story concerning Hack's day that "the showering of tokens will be resumed this afternoon when Nick Strincevich, who is scheduled to start for the Pirates against Doyle Lade, will be presented with an automobile by his Gary, Ind., neighbors. Tomorrow, Bert Haas of the Reds will receive a car from fans of his home town, Naperville."

It would have been nice if the players could have reciprocated with some gifts of their own, but the season came to an end with 69–85 record. In the baseball off-season, the Bears finished a much more respectable 10–2, but they and their equipment chewed up the field so badly that groundskeeper Bobby Dorr and his chief assistant Harry "New York" Hazelwood had to oversee the planting of fifty-five hundred square yards of sod on the portion of the field that had been used by the Bears.

THE BIGGEST PAID CROWD

Despite the Cubs' years of dreary play, the crowds still came. As noted, on May 18, 1947, 46,572 fans crammed their way in to see Jackie Robinson. A bit more than a year later, on Memorial Day, May 31, 1948, a throng of 46,965 stuffed Wrigley Field to see the Cubs and Pirates split a doubleheader. On that day, major league baseball shattered its all-time single-day attendance record—raising the possibility that postwar crowds were simply crazy for baseball, whether or not it was well played. Baseball had become such an established part of the culture that the papers barely commented on the attendance record the next day. Was loving the Cubs no longer a story?

What was a story was the August 26, 1948, near-riot in a game against the Boston Braves, who would go on to win the National League flag. This time, 27,315 were on hand for the doubleheader. After the Cubs took the first contest 5–1, Phil Cavarretta came up in the third inning of game 2 with Chicago down 1–0. With two men on, Cavarretta lined a shot to left field. Jeff Heath, Boston's left fielder, couldn't find the ball; he thought it had gotten stuck in the ivy. Cubs catcher Bob Scheffing, sitting in the bullpen, claimed that the ball was on the ground the whole time. Cavarretta circled the bases for an apparent three-run inside-the-park homer. The Braves protested, and the umpires ruled the play a ground-rule double, which allowed just one man to score.

"Straw hats, bottles, and paper sailed out of the grandstand and bleachers," reported Harry Warren in the August 27 *Tribune*. "Umpire Jocko Conlan tried to take command and raced across the diamond to berate a policeman in the Cubs' dugout for not stopping the noise." Once Chicago skipper Charlie Grimm emerged from the dugout to protest Conlan's actions, the fans booed again, throwing more hats, bottles, paper cups, and scorecards. "Because of the debris in center field," Warren continued, "the umpires announced that any ball that fell in the paper would be a double. [Boston] Manager Billy Southworth protested this and refused to permit the game to continue until the field was cleared. This was done." After Andy Pafko was intentionally passed, Peanuts Lowrey hit a bases-clearing triple off Vern Bickford. Chicago won 5–2, and the crowd was mollified. The Cubs finished that year a lowly 64–90, but it doesn't seem that there were any riots on that account.

GIRLS, GIRLS, GIRLS

Among the crowds were, as ever, lots of ladies. A September 13, 1952, photo essay on Ladies Day at Wrigley in *Collier's* showed that many of these "ladies" were teenagers. Some wanted autographs; others spelled out players' names in masking tape on their blue jeans. Some fought hard to reach foul balls. This was not a particularly genteel crowd.

"There's a lot of shrieking, and screaming," said then-manager Phil Cavarretta, "but you know the women are behind you on every play."

Well, not all of them. In 1949, one young lady had a much more negative influence on the team. Ruth Steinhagen, born in suburban Cicero in 1929, was an obsessive Cubs fan. First, she had a crush on outfielder Peanuts Lowrey, who had once been a child actor in the *Our Gang* comedies; later, she turned her attentions to Eddie Waitkus, a slick-fielding first baseman who had joined Chicago in 1946.

The Cubs dealt the popular and handsome Waitkus to the Phillies in December 1948. By the next June, when Philadelphia visited Chicago, the disturbed Steinhagen had become obsessed with Waitkus, whom she had never met. She hatched a plot to kill him, believing that if she couldn't have him, nobody should. On June 19, Steinhagen booked a room at the Edgewater Hotel, some twenty blocks north of Wrigley Field, and lured Waitkus upstairs by leaving him a note signed by a "Ruth Ann Burns," whom the player thought might be a relative of an old ballplaying friend of his from Boston. When Waitkus reached Steinhagen's room, she pulled out a rifle and fired a bullet through his chest.

Waitkus survived, but barely. It scarred him for life, both physically and emotionally—though through the version of his story told by Bernard Malamud in *The Natural*, he became a baseball icon. According to Waitkus biographer John Theodore, Steinhagen was institutionalized in Kankakee, south of Chicago, until 1952. Waitkus passed away in 1972, but Steinhagen lived on the near Northwest Side of Chicago until December 2012, when she died.

This wasn't the first time that a female fan had gunned down a Chicago player. During the 1932 season, a showgirl named Violet Valli shot Cubs infielder Billy Jurges at the Hotel Carlos where they both lived, just a little bit north of Wrigley Field. Valli had wanted a relationship with Jurges, who demurred. Jurges was not seriously injured, and in fact did not even wish to prosecute the case.

SOME OLD BUSINESS

Prior to the beginning of the 1951 season, the Cubs finally rotated the box and grandstand seats down the right-field line toward home plate, completing a process begun in 1938. The renovation, which involved ripping out huge sections of the grandstand and boxes, rebuilding the cement foundation, and reinstalling new seats at a different angle, was made only to the lower deck, although the Cubs did install new bolted-in folding chairs for the upstairs patrons.

Workers also spent the 1949–50 and 1950–51 off-seasons installing new box seats in various sections. A crew of 150 worked tirelessly through March and early April 1951 to complete the new lower deck, made of monolithic reinforced concrete, in time for the season. The weather had been very poor in the late winter and early spring. In addition, the outfield grass did not grow and had to be resodded close to Opening Day. On April 14, 1951, the day of a city series game against the White Sox at Wrigley and three days prior to Opening Day, the Cubs announced that the repairs were complete. (The postseason city series was suspended in 1942 due to World War II and never regained traction despite several further attempts.) The club invited the workmen and their wives or girlfriends to attend the Cubs-Sox exhibition held at Wrigley on Sunday, April 15. Unfortunately, the temperature was just thirty-seven degrees and many workers elected to stay home. The April 16 *Sun-Times*'s John Hoffman reported that the Cubs sold six hundred gallons of coffee to the sixty-three hundred fans on hand.

SLAMMIN' SAMMY

The Cubs' April 17, 1951, Opening Day ceremonies included a 450-foot hit that sailed over the huge center-field scoreboard. Unfortunately the drive came not from one of the Cubs but from, prior to the game, golfer Sam Snead, who—in his street clothes, with a recently broken left hand, and not using a tee—used a four-iron to hit a golf ball off the scoreboard from home plate. He then used a two-iron to clear the scoreboard from the same spot.

It was another cold day, but the 18,211 fans left happy because the Cubs beat the Reds 8–3. Old-timers Gabby Hartnett, Freddie Lindstrom, and Charlie Root were all on hand, the latter as the Cubs' new first-base coach. Also present was seventy-eight-year-old semipro entrepreneur Billy Niesen, still spry and full of vinegar as he shook hands, told jokes, and brought up memories of the old days. As president of the local Old Timers' Baseball Association, Niesen presided over many an annual off-season banquet and beer bust for Chicago fans, writers, and players.

It was all downhill from here, as the Cubs finished last, at 62–92.

OLD-TIME BASEBALL

The 1952 season started soggily. After a week's worth of rain, which canceled some of the preseason Cubs-Sox series and made a mess of Bobby Dorr's newly seeded field, the Cubs opened at home on April 18, bare patches in the outfield and all. "The Cubs are introducing one refreshing novelty to the usual opening-day ceremonies," noted the *Sun-Times*'s Edgar Munzel that morning. "There will be no first-ball pitching by any of the politicians who are posturing and mugging with or without benefit of television in this election year."

Cubs GM Jim Gallagher decided that a loyal fan should toss out the ceremonial first pitch. The initial rooter chosen for this honor was fifty-three-year-old Eric Johnson of upstate Rockford, attending his thirtieth straight opener at Wrigley Field. After the first pitch, and the customary band music and flag raising, the Cubs—down 4–1 in the last of the ninth—rallied for four runs and won 5–4 on a two-run double by Bill "Willie the Whip" Serena before 20,396.

Gallagher's choice became a regular feature on Opening Day. Mrs. Adele Karstrom, a widow living in suburban Evanston, threw out the first wild one of the 1953 season. Ms. Karstrom had seen every Cubs home game since 1933 with the exception of the year 1942, when she lived in Los Angeles—and that year watched every contest at that city's Wrigley Field.

The following year, sixty-one-year-old South Sider Dan Kelly tossed out the first ball a few days after three thousand rooters welcomed the Cubs and White Sox home from spring training with a downtown ceremony.

CLOSED FOR GOOD

On April 20, 1952, the Cubs announced that they were closing off four center-field bleacher sections at the request of Cardinals manager Eddie Stanky. The Cardinals skipper claimed that he wanted the sections blocked off because his hitters couldn't see the ball. According to the next day's *Sun-Times*, when Stanky requested that the Cubs keep the bleachers unoccupied for a hitting background, Chicago manager Phil Cavarretta was all for it, and GM Jim Gallagher gave his okay. The Cubs themselves had been complaining about the visibility problem since 1937, and it is likely that the team put the onus on Stanky to deflect criticism for what really was an internal decision. Cardinals superstar Stan Musial was pushing for the change, too. "When people are sitting in the middle sections of the center field bleachers, it's just impossible to follow the ball," he said. "That's why Roy Campanella was beaned here last fall."

"Eddie Stanky has 2,200 individual enemies in Chicago," quoted an uncredited article in the following day's *American*. "That's the number of persons a Stanky request deprived from sitting in the sun yesterday at Wrigley Field." Nevertheless, this time, the Cubs' decision to reduce the bleacher count stuck, although the amount of lost seats would be decreased.

On April 25, with the Cubs entertaining Cincinnati, Jim Gallagher announced that three of the four centerfield sections of the bleachers, consisting of some twelve hundred seats, would be closed for the remainder of the season (fig. 21), leaving the

FIGURE 21. While conditions at Wrigley—even for this Sox-Cubs Boys' Benefit exhibition game—were better than many at other major-league parks, they would be woefully inadequate today. This picture dates from between 1952 and 1960. By this time, the center-field bleachers had been permanently closed. (Credit: National Baseball Hall of Fame and Museum)

bleacher count at three thousand. "Closing the sections will mean a sacrifice of $750 on days when the bleachers ordinarily would be jammed," the *Tribune* reported on April 27.

With the improved visibility for hitters, home runs and runs scored at Wrigley Field almost immediately increased. Wrigley didn't, however, become one of the best parks in baseball for hitters until other, smaller parks, such as the Polo Grounds, Ebbets Field, Braves Field, and Shibe Park were shuttered and larger ones, like Dodgers Stadium, Milwaukee County Stadium, and Candlestick Park were built.

SINKING

Even with their improved offense, the Cubs in the early 1950s had become almost a joke, nearly irrelevant in their hometown. Meanwhile, the White Sox had gotten off the mat in the junior circuit. That doesn't mean that nobody came out to see the Cubs, but the team often had to give tickets away. Ladies Days (Wednesdays in 1953) remained staggeringly popular, with this the first year that the ladies did not have to pay tax or service charges on their freebies. The Cubs for several years after World War II also distributed up to five hundred tickets a game, through the USO, to military veterans.

During these years, Opening Day festivities at Wrigley Field were trimmed to a minimum. Ceremonial first pitches and the raising of the American flag by marine color guards were all that was left of the elaborate ceremonies of previous decades.

One development that did prop up interest in the team was the move of the Braves franchise from Boston to Milwaukee in 1953. In the middle and late 1950s, when Milwaukee was manic over its new club, busloads of fans traveled to Wrigley Field for Braves/Cubs contests. Chicagoans would travel to Milwaukee as well, though not in such great numbers. On August 16, 1953, Wrigley Field hosted 39,903 fans as the surprising Braves, second in the NL, swept the Cubs in a doubleheader. As a sign of the times, fan loyalties were divided.

PAY FOR PLAY

As the team continued to sink, it was not only management that was concerned about revenue. Prior to the Cubs' 1954 home opener, Chicago player representative Ralph Kiner announced to the media that he and his teammates would forthwith demand a $100 fee for any radio or television interview appearance. Kiner stated that this was not intended as a shakedown. Rather, he explained, "Most of the players would just rather not go on those programs which come when we have to interrupt fielding or batting practice before games." Amazingly enough, Cubs personnel director Wid Matthews stated that he agreed with the players in this regard. (Imagine a front office today telling the press that they'd have to pay for interviews.)

Broadcasters, unhappy with the idea of having to pay players for their time, used this opportunity to begin soliciting gifts (clock radios, etc.) for prospective guests on pregame shows. In a juicy irony, Kiner, while a broadcaster for the Mets, attempted in 1964 to interview Phillies pitcher Jim Bunning, who had just tossed a perfect game. Bunning greeted Kiner with a request for payment before he went on screen.

BLOWUP

On Opening Day 1954, April 15, rain delayed the start of the game, chopped batting practice in half, and made the field a mess. In addition, the 17,271 spectators were surprisingly rowdy. Ed Prell in the *Tribune* called it "one of Wrigley Field's most exuberant Opening Day crowds" and noted that it was quite raucous. Pat Pieper had to warn the fans several times not to throw papers onto the field. Several fans exploded firecrackers in the stands.

The fireworks did not extend to the Cubs offense, as the Reds blasted the Cubs 11–5—the first of ninety losses that year. Popular outfielder Hank Sauer had a good year, with forty-one home runs. Even better for him, on August 22 he was honored with a sports car, a hunting dog, and—courtesy of Mary Joseph, the president of his local fan club—a huge tub of sauerkraut. During the game, a 12–6 loss to Milwaukee in which Sauer went an inconsequential one-for-five, fans threw packets of chewing tobacco onto the grass in right field. This gifting delayed the game for about two minutes while Sauer and center-fielder Bob Talbot collected the packages and, according to the *Tribune*'s Irving Vaughan the next day, "stored them in the ivy vines on the right-field fence for safe keeping until the end of the game."

These sorts of celebrations in which fans, fellow players, club officials, and sometimes members of the press contributed to buy gifts for popular star-quality performers, disappeared from the

American sports scene by the early 1970s; the Cubs held one for Ernie Banks in 1964, one for Billy Williams in 1969, and another for Ron Santo in 1971. With baseball players now making salaries far higher than most fans, writers, and even team officials, there seemed to be no need to give them anything but applause and respect. Besides, in the interim years, there weren't many Cubs worthy of the honors.

ROBBERS' QUARTERS

Prior to the 1955 campaign, the Cubs repainted most of the ballpark, as they often did between seasons. The job wasn't finished until early April, but the lower exterior of the park and the ninety-foot-tall foul poles, among other things, were done. The mild winter of 1954–55 allowed Bobby Dorr to resod the entire field with uncommon success; the field was in remarkably good shape by Opening Day. But the biggest change at Wrigley Field for 1955 was a new room for umpires. Previously pent up in a small anteroom off the visitors' clubhouse behind first base, the arbiters now moved to new quarters under the stands down the left-field line. This $30,000 room was, according to the April 9 *Tribune*, "Plush with a capital P." Unlike any other umpires' quarters in baseball, the Wrigley Field sanctuary included a television, a new shower room done in marble, natural birch cabinets, and a sitting room with Naugahyde cushions, end tables, and a writing desk. Otis Shepard, the Wrigley Company's the art director, designed the room.

Another innovation at the stadium that year was the debut of in-house audio. The team piped in the sound from the Cubs' TV broadcasts—usually the voice of Jack Brickhouse—via speakers to a section of the left-field bleachers. This feature appears to have lasted until the early 1960s.

This was a benign enough innovation—and America in the 1950s was awash in innovations, whether or not they were was actually useful. P. K. Wrigley presented another ballpark "first" on July 21, 1956, when the Cubs debuted a "speedwalk" in the aisle leading to the upper deck on the right-field side. Like the moving walkways used at airports, this device carried fans up but not back down. (The first day the speedwalk operated, a torrential rainstorm hit Wrigley Field. High winds snapped a huge bolt of metal off one of the eight-foot flagpoles on the grandstand roof and sent it flying into a box seat, slightly injuring a twelve-year-old boy and a thirty-seven-year-old man. The game between the Giants and Cubs was eventually called off.)

The speedwalk, fraught with mechanical problems, never really caught the fans' imagination after the first wave of novelty wore off. The late park doyen E. R. "Salty" Saltwell recalled that it was shut down around 1960.

THE SAD YEARS

Despite the general dearth of quality players in this time, Sam Jones—nicknamed "Sad Sam" both for his expression and his demeanor, and "Toothpick" for the ever-present wedge of wood between his teeth—was a memorable pitcher for the Cubs during the 1950s. As a rookie in 1955, he paced the NL in both strikeouts and walks; he won two more strikeout crowns before his career ended in the early 1960s.

Before his start on May 12, 1955, WGN-TV's Harry Creighton bantered with Jones, promising to buy him a solid gold toothpick if he no-hit the visiting Pirates. Jones apparently took Creighton seriously. Only 2,918 fans were at the ballpark on the overcast afternoon, but all of them were on their feet in the top of the ninth. Jones hadn't allowed a hit and had gone two-for-four with an RBI as the Cubs led 4–0. Jones walked the first three hitters he faced in the ninth—Gene Freese, Preston Ward, and leadoff man Tom Saffell. Rearing back for a bit extra, he then struck out Dick Groat and right-fielder Roberto Clemente, then in his first season. Frank Thomas, the Bucs' top slugger, stepped to the plate. Jones whiffed him on a 1–2 count and became the first African American to toss a no-hitter. This was the first such gem at Wrigley Field since 1917. He got his gold toothpick.

Sam Jones opened the following season with another gem: a complete-game four-hitter. Despite a high of forty-one degrees, the Cubs whipped the Reds 12–1. Everett Gregerson, a local cabbie who had gone to all but twelve games at Wrigley since getting out of the Army in 1946, threw out the first pitch with a replica of the ball Albert Spalding made for the National League back in 1876. Once again, however, the season that unfolded from there was a disappointment, with the Cubs finishing last, at a dismal 60–94.

Nevertheless, fans came back the following year for another opener. Eighty-one-year-old William Klose, who had been to his first Cubs game back in 1886, handled the ceremonial first pitch, whipping the ball from the mound on the fly to Cubs catcher Cal Neeman. The Cubs could have used his arm in the season that followed, in which they won only two more games than in the previous year. That day, a Marine Corps reserve corps raised the flag, and Mayor Richard J. Daley, Illinois Governor William B. Stratton, NL President Bill Giles, and 23,674 fans watched the Cubs lose 4–1 to the Milwaukee Braves.

At least the team was prettier to look at in 1957. The newspapers were abuzz because for the first time in many years, the Cubs took to the field in pinstriped uniforms, a style they have kept to this day. The Cubs' new caps, though, were another matter; the odd-looking hats featured six strands of white piping from top to bottom.

The appearance of Wrigley Field itself was also a factor; Phil Wrigley had been letting the ballpark slip. Bill Veeck Jr. later wrote: "By 1959, Wrigley was no longer keeping the park freshly painted. The neighborhood had deteriorated badly. None of that mattered. People came into Wrigley Field *knowing* they were comfortable." There is some truth in that statement, but people weren't coming to Wrigley to be comfortable; not many were coming at all. From 1956 through 1958, the Cubs' attendance was seventh among eight NL clubs. They ranked sixth in 1959, last in 1960, seventh in 1961, and when the league expanded to ten teams in 1962, Chicago's attendance ranked last.

And not all of this can be blamed on larger trends, like white flight and television, because people were still going to see the White Sox. Between 1953 and 1967, the White Sox' attendance ranked better among AL teams than the Cubs in the NL every single season.

Few people recall as "glorious" the days when the Cubs were a horrible team watched by progressively fewer people (fig. 22). The Cubs seemed to have become irrelevant even to baseball, and this perception didn't abate until the Cubs became competitive in 1967. The lesson of the postwar era is one that they should have learned before—that building a good team and taking proper care of the park was difficult but necessary.

PASS THE SALTY

Things needed to be fixed, and in 1958 some good steps were taken. The Cubs began another park improvement program, this time replacing most of the original brick walls from the 1914 construction with buff-colored concrete. Wrigley budgeted $1 million for the effort, which also included sprucing up the ticket windows.

Salty Saltwell worked as an executive in Des Moines and other outposts in the Cubs farm system during the 1950s. In 1958, Wrigley summoned him to Chicago and hired him as the team's assistant secretary-treasurer—he was to go on to hold some thirteen different positions with the team until his retirement in 1990. Saltwell's first order of business was to straighten out some shady business practices in the Wrigley Field ticket and concession offices. Apparently, some individuals in the offices had been siphoning revenue, although Saltwell never publicly disclosed the names of the guilty.

After longtime traveling secretary Bob Lewis fell ill, Saltwell assumed those responsibilities for the 1959 and 1960 seasons.

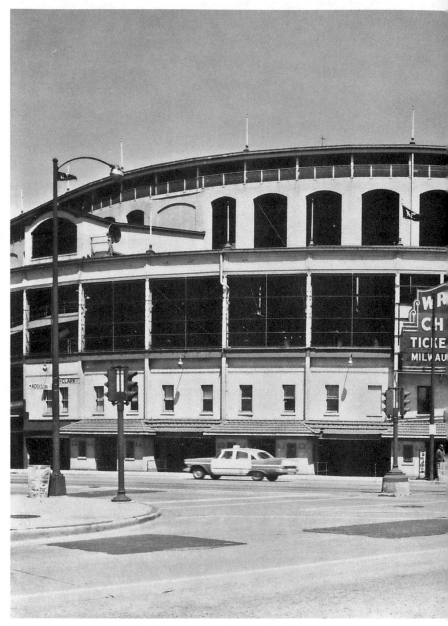

FIGURE 22. Few fans are bothering Wrigley Field's ticket agents in
this 1958 photo of a very sleepy Clark and Addison.
(Credit: National Baseball Hall of Fame and Museum)

When replaced as traveling secretary in 1961 by Don Biebel, Saltwell returned to his true bailiwick, park operations. At that point, he pushed for and helped oversee several critical improvements to the park, including permanent seating, new painting, and new rest rooms, in the space of a few years. When the Cubs started to win again in 1967, the park was ready.

TAKE ME OUT TO THE BALL GAME

Miss Lavon Carroll served up the first song of the 1958 season at Wrigley Field on April 18 at 1:00 P.M. But rather than singing "The Star-Spangled Banner," she belted out "Take Me Out to the Ball Game." Five marines marched out to the right-field corner and hoisted the flag. Seventy-three-year-old Frank P. Carter tossed out the first pitch. "Carter, a brown-suited, white-haired fellow, removed his topcoat and hat, seized the baseball, and lofted it from his third-base box into the north wind and onto the field," reported David Condon in the April 19 *Tribune*. In his column, Condon also found it necessary to mention—twice—that Miss Carroll had a twenty-three-inch waist. You can hardly blame the man for being uninterested in the nominal main attraction in these years.

The Cubs did win that day, 11–6. But after a hot start, they cruised to an eventual sixth-place finish. Even the sportswriters were complaining. Robert Cromie complained in the *Tribune* on July 2, "Heaven knows how many ulcers or cases of extreme dyspepsia got their start in press boxes during those interminable double headers from the cold cheese sandwiches on stale bread, tepid hot dogs, and acid coffee." Of course, Cromie and the others should have had little reason to complain; in those days, they ate free at the park.

One of the high points of this season at Wrigley involved not playing at Wrigley. The words "subway doubleheader" are two of the sweetest words in the English language to Chicago baseball fans. Those rare days when both Chicago teams are at home, one playing in the afternoon and the other at night, provide a great contrast between ballparks, neighborhoods, and styles of play.

The first such day came on July 1, 1958. The White Sox pulled in 16,639 fans for a night game at Comiskey Park while the Cubs and Giants drew 16,549 at Wrigley Field. The Cubs took the day game 9–5, with the biggest kick coming in the home half of the first. Tony Taylor grounded a ball past third base and toward the left-field corner. Giants left-fielder Leon Wagner chased the ball but lost sight of it. Cubs pitchers in the bullpen jumped from their perches and made it seem as if the ball were rattling around the bench. Wagner took the bait, looking behind the bench, thinking that the ball would be a ground-rule double—not realizing that the ball was sitting some ten feet past the bench near the foul line. One fan tried to point Wagner in the right direction while Taylor sped around the bases. Only after Taylor rounded third did Wagner locate the ball. The Giants protested, but the home run stood.

For once in these years, the Cubs had the better day, as the White Sox lost to the Yankees, 7–0.

ECCCH

The Cubs were at the point where they would try anything—anything, that is, apart from getting better players. Since 1945, they had finished third once (in 1946) and fifth once (in 1952). Otherwise, it was sixth, seventh, or eighth every season until 1966 (fig. 23).

In 1959, the Cubs tried altering their game starting times, opting for 2:00 on weekdays and 1:00 for Saturday and Sunday games. The reason given was that the times seemed to work well for pro football. The new start time didn't prevent an April 10 snowout on Opening Day 1959, the first cancelled Cubs opener in years. Presumably even Everett Lee, who first saw the Cubs play in 1903 and threw out the first pitch on April 11, didn't remember dropping a game due to snowfall.

OFFICIAL PROGRAM 10¢

CHICAGO CUBS · WRIGLEY FIELD

FIGURE 23. Graphic artist Otis Shepard's lovely designs, which graced Cubs scorecards for many years, were often more attractive than what was on the field. (Credit: National Baseball Hall of Fame and Museum)

But the biggest news at Wrigley Field that April was the last-minute evasion of a possible vendor's strike. Vendors union local 236 asked Cubs management for a guarantee of $5 per vendor in case of games called by rain as well seeking a hike in commissions. The Cubs agreed on the guarantee but balked at the commission raise. The two sides came to an agreement before Opening Day.

The most memorable moment of that season came on June 30, when somehow two balls were in play at once. Cardinals star Stan Musial walked in the fourth inning. The Cubs argued that ball four, which sailed by catcher Sammy Taylor, actually had grazed Musial's bat—meaning that Musial should not have been given first base. Taylor didn't chase the ball, however, and Musial, with no one stopping him, alertly headed for second. Plate umpire Vic Delmore absent-mindedly handed pitcher Bob Anderson a new ball, while third baseman Al Dark retrieved the original ball from the Cubs batboy. Clearly, the original ball was still in play, despite Delmore's error. Both Dark and Anderson, intending to retire Musial, fired balls toward second at the same time. Anderson's throw sailed over second baseman Tony Taylor's head, but Dark's toss bounced to Ernie Banks, who tagged out Musial between second and third.

Players and managers from both clubs ran onto the field and began arguing. The whole episode succeeded in "promoting perhaps the most hilarious moments ever witnessed in the staid North Side park," in the words of the *Tribune*'s Ed Prell the following day. "Not even Bill Veeck of the White Sox"—who by now had an epic reputation for ridiculous stunts—"could have conjured up such a zany episode."

The umpiring crew eventually ruled Musial out, but the resulting Saint Louis protest was rendered unnecessary as the Cardinals won 4–1. The National League cashiered umpire Delmore over the winter.

THE LONGEST

The Cubs did set one NL record in 1959. On August 14, Chicago blew out the visiting Giants 20–9. The nine-inning contest took three hours and fifty minutes to complete, the longest period ever for a regulation game. Pitchers from both teams combined to walk nineteen hitters. The clubs combined to belt eight homers and leave twenty-one men on base. The Giants actually led 7–6 after three innings, but the Cubs scored four in the fourth, two in the sixth, six in the seventh, and two in the eighth. They scored in seven of their eight frames. A crowd of 17,963 witnessed the carnage.

INSIDE JOB

The renovations begun in 1958 continued in various forms. In 1960, the Cubs clubhouse was relocated from on the mezzanine level on the third-base side to a new structure in the left-field corner that came complete with a lounge, a trainer's room, and a separate manager's office. (The old upstairs cubbyhole is now the ballpark's security headquarters.) The visitors' clubhouse was also expanded and spiffed up. The Cubs built the new dressing room in the corner because it was, according to Salty Saltwell, the only space available. "That was still inadequate," Saltwell said of the left-field corner clubhouse, which remained in use until 1983. "With the clubs now, [it's] not only the 25 players on the active roster; [you have] your training rooms, your weight rooms, a whole new situation."

In addition, the club rebuilt more than a quarter of the lower grandstand in winter 1959–60, laying new concrete foundations and seat slabs. The foul screen behind home plate was replaced, with the new screen laid at a sharper angle. Workers also constructed a new fan entrance, with new ticket booths and facade, at Clark and Addison. Finally, the club repainted the scoreboard and resodded the playing surface. The team estimated the cost of the repairs to be $400,000.

NOTHING TO HIDE

All the renovations to the interior did nothing for the results on the field. Hopes spring eternal, however. On April 22, 1960, the weather was the best that anyone could remember for a Cubs opener, reaching eighty degrees. Eighty-three-year-old retired fireman John Miller and his wife threw out first pitches, and Pat Pieper began his fifty-seventh year as the Cubs' field announcer. (He really did make his public address statements from the field, sitting near the backstop, close enough to hear the umpire officially announce new players into the game.) The Cubs lost to the Giants, 10–8, but Dick Dozer in the April 23 *Tribune* reported that the bleachers were the real center of activity as "a young lady did an impromptu—and complete—striptease."

The next day, the Giants destroyed the Cubs 18–2 in front of, in Dozer's words, "an unbelieving assemblage of 24,703." He continued: "Spectator shenanigans have been at a new high in the balmy weather the last two days . . . one damsel was escorted from her box seat near first base due to over-imbibing. Youths have been climbing the new backstop screen to wrestle baseballs thru the mesh during the game's progress, and Saturday, hundreds of youngsters trampled over the field to hamper a TV crew attempting to make a film."

At least someone was having fun. Elsewhere, beyond the stands, ineptitude reigned. On April 24, George Altman of the Cubs walked on just three balls. Umpire Ken Burkhart forgot the count after calling a balk on Giants pitcher Billy O'Dell.

HIGHS AND LOWS

The Cubs obtained hard-throwing right-handed pitcher Don Cardwell from the Phillies on May 13, 1960, in a four-player deal. Two days later he made his first Chicago start in the second half of a Sunday doubleheader at Wrigley Field against Saint Louis. An unexpected throng of 33,543 showed up.

After walking Alex Grammas in the first inning, Cardwell mowed the Cardinals down one by one without allowing a hit. In the eighth, Jerry Kindall at second base made a terrific play against Daryl Spencer, and Cardwell fanned pinch hitter Stan Musial to retire the side.

The ninth began at 5:45 P.M. with the Cubs ahead 4–0 and shadows breaking across the field. Carl Sawatski lined hard to George Altman in right as the fans roared. Pinch hitter George Crowe flied to Richie Ashburn for the second out. Cardwell went to three-and-two on Cardinals leadoff man Joe Cunningham as the fans screamed. Cunningham rapped the next pitch to short left field. Slow-footed outfielder Walt "Moose" Moryn ran toward the infield in pursuit. "Come on, Moose!" exhorted telecaster Jack Brickhouse. Moryn picked the ball off his shoe tops and ran in holding the spheroid aloft, a huge smile creasing his face. Hundreds of fans broke onto the field to mob Cardwell.

Radio color man Lou Boudreau could barely get to Cardwell but did eventually carry on a short postgame interview as thousands of fans milled around the field, chanting and cheering. It was, as Jim Enright wrote, "Cubs' fans' biggest on-the-field celebration since Gabby Hartnett's famous homer in 1938." Edgar Munzel in the May 25 *Sporting News* observed, "It looked as if Cardwell actually was in danger of injury as the fans tried to get near their newfound hero." Eventually, Cardwell finished the interview with Boudreau and made it to the clubhouse.

Videotape exists for the last two innings of this game. It is apparently the oldest visual document of a regular season no-hitter. At the time, WGN-TV used just three cameras at Wrigley Field. One camera was behind the plate at field level, one was placed in the vacant center-field bleachers looking toward the plate (a WGN innovation), and the third took shots from the first row of the upper deck on the third-base side. The next year, WGN added a fourth camera, behind the plate in the upper deck.

Longtime Cubs fan Ray Kush, a nephew of 1940s Cubs pitcher Emil Kush, was thirteen years old in 1960 and happened to be at the ballpark that magical day. He recalled:

> Because of the doubleheader, it was a big crowd. During the second games of doubleheaders, a lot of fans would leave early. But because of the no-hitter, many more stayed. The shadows were falling, and it was about 6:00 when the Cubs made the last out. It was so exciting, my friend Bucky and I just followed a lot of other fans right onto the field.
>
> Did we go through the door, or just jump over the wall? I think we went over the wall. It was just a few seconds and the whole infield was full.

Kush became part of the milling mob that nearly squashed Cardwell and Boudreau. "I'd never do something like that now," Kush remarked.

Cardwell's achievement and the momentary ecstasy it induced aside, the Cubs were bad in 1960. On August 1, Jerome Holtzman of the *Sun-Times* took aim at Phil Wrigley as Chicago's NL entry staggered along in last: "One of the intriguing aspects of the Cubs is the myth which P. K. Wrigley has successfully created about himself. In this myth, P. K. pictures himself as a 'hands-off' owner . . . that he is merely a figurehead with his subordinates making all the important decisions. But this is simply not true. It's Wrigley, himself, who sits at the head of the table and makes the final decisions. That the Cubs are dying is not news, but they are disintegrating like a tree. They are dead at the top."

The on-field madness continued four days later, when Cincinnati Reds infielder Billy Martin took exception to a high and inside pitch and punched Cubs pitcher Jim Brewer in the face, smashing the orbital bone near Brewer's right eye. The Cubs won 5–3 anyway to move within twenty and a half games of first place.

OUTSIDE ATTRACTIONS

The following year, 1961, was no better. On the field, the team debuted the preposterous "College of Coaches," in which eight hapless men were tasked with rotating the job of manager. It didn't help—in fact, it led to total chaos and a dearth of leadership rather than an excess of it.

As in too many other seasons, the highlights were off the field. During the sixth inning of an otherwise sleepy 6–5 Cubs loss to the Giants on May 28, a kerosene-powered hot dog cart exploded in the box seats down the right-field line. The cart shot flames twenty feet into the air, and ballpark personnel could not extinguish the conflagration. It took the men from Engine 78, the firehouse just down the block on Waveland Avenue, to drop a hose over the right-field stands and quickly put out the fire.

A more significant off-field development came in November, when the Collins and Wiese Coal Yard, which had operated just west of the ballpark since the early 1900s, moved about twenty blocks south, selling the property to fast-food franchiser Henry's Drive-In. Henry's spent some $700,000 on property acquisition, demolition of the coal facility, and paving. The company was already operating successful locations near Comiskey Park, Chicago Stadium, and the popular Riverview amusement park, some fifteen blocks west of Wrigley, and had more than a hundred locations nationwide at the time. The new Henry's lot had enough space for two hundred cars. It remained open next to Wrigley Field into the early 1970s, by which time then the novelty of drive-ins had faded. After Henry's closed down, the fast-food gap was filled by Yum Yum Donuts.

A COLD START

As bad as things had been, no quantity of fast food could soothe the desperation of 1962. Opening Day at Wrigley Field was Friday, April 13—indeed an omen, as the team was about to suffer through its worst season. As baseball teams do, the Cubs entered the season full of optimism, but they dropped three straight at Houston to the brand-new Colt .45s, then returned home to find only 9,750 fans waiting at freshly painted Wrigley Field on a bitterly cold day. Before the Cubs and Cardinals took the field, long-time traveling secretary Bob Lewis, who had retired after thirty-three years, tossed the first ice ball.

It was so frigid that Saint Louis manager Johnny Keane built a fire under the stands so that his pitchers could stay warm. To make everyone on the premises even more miserable, the contest went on for fifteen innings—four hours and forty minutes—and the Cubs lost 9–5. Rookie outfielder Lou Brock led off the Cubs first inning with a home run onto Sheffield Avenue. (Later that season, Brock homered into the Polo Grounds' center-field bleachers, some 460 feet away, becoming only the second player ever to do so.) For the year, he hit .263 with nine homers. Management was disappointed.

The most important event of 1962 at Wrigley Field occurred on July 24, when the first intercontinental broadcast, carried around the world via the Telstar broadcast satellite, brought a short piece of a Cubs-Phillies game to an estimated 200 million viewers. WGN's Ward Quaal, a critical figure in Chicago's early television broadcasting history, had offered the U.S. Information Agency some representative programming for the Telstar, and by luck a game happened to be on the schedule the very day of the international broadcast.

As millions watched, most of them in countries with no concept of baseball whatsoever, longtime Cubs telecaster Jack Brickhouse described Philadelphia infielder Tony Taylor's flyout to George Altman and Johnny Callison's single to right. The entire segment at Wrigley Field lasted just over ninety seconds. "Our translators are at this moment going out of their minds trying to figure out how to say 'runs, hits, and errors' in Italian and Swedish," Brickhouse joked.

WGN's Carl Meyers explained the complex setup in the next day's *Tribune*:

> The voices of Brickhouse and others were picked up from the WGN booth high in the Wrigley Field stands. The pictures were picked up from the four regular camera positions on the field and overlooking it. The signals then were sent by wire and coaxial cable to the big remote control truck situated under the stands.
>
> From the truck, by wire and coaxial cable, the TV signals were sent to the Illinois Bell Telephone company headquarters downtown, and then, in turn, to WNBQ [now WMAQ] in the Merchandise Mart; the New York network headquarters, where all segments of the three-network pool pickup were assembled for transmission over land lines or micro-wave relay to Andover, Me.; and then to Telstar, 3,000 miles up in the air.

Telstar was a much bigger hit that year than the Cubs. On December 22, the surf-music instrumental "Telstar," written by Joe Meek and recorded by the Tornadoes, became the first song by a British group ever to hit number one on the *Billboard* charts—a full thirteen months before the Beatles did.

The Cubs were getting a fair amount of media attention,

despite their wretched play. Less than a week after the Telstar broadcast, the Cubs hosted 1962's second All-Star Game (in 1960 1961, and 1962, two All-Star games were held per year) and the first in Wrigley since 1947. This was a big enough deal that for the first time in a decade (and the last time to date) Chicago management chose to open the center-field bleachers. Sacrificing the quality of play for a few more cheeks in seats at an exhibition game seems especially mercurial, even for baseball, but the player representatives approved the plan; more people in the park meant more proceeds for the players. The best box seats cost $8 and $6, depending on location.

Barry Gifford, a writer who grew up going to Cubs games, recalls waiting in line for All-Star tickets in his memoir, *The Neighborhood of Baseball*: "Steve [Friedman] and I were determined to have our regular bleacher seats for the game and so joined an already considerable bleachers box office queue at four o'clock the morning of the game. Fans had set up card tables, playing by lantern light; some were wrapped up in sleeping bags; others were crouched down against the wall passing wine or whiskey bottles. The ticket sale began about ten." Some 38,359 fans jammed Wrigley Field for the contest. The bleachers were filled by 11:00, two hours before game time. Friedman and Gifford both got their seats.

This was the biggest game in Wrigley since 1945. The jammed press bus received a motorcycle escort from the journalists' hotel to Wrigley. Andy Frain hired 350 ushers, who were on hand at 7:00 A.M. for training. A Chicago Police battalion was also on hand. Arch Ward's widow, Helen, threw out the first ball, while dignitaries, including Joe Cronin, Will Harridge, Stan Hack, Ray Schalk, Bill Nicholson, and Cal Hubbard, looked dignified. Amazingly, Cubs Ernie Banks, Billy Williams, and George Altman all appeared in the game. In the eighth inning, Banks tripled off the center-field wall and scored on Williams's groundout. The National League still lost 9–4.

Years later, Jerome Holtzman noted that, when asked by the *Daily News*'s Jack Kuenster if he was going to attend the game, Phil Wrigley demurred. The peculiar Cubs owner commented that he'd rather a fan have the tickets and that he'd get a better view of the game if he stayed home and watched it on television. This comment, of course, led to derision. Bill Veeck, who had operated the crosstown White Sox until the previous season, gloated, "He's telling the fans to stay home and watch the game on television!"

This was, of course, what Cubs fans all over the city were already doing—or at the very least, they were staying home. Overall attendance at Wrigley fell that year to 609,802, the lowest of any club in the majors and the franchise's worst since 1943. And no wonder: the team went 59–103, its poorest record ever. They had the distinction of finishing ninth (out of ten teams) for the first time—possible only because of the new expansion franchises that year in Houston and New York. Embarrassingly, Houston won five more games than the Cubs; the Cubs did manage to outperform the Mets—whose bumbling 1962 squad was one of the very worst teams of all time. Bravo.

I'M A LOSER

What, to put it plainly, was Philip Wrigley's problem?

When he went to watch games—and he did, contrary to popular belief—P. K. Wrigley tried to blend in with the crowds, sitting in grandstand seats rather than drawing attention in his field box. Said Claude Brooks, secretary of the Wrigley Company in 1977, "He always tried to go incognito because he wanted to be in the position of the fan. He said you would never find out how the fans were treated if you went and sat in the owner's box." Wrigley was willing to risk ridicule, or outright assault, from fed-up fans, even though he had plenty of reason to hide.

The Cubs were at their lowest ebb in decades. With a ridiculous managerial system—the College of Coaches had not been abandoned—a club of mediocrities, a fan base shrunk by poor management, and the contrasting strong play of the White Sox, the North Siders didn't seem to have a hope. Wrigley said at the time, "When the bulldozer breaks down, it's time to change the driver." As Jerome Holtzman wrote later, "What he didn't realize, or refused to acknowledge, was that it was the bulldozer that required repair."

Crowds in the low thousands were common. As George Castle pointed out in *The Million-to-One Team*, Wrigley often lost money just by opening up his gates for the few thousand who might trickle in—an amazing feat for a baseball team.

Did P. K. Wrigley care? Of course he did. He had a competitive streak just like anyone else, as well as a cast-iron ego. But did he care enough to risk his ego, get rid of the dead wood, hire bright new people, and risk hearing "no" from his subordinates?

Wrigley was an innovator, an inventor, a tinkerer. He certainly wasn't afraid to try new things—the College of Coaches is evidence of that—but any new ideas he would try were his own. He didn't want to be forced by public opinion, the press, changing social conditions, or the National League into adopting any new strategy he didn't want to implement unless it became absolutely necessary.

P. K. Wrigley put the "no" in "nowhere man." Integration? Not his idea. Night baseball wasn't his idea. Selling the team wasn't in his plans—though he was approached over the years by, among others, Ray Kroc, the mastermind behind McDonald's and friend of George Halas, owner of the Bears; Wrigley said no. Responding to player and press entreaties to fire manager Leo Durocher during the clubhouse wars of the early 1970s wasn't Wrigley's idea either. Nothing changed at Wrigley Field until Wrigley said it would change.

Wrigley appears to have been afraid of several things—of the media, of the public, of letting things get out of his hands. Hence, he created an organization full of yes-men afraid to tell him when his ideas were bad. And by the 1960s, they were. He may have known how to sell gum and even how to sell the ballpark experience, but his knowledge of baseball was simply inadequate.

Some have attributed his lack of innovation in hiring real baseball people to a generous streak, a paternalistic desire to provide security for his employees. Charlie Grimm said in 1977, "The reason he worked out that ten-coach system was just to give the men involved security. He confided that to me one time." While that kindness helped feed the families of Wrigley's baseball men, it didn't help the Cubs win—and in fact, it all but guaranteed that they would lose.

OFF THE BASES

Useful innovations did still crop up occasionally, though. Having been far from the head of the pack integrating on the field, the Cubs nevertheless hired the first black coach in Major League Baseball (MLB) history, Buck O'Neil, on May 30, 1962. Famous for many years for his goodwill, great storytelling, excellent Negro Leagues playing career, and pioneering work in scouting blacks for the majors, O'Neil joined the Chicago staff but was not part of the College of Coaches managerial rotation. O'Neil felt that GM John Holland and longtime Cubs fixture Charlie Grimm looked for any excuse to keep him under a bushel, despite his talents. In his autobiography, O'Neil recalled a game in Houston when two coaches in the Cubs' rotation were ejected. Grimm, sitting in the press box, directed pitching coach Freddie Martin to man the third-base coaching box rather than O'Neil.

Moreover, even though the Cubs had hired O'Neil, they could still be racist. George Castle quoted O'Neil as saying: "I got all these players, but they weren't playing them at the same time. I told Mr. Holland we'd have a better ball club if we played the blacks. Then he showed me a basket of letters from fans saying, 'What are you trying to do, make the Cubs into the Kansas City Monarchs?' We weren't appealing to the black fans anyway, playing on the North Side of Chicago."

If Holland and Grimm allowed their personal viewpoints, or

those of few prejudiced fans, to dictate on-field policy, then the Cubs organization was craven at best and racist at worst—and if they weren't fielding their best team or using their coaches effectively, then they weren't even doing the most basic part of their job. And Phil Wrigley bears responsibility for that—even as he gets credit for having hired O'Neil at all.

What Cubs fans wanted then—just as they want now—was a winning team. They took to Ernie Banks. They took to Billy Williams and Fergie Jenkins and Bill Madlock, just as they would later take to Andre Dawson and Sammy Sosa and Derrek Lee. They took to winners.

THE BEATINGS WILL CONTINUE
UNTIL MORALE IMPROVES

As a military and college man, Phil Wrigley had his own viewpoint on morale—much as he had his own viewpoint on pretty much everything. He decided that, for the 1963 season, the Cubs needed an athletic director. Apparently, nobody told P. K. that what might work for a college athletic program was a terrible idea for a major-league baseball team, so he hired six-foot-five, 230-pound former Air Force colonel Robert Whitlow to supervise the Cubs' field operations, training, conditioning, and the like. Bringing a crusty military man with no baseball experience into the already competitive College of Coaches was foolhardy, especially when Whitlow presumptuously took the field during workouts, toting a fungo bat and wearing jersey number 1.

On Opening Day that year, April 9, Whitlow did field drills with the players before the game. Some 18,556 fans braved temperatures below forty degrees and seventeen-mile-an-hour winds from center field—as did the players: at this time, the dugouts at Wrigley weren't heated. During the game, the band playing in the stands broke into a rousing chorus of "Jingle Bells," much to the chilled fans' satisfaction. Eight-year-old Linda Cody, Chicago's Easter Seals child of 1963—the charity had a poster child each year—tossed out the first ball.

The Dodgers won 3–2, but perhaps the biggest story of the day was that while Arthur Allyn, owner of the White Sox, was on hand, P. K. Wrigley was not. Whitlow admitted that the absence was troubling, but he said that the sixty-eight-year-old Wrigley had just undergone a hernia operation.

The first tangible evidence of Whitlow's effect on Wrigley Field came June 18 when the team, under his direction, installed a wire fence, painted green, atop the outfield wall in center field. This fence, measuring eight feet high and sixty-four feet wide, spanned the closed-off bleacher section. Ivy was planted on the fence to make it appear more natural. With the wire fence in place, the height now needed to hit a home run into the center-field bleachers was nineteen and a half feet.

According to Whitlow, Cubs players had requested the new fence. Cubs head coach Bob Kennedy, however, said that the fence was news to him, effectively distancing himself from Whitlow's decision. Meanwhile, GM John Holland, according to an unattributed note in the June 19 *Tribune*, claimed that both Chicago and opposing players wanted an even better hitting background. "We've changed the color of the vacant seats several times in the last several years trying for compatibility," he said. "We just hope this new dash of ivy does it." The fence remained through the 1963 and 1964 seasons then removed with little fanfare.

The fence was just one sign of the tension and lack of communication among Whitlow, Kennedy, and Holland. By Opening Day 1964, it was no secret that the dissension in the organization had reached a boiling point. Whitlow and one of the team's coaches came to blows on at least one occasion. The *Sun-Times*'s Jack Griffin spent some of his Opening Day with a photographer in tow, interviewing fans about their feelings concerning the front office. One fan, Allan Jones, noted in the April 18 issue, "I don't think we should have an athletic director. You got three guys telling everyone what to do. So who's going to listen to whom?"

To be fair to Whitlow, he tried to bring new thinking into the game, applying statistical analysis and planning that forty years later became an industry standard. But he was too early for the party and did not have the support of the traditional baseball minds of the organization. Wrigley, for his part, spent much of his summer at his home in Lake Geneva, Wisconsin, and was far removed from the front office tension. He simply allowed the Whitlow/Kennedy/Holland battle to continue.

STILL IN THE DARK

By the early 1960s, Wrigley Field wasn't crowded with fans, and other NL owners were noticing. Dodgers owner Walter O'Malley claimed, at the 1962 MLB winter meetings, that he lost money every time he brought his team to Chicago and that something should be done about that park without lights. While O'Malley probably would have commanded his limousine driver to stop so that he could pick up a penny from the street, his fellow owners were hardly less money conscious, and they also pressured Wrigley to add lights to his park.

Stubborn, determined, and civic minded as always, Wrigley asked the Lake View Citizens Council (LVCC) to come up with a petition against the idea of night baseball. Once the group collected five thousand signatures, Wrigley pointed to them and said there could be no lights at Wrigley Field. Asked in early 1964 why he refused to put lights in his park, Wrigley told Charles Chamberlain of the Associated Press, "Kids are our future fans. One reason we play in daylight is that they can see the games. They should be home at night. Another reason is that night baseball would have a deteriorating effect on the neighborhood. Another reason is that I think the game should be played in daytime."

HUBBS FANS BID KID ADIEU

As bad as things were when the Cubs played, they sometimes were worse when they didn't. Second baseman Kenny Hubbs wasn't much of a hitter, but he had been part of the 1963 team that had improved by twenty-three games from the previous year to finish 82–80, the team's best record since 1946. Hubbs crashed his small plane on February 13, 1964, outside of Provo, Utah, and died at age twenty-two. His death dispirited the club, ruined the defense, and shot Chicago into another down cycle that delayed progress until 1967.

A day after the home opener on April 18 (when the thermometer read eighty degrees), the *Tribune*'s Robert Markus reported on the pregame ceremony honoring Hubbs:

While the competing Cubs and Phillies stood at attention, heads bowed, along the third and first base lines, the Opening Day crowd of 18,868 rose for a minute of silent prayer. The storm clouds overhead gave an extra aspect of gloom to the proceedings.

As the announcer intoned, "Amen," a sudden gust of wind raised a whirlpool of dust over the second base area where Kenny Hubbs performed so brilliantly for the Cubs. Then it was gone . . . just as Hubbs is gone.

COMFORT STATIONS

The stadium itself was improved in one way prior to the opening of the 1964 season. While Wrigley Field did not get its usual coat of fresh paint, it did get its customary new sod (courtesy of Bobby Dorr's successor, Pete Marcantonio) and, most important, renovated rest rooms behind home plate. Facilities judged above average in 1947 were distinctly below par by 1964, with clubs in Milwaukee, Los Angeles, San Francisco, New York, and Houston playing in newer parks. Changes to Wrigley included new tiles on the walls; fluorescent lighting that was much brighter than the old bulbs; seven private stalls in the men's room and presumably more in the ladies' room; and a stainless-steel circular washstand (a technology still in use at Wrigley) operated by a treadle that allowed several people to wash their hands at the same time.

In the April 18 *American*, Bill Gleason remarked, "you have to say this for P. K. Wrigley. When he does something he does it in a big way . . . he has installed the major leagues' most modern comfort stations. Long after the score of the Cubs' '64 home opener has been mercifully forgotten, many fans will remember their first visit to the lavish new facilities that are located under the stands behind home plate." Similarly, Dick Hackenberg of the *Sun-Times* declared on April 18 that "the new men's rooms are the last word in relief stations. A new hand-washing gadget seems too readily convertible to a shower bath, but nobody was complaining. The women's rooms, too, are the acme of perfection, but this will have to come to you as pure hearsay from an unimpeachable source."

In addition to greater comfort at the stadium, some suburban fans could now enjoy easier access to it as well. On April 20, 1964, the Chicago Transit Authority debuted a new train line, the Skokie Swift, which ran nonstop from the Dempster Street depot in suburban Skokie to the Howard Street station at the north border of Chicago. Over the years, hundreds of thousands of Cubs fans from Skokie, Morton Grove, Lincolnwood, and other suburbs have taken the Swift to the Howard line (now the Red Line), which then transported them to Wrigley Field. Fares at the time for the Swift were forty-five cents for adults and twenty-nine cents for kids and students. Transfers to the Howard line were free.

OUT OF COMMISSION

The minimal changes to Wrigley Field in these years and the overall downturn in its upkeep seemed to be hinting that Chicago was soon to join a larger trend. During the 1960s, many cities spent millions of dollars on new multipurpose "superstadia." The National Football League was growing in popularity as baseball's influence was seen to be waning. Such new multiuse facilities had either opened or were planned in the New York region and Saint Louis, Oakland, Philadelphia, Pittsburgh, Houston, and Cincinnati, among other cities. All of these parks would host both football and baseball, just like Wrigley Field, but had the advantages of being larger, with better parking facilities, and in many cases, outfitted with artificial turf.

Chicago mayor Richard J. Daley was interested in a superstadium, too. He formed a commission in 1964 to investigate the matter. P. K. Wrigley and White Sox president Arthur Allyn, among others, were members of the group. At the Cubs' January 1964 media social, Wrigley told a pool of reporters, "I am in favor of building a community stadium in Chicago, something like the domed arena going up in Houston. It would be a civic enterprise. The Cubs, White Sox, and Chicago Bears would play there." The owner continued, somewhat shockingly, "We would play night games there. We would tear down Wrigley Field and sub-divide it for residential use. But I don't think there is much chance of it at all."

Wrigley was correct, at least, that no such stadium was to come. After Allyn quit the group, wishing to keep the Sox in their own park, and Wrigley bowed out citing an unspecified conflict of interest, the commission folded. The Bears did, however, leave Wrigley Field for Soldier Field at the end of the decade—actually going against the trend of consolidating teams in a single stadium.

(I WISH IT COULD BE) 1965 AGAIN

On January 8, 1965, Colonel Robert Whitlow, utterly frustrated, resigned his post as athletic director, effective January 31. The job of athletic director died with him, never to be reanimated. It was a bad winter. On the field, the sod didn't take, and for Opening Day the crew hurriedly sprayed green vegetable dye on the brown grass. That day, fans watched Al Jourgensen, a Cub employee for forty-one years, throw out the first ball. Jourgensen had worked as an usher, grounds crew member, office boy, press box attendant, and from 1946 on, scoreboard operator. Those in the first ten rows of the box seats sat in new "pop-up" plastic chairs, replacing the less comfortable, barely bolted-in seats of previous years. At last, the most expensive tickets bought the best seats. No batting practice was held, as the tarp remained on the field in threatening and chilly conditions.

The gloom lent extra poignancy to a short pregame memorial to radio voice Jack Quinlan, a rising star who had been killed in a spring-training auto crash in Arizona. Vince Lloyd, formerly the number-two man on Cubs telecasts with Jack Brickhouse, shifted to the radio booth to fill the vacancy and began his long and successful tenure as the "Voice of the Cubs," teaming with the equally popular Lou Boudreau.

The game, between the Cubs and Cardinals, was a cracker, going eleven full innings before being called a 10–10 tie due to darkness. The Cardinals plated five runs in the first, but the Cubs came back and eventually knotted things up with three runs in the last of the ninth on Ernie Banks's two-out home run off former Cub Barney Schultz. The 19,751 cold but enthusiastic fans also saw Saint Louis center-fielder Curt Flood make one of the greatest catches in the history of Wrigley Field, leaping the wall in left-center to snare a line drive hit by Len Gabrielson. "Never seen anything like it! *Never* seen anything like it!" screamed Cardinals radio man Harry Caray. Each team scored once in the eleventh before the umpires called it a day.

WHAT COULD BE SIMPLER THAN THE CUBS?

Despite the occasional exciting moment, the Cubs had grown—or fallen—into the role of lovable losers. Columnist Armand Schneider, in the April 12, 1965, *Daily News*, heralded Wrigley Field as the favorite playground of the "night shift," both ridiculing and romanticizing the pathetic state of the club and its dwindling fan base:

> The Cubs and the people who work at night deserve each other. During the daylight hours, they live in a perpetual stupor, clinging to each other like lost brethren. Each comes out of winter hibernation into the sunshine.

The Cubs are the comedy act for the night people, who sleep through such intellectual pastimes as the "Beverly Hillbillies" and "McHale's Navy" and "Peyton Place."

There is no other place to sit for the night people but in the bleachers . . . to sleep while the sun radiates its warmth into the open bleachers is almost sinful.

If the guy is really a swinger he sits in that little nook in the upper portion of the right-center field bleachers where the gamblers hang out. It's like a poor man's Las Vegas. Every pitch means a bet.

The White Sox are Chicago's sports equivalent of such deep-thinking stuff as Vietnam and the Berlin Wall and tax reform. Everyone takes the Sox too much to heart. It's the simple life a guy yearns for after a hard night's work, and what can be more simple than the Cubs?

As true as this was, the franchise was about to turn a corner. The first twenty years of the postwar era hadn't produced much but bafflement at the ways of P. K. Wrigley, but Cubs fans would soon have reason to hope.

NEW WINE IN OLD BOTTLES
WRIGLEY FIELD, 1966–1981

LIP SERVICE

Following the 1965 season, even P. K. Wrigley was forced to admit that the College of Coaches had failed, even with "head coach" Bob Kennedy mostly in charge for the last two years. So Wrigley made a big splash, hiring Leo Durocher, former manager of the Dodgers and Giants, known throughout the game for his fiery demeanor and unwillingness to take guff from anybody. He was as far from a collegial coach as could be.

On April 19, 1966, with Durocher holding the reins, the Cubs played their home opener against the Giants—though Durocher was in a minor car crash on the way to the park. One important change the Cubs made to the old yard was the installation of a new foul pole in left field. The previous pole had actually sat a few feet behind the left-field wall, which had led to some confusion on home-run calls. The new pole, like the right-field pole, sported a Cubs flag. Once again, a rather bitter spring had created problems for the sod, and Dick Dozer reported in the April 19 *Tribune* that a team painter "was spraying new sod in the outfield a bright green, and a ground crew member explained, 'They like it pretty for the color TV nowadays.'" After Louis Sudler sang the national anthem, backed by Henry Brandon's band, former Cub batboy Al Bluhm, who had been going to Cub openers for fifty years, threw out the first ball. Due to rain, only 15,396 fans watched the Cubs lose 11–10. Pinch hitter Ty Cline whiffed with the bases loaded to end the game.

Many more losses followed. Despite the presence of Ron Santo, Ernie Banks, and Billy Williams, the Cubs were a second-division club. A squad of has-beens including George Altman, Billy Faul, Wes Covington, Carl Warwick, Billy Hoeft, Frank Thomas, Lee Thomas, Harvey Kuenn, and Ernie Broglio failed out of the gate, and Durocher saw the writing on the ivy-covered wall: he had inherited a loser. By the end of the campaign, the Cubs were 59–103, tying the team mark for the most losses in history. Chicago was last, even behind the Mets—who, up to that season, had never finished ahead of anyone. Just as alarmingly, attendance plunged yet again to 635,891, the club's second lowest total since 1943. Only the AL's doormat, the Washington Senators, kept the Cubs from being the game's poorest-drawing attraction in 1966.

So who was bothering to show up? Gamblers. William Furlong wrote in the July 1966 *Harper's* about the investors in Wrigley's right-center-field bleachers: "Just inside the bleacher entrance to Wrigley Field in Chicago is a sign that warns: 'No gambling.' On the ramp leading up to the bleacher mezzanine is another sign that warns: 'No gambling.' At the top of a ramp, patrolling the aisle of the mezzanine, is a cop whose presence warns: 'No gambling.' In the right-center-field bleachers are Stace and Sambo, Jonesy and Zsa-Zsa, Dynamite and The Preacher—all there to sit in the sun and enjoy the National Pastime: gambling on baseball." Furlong notes that undercover cops had made dozens of arrests in order to shut down ballpark gambling. But the wagerers had "finger signals as abstruse as the bidding at Sotheby's" to exchange information, which helped throw off law enforcement.

Once again, the major attraction at the park was not on the field but in the stands. This was especially true on September 21, 1966, and not because the Cubs beat the visiting Reds 9–3. On that overcast Wednesday afternoon, only 530 fans visited Wrigley Field—the smallest crowd in the majors that year, and in fact for many years hence. But from small things, big things come. A cadre of ten left-field fans, some of the forty or so hardy bleacherites in attendance that day, decided that they were a gang of sorts. The next year, one of them, a lady named "Ma" Barker, brought to the park a bedsheet with a hole cut in it. On the sheet was written, "Hit a Bleacher Bum," with the idea that Cub hitters would knock home runs right at the fan whose head stuck through the hole. Thus was born a lasting term. The "bleacher bum" had come to Wrigley to stay.

RESURGENCE

Following their pathetic performance in Durocher's first year, things *had* to get better; they couldn't get too much worse. And the team did play much better as the 1966 season went on, debuting some interesting young players, including pitchers Fergie Jenkins (swiped from the Phillies in an early-season deal), Bill Hands, and Kenny Holtzman, catcher Randy Hundley, and outfielders Adolfo Phillips and Byron Browne. Browne's loopy swing, poor fielding, and bum shoulder soon landed him back in Triple-A, but the others stuck around and played big parts in the team's resurgence. Notably, however, many of these players were not developed by the Cubs' moribund farm system but rather liberated from other teams.

Things turned around in earnest in 1967. The year got off to a promising symbolic start, with the resurrection on April 8 and 9 of the city series, which had mostly petered out after 1957. Then, on April 11, 1967, a sparse and chilled Wrigley Field Opening Day crowd saw a 4–2 Cubs victory over Philadelphia. The first pitch had been tossed not by a local fan but by Vietnam veteran Ronald Centers, from the nearby Great Lakes Naval Training Center, where P. K. Wrigley had served many years before, and the crowd included dancers from Billy Minsky's chorus line, who took in the game from the box seats behind home plate. The Cubs' new full-time organist, Jack Kearney, sat behind a brand-new keyboard in the football press box on the third-base side, playing, among other tunes "The Star-Spangled Banner," which was soaring in popularity. Also new this year—though not ready for Opening Day—was a new public address system.

But the important thing was new faces and new success on the field. Bolstered by the sudden development of Jenkins, Hands, and Holtzman into top-flight starters, the Cubs rose from the ashes to contend in the NL. Perhaps inspired by this, the club began a seven-year, $3 million initiative to improve the park. One cheap but important—and even arguably stylish—change had to do with the hitting background. In early May the team laid a huge bright green sheet of AstroTurf on the vacant center-field seating sections. The background was notably improved by the uniformity of the AstroTurf and was even attractive in a 1960s sort of way. At the same time, the Cubs decorated their dugout with a green AstroTurf carpet.

By Sunday, July 2, the city had Cubs fever for the first time in decades. That day, fans gathered at the ticket windows as early as 8:15 A.M. The gates had to be closed at 12:45 when all standing-room tickets had been sold. Ten thousand fans were turned away—the biggest group to seek tickets unsuccessfully in many years. For the first time in recent memory, dozens of fans parked themselves on rooftops and fire escapes past the left-field and right-field walls, soaking up the sun—and some winning baseball. Durocher said later, "I can't remember seeing people over there since the early 1930s."

The Cubs obliged their fans by beating the Reds 4–1, for their thirteenth win in fourteen games, including an 11–1 home stand. Following the game, most of the 40,464 paid remained in the park to learn the results of the Cardinals' game at New York. When the Mets' 5–4 win was posted on the scoreboard, the crowd went crazy, and some fans streamed onto the playing field in joy: the Cubs had moved into first place by a half-game. The fans wouldn't vacate the park until the flags above the scoreboard were changed to reflect the Cubs' first-place standing. A parade of celebrators descended on the local taverns.

"Who ever heard of an entire city wanting to sleep inside a baseball stadium after the game was over?" asked Brent Musburger in the July 3 *American*. He went on to discuss the reaction of the players:

> The players, tho, guzzled beer, ate Ron Santo's pizza, dealt cards, and raved endlessly about the fans, many of whom were still milling about outside the dressing room, chanting "We're No. 1 . . . We're No. 1 . . ." or "We Want Leo." [Cubs reliever] Dick Radatz . . . put a Nazi helmet with "Hell's Angels" lettered across the top, stepped outside the dressing room door, and held up both hands in the politician's familiar "V" for victory sign. The crowd threw Radatz kisses in return.

"From now on, I'm going to demand combat pay before I work in Wrigley Field," one usher told Musburger.

Chicago's lead lasted only a few hours, as the Cardinals later that day beat the Mets in the second game of a doubleheader to come back into a tie with the Cubs. Chicago went on the road the next day and beat Atlanta, but beginning July 4 they dropped seven in a row. Back at home on July 22, the Cubs—down 5–4 in the last of the ninth—came up with two runs to edge the Giants, creeping back into a tie for the top spot in front of 29,079 manic rooters. Jack Brickhouse yelled on WGN-TV after Randy Hundley's single scored the winning run, "Watch Wrigley Field go out of its mind! Andy Frain ushers [are] in the outfield to keep the fans from jumping over the fence! Some of those fans want to jump *right out of the stands!*"

Insane last-minute finishes, which became a staple of the club during the latter part of the 1960s and early 1970s, helped build tremendous excitement among the club's reconstructed fan base—and led to endless anxiety attacks. From 1967 until the mid-seventies, the fans couldn't get enough of their resurgent Cubs.

On July 23, some fans arrived at the park at 4:00 A.M. to line up for tickets to the day's doubleheader against the Giants. By the time the sun came up, approximately a hundred fans were by the bleacher gate. David Claerbaut quoted young Cubs lefty Rich Nye about the crowds that had returned to Wrigley in 1967. "The players parked their cars near the firehouse across the street from the left field wall," recalled Nye, "and walked across Waveland to the bleacher entrance. By 9:00 people were lined up for bleacher seats, and you couldn't get through without being besieged by autograph seekers." This day, nearly thirty-five thousand screamers filled the park for the doubleheader split. The Cubs would not reach first place again, eventually finishing third, fourteen games out—the franchise's best finish in more than twenty years.

Cubs ticket manager Jack Maloney was all smiles. He had told Bob Billings in the *Daily News* on July 1, "If they keep it up, we're a cinch for a million. I had figured on about 800,000, but this could really percolate . . . when you've got a good team it isn't hard to get a million in here. That's without night games. It proves that you don't need night baseball to draw fans. It's the team that counts." By the end of the season, attendance vaulted to 977,226, the team's best in a decade and the last time to date they have been below a million over a full season.

THE TEAM PLAYED ON

The year 1968 was one of the most traumatic in modern American history. Racial tension, already at a boiling point, exploded with the April 4 assassination of Dr. Martin Luther King Jr., and on June 6, Bobby Kennedy was shot down after capturing the California Democratic presidential primary.

In this environment of unrest and upheaval, baseball became something of a normalizing factor. Though President Lyndon B. Johnson's declaration of a national day of mourning for Dr. King shelved the Cubs/Sox exhibition slated for April 7, the Cubs opened with a win and a loss in Cincinnati. That year's home opener, on Saturday, April 13, was a nationally televised affair against Saint Louis. Despite intermittent rain, 33,875 fans crammed into Wrigley, the biggest opening-day crowd in many years. Two more Vietnam vets, David Shields and Michael Wid-halm, tossed out first pitches. (At various times, including in 1966 and 1967, the Navy held a "recruit day" at Wrigley Field, where a hundred or so cadets took their induction oaths and officially joined the Armed Forces. These events continued into the 1970s.) Despite Ron Santo's two hundredth homer, the Cubs blew a 4–0 lead and lost 8–5, setting the tone for much of the season.

Santo, later a voluble and highly entertaining radio color man for the Cubs, never received the unbridled love the fans' dem-onstrated for players like Ernie Banks and Billy Williams. While "Captain Ron" had his boosters, including some fans who named Wrigley "Santo's Village" in homage to local amusement park "Santa's Village," as well as some who called for "Pizza Power" (Santo's frozen pizzas were sold at the park), he also had detrac-tors who accused him of not hitting in the clutch and not play-ing hard. Even happy Cubs fans are a tough crowd. But when they loved someone—like they loved Leo Durocher—there was no ambiguity about it. The April 14 *Tribune* remarked that dur-ing Opening Day ceremonies, "Durocher got such a deafening, standing ovation that the public address man, WGN's Roy Leon-ard, had to delay the introduction of the rest of the Cubs for a few moments."

(Durocher's relations with the media weren't always smooth. He rarely gave interviews, since he had his own radio show, "Du-rocher in the Dugout," on WGN. Before one game, WMAQ-TV sportscaster Johnny Erp pretended to speak off-the-cuff to Du-rocher down the left-field line near the Cubs bullpen. Erp was carrying a hidden microphone, however, and a crew filmed the conversation with a zoom-lens camera set up near the dugout. When Durocher found out that he had been "interviewed" with-out his knowledge, he raised holy hell.)

The Cubs lost twelve of thirteen and, in June, set a senior cir-cuit record by going forty-eight innings without scoring a run. On June 28, after falling to the Cardinals, the 31–41 Cubs were in ninth place. At that point, the team woke up. From July 5 through the end of the year, the Cubs' 49–33 record was the best in the league. On July 6 and 7, they swept back-to-back doubleheaders from the Pirates, ending the first half of the year in a flash and sending the Bucs on a ten-game losing skid. (In the second twin bill, both wins came in the bottom of the ninth, with reliever Phil "The Vulture" Regan notching the victories.)

North Side fans were excited to have a competitive team to watch after many lean years. Perhaps the real sign that the Cubs had reclaimed their fans' hearts came July 28, with the dull ninth-place Dodgers in town for a Sunday doubleheader. The Cubs battered Los Angeles 8–3 and 1–0 before 42,261 screaming rowdies, who spent six hours chanting, yelling, cheering, and drinking. "Try to argue with the 42,261 fans who jammed Wrigley Field yesterday and the thousands that were turned away that the Cubs are not on the move," wrote George Langford the next day in the *Tribune*. "The largest baseball crowd to overrun Wrigley Field in 20 years came out because of the Cubs, a fifth-place team almost in fourth, a half game out of third and 2½ lengths from second place."

For the first time in many years, the streets around Wrigley Field were beset with traffic jams. Buses to the park ran well behind schedule because of the influx of cars. The *Tribune* reported the following day that the fans "stood four deep on the ramps, perched on railings, and sat in the aisles. And several thousand were turned away at the gates," even though the Cubs had increased capacity after 1967 by selling more standing-room seats.

When the league-leading Cardinals came into town on August 12 for a four-game set, Wrigley Field was packed even though Chicago was fourteen games out. Over the four-game set, 121,740 fans filled Wrigley Field—a record at the time for a four-game set at the park, and all the more remarkable for a weekday series. Fergie Jenkins in his first autobiography remembered: "Before the third game of the series, Cardinal left fielder Lou Brock brought a towel with the words 'We're No. 1' written on it to the outfield to flash at the bleachers. Center fielder Curt Flood pulled the towel off Brock's shirt and waved it at the fans, particularly the Bleacher Bums, who had been on Brock and Flood the entire series. The fans went wild, showering Brock and Flood with beer cans, flashlight batteries, milk cartons, and whatever else they could get their hands on." Success had created something exciting, yet more than a little threatening.

Less than a week later came one of the biggest controversies at Wrigley Field in many years. In the first game of an August 18 doubleheader between the Cubs and the Reds, plate umpire Chris Pelekoudas, upset at what he felt was a proliferation of spitballs and other illegal pitches, ruled without any evidence that Phil Regan—often accused of tossing a spitter—had issued three illegal deliveries. ("This man defied us," Pelekoudas said later. "I wanted to make him suffer.") He allowed Pete Rose and Alex Johnson, who had made outs, to come to bat again. Rose singled after his swinging strike three was disallowed.

The fans hurled debris at the umpires. That the Cubs eventually lost both games of the doubleheader made them all the hotter. National League president Bill Giles flew to Chicago for an investigation and upbraided Pelekoudas for making a call without physical evidence. General Manager John Holland, according to George Vass in the August 19 *Daily News*, was "alarmed" by the angry reaction of the crowd, however. Now that the Cubs were serious about winning, their fans were serious, too—perhaps to a fault.

The Cubs' rally in the second half wasn't enough to propel them to the top—they finished third overall and then only by winning their last five games. But their popularity was on the rise. By the end of the season, 1,043,409 fans had clicked the Wrigley Field turnstiles. The team hadn't drawn so many since 1950. But even with over a million, the Cubs' attendance still ranked fifth among ten NL teams; they were outdrawn by, among others, ninth-place New York and last-place Houston.

THE FUTURE IS IN PLASTICS

Chicago Bears star running back Gale Sayers tore up his knee on muddy Wrigley Field turf in 1968. The injury essentially destroyed his career, and in the wake of it, Bears owner George Halas and P. K. Wrigley began serious discussions about installing artificial turf, which at the time was sold both as a way to decrease groundskeeping costs and as a way to prevent sports injuries. At this time, the only major-league baseball park with plastic was the Houston Astrodome, for which AstroTurf had been invented. Others were on the way, however—in 1970–71, new parks in Cincinnati, Pittsburgh, and Philadelphia would open using artificial turf, and three existing parks also soon converted. Even the White Sox partially converted Comiskey Park in 1969.

Wrigley told a *Sun-Times* reporter on November 11, 1968, "There's no doubt that these artificial surfaces are the coming thing. We have been studying developments of it and there's no doubt that it would pay for itself within a few years, because maintenance of grass turf is expensive." At this time, it cost some $400,000 to install AstroTurf (or its competitor, Tartan Turf, which Wrigley was considering using) on a regulation field. The *Sun-Times* article also revealed that "baseball is so convinced that artificial grass will soon become universal that at the general managers meeting recently in Colorado Springs, Colo., a subcommittee was appointed to study the matter."

The experiment never fully convinced fans or players, although artificial turf is still in use in some stadiums. Among the merits of artificial turf touted in the 1960s was that it would prevent knee injuries like Sayers's. In later years, however, most baseball people tended to feel that plastic grass, with its intractability and lack of sponginess, actually facilitated injuries. This is among the reasons that the fake stuff faded from use by the 1990s. The Pale Hose removed their AstroTurf infield in 1975, and plastic hasn't shown up on a Chicago major-league baseball field since.

If we could put a man on the moon, you would think we could put the Chicago Cubs atop the National League. And in 1969, both seemed possible. The Cubs jumped off the mat that year and, for 155 days, led the newly created NL East—consisting of, in addition to the Cubs, the Phillies, the Pirates, the Mets, the Cardinals, and the newly created Montreal Expos. Unfortunately, they were the first 155 days of the season rather than the last.

The story of the ill-fated 1969 squad has been told over and again. Any Cubs fan old enough to remember the season still cringes, as do many of the pennant race's participants. Even years later, third baseman Ron Santo could not discuss the club's collapse down the stretch without becoming emotional.

The ill-fated sixty-nine season began on April 8, with the Phillies in town. After 1968's strong second half and with double the number of playoff teams as a result of realignment, many pundits and fans believed that this was the Cubs' year. Pennant fever began to manifest at 8:00 A.M. on Opening Day, when fans began lining up outside Wrigley Field's ticket windows in hopes of obtaining one of the five thousand bleacher seats or twenty-two thousand general admission tickets put on sale the day of each game. The next day's *Tribune* reported that "sale of bleacher tickets was cut off long before game time. Standing room tickets were sold in the outer precincts and standees packed the walking area behind the lower deck stands." The crowd of 40,796 was reported to be the largest ever at a Wrigley Field opening, although some games in the 1920s probably attracted more.

The Cubs decided to "go Hollywood" for their opening ceremonies; showbiz veteran Jimmy Durante came out and told a joke or two, and veteran sportswriter Edgar Munzel of the *Sun-Times* tossed the first pitch. Loyola Academy High School provided the band, and the crowd observed a moment of silence for former president Dwight Eisenhower, who had died on March 28.

It was the same old field, though part of the upper deck had been rebuilt as part of a four-year infrastructure project begun the previous fall, and there was new carpet in the Cubs' dugout. On the field, the Cubs played their typical game of the era, getting out to a big early lead, blowing it in the late innings, and putting on a wild finish. Ernie Banks hit two homers in the first three innings, driving in five runs. In the ninth, up 5–2, the Cubs coughed up the lead. Rookie Phillies infielder Don Money's three-run homer off a tiring Fergie Jenkins knotted the score.

In the eleventh, the Phils went up 6–5 on a double by Money. In the Cubs half, Randy Hundley singled off Barry Lersch with one out. Left-handed-hitting "Wonderful" Willie Smith, batting for Jim Hickman, launched a 1–0 fastball into the right-field bleachers. Fans danced in the aisles, and the entire Cub bench mobbed Smith. Jack Griffin of the *Sun-Times* said on June 27, concerning the Cubs' penchant for late-inning wins, that the explanation must be mass hypnosis. "[Starter] Dick Selma or [reliever] Hank Aguirre waves a forefinger above his head, and Leo Durocher says a magic word, and the organ grinder plays a special tune. And everybody goes home in blind hysteria."

From this point, it was "ignition on" for the Cubs, who won eleven of their first twelve. By May 16 the Cubs were 24–11 and up by six in the National League East.

With success, and more fans, came a new series of challenges relating to crowd control. The left-field bleachers had become the territory of the Bleacher Bums, an assemblage of mostly young, mostly male, mostly politically conservative fans who wore yellow hard hats, drank beer in copious amounts, chanted slogans, insulted opponents, and deified their Cubs. One of their inspirational cheers, calling for a double play from Santo, Kessinger, Beckert, and Banks, went: "14, 11, 18, 10: come on, infield, do it again!" Some of the Bums' fun was harmless; most of the chants, clapping, cheers, throwing back of opponents' home runs, and good-natured razzing usually didn't bother anyone. But they could be insensitive to fans who wanted to watch the game, insulting and sometimes assaulting supporters of other teams. Some Bums learned the names of opposing players' girlfriends or wives and screamed insults about them. At times, the Confederate flag flew in the bleachers (ostensibly honoring southern Cubs like Jim Hickman and Randy Hundley); at others, the Bums co-opted the Black Power chants of the day ("Abeebee! Ungowa! *Cub* Power!"). The more the beer flowed, the more obnoxious the Bums got.

In the June 29 *Sun-Times*, Jack Griffin quoted a Saint Louis fan sitting at the nearby tavern Ray's Bleachers: "Those people frighten me. First day in, one of our guys is signing autographs for them in left field. Being a nice fellow. There is no being a nice fellow with those people. While he is signing autographs somebody pelts him on the head with a large rubber ball. Right on the head." Mudcat Grant, with the Cardinals that season, simply said, "You oughta put a cage over 'em."

Many bums loaded up before the games at Ray's Bleachers at Sheffield and Waveland. Ray and Marge Meyer, who bought Ray's in 1962, had great memories of the Bums. Marge told Bob Ibach and Ned Colletti in 1983, "So much of their lives revolved around what the Cubs did. Not only did they go to the games, but they hoped to have breakfast with a player . . . or maybe a nightcap at the bar." Durocher had labeled the tavern off limits for Cubs players, but he was only the manager.

Cubs players seemed to get along fine with the Bums. Pitcher Dick "Moon Man" Selma quickly became a Bum favorite as he led cheers from the bullpen. Ron Santo curried favor with the fans by running toward the left-field corner clubhouse after games and leaping into the air, clicking his heels. The Cubs' opponents thought it was bush league, but the fans ate it up. And one reserve outfielder must have loved the Bums's rendition of the last verse of the "Star Spangled Banner" as "Oh, say does that *Al Spangler* banner yet wave. . . ." The Cubs seemed to respond well to the love in 1969, churning out a 49–32 home record.

Compared with many of the players today, Cubs players of that era were closer to the fans, and the players remained local heroes even if they didn't actually win. George Castle wrote, "The majority of the players kept their off-season homes in Chicago; they were part of the community. You could drink with the Cubs at Ray's Bleachers behind the center-field scoreboard or watch their off-season basketball team perform. That's why their failure to get to the World Series is so painful."

The Cubs players may have been more a part of the community, but that community was continuing to change. The U.S. Census Bureau estimated that in 1950 approximately 125,000 people lived in Lake View in an estimated forty-five thousand housing units. By 1970, the population had dropped to 120,000 but the number of housing units had risen to near fifty-five thousand. By this time Lake View was really two separate neighborhoods—east of the ballpark and west. Lakefront property to the east remained valuable though gangs occasionally troubled the area, and over time the neighborhood attracted a young, upscale, singles crowd into what would soon be called New Town, so named for its relative proximity to the city's popular Old Town. The area, which featured plenty of trendy bars and restaurants, also became a nexus of Chicago's gay community and much of it is today known as Boystown.

Meanwhile, increasing numbers of recent immigrants settled in the countless graystones and brick two- and three-flats that stand on the main thoroughfares, as well as in the single-family houses that line the side streets, of the western portion of Lake View and immediately south of Wrigley. By the latter half of the 1960s, the Lincoln-Belmont area had turned largely Latino. Dominic Pacyga and Ellen Skerrett note that "in 1974, there were 2,000 Spanish-speaking people living in the area around Wrigley Field between Halsted and Racine."

Citizens of Korean and Japanese descent, who had begun arriving in Lake View in the 1930s and 1940s, increased their presence in the area during the 1960s as well. There were still few blacks in the area, apart from those on the field.

One of the most popular players of this time, white or black, was All-Star outfielder Billy Williams. The team honored him at a doubleheader on Sunday, June 29, against the Cardinals. A crowd of 41,060 attended, with security personnel turning away ten thousand more. The Cubs and his teammates—as well as the writers!—lavished him with an array of gifts. Williams then went out and drove in Ernie Banks with the winning run in the bottom of the eighth of game 1. In game 2, he had four hits—a single, a double, and two triples—to drive in three runs. Sweeping the twin bill 3–1 and 12–1, the Cubs moved eight games in front of the second-place Mets. Everything was falling into place.

ONE GIANT LEAP FOR KEN HOLTZMAN

The pitching was in gear, too. Since coming to the Cubs in 1966, lefty Kenny Holtzman had been touted as a "new Koufax." On August 19, 1969, he finally did something Koufax did four times: he threw a no-hitter. Without anything but a fastball, Holtzman shut down the eventual NL West champ Atlanta Braves 4–0 before an overflow crowd of 41,033. When Glenn Beckert threw out Hank Aaron for the last out, hundreds of fans—mostly young men—jubilantly jumped from the stands and ran onto the field. Ushers and policemen couldn't stop the fans from swarming the Cubs, and Holtzman was nearly choked in the mayhem. After the on-field melee, the players gathered in the cramped clubhouse and celebrated. Backup catcher Gene Oliver not so subtly hinted, for the assembled press corps to hear, that Holtzman should charge for interviews. One local car dealership even phoned in to give the lefty a new automobile.

Cubs players were not used to mic-wielding interviewers in 1969. The media environment was not yet what we have become accustomed to, with detailed broadcast coverage of every game. Few broadcasters even came to the park in those days except on special occasions, and rarely did TV crews conduct postgame interviews. Martin "Red" Mottlow—the first radio reporter to cover games regularly at Wrigley Field—was the only radio reporter in the ballpark for most of Holtzman's no-hitter. Others, including Brad Palmer, then with WBBM radio, sped to Wrigley only when the game reached the eighth. As a result, Mottlow could easily navigate the crowded Cubs clubhouse and get to Holtzman.

Following the game, Braves hitters and even the sportswriters credited the Cubs grounds crew with making the no-hitter happen. Edgar Munzel wrote in the August 20 *Sun-Times* that "the long grass of the infield also played a part in foiling the Braves in several instances." Grounds chief Pete Marcantonio insisted, however, that the grass was no longer on August 19 than at any other point during the season. Marcantonio did note that his crew had placed new sod on the infield, but the grass had recently been cut to its normal height of two inches.

Whatever the cause, the Cubs' success was roping in the fans. Two days later, the Cubs drew their largest crowd of the season: 42,364, a Ladies Day assemblage. For the three-game Braves series, the Cubs pulled in 119,089.

CRUMBLE

From this high point, the season devolved.

After winning a suspended game and a regular game at Cincinnati on September 2, the Cubs led the Mets by five. But a three-game home series September 5–7 against the Pirates proved a turning point. On Friday and Saturday, the Pirates destroyed the Cubs, 9–2 and 13–4, knocking Holtzman and Jenkins silly. Saturday was Boy Scout Day, with three thousand scouts among a surprisingly small crowd of 27,791. Meanwhile, the Mets had won two of three from Philadelphia and were now only three and a half games behind the Cubs.

Sunday afternoon's contest appeared to be the kind of game that the Cubs had won all season. Down 4–3 in the eighth, Chicago went ahead on Jim Hickman's dramatic two-run eighth-inning blast against former Cubs reliever Chuck Hartenstein. In the ninth, closer Regan retired Matty Alou and Gene Alley then went 2–2 on Willie Stargell. The next pitch, in Regan's words, was "a sinker that didn't sink." Boom. Onto Sheffield Avenue, over the right-field wall, as 28,698 fans sat stunned. (This was, again, an oddly small crowd; on a Sunday, many may have been watching the Bears on television.) In the eleventh, Don Kessinger's error on a grounder let the lead run score, and Richie Hebner knocked in another with a single. The 7–5 defeat, and the Mets' 9–3 win over the Phillies, cut the Cubs' lead to two and a half.

The Cubs went on the road for nine games, going 2–7. By the time they came home, they were four back of the streaking Mets, and the race was over. Most of the exhausted regulars played poorly in September, and manager Leo Durocher, no calm presence in a storm, seemed powerless to deal with the situation. The Cubs of 1969 are fated forever to be the Team That Should Have. They were popular, though: 1,674,993 Cubs fans turned out that year, fourth most in baseball.

THE BATTLE AT HOME

The more things change, the more they stay the same. The Cubs buffed up the park for 1970 (fig. 24). As part of the continuing work to reinforce the structure of the nearly sixty-year-old stadium, workers installed seventy-five hundred new chairs and re-laid concrete over the stadium's foundation and walkways.

On Opening Day, April 14, Lou Boudreau, WGN radio color man and recent Hall of Fame inductee, tossed out the first ball to Gabby Hartnett. Comedian Milton Berle stopped by, the Cavaliers Drum and Bugle Corps performed, and Louis Sudler sang "The Star-Spangled Banner" after a local Boy Scout recited the Pledge of Allegiance.

Pitcher Dick Selma, unofficial leader of the Bleacher Bums cheering section in 1969, had been dealt to the Phillies that winter. On Opening Day 1970, he led cheers before the game in his Phillies uniform and a yellow hard hat. During batting practice, fans threw coins at him. According to E. M. Swift in a 1980 *Sports Illustrated* article, Selma scooped up the coins and, after the game, went to Ray's Bleachers, threw the coins on the bar, and bought drinks for the house.

FIGURE 24. This 1970 shot of a packed Wrigley watching the Cubs take on the Reds has treats for the historian: the auxiliary press section (now housing luxury boxes), the padded walls down the right-field line, the right-field "catwalk," and the Schlitz ad on the building across the street. In addition, the el train is visible because at this time, the far portion of the lower-deck right-field stands had no seats. (Credit: Blake Bollinger, Wikipedia Commons)

Despite the patriotic festivities, the 1970 home opener was one of the most unpleasant days ever at Clark and Addison. The violence that had buffeted America during the late 1960s had missed Wrigley Field, viewed at the time as a bastion of conservative American values: baseball, short hair, orderliness, and beer. Rock music, political upheaval, and nonalcoholic drugs hadn't yet penetrated this most old-fashioned of Chicago's public arenas. And yet, for the first time, the violence of the era manifested itself on Opening Day, even though baseball itself had little to do directly with Vietnam, civil rights, drug laws, recession, and urban poverty.

This day, angry young fans (many of them drunk or stoned school-skippers) and others massed early in the morning by the left-field and center-field bleacher entrances. Things began to get rowdy; some fans were pushed out of line, and one suffered a broken leg. More than one ticket seeker fainted in the crush of humanity and had to be passed, end over end, to the outer rim of the crowd.

Inside, there were fights. These had happened before, but not on this scale. "Intermittent fisticuffs among fans in deep left field occupied the attention of the Cub bullpen during the game," reported Cooper Rollow in the April 15 *Tribune*. Dick Dozer, also in the *Tribune*, noted that "isolated fistfights had erupted continually during the game, taxing the Andy Frain fully staffed ushering crew and officers of the Burns Agency." Bands of teenagers roamed the bleachers and upper deck, buying beer where possible and, in some cases, terrorizing fans. As Ron Grousl, lead spokesman for the Bleacher Bums, said later, "They try to look like Bums, but they're just bums." Once the game ended (Cubs 5, Phillies 4), the Cubs were herded from the field through a cordon of ushers.

Rowdy aggression merged at this moment with political controversy as some Vietnam War protestors jumped over the right-field bleacher wall and swarmed onto the field. Three fans knocked down second baseman Glenn Beckert. One teenage usher was kicked in the face repeatedly by members of the mob.

At that time, Chicago police did not enter private premises to restore order unless asked in. No one asked them. As a result, they didn't come into the park to fix things until the worst had already transpired. Told that the Chicago police had fifty officers on hand, Salty Saltwell told Cooper Rollow in the April 15 *Tribune*, "The only trouble is that they were all out directing traffic when we needed them." Worse, Saltwell recalled to George Castle years later, the police knew about the protest group and had reason to think they would come to Wrigley Field, but nothing was said to Cubs management.

Rick Talley wrote an angry editorial in the Chicago *Today* on April 15:

It's a certain type of spectator . . . the lout, or clod, or exhibitionist, or whatever you want to call him, who thinks that for the price of a ticket, he's free to (1) get drunk, (2) throw things, (3) pour beer on people, (4) leap over walls onto the playing field, (5) knock down ushers, (6) snatch a ballplayer's hat, or glove, or tear his shirt, and (7) see a picture of himself in the next day's newspaper . . . we've got thousands of people—mostly young people—who are more concerned with performing, rather than watching the performers in Wrigley Field.

One note of humor graced the gray, cold, threatening day. In the fourth inning, public address announcer Pat Pieper advised, "Will fans in the left field bleachers please take their clothes off . . . [*dramatic pause*] the bleacher wall."

On the whole, however, Cubs management was displeased and baffled. How could this have happened? What could the club do to control drunks, unruly kids, and protesters? This was not the kind of friendly thrill-of-victory field swarming familiar to Cubs fans from 1938, 1960, or even 1969. Salty Saltwell talked with his counterpart in Saint Louis, Joe McShane, who had built a basket in front of the Busch Stadium wall. Soon, Saltwell proposed a wire fence jutting straight up from the top of Wrigley's outfield wall, though it would block fans' view. The concept needed refining, but something was going to be done.

In the meantime, Wrigley Field attracted a different kind of protestor. On May 5, a group of aggrieved Native Americans camped out kitty-corner from the left-field gate on the northwest corner of Waveland and Seminary. The group, led by Michael Chosa, was protesting housing conditions for poor Native Americans in the neighborhood. The group, which grew from five to more than sixty, remained at the corner for a month, setting up teepees and other shelters. On some nights, while campfires crackled, media, sympathizers, and other visitors stopped by, including, on at least one occasion, Ernie Banks and Billy Williams. The community eventually fell apart when other squatters, not Natives, began encroaching on the land used to park cars for games at Wrigley. This led to arrests. Eventually, the police evicted the protesters, who offered no opposition despite earlier threats to resist with violence if necessary. "Any day is a good day to die," Chosa had told reporters.

On the same day as the Native American protest began, the Cubs installed a new organ on the press-box concourse as well as new loudspeakers. The equipment was so heavy that it had to be hauled in by helicopter, deposited on the roof, and then hooked up. And then, the next day, according to the May 7 *Tribune*, "finishing touches were applied to a new oblique screen which is angled 42 inches out over the playing surface to help control littering and keep exuberant patrons from leaning onto the field." The wire fencing would add "into the basket" to the Wrigley lexicon every time a fly ball landed there. Such balls were ruled home runs.

Few seemed to be bothered by the new fence. Bleacher Bum Don Alger, for example, told Bill Jauss in the May 7 *Daily News*, "It's a great idea. Now those idiots won't be jumping down on the field." Management also erected a foot-high plastic barrier atop the brick outfield wall, but this blocked the view of the field for some bleacher fans, and due to public outcry was removed almost immediately.

The Cubs took several other measures to improve security at the friendly confines. Edgar Munzel laid them out in the May 16, 1970, issue of the *Sporting News*:

- The Cubs installed of a video monitoring system, with zoom-lensed video cameras recording several locales in the ballpark at once.

- Beer sales by vendors in the bleachers were prohibited. To purchase beer, fans would have to leave their seats and visit the concession stand at the back of the bleachers.
- Standing-room tickets were no longer sold for the bleachers.
- Bleacher gates were to open at 9:00 A.M., rather than at 8:00 A.M. as they had previously.
- Chicago police agreed to station officers inside the park for weekend and holiday games.

General Manager John Holland told Munzel, "The most effective thing will be the introduction of these video cameras. They will enable us to pinpoint where the disturbances are and also the troublemakers involved. Our security men will be equipped with walkie-talkies so that they can move in within a matter of seconds." Rumors had the Cubs using their new security equipment to zero in on gamblers in the right-field bleachers—who flashed signs to their counterparts in the left-field bleachers. Whatever the truth of that, Wrigley Field had quickly come to seem a lot less friendly.

Gambling and protestors were not the only topics at Wrigley Field in the spring of 1970. Alcohol was, too. The Cubs had suffered another public relations hit when the *Daily News*'s John Justin Smith broke the story on May 6 that the team had been selling near beer (3.2 percent alcohol) ever since the end of prohibition back in 1933. The vending of the low-caliber brew was intended "as a crowd control measure," though the White Sox had long trusted their fans to handle 3.8-caliber Meister Brau. P. K. Wrigley told John Holland, "I don't care who knows it" when the news came out, although city commissioner of sales (and later mayor) Jane Byrne felt that the public was being bilked.

Ron Grousl of the Bleacher Bums had the last word about the 3.2 controversy. "I heard rumors to that effect," he commented. "But it doesn't make any difference to me. I drink mine at Ray's Bleachers across from the park before the game."

500

Meanwhile, there was baseball to be played. Ernie Banks had entered the 1970 campaign with 497 dingers, and he connected again on April 25 and May 9. Then, in the bottom of the second inning of the May 12 game, before just 5,264 fans at misty Wrigley Field, Banks lined Pat Jarvis's 1–1 fastball just over the left-field wall. The ball was gone almost before anyone could grasp the significance of what was happening. The ball bounced in and out of the half-filled bleachers to left-fielder Rico Carty, who threw it toward the Cubs bullpen. Banks received a standing ovation from the fans as well as from the assembled press corps, and the game was held up for a short ceremony. Later, in typical fashion, trailing 3–2 in the last of the ninth, the Cubs rallied. Billy Williams connected off Hoyt Wilhelm to knot things up, and in the eleventh, Ron Santo's seeing-eye single—so named because this softly hit ground ball appears to elude the fielders as though guided by unseen force—scored the 4–3 winner.

But the season was short on such sweet moments. The team finished at 84–78, five games behind the Pirates.

SUCCESS HAS MADE A FAILURE OF OUR HOME

The Cubs continued to contend into the early 1970s but did not take a division crown until 1984. Much has been written about why they didn't win, with some analysts blaming the Cubs' schedule of eighty-one day games for wearing the club down in the stretch. Players from the era have taken each side of the argument over day games; some believe that the Cubs were disadvantaged by playing all their home games in the greater heat of an afternoon contest, while others feel that it was actually the visiting clubs that had to struggle to adjust to the sunshine and heat when they came to Chicago. The many factors involved—both measurable and immeasurable—have made it difficult to come up with a clear statement as to whether playing day games helped or hurt the Cubs.

Looking at the difference between the Cubs' home and road winning percentages from 1940 through 1988 (when the team put in lights), it's clear that when the Cubs were bad, they had a very high differential between their home and road winning percentages. In some years, they won fewer than 30 percent of their road games, even while posting records above .500 in Wrigley Field. The only time in that nearly fifty-year span that the Cubs were consistently good was from 1967 through 1972. In those years, the differential went way down—that is to say, their home and road winning percentages were more comparable, largely because they had talented players who were good on the road as well as in Wrigley.

NOT GOOD ENOUGH

Fans saw enough reason for hope, though, and they still lined up early in sleeping bags to get Opening Day tickets—Elmwood Park cabbie Randy Bratu was first in line in 1969, 1970, and 1971. Opening Day, April 6, 1971, featured forty-degree temperatures and twenty-five-mile-an-hour winds, but 41,121 thrilled to the eleventh-inning homer by Billy Williams that provided a 2–1 win.

Some thirty-six hundred purchased $1 bleacher tickets, with another several hundred refused entry. "It was a mad scene," said Andy Frain usher Dave Noren. "But it was nothing like last year." John McHugh of the April 7 Chicago *Today* reported that "the pile of debris at the gates was ample testimony to the mad scramble to get in the bleachers. Blankets, knit caps, gloves, clothing, playing cards, [and] shoes were among the items left behind." At least one usher was assaulted and had his uniform torn in the mayhem of spectators trying to get in.

With the 1971 season, Leo Durocher was in his sixth year as manager. The first serious sign of dissent in his administration came August 23. With the Cubs struggling to stay in contention, Durocher held a fractious pregame meeting in which he invited his players to speak their minds—then ripped those who did.

Veterans Milt Pappas and Joe Pepitone already had reputations as clubhouse lawyers, and both got in shots before Durocher took the floor and fired back at them and at several other Cubs, including Ron Santo.

Santo, an emotional man, had wanted a "day" of his own. Durocher used Santo's vulnerability to make him look bad during the meeting, claiming that the only reason that the Cubs were staging such a day later in the week was that Santo had begged GM John Holland for it. Santo nearly came to blows with his sixty-six-year-old manager, and the blowup got into the papers, soon forcing P. K. Wrigley's hand. As the team fell further from first place, P. K. took out ads in all Chicago papers supporting Durocher, telling those who wanted to get rid of him that they had best "give up." Wrigley also threatened to deal any unhappy players—though he would have had to trade at least half the club.

Saddest in Wrigley's public letter was the postscript: "If only we could find more team players like Ernie Banks." Perhaps the aging owner was unaware that Durocher—said to be jealous of Banks's stature—had more than once embarrassed the future Hall of Famer, making him face tough right-handers while sending in pinch hitters for him when lefties were on the mound.

The Cubs did hold Santo's day on Saturday, August 28, with the Braves in town. The third baseman received a new car and a speedboat from the club, while his wife, Linda, was given a mink coat. Santo's teammates presented him with an engraved shotgun, which he did not use on his manager. Unfortunately for the Cubs, Atlanta won 4–3 and kept the Cubs in their fatal spiral. They eventually finished third, fourteen games back.

AN UGLY SEASON

Through the early 1970s, values continued to change even at Wrigley Field, bastion of the traditional. Player/owner labor squabbles, which first began to surface in 1969, blew up in 1972 with the first Major League Baseball Players Association strike over benefits, salaries, and other contractual details. The labor action canceled the first few days of the regular season and left a bitter taste in many mouths. On the scheduled Opening Day, April 11, several dozen fans picketed in front of empty Wrigley Field to protest the absence of baseball.

While the Players Association and the owners argued, the players themselves tried to stay in shape. Prohibited from working out in Wrigley Field, several Cubs let the press know on April 9 that they'd love to work out with the White Sox at Comiskey Park. (The Pale Hose had defied American League president Joe Cronin's order to lock the doors to players.) Unfortunately, the potentially fascinating scene of Cubs and Sox working out together never came to pass. The strike was settled on April 13 when MLB owners agreed to add $500,000 to the players' pension fund—what seems an almost ridiculously small amount considering that the owners lost some $5 million in revenue from the eighty-six canceled games. The Cubs opened at Wrigley on April 15 against Philadelphia.

There was no glitz or hoo-ha on Opening Day in 1972; resentment over the strike meant that only 17,566 fans showed up for Chicago's 4–2 loss to Steve Carlton and the Phils. The newspapers were full of quotes from angry fans wishing ill to the players, and, perhaps for the first time, people began to wonder whether the fun had gone out of baseball.

John Husar of the *Tribune* quoted Bill Duncan, a bartender at Ray's, on April 16. "I'm really bitter about this, myself. I lost money by not working this week. Those players lost money, too, but they can afford it." (It's not clear from Husar's article whether Duncan ever thanked the players for performing their jobs the rest of the time, when people actually came to Ray's and paid his salary.)

Attendance sank some 300,000 on the season to 1,299,163. The strike was certainly to blame, but the Cubs also did not play well, despite their second-place finish. Despite some stellar defensive moments from the trio of Ron Santo, Don Kessinger, and Glenn Beckert, the rapidly aging club was on the way down. Leo

Durocher was forced out of the manager's position on July 24, and the Cubs never contended. To make matters even worse, in 1972 the Cubs debuted strange new uniforms. The home jerseys, formerly stylish button-downs, were altered to double-knit pullovers with atrocious big blue built-in polyester belts—which emphasized pot bellies—while the club's road uniforms resembled beer-league softball suits.

The home uniforms must not have bothered the pitchers too much, though, since two of them threw no-hitters at Wrigley Field in 1972, the last ones to date at the park. On April 16, the second day of the season, Burt Hooton tossed a 4–0 no-no (i.e., no-hitter), fanning seven, against the Phillies as 9,583 cold, wet loyalists watched—one of just two Cub wins in their first eleven games. Then, on September 2, with the Cubs well behind the NL East champion Pirates, veteran Milt Pappas fired an 8–0 no-hitter against the visiting San Diego Padres. Pappas set down the first twenty-six hitters, coming just *that* close to a perfect game, before walking pinch hitter Larry Stahl on a 3–2 delivery that sailed a few inches low of the strike zone. After yelling angrily at plate umpire Bruce Froemming, Pappas retired former Cub Garry Jestadt on a popup to second to complete his no-hitter in front of 12,979.

INTO THE WOODS

As the Cubs stars of the late 1960s got old or were traded, the team sank into another stretch of mediocrity. Changing managers every couple of seasons, trading undeveloped future stars, and bringing in a parade of aging former stars to prop up a poor talent base, the Cubs finished below .500 every year from 1973 through 1983, with the exception of 1977, when they ended 81–81.

The Cubs did continue to work on the ballpark, although the maintenance schedule was nowhere near what it had been long ago. Prior to the 1972 season, the club spent $500,000 on turning more seats in the right-field grandstand toward home plate, finishing the project begun some two decades before. In making this change, Cubs management razed the large aisle in the back of the right-field boxes and added another thousand seats to the right-field grandstands, filling a section in the deep right-field corner of the lower deck that had been empty for years. Subsequently, Wrigley spent $385,000 remodeling upper-deck seats.

On April 6, 1973, Opening Day jazz chanteuse Sarah Vaughn sang the national anthem and a former prisoner of war in Vietnam, Lieutenant Commander Robert Naughton, tossed out the ceremonial first pitch. With temperatures reaching sixty-five degrees and no clouds in the sky, 40,273 fans saw the Cubs emerge with a 3–2 win by plating two runs in the bottom of the ninth. Pinch runner Tony LaRussa scored his only Cubs run ever on Rick Monday's bases-loaded walk that won the game. This was perhaps the high point of that season, as the Cubs finished 77–84. From 1974 to 1976, attendance dipped sharply, as the North Siders barely cleared a million fans each season.

COLD TEAM, COLD FANS

Come 1974, the team had rid itself of most of its veteran players in favor of younger, cheaper talent. This rebuilding phase, meant to keep costs down, was sold to the fans as a first step in returning to contention.

Despite the lowering of the payroll, the Cubs raised prices on most concessions. Twelve-ounce bottles of beer went from fifty-five to sixty cents, the first price increase since 1971. Both popcorn and scorecards were raised from a nickel to twenty cents (although a free pencil nub came with the scorecard). The only souvenirs sold at Wrigley at the time were pennants, T-shirts, sweatshirts, and caps, and for all of them except pennants, the Cubs raised prices by a quarter.

Sarah Vaughn again sang the Opening Day anthem, appearing with an all-service color guard. Prior to the game, the two hundred–member Dundee High School band performed, and the Proviso East state basketball team (led by Joe Ponsetto, later a star for DePaul University) flung ceremonial first pitches. In the game itself, Bill Bonham shut out the Phillies 2–0 in forty-degree temperatures in front of 30,601 fans. But as expected, the Cubs fell to the basement for the first time since 1966, finishing 66–96. The rebuilding was off to a slow start.

Veteran field announcer Pat Pieper, on the job for fifty-nine years, would not be around to see the next good Cubs team, passing away October 22, 1974, at age eighty-eight. For the last few years of his career, Pieper had worked from the press box, after spending most of his career making announcements from the field. Jim Enright, longtime Chicago sportswriter who for several years served as an official scorer, took over public address duties.

SICK MUSTARD, SICK COW

The following year, 1975, was a slight improvement, at least in the quality of the play. But two off-field forces had negative effects on the game that year. The first of them was a snowstorm, which caused a rare cancellation of the home opener. With the white stuff piled up outside the ballpark, some 19,239 fans braved near-freezing temperatures all the same. When the club finally got things going on April 10, after two snow days, the Pirates clubbed four homers in an 8–4 win. Columnist David Condon, in the April 11 *Tribune*, noted that "the outfield grass was as jaundiced as sick mustard . . . vendors found icebergs in the hot coffee." The Cubs got out of the basement that year but not much more than that.

The other surprise of the year came on September 15, with the Pirates back in town to formally eliminate the Cubs from the NL race with a 9–1 win in the second game of a doubleheader. When popular Cubs center-fielder Joe Wallis, nicknamed "Tarzan" by fans and teammates, pinch-hit in the first game, the public address loudspeaker blared out a Tarzan yell that, in the words of Cubs traveling secretary Blake Cullen, sounded like "a sick cow."

Wallis was horrified, saying after the game, "That's embarrassing. I don't even *like* the name 'Tarzan.'"

This was the first known instance at Wrigley Field of the pre-recorded antics so common now at most parks. It is, to some, a grim innovation. *Ev-ry-bo-dy clap your hands!*

Possibly still traumatized by the noise, the Cubs were plastered by the Pirates the next day, 22–0, the biggest margin in a shutout since 1883. Infielder Rennie Stennett of the Bucs went seven-for-seven, becoming the first player ever to do so in a nine-inning contest. Only 4,932 fans were on hand, however, to see the sad spectacle.

LEFT FIELD SUCKS

While the left-field Bleacher Bums got the attention in the late 1960s and early 1970s, many claim that the real fans—the long-time sufferers—have always been in the right-field seats. That's where, for example, author Barry Gifford and screenwriter "Big" Steve Friedman yelled at their favorite Cubs during the 1960s. Fans in the bleachers have long had a good-natured rivalry involving a consistent stream of back-and-forth insults; for years, barely a game went by without a group of fans from left field yelling "Right field sucks!" and their counterparts in the sun answering in turn. This custom appears to have begun in the 1980s.

In the 1970s and 1980s, recalls veteran fan and writer George Castle, old-timers like Caleb "Chet" Chestnut, Papa Carl Leone, and Marvin Rich sat out there and passed on baseball traditions. Chestnut, an African American born in 1896, puffed a pipe while dispensing baseball knowledge. His presence as a black man was in itself a rare event in the mostly white "cheap seats." Rich, a relative youngster born in 1930, consistently sat in the first row of the right-field bleachers. Leone occasionally tried to help out the ushers. George Castle wrote in August 1980 that "on Opening Day 1978, [Leone] . . . tied ropes to posts next to the bleacher benches, next to the top of the stairway in right field, to prevent portions of the near-riotous mob of 45,000 from stepping over the people in his section." The next year, Leone reported to Wrigley Field at 3:30 A.M. for a Cubs-Reds doubleheader scheduled to begin eight and a half hours later.

The well-known right-field denizens of those days are gone—as is, generally, the significant crowd of gamblers who sat in the back rows near the concession stand. Chestnut passed away early in the 1977 season. Papa Carl Leone died in 1986. Marvin Rich left the earth midway through the 1989 season and did not see the team's first-place finish. They were just three of the millions of long-suffering Cubs fans. Right field has been full of them.

SALT OUT OF WATER

With the rebuilding process not looking good for 1976, General Manager John Holland was eased out of the job and became a "consultant." P. K. Wrigley—aging, out of touch with his peers, and reluctant to hire outsiders—simply looked down the executive depth chart and assigned the job to Salty Saltwell, who was entirely unsuited for it. (As former Cubs pitcher Jim Brosnan said about the College of Coaches, "Wrigley was perfectly willing to hire his old athletes instead of bright, hardworking people.") Holland assistant Blake Cullen had been the favorite for the GM job, and Saltwell's appointment surprised almost everyone, including him. Derided by the media as simply a "peanut vendor," Saltwell went back to supervising ballpark and business-side operations after the '76 season, in which the Cubs were again below .500.

THE BICENTENNIAL MINUTE

The 1976 season had its moments, to be sure—but once again few of them involved Cubs victories. That year, baseball wrapped itself in the red, white, and blue to celebrate America's two hundredth birthday—and perhaps to distract fans from the ongoing player/management battles that were leading, step by painful step, to a new policy of player free agency. The Cubs sewed commemorative patches on their uniform sleeves and did their best to associate themselves with the past instead of the present. On Opening Day, April 13, the daughter of Cap Anson—a major figure in the Cubs nineteenth-century exploits who had himself thrown out the Cubs' first pitch in 1908—threw out the first ball. Not to say that the Cubs were out of touch with the times, but their selection to sing the national anthem was James Darren, a former teen idol whose moment in the spotlight had come some fifteen years before.

(These are just some of the many pieces of evidence that the Cubs were resistant to the modern world. To give another example: George Castle notes that, in the mid-1970s, Bill Bonham, Pete LaCock, and Bob Locker of the Cubs began doing yoga exercises to stretch out before home games but were soon commanded to take their hippie business off the field and to a small room near the clubhouse.)

Optimistic forecasts had thirty thousand rooters turning out for the game, but good weather led to a huge walk-up crowd. By game time, 44,818 had passed through the turnstiles, the largest paid total to see a game at Wrigley in nearly thirty years. It's not clear why so many came to the park, but most of the attendees went home happy as the Cubs edged the Mets 5–4 with a run in the last of the ninth.

The Cubs won the next day, too, remarkably enough, but of even greater note was what Dave Kingman of the Mets did to a 1–1 Tom Dettore fastball in the sixth inning, riding it over the left-field wall in the sixth inning for perhaps the longest four-bagger ever at the ivy-covered grounds. As Eddie Gold wrote: "The usual gang of kids was waiting outside with gloves poised. But the ball sailed over their heads. They turned and started running north on Kenmore Avenue. The ball struck the porch of the third house from the Waveland Avenue corner and was caught on the rebound by Richard Keiber."

Babe Ruth, Bill Nicholson, Ransom Jackson, Hank Sauer, Roberto Clemente, Hank Aaron, Jim Hickman, Willie Stargell, Ryan

Klesko, Glenallen Hill, Sammy Sosa, and Anthony Rizzo, among others, have clubbed monumental homers at Wrigley Field, but Kingman's may be the longest. (Some will argue for Sosa's mammoth blast against Milwaukee in June 2003.) Two years later, Kingman brought his talents to the Cubs and in three years there hit ninety-four homers, including a league-leading forty-eight in 1979.

Despite the team's hot start, attendance barely cleared a million. After the big gathering on Opening Day, the Cubs' largest crowd the rest of the season was 28,287 on April 17; they were rewarded with the sight of the Cubs blowing a 12–1 lead to lose to the Phillies 18–16 in ten innings, with Philadelphia's Mike Schmidt clubbing four homers, in the fifth, seventh, eighth, and, critically, tenth.

The Cubs were never a factor in the NL East race; they were already nine games back by mid-May and finished the year twenty-six games out.

OUTLIVING MY USEFULNESS

Philip K. Wrigley died on April 12, 1977, at age eighty-two. His death, just five days after Opening Day, was not unexpected; once a tireless worker, he had not been into his office in nearly half a year. "Everything has changed," Wrigley said shortly before passing on. "I have outlived my usefulness."

His death marked the end of an era. Wrigley was nearly the last of his kind; of the remaining Major League owners, only the similarly old-fashioned Calvin Griffith of the Twins could be compared to him, and Griffith had never shown the concern for the fans that Wrigley had. The game got away from Wrigley in the seventies with the advent of free agency and the influence of national television. He tried to hold down salaries and costs but didn't try to adapt to the time: he remained opposed to lights for the park and still believed in baseball as a great way to market a healthy lifestyle.

When Wrigley passed, flags at the Wrigley Building and Wrigley Field were lowered to half-mast. The Cubs were in Philadelphia; outfielder José Cardenal sat in his hotel room and cried. "I don't know why more players didn't take the time [to know him]," Cardenal said. "Too many of them thought about him only on the first and the 15th of the month, when the checks came with his name on them. But Mr. Wrigley's door was always open. He loved when a player came to talk to him. I think he was a little lonely."

The Cubs went to Wrigley's only son, Bill, who had taken over the gum operations in 1961. To ease tax burdens on his son, P. K. Wrigley had willed that his devoted wife, Helen, would receive half of the estate, but she passed away only two months after her husband. Estate finances would preoccupy Bill for the next three years—and lead him to a dramatic decision.

SEASON IN THE SUN

Following P. K. Wrigley's passing, the Cubs began to hold more promotional days. On Saturday, June 25, 1977, they held "A Day of Fame," which the team called "the first old timers' game played within the friendly confines of Wrigley Field." (It wasn't—such games had been held back in the 1930s—but the claim made good copy.) The team was off to a surprisingly good start, thanks to the pitching arms of starter Rick Reuschel and closer Bruce Sutter, and held a seven-game lead in the National League East, so a huge crowd was expected for the three-inning exhibition, even though the opponent in the "real" game to follow was the last-place Mets. On this warm and sunny day, 33,130 fans watch the Cubs old-timers whip a group of Hall of Famers, 5–1. Ernie Banks got the loudest ovation, but former Cub hurler Moe Drabowsky made the funniest entrance, running from the Cubs dugout and sliding into home plate. Charlie Grimm managed a team with pitchers Drabowsky, Dick Ellsworth, Don Elston, Rich Nye, Johnny Klippstein, Dutch Leonard, Phil Regan (ejected by umpire

Tom Gorman for protesting a ball call), Dick Drott, Bill Hands, and Larry French. The position players included Paul Popovich, Ron Santo, Jerry Kindall, Walt "Moose" Moryn, Clyde McCullough, Bob Will, Gene Baker, and Andy Pafko. Banks, as well as Billy Herman and Fred Lindstrom, played for the Hall of Fame club. Retired *Tribune* sportswriter Ed Prell, asked back to cover the event, noted on June 26 that "the old-timers' 'clubhouse' was the Ambassador West [Hotel], and the group arrived at Wrigley Field in an open-air bus, slightly remindful of the era when visiting teams came to the ballpark in horse-drawn hacks."

Following the warm and fuzzy exhibition, the Cubs went out and fell behind to the visiting Mets. But, down 4–1 in the ninth, the Cubs rallied. With Banks sitting next to Chicago mayor Michael Bilandic in the left-field bleachers, Steve Swisher singled. With one out, Ivan DeJesus doubled Swisher to third, and Larry Biittner doubled to right to plate two runs. Bill Buckner then hit a fly ball to left-center. The wind whipped the ball around, and as Banks, Bilandic, and the other bleacher fans screamed, Mets outfielders Steve Henderson and Lee Mazzilli collided. The resulting double scored Biittner. Two walks later, Manny Trillo hit a bases-loaded roller to third. Doug Flynn bobbled the ball, and by the time he threw to first, Trillo was safe, pinch runner Mick Kelleher scored, and the Cubs had won.

The Cubs' success continued through July. On the twenty-seventh, both they and the White Sox were in first place and playing at home. The Cubs split an afternoon twin bill with the Reds, drawing 42,342 sun-baked fans, while the White Sox pulled in 39,177 to a night game they lost to Detroit. The combined 81,519 turnstile clicks set a record for the biggest one-day baseball crowd in Chicago.

The next day, the Cubs vanquished the Reds, 16–15, in an insane thirteen-inning contest that some possibly hyperbolic members of the Chicago press called "the most exciting game ever played." With 32,155 fans on hand for the four-hour-and-fifty-minute struggle, the Cubs and Reds pulled out all the stops. Cincinnati scored six in the top of the first, but the Cubs tallied four in the bottom half. Trailing 13–12 in the last of the ninth, Chicago knotted the contest on Steve Ontiveros's RBI single. After the Reds scored in the twelfth, Cubs catcher George Mitterwald hit his second homer of the game into the right-field bleachers to knot things again. One inning later, pitcher Rick Reuschel, on in relief after defeating the Reds two days before, singled to center, advanced to third on Ontiveros's single, and scored on another hit by infielder Davey Rosello.

By the time the game ended, the Cubs had used twenty-one players and the Reds sixteen. Reuschel scored the winning run just after 6:00 P.M., and Chicago players ran to the center of the diamond and celebrated. As Tom Fitzpatrick wrote in the next day's *Sun-Times*, "The fans stood on their feet and kept cheering at the top of their hoarse voices and pounding their hands together. As the Cubs trotted through the dusk of the early evening, the fans remained, chanting in unison: 'We're No. 1. We're No. 1.'"

This was the high point of the season. The team was playing over its head, and after Bruce Sutter went down with a shoulder injury, the Cubs collapsed, finishing at 81–81. Sutter T-shirt sales continued unabated, however, although unfortunately for the young right-hander, he wasn't cut in on the action. At Sutter's request, the Players Association filed suit to stop two women from selling shirts reading "Only the Lord saves more than Sutter."

TAKE YOUR FUN WHERE YOU CAN FIND IT

The following season, 1978, featured one of the wildest openings on record. In 1996, George Castle recalled the day: "4,000 showed up at dawn for bleacher seats. Fearing a riot from the impatient throng, ballpark officials opened the bleacher gates at 8 A.M. . . . fans kept storming ticket windows until 45,777 squeezed into Wrigley Field. That meant 8,000 were either standing, lap-sitting, or blocking aisles." By all accounts, it was a mad day at Wrigley—and the last Opening Day to feature day-of-game bleacher sales.

Joe Goddard noted in the April 15 *Sun-Times* that "many had slept overnight at the gates." To accommodate the early crowds, Ray's Bleachers opened for business at 7:00 A.M. and was jammed two hours later. By then, all bleacher seats were filled. Once the grandstand gates opened, two turnstiles actually broke down in the crush, which delayed entry for some fans and held up the official ticket count.

The game was crazy, too. Pirates infielder Jim Fregosi was almost hit by a small chain thrown from the seats. Larry Biittner's ninth-inning homer off Jim Bibby carried the Cubs to a 5–4 win. Later, in the clubhouse, Cubs manager Herman Franks and a local radio reporter engaged in a shouting match.

The Cubs landed under .500 this year, and again in 1979, and once more in 1980, when they finished a lousy 64–98.

These years saw more promotional events and other distractions, which was probably just as well. One of these came on August 17, 1979, when a team of actors and producers from the staggeringly successful ABC-TV series *Happy Days* came to Wrigley Field to take on a contingent of Chicago media figures in a pregame softball contest. Rain washed out the proceedings after just two innings, but the game was completed two days later. In a seven-inning contest, the *Happy Days* team (featuring Henry Winkler, Ron Howard, Anson Williams, Tom Bosley, Marion Ross, Donny Most, Erin Moran, Scott Baio, and Garry Marshall) and the Chicago media club (managed by Lou Boudreau) tied 4–4. Prior to the August 17 exhibition, Bosley—who attended Lake View High School four blocks north of Wrigley—received the Sword of Hope from the American Cancer Society for his work in raising money for cancer research.

More and more people came to the park less in the expectation of seeing good baseball than in the hopes of having a few beers in the sun. On Opening Day 1980, April 17, even that hope was dashed. The Cubs did win, 4–1 in front of a relatively small crowd of 33,313, but did so in such rapid fashion—the game took only an

FIGURE 25. The Cubs and Houston Astros go at it in the early 1980s. Soon the team would replace the press-box level with luxury boxes and install lights on the upper-deck roof. (Credit: National Baseball Hall of Fame and Museum)

hour and fifty-eight minutes—that beer drinkers, according to Rick McArthur in the next day's *Sun-Times*, were "barely left time for the foam to subside in their cups." At least one fan, Sigmund Walsch, had a great time with his friends in what had become one of the world's largest outdoor saloons. "We really got primed," he told the paper. "I took the day off from my job, and we're gonna break the record of 17 [beers] in one game—all 12 of us. There's no doubt about it. This is the greatest day of the year."

The Cubs were once again an afterthought in their own stadium (fig. 25)—and, as it turned out, in their own history. On June 14, 1980, the team presented a thirty-fifth anniversary celebration of the team's last appearance in the World Series. Teams of ex-Cubs and ex-Tigers took the field for an exhibition, and the Tigers made history repeat, winning 4–1. For extra humiliation, before the game Eddie Mathews defeated Ernie Banks in a home-run hitting contest.

SOLD! TO THE HIGHEST BIDDER . . . WELL, THE ONLY BIDDER

The real looming issue for the Cubs in this period was in the front office. Bill Wrigley had never gained his footing as head of the organization. Despite some fortuitous trades that had brought in young talent in the mid-1960s, years of farm neglect and poor personnel decisions had rendered the Cubs unable to compete on a high level, and it did not seem that, given all the estate issues he was facing, Wrigley would be spending the money to create a contender.

He did make a few structural improvements, enlarging both the home and visiting dugouts at Wrigley Field. "We'd always been criticized for having such small dugouts," recalled Salty Saltwell in 2003. "The dugouts *were* inadequate." But without real investment in the team, this had just made more room for mediocrities.

Wrigley's primary concern was the estate. Taxes from his inheritance of the Cubs and, soon after, Wrigley Field threatened to run to $40 million. Most of the taxes had been paid, but Wrigley needed additional funds to pay the rest of the bill. During the three years that he was negotiating with the Internal Revenue Service, Wrigley came to realize that he simply could not retain the team, especially with attendance down, the club performing badly, and little talent en route from a still-barren farm system. Therefore it was a shock, but not a surprise, that he decided to sell. Alice Bright, an attorney who helped administer the Wrigley estate, noted that there was nothing that Bill Wrigley could have done to settle the tax bill and keep the team under his control: "It was a great family tradition, and it's rather sad that taxes can break it up."

The front page of the June 17, 1981, *Chicago Tribune* trumpeted the big news: the Tribune Company itself had purchased the Cubs. Mark Starr reported that Bill Wrigley had made no public offers of the team, instead choosing the Tribune Company as the first and only suitor. Many others would have entered the bidding in an open sale; contentious Oakland Athletics boss Charlie O. Finley stated immediately that he would have loved to have known that the team was on the block, though the thought of the Indiana native—known for his extravagant innovations and battles with players—owning the staid Cubs boggles the mind.

Tribune Company president and chief executive office Stanton Cook announced the purchase, which totaled $20.5 million. (In 1980, the Cubs had claimed to be worth $2.2 million.) That amount covered the baseball team's assets and most of its liabilities, as well as Wrigley Field itself, but it did not include the Chicago Cubs corporation, in order to provide the Tribune Company with additional tax advantages. Writing off player salaries against company earnings would allow the Tribune to save around $1 million a year for a five-year period. The deal also did not include the land on which the stadium stood, though it did include an option on it, which the Tribune exercised a few months after the sale. Since Bill Wrigley controlled 81 percent of the team's stock, approval of the sale by the Cubs' board of directors was a mere formality, even though the Cubs were the only publicly-held team in baseball. The news was excellent for the club's minority shareholders, who were paid $2,050 per share from the transaction.

But would the *Tribune* newspaper be able to report on the Cubs objectively? According to sports editor George Langford, "We will cover the baseball news as diligently as possible and critique the management and ownership when appropriate." By and large, the newspaper did a good job of this. There were times, however, when the paper soft-pedaled legitimate criticism or beat the drum for unpopular or unwise public-policy decisions that just happened to benefit the ball club.

At the time of the sale, most everyone—including the *Tribune* itself—acknowledged that the Cubs were meant to be a center-piece of the company's presence in the growing cable TV field. And indeed, the company's over-the-air station, WGN, had gone on basic cable systems all over the country just a short time before and was soon pulling in huge ratings and advertising dollars by telecasting more than 140 Cubs games per season. After the WGN contract ran out at the conclusion of the 1983 season, the Tribune Company chose to keep games on the superstation rather than move them elsewhere in the cable arena. (In fact, the Cubs didn't televise a game solely on cable until 1993, when the Tribune's local cable news channel, CLTV, began beaming blacked-out Wednesday night contests to the Chicago area.)

While Cubs fans were shocked by the sale, they weren't necessarily saddened. It had been four years since P. K. Wrigley's death, and with the Cubs continuing to wallow in mediocrity, public sympathy favored anyone taking over if they could render the franchise more competitive. Some area residents were happy that the big boys had bought into the neighborhood. A *Tribune* story on June 18, the day after the sale, painted a picture of fans celebrating the sale at the Bleachers Bar—formerly Ray's and soon to be renamed Murphy's: "The fans who sit in the bleachers at Wrigley Field often are the same people who have a hot dog and a beer before the game at the Bleachers Bar," wrote Michael Tackett. "These people, the fans said, would go to the games no matter who owned the team."

Many locals were afraid, however, that the new owner would attempt to install lights inside the baseball shrine at Clark and Addison. With this in mind, in July 1981 the Lake View Citizens' Council named Christy Cressey chairperson of its committee against lights at Wrigley Field, which soon morphed into Citizens United for Baseball in the Sunshine (CUBS). At the time, Andrew McKenna, a paper company executive whom the Cubs appointed chairman of the board, promised neighborhood activists that year that there would be no lights installed at Wrigley Field for at least three seasons. This wasn't nearly good enough for some. Another local, Charlotte Newfeld, became an anti-lights activist around this time and remained a strong presence in Wrigley matters for most of the next two decades. "They can play night ball," she told the *Tribune*'s Daniel Eglar in an August 24, 1982 story, "but not in our neighborhood." Citizens United for Baseball in the Sunshine made quite a splash in the 1980s, distributing popular yellow T-shirts with the words "No Lights!" in bright red letters. These became popular in the bleachers, and even celebrities began to sport them. Bass guitarist Mike Mills of the Georgia rock band R.E.M., a longtime baseball fan, donned one of the shirts for an album signing at a Rose Records location just a few blocks from Wrigley in June 1984.

But even as Lake View residents were sizing up the new owner, the owner was sizing up Lake View. Frank Maloney, for many years the Cubs' director of ticket operations, joined the organization in 1981. He noted, in a 2002 interview conducted by Shamus Toomey, that, "when I started here, I wasn't sure that this neighborhood wasn't going to become a slum. We were located between [upscale] Lincoln Park and [lower-middle-class] Uptown, and there's a major difference between the areas on a socioeconomic level. I came in and thought: 'Which way is it going?'" Maloney is right that the Lake View neighborhood was economically and socially diverse, but at no point was the area around Wrigley truly dangerous. In fact, by the 1980s, the real estate market in Lake View was bouncing back. According to Michael Miner in the April 12, 1985, Chicago *Reader*, "a Sheffield Avenue three-flat that cost $18,000 in 1971 was appraised last year at $175,000."

Whatever the reality of the neighborhood, the Cubs now sought to improve the perception of it. All the organization, and the area, needed was a spark—and Chairman of the Board Andrew McKenna had just the man in mind. What Leo Durocher had been to the Cubs resurgence in the late 1960s and early 1970s, Dallas Green would be the team in the 1980s.

At least that was the hope.

THE EMPIRE OF THE *TRIBUNE*

WRIGLEY FIELD, 1982–2009

BUILDING A NEW TRADITION?

Shortly after the Tribune purchase, Andrew McKenna hired Dallas Green, fresh from helping turn the Phillies into a world championship club, as the Cubs' new general manager. Perhaps a little too eager to put his stamp on the club, the blustery, hard-bitten Green cut all organizational ties to the 1969 club as part of his Building a New Tradition campaign. In a move that won enmity from fans and the media, Green even exiled the most famous Cub of all, Ernie Banks, who since his retirement in 1972 had been associated with the club in various capacities, mostly in the group ticket sales department, where he schmoozed high-volume customers. The new general manager apparently did not understand the hold that past Cubs greats have on their fans. Even ten-year-olds knew Ernie Banks and Ron Santo, but nobody clamored for Dallas Green.

The new tradition looked a lot like the old tradition at first. Under Green's handpicked skipper, Lee Elia, the Cubs were 73–89 in 1982 and got off to a poor start the next season. Following a 4–3 loss to the visiting Dodgers on April 29 that dropped the team to 5–14, Elia had had enough—enough of the press, enough of bad baseball, and enough of Cub fans, whom he saw as lazy, backstabbing, violent-tempered ignoramuses. He vented that day to veteran radio man Les Grobstein:

"They're really, really behind you around here." *My f***ing ass!* What the f*** am I supposed to do? Go out there and let my f***ing players get destroyed every day? And be *quiet* about it? For the f***ing nickel-dime people that show up here? The motherf***ers don't even *work!* They ought to go out and get a f***ing *job* and find out what it's *like* to go out and earn a f***ing living. 85 percent of the f***ing world's working; the other 15 come out here. It's a f***ing *playground* for the c***suckers!

Rip the motherf***ers! Rip them c***in' c***suckers like the f***ing players. Got guys bustin' their f***in' ass and them f***in' people boo. And *that's* the *Cubs?* My f***in' *ass!* They talk about the great support the players get around here. I haven't seen it *this* f***in' year! The changes that have happened in the Cub organization are *multifold!* [*sic*] All right, they don't show because we're 5–14. And unfortunately, that's the criteria of them dumb 3,000 f***ing fans who come out to watch day baseball. The other 85 are earning a living!

This may not have been what Green meant by "a new tradition," exactly, but it was one of the more entertaining, and honest, rants ever made by a sports figure. Unfortunately, the nationally publicized incident made the Cubs and Elia even more of a mockery. It also effectively ended the skipper's career in Chicago. He was mercifully relieved of his job on August 22, with the Cubs at 55–69. The 15 percent, however, weren't going anywhere—and they would soon multiply.

ENTERING THE MODERN ERA

Beyond hiring Green, the Tribune Company made investments in the infrastructure. (By 2000, the company had spent approximately $35 million refurbishing the field.) They started with the clubhouses, which for decades had been inaccessible from the dugouts—with the effect that players were sometimes seen walking down the foul lines toward the clubhouse entrances during games, to get to the bathrooms (fig. 26). Furthermore, the

FIGURE 26. Until the early 1980s, the Cubs could only access their clubhouse by walking to the left-field corner and entering this door. These days, the area stores groundskeeping tools.
(Credit: Andrea Giafaglione)

showers were small, rats ran wild, and the facilities hardly had room for the players, much less the press.

Dallas Green made new clubhouses a priority. "It was one of the first things Dallas wanted to do," Salty Saltwell recalled. It was an expensive project, requiring excavation behind the dugouts, but at Green's urging the Tribune Company coughed up, though the project wasn't completed until 1984. The new dressing room was an indication that the Cubs were serious about modernizing—or at least in making things better for themselves, since the visitors' quarters remained cramped and unventilated.

"We've put in a beautiful new clubhouse for our team," Green said at the time. "I considered doing the same thing for the visitors, but then I said, 'Nah, let 'em suffer.'" The Cubs did install canvas around both sides of a walkway that ran above the concourse to protect visiting players from the barbs of fans. The netting also kept fans from climbing the wall to access the visiting clubhouse; equipment had been disappearing from the visitors' quarters.

Not all of the Tribune investments were as welcome. Shortly after Opening Day 1983, the Cubs added an electronic message board to the bottom of the legendary scoreboard. The board was nominally intended to provide statistical information about players, but its real intention was to convey between-inning advertisements. To make things worse for purists, management chose to have beer ads hooked to each side of the new electronic board, blocking the view from the last rows of the center-field bleachers. The beer signs were removed prior to the 1986 season, but the message board remained.

A SPECIAL SEASON

Things began to turn around in 1984, though the season did not begin smoothly. Two spring training fights between teammates and a big late-March trade with the Phillies kept the Cubs up in the air as the season began. But it would soon become clear that this was a special season. The Cubs started hot, as did the usually moribund New York Mets, but the Cardinals lost seven in a row in April and fell out of the race, as did Pittsburgh, Philadelphia, and Montreal.

The rising star of the 1984 team was second baseman Ryne Sandberg, in his third season with Chicago. No game did more to cement his reputation—and that of the rising Cubs—than the nationally televised June 23, 1984, tilt against visiting Saint Louis. A six-run Cardinals second inning had knocked out lefty Steve Trout, and Willie McGee was working on the cycle. But ahead 7–1 in the fifth, the Cardinals' pitching weakened. During a five-run Cubs rally in the sixth, Sandberg hit his third single of the day (and drove in his third and fourth runs). With Saint Louis ahead 9–8 in the bottom of the ninth, former Cub Bruce Sutter tried to finish the game. Sutter had been on the mound since the seventh, and Sandberg took him deep to lead off the ninth. In the Cubs tenth, with the Cardinals up 11–9 and Sutter still on the hill, Bob Dernier worked a walk with two out. Sandberg then came up and drilled another Sutter splitter over the left-field wall to tie things *again*. Sandberg had hit last-ditch game-tying home runs in consecutive innings off the best closer in the game—a hysterical crowd of 38,079 howled; NBC broadcaster Bob Costas couldn't believe it; Harry Caray, in the Cubs radio booth, yelled, "Sandberg did it *again!*" Five for six, two homers, seven RBI. The Cubs went on to win, but that was almost a footnote to Sandberg's heroics.

And when the Cubs won, the fans came back. In 1984, the Cubs broke two million for the first time, drawing 2,107,655 to finish second in the league in attendance, up about 700,000 from the previous year. Only once since then, in 1986, have the Cubs drawn fewer than two million fans over a full season, and it has become routine for them to see close to three million every year. The club also reaped benefits on TV. Broadcaster Harry Caray with his good-time, beer-drinking persona was immensely popular, and Cubs games on WGN were among the most highly rated shows on cable.

But television was also a problem. For the first time in the era in which people expected to watch the playoffs on national television, the Cubs were breezing toward the National League East division title, which they nailed down with a 96–65 record. Broadcast muckety-mucks in New York were aghast at the possibilities. What if the Cubs made the World Series? And had to play in the *daytime*? NBC, which held the broadcast rights to the series, and Major League Baseball itself fretted that games played on weekdays would draw millions of dollars less advertising revenue than night games—and they saw no silver lining in the potential novelty of postseason day games.

This was quite a turnaround. Night games had been introduced to the World Series only as recently as 1971, raising concerns that children would not be able to stay up late enough to watch, and that the game would become too controlled by advertisers. While the sky hasn't fallen, it is clear in retrospect that those concerns were well founded. Television contracts forced baseball to abandon its tradition of daytime postseason play, making the game just another nighttime show. But people adapted—though ironically people in the media now sometimes complain when games run too late—and by 1984 the landscape had shifted so much that the Cubs, in their old-fashioned brick ballpark with no lights, threatened the existing order.

So baseball commissioner Bowie Kuhn said to hell with tradition and, more significantly, to hell with fairness. Showing that television really did run the game, Kuhn ruled that should the Cubs get to the World Series, they would be denied home-field advantage, which was to have been the National League's that year. (At the time, home-field advantage alternated.) To protect NBC's advertising revenues, Major League Baseball would force the Cubs to play the middle three contests at home rather than the first two and last two, so that there would potentially be more night games. When told that the games would be rescheduled, Cubs manager Jim Frey had it exactly right. "When baseball and TV signed the contract, didn't they know that the Cubs were in baseball and this might happen?" he said. "Did they just find out in the last week that we're in the league?"

Unfortunately, the Cubs made the controversy moot. After winning the first two playoff games against the Padres at home, 13–0 and 4–2, before capacity throngs of 36,282, they went to San Diego and dropped three straight, the last two, in particular, heartbreakers.

That series was notable not only for its role in the saga of the lights but for a moment in the evolution of the rooftops across the streets from the park. In 1985, a high school history teacher, Bob Wood, visited all the Major League ballparks and wrote a book about his adventures. In Chicago, he talked his way onto a Waveland Avenue rooftop, where building residents and their friends sat; the rooftops were not yet the province of private clubs. He describes a "lawyer who during the '84 play-offs had brought suit against the owner of the building[, who] had barred his tenants from the roof for the Padres games. Instead he planned to rent it out for high-priced parties . . . [the lawyer] went to court and got an injunction to stop the bum . . . Through the entire trial the bleacherites across the street would turn around in unison and chant, 'Landlord sucks,' followed by a round of applause." This, too, was a story with more chapters yet to be written.

LIGHT UP THE NIGHT

Major League Baseball was losing patience with the darkness at Wrigley Field. Brand-new commissioner Peter Ueberroth began making not-so-veiled threats against the Cubs, directing them to install lights under penalty of having future series games transferred to other parks. "It's not just a question of lights in Wrigley Field. It's a question of *if* Wrigley Field. If Wrigley Field, in my opinion, doesn't have lights . . . at some time in the future, it won't *be* a field," Ueberroth told the National Press Club early in 1985.

Local media responded with appropriate venom, but the Tribune Company wasn't unhappy at all. They and Dallas Green—who was in the faction that believed that playing eighty-one home games in the sun was a disadvantage—had always wanted lights installed, and the inexorable march toward artificial illumination began. The day after Ueberroth's threat, the Cubs filed suit in Cook County Circuit Court to keep the city from enforcing city and state laws banning night ball at Wrigley Field.

This act, along with the arrogance and aggression of Major League Baseball, galvanized the No Lights in Wrigley movement. Neighborhood opposition to the Cubs, and to baseball itself, grew sharply. Part of what made Wrigley Field special in the 1970s and 1980s was the way it reminded people of the pretelevision days of baseball. The Cubs had traded off that image for a long time, and the Lake View neighborhood had a right to fight for it. At the same time, some members of the antilights faction wanted simply to make life as difficult for the Tribune Company as possible; some didn't even care if the Cubs were forced to leave Wrigley Field. The loudest and most uncompromising of them tarnished the movement.

On March 25, 1985, Chicago judge Richard Curry rejected the Cubs' lawsuit to reverse the ban on night ball at Wrigley. He asserted that lights would destroy a residential community to make sports team owners richer in an act "repugnant to common decency." Yet why were the Cubs held to a different standard than the White Sox, who had been playing night ball near the residential neighborhoods of Armour Square and Bridgeport for more than forty years at the time?

A Cubs fan and a traditionalist, Curry used all sorts of baseball imagery in his ruling, none of which explained why the misery he alleged would occur with the installation of lights was acceptable to South Side fans but not to North Siders.

The Cubs immediately appealed Curry's decision. The saga of the lights was a long way from over.

CASHING IN

The Cubs new success and popularity was having other effects on the neighborhood. Rehabilitation and gentrification came to a part of town more recently known for its dilapidation. Suddenly, the race was on to rehab old apartments and turn them into condos, to tear down old structures and rebuild on the sites, and to open new bars, stores, and restaurants. By the mid-1980s, young people flocked to rock shows at the Metro (a nightclub formerly known as Stages) as well as at the Cubby Bear, the Wild Hare, and Exedus. Both local and national acts performed at these clubs, and parking was often scarce.

Sometime during the decade, according to Forty-Fourth Ward alderman Bernie Hansen, local real estate agents began referring to the area as "Wrigleyville"—though some hold that developers coined the term back in the 1970s. Whatever its genesis, the name has stuck.

A few smart investors had begun buying property around Wrigley Field in the late 1970s. Two of the most well-known speculators were George "Gus" Loukas, who by the early 2000s owned nearly twenty buildings around the park, including the Cubby Bear and Sports Corner, and Jim Murphy, a former policeman who bought Ray's Bleachers in 1980.

Some of the newcomers took drastic actions to improve their holdings. A series of "mysterious" fires gutted several old buildings in the area during the early 1980s, providing insurance money for rebuilding. "We'd get two or three fires a day," remembered fireman Marc Patricelli of Engine Company 78 in 2002.

Another ugly aspect of the influx of money into Lake View was the displacement of locals—that is, gentrification.

Some folks no longer able to afford Lake View moved north to Uptown, a diverse but struggling neighborhood. Others went west, or even to the suburbs, many of which now are home to substantial Latino populations. In their place, much of the area now hosts a constant turnover of young, mostly white, postcollegiates looking for an "authentic" city experience. Such youngsters, with skin ready for tanning, money to spend, and copious appetites for alcohol, seem to become instant Wrigley Field converts. Each year a fresh class of affluent twentysomethings seems to glom onto Cubbie fandom—or something akin to it.

THE IN-CROWD

The Cubs had become genuinely popular. For the first time in years, the Cubs, their park, and their fans were media darlings. The peculiar habits of Wrigley's bleacher denizens—tossing back enemy home runs, tossing back beers, and tossing around bets with fellow fans—became draws in their own right.

Bill Veeck, having divested himself of the White Sox for a second time, became a semiregular at Wrigley in the 1980s, enjoying his dotage by sitting shirtless in the bleachers with a frosty beverage. His words on the bleachers in 1984 came to embody many people's feelings about Wrigley Field: "The scent of suntan oil, broiled hot dogs, and spilled beer create a wondrous feeling of euphoria—a feeling that neither crowds, hard benches, long ticket lines, nor the endless trek to distant toilets can diminish. The bleachers aren't just concrete and steel, cheap seats, and concession stands; they're a state of mind, a way of life, the best of summer."

The euphoria wasn't confined to the bleachers. Announcer Harry Caray turned the middle-of-the-seventh tradition of singing "Take Me Out to the Ballgame" into a boozy, high-spirited sing-along, creating another special ritual of Wrigley Field. Bob Wood put it this way: "Harry sings, everybody else joins in. They stand, in the box seats, upper and lower, in the crowded bleachers, on the rooftops across the street, and on Waveland below. All sing from the heart, for they truly don't care 'if they ever get back.'" Never mind that Caray started the sing-along when he was an employee of the White Sox.

To accommodate more fans, in July 1985 the Cubs added more than two hundred seats to the outfield "catwalks," which ranged from the foul lines to the curves in the wall in left and right center. These had never before featured seating, serving instead as egress walkways, letting fans out onto the street after games and allowing security personnel into the bleachers from outside or the grandstand if necessary. No more would Cubs announcers call home runs slugged "onto the catwalk." Prior to the 1986 season, three rows of these seats were designated as no-alcohol "family" sections—perhaps to answer neighborhood charges that the team's drive for night baseball was really a drive for night beer revenues. A few years later, citing low attendance in the section, the Cubs lifted the designation on the right-field side. The one in left field remained open through the 2010 season, albeit at prices higher than any other nonbox seats in the park. After 2010, the no-alcohol section was cashiered.

HAWK DOWN

Free agent outfielder Andre "The Hawk" Dawson, nearly locked out of baseball by owner collusion despite stellar years with the Montreal Expos, signed a ridiculously cheap $500,000 contract with the Cubs in spring 1987. The hustling Dawson became an immediate favorite with right-field bleacher fans in Wrigley, and he shared the love by hitting forty-nine home runs, a performance that garnered him National League most valuable player honors despite the team's last-place finish.

Perhaps the most memorable moment of the Cubs' poor 1987 season was scary rather than triumphant. On July 7, Dawson clubbed a homer in the first inning against the Padres' Eric Show; it was his twenty-fourth of the year and seventh against San Diego. When Dawson batted in the third, Show beaned him on the left side of his face. Dawson went down, bleeding from a wound that would eventually require a trip to the hospital for twenty-two stitches. As angry murmurs came from the crowd of 26,615, Cubs pitcher Rick Sutcliffe charged out of the dugout to attack

Show. Both benches emptied, and a real fight—not the milling-about kind often seen in baseball—broke out while trainers examined Dawson. By the time Dawson came to, the fight had abated. But Dawson lurched to his feet and tried to charge Show, who was quickly led from the field by umpire Charlie Williams as the crowd roared.

Following the incident, a seemingly contrite Show released a statement in which he disclaimed any desire to hit, or even throw at, Dawson (or any other hitter). The Cubs didn't think much of the apology. Padres manager Larry Bowa, a former Cub, simply said, "The Cubs don't know Eric Show too well. Knowing Show, he tried to pitch inside. He did not try to hit the guy."

Whatever the case, the Cubs won that one, 7–5.

HELL BENT ON COMPROMISE

Outside the park, an all-out war was brewing. The team was still pushing for lights in the park, and much of the neighborhood was still against it. Prompted by local outrage, in June 1985, the Illinois House of Representatives and Senate voted to prohibit night ball at Wrigley Field. In response the Cubs immediately rat-tled their sabers, threatening to junk the stadium if need be. Dal-las Green and the Tribune Company, unburdened by sentimen-tal feelings, spoke of their frustration in not being able to play night games at home as every other team could. Vague threats of moving to a suburban location emanated from the mouths of Cubs' lawyers, officials, and lobbyists, but that idea didn't play well downtown. Mayor Harold Washington said in June 1985 that he would keep Chicago's borders guarded "like Horatio at the bridge" to ensure the team didn't move.

The mayor understood, however, that some sort of compro-mise would have to be worked out. So he, the Cubs, neighbor-hood groups, and lawmakers set about brokering an agreement. The Cubs embarked on a long campaign of lobbying state and lo-cal politicians that eventually led to the announcement, in early 1987, that the club could accept a limit of eighteen night games a season, were any to be permitted at all. The House and Senate then voted to exempt postseason games from the antilights bill. This inching along turned into a leap forward when Harold Washington announced in November 1987 that he endorsed the installation of lights. Washington's sudden death on November 25, complicated matters some—he was no longer there to strongarm any plan—but his successor, Eugene Sawyer, also endorsed the idea. Sooner or later, this was going to get done.

What had turned the tide? Money, as always—Major League money. The Cubs had recently applied to Major League Baseball to host the 1990 All-Star Game, perhaps hoping that the public relations windfall from bringing extra money into the city would push politicians toward agreeing to light up Wrigley. Baseball commissioner A. Bartlett Giamatti informed Mayor Sawyer on February 24, 1988, that the Cubs wouldn't get the All-Star Game unless the Chicago City Council approved the lights resolution—and quick.

The next day, two weeks after a *Tribune* editorial blistered "political bums" working against the lights proposal, the City Council voted 29–19 to approve the installation of lights at Wrigley Field and, not coincidentally, make the 1990 All-Star Game and its attendant festivities possible. That alone was estimated to be a $40 million windfall for city hotels, restaurants, cabbies, and taverns.

On February 26, the Cubs signed an agreement to stay at Wrigley Field through 2002—given the stipulation that the neighborhood was not voted "dry." In that event, the Cubs had an escape clause.

With city approval and team commitment in hand, the night game plan allowed the Cubs to schedule eight night contests in 1988 and eighteen each season from 1989 through 2002. This gave the Cubs the opportunity to make more money off their gate and their television broadcasts and allowed for night postseason games if necessary. The war was over—though ironically, perhaps, Dallas Green, the Tribune's chief engineer in bringing the team out of the past, was no longer with the club having quit after the 1987 season over "philosophical differences."

LIGHT, MORE LIGHT

Now that the lights had been approved, it was time to actually install them. In fact, the process of designing of a lighting system and constructing light towers had begun long before the politicians hammered out their compromise. As a result, the Cubs were able to begin installing the lights just a few weeks after the deal went down. The Cubs' goal was to build a functional structure that disturbed the neighborhood as little as possible. A trade magazine later noted that "minimizing light trespass into the surrounding neighborhood was a prime objective in the design process. The narrow NEMA 2 beam spread of the floodlights allows precise aiming and control of light output. A matte-black metal band around the outer edge of the reflector surface minimizes stray light." Cleveland's Osborn Engineering Company built the structural system, and General Electric provided the lighting system.

On the evening of April 6, 1988, trucks transported the structural steel of the light towers to the players' parking lot at Wrigley Field. The next morning, a helicopter lifted, to the upper deck roofs, the first in a series of girders to hold the six lighting structures (three on each side of the roof). A helicopter crew worked to lift the pieces from 8:30 A.M. to 4:00 P.M. for several weeks. The third-base-side towers were installed by April 26, the first-base-side towers by June 21, and the wiring finished in July. The lights themselves, heretofore stored in a nearby warehouse, were lowered into place—again by helicopter—after each tower was completed. It took thirty minutes to bolt in the first series of light banks, according to former Cubs publicist Bob Ibach, but by the end of the process, workers were installing the banks in four minutes. The six light towers held 546 floodlights. The lamps, which had an average life of three thousand hours, could last for up to five hundred games. General Electric estimated a cost of $518.40 per night game.

The Cubs also bolted eight lights to the top of the scoreboard and installed lights both in the stands and under them to make sure that fans could find concession stands, rest rooms, and exits. The team also fitted the parking lots and the outside of the stadium with lights. According to the Cubs, the project cost $5 million.

On the evening of July 25, the Cubs held a benefit for Cubs Care (the club's charity arm) at Wrigley Field before three thousand spectators. This allowed the club to troubleshoot the lighting fixtures one final time. Mickey and the Memories, a popular 1950s/1960s-styled rock and soul cover band, played on a stage in right field. Billy Williams and Ernie Banks signed autographs, and the two teamed with Andre Dawson and Ryne Sandberg for a home-run hitting contest. Everyone could see just fine.

LIGHTS ON

August 8, 1988, was hot and humid. Ninety-one-year-old Cubs fan Harry Grossman flipped the light switch at 6:06 in the evening, and the lights came on. A throng of 565 reporters was on hand for the occasion, making this the most widely covered regular-season baseball game in history.

In the bottom of the first, Ryne Sandberg stepped into the batter's box only to be greeted by the bouncing breasts of Morganna, the "kissing bandit" who made a habit in the 1970s and 1980s of running onto various athletic fields to plant wet ones on pro athletes. Cubs security led her off the field before she could plaster the beloved Ryno.

Despite the excitement of the evening, the fans went home without a result. During the fourth inning, with the Cubs leading the Phillies 3–1, a hard rain began to fall, delaying the game. More than a dozen fans jumped out of the stands to slide on the wet tarpaulin; one fan careened so quickly that he crashed into the brick wall behind third base and had to be carted off on a stretcher. Cubs pitchers Greg Maddux and Les Lancaster slid on the tarp as well, but without injury. After two hours of rain, umpires called the game at 10:15.

The first official night game was played the next evening, when the Cubs topped the Mets 6–4 before 36,399. "I've never been to a night game before," eighty-six-year-old bleacher regular Carmella Hartigan told United Press International. "But you know, times change and you can't be a stick in the mud." Acquiescing to neighborhood concerns, the Cubs cut off beer sales at 9:20 P.M. and halted organ playing half an hour later in order to keep things a bit quieter.

And you know what? The world did not crumble. In fact, night games at the ballpark became real events, special in their novelty and relative scarcity.

LUXURY TAX

Flush with success, the Cubs went to stage two of their modernization campaign in 1989, spending $14 million to install luxury boxes, build a new press box, establish a permanent upper-deck concession stand, and construct a balcony in the upper deck. The architectural firm of Hellmuth, Obata, and Kassabaum, which two years later gained fame by designing Camden Yards in Baltimore, the first of the "retro" stadiums, planned the Cubs' renovation. Turner Construction of Chicago did the building.

For the luxury boxes, which were a top priority, the team installed sixty-seven high-rent seating areas above the lower-deck stands, from foul line to foul line, taking over what had been the press box. Each suite was, at the time, rentable for between $45,000 and $60,000 a season, depending on its size and location. Local corporations such as Beatrice, Baxter Healthcare, and First Chicago signed up. Along with prime seating (protected from the weather by windows), the luxury boxes came with meals, beverages, and a dizzying array of freshly prepared desserts.

To accommodate the press, ejected from their perch above the lower deck, the Cubs tore out a chunk of upper-deck grandstand seats behind home plate and built a new press box that could hold 130, some fifty more than the old one. For those used to the old, cramped press box, the new rest rooms, larger dining area, and upgraded facilities were a welcome change. (To ameliorate the loss of the upper-deck grandstand, the Cubs added around four hundred new seats behind the last row of the previously existing upper-deck boxes—and thus came out ahead.) The new press area, however, had no elevator. The writers, who often must walk up to the press box two or three times a day as part of their jobs, complained—justifiably—of exhaustion. And when, on April 8, 1989, veteran *Trenton Times* writer Harold "Bus" Saidt—who had just covered the Phillies during the season-opening series at Wrigley—passed away after returning to the East Coast, the Baseball Writers' Association of America formally protested the lack of an elevator to Cubs President Don Grenesko. Grenesko claimed that installing an elevator would damage Wrigley Field's facade. One was finally installed in 1996, after four wheelchair-bound Cubs fans had filed suit in federal court, claiming that they had inadequate access to their seats in Wrigley Field. At that time, to bring Wrigley Field into compliance with the Americans with Disabilities Act, the Cubs also doubled the reserved seating for the disabled from forty-four to eighty-eight and built more wheelchair-accessible rest rooms and concession stands. Not that this did Bus Saidt any good.

A major portion of the rebuilding involved concession stands. The Cubs built a permanent concession stand under the new press box; in previous years, upper-deck fans could buy concessions only from carts near the rest rooms. In addition, the Cubs constructed a balcony, facing southwest, behind the home-plate section of the upper deck. The balcony offers a great view of the city; groups can rent the space for pregame parties.

When, in the 1980s, Tribune Company types discussed the Cubs' "need to be competitive," they were talking in code about night games and luxury seating. Having accomplished both of these goals, the Cubs got ready to reap the profits.

WILD TIMES

The Cubs, surprisingly, rose again in 1989. Nobody expected the Don Zimmer–led team to do much, but fine seasons from Sandberg, Dawson, rookie outfielders Jerome Walton and Dwight Smith, first baseman Mark Grace, and a sharp pitching staff put the club into contention. Smith was not only a good player but also a fine singer. He belted out the national anthem on July 21, becoming the first Cub player to do so since infielder Carmen Fanzone took the field with his trumpet on June 18, 1972.

The fun began Opening Day, April 4. As 33,361 fans shivered, the Cubs took a 5–4 lead into the ninth. Newly acquired closer Mitch "Wild Thing" Williams—one of the most aptly nicknamed pitchers in baseball history—gave up consecutive singles to Philadelphia's Bob Dernier, Tommy Herr, and Von Hayes to load the bases. And then he fanned Mike Schmidt, Chris James, and Mark Ryal to send the crowd into an uproar.

Following Opening Day, injuries to key players and some inconsistent play dropped the Cubs as low as fourth by mid-May, but the team battled back, claiming first place for good in early August. The August 29 game indicated that it really might be the Cubs' year. Houston came into Wrigley Field and blew Mike Bielecki and Dean Wilkins off the hill with two runs in the second, two more in the fourth, and five in the fifth. Trailing 9–0, the Cubs looked done. But in the sixth, the Cubs scored a pair, and they tallied three more in the seventh on Lloyd McClendon's two-run homer and Dwight Smith's pinch-single. In the eighth, still down 9–5, the Cubs rallied for a tie on RBI singles by Sandberg, McClendon, and Grace and a sacrifice fly by Smith. In the last of the tenth, Walton walked, McClendon singled him to third, and Smith lashed a single to right, driving in his third run in four innings. The 10–9 win, the Cubs' first comeback from nine runs down since 1930, was probably their most dramatic victory since the so-called Sandberg game in 1984.

The Cubs began to pull away, and ended the season with a six-game advantage over the Mets. Winning the 1989 division title meant that the Cubs would play their first postseason night games at Wrigley Field, squaring off against the San Francisco Giants in a best-of-seven series.

On Wednesday, October 4, a sellout crowd of 39,195 filled the venerable park for game 1. The Giants' Will Clark had four hits, including two homers (one a grand slam), and six RBI as he and his team stormed Greg Maddux and the Cubs 11–3. The next day, the Cubs blew former teammate Rick Reuschel out of the box, scoring six runs in the first inning en route to a 9–5 win. Again, fans jammed Wrigley Field to capacity. Unfortunately for the Cubs, the Giants took the next three contests at Candlestick Park and captured the National League pennant.

THAT'S WHAT I WANT

When the Wrigleys owned the team, the Cubs had only one consistent promotion: Ladies Day. While other teams threw events such as bat day, cap day, or banner day, the Cubs held fast to non-promotion. The Cubs did hire a full-time director of promotions, Marea Mannion, in 1977, but only nine "special days" were held that year, and the concept of giveaway promotions was shelved.

Once the Tribune Company bought the team, however, everything changed. For the first time, the Cubs built a marketing department, realizing that with the team so often in the dumps, other measures were necessary to bring in fans and dollars. In 1982, the Tribune brought aboard veteran baseball front-office man Jeff Odenwald and made him director of marketing. In 1984, the Cubs began an aggressive campaign of special dates, giving fans such items as calendars, batting helmets, sports bags, tote bags, caps, toiletry kits, ponchos, floppy hats, big sunglasses, mesh shirts, thermoses, sun visors, backpacks, baseball cards, and scarves. The items were, of course, decorated with the logos of whatever company paid to have them manufactured. Companies like Rawlings, American Girl, Bowman, Topps, and Mattel have presented Cubs fans with tchotchkes ranging from the traditional pennants, balls, cards, T-shirts, and plastic cups to newer novelties like magnetic schedules, dolls, growth charts, water bottles, and pins. In addition, the Cubs have allowed fans on Wrigley Field's surface itself for camera days, and kids have participated in on-field pregame baseball games and clinics.

Sometimes, the giveaways work too well. When the team gave away Beanie Babies, Precious Moments, or Cherished Teddies dolls decorated with Cub themes, for example, many of the "fans" waiting to be among the first five or ten thousand to get them simply left the park once they had secured their dolls. Other times, the giveaways backfire. On separate occasions, both Mark Grace and Randy Myers got to watch thousands of posters featuring them come sailing onto the field when they performed less than stellarly.

Some early 1980s promotions, such as father-son (or -daughter) games and Farmer's Day, didn't catch on, but Ted Giannoulas, the San Diego Chicken, made several well-received appearances. While Giannoulas was not the first team mascot in the major leagues, his wacky antics made overstuffed animal costumes de rigueur at most parks, although Wrigley Field sported only one—a creature called Cubbles—for a short time in the late 1970s. Later kitschy promotions, such as '70s Night, became very popular, featuring rock groups such as Sister Sledge and KC and the Sunshine Band. The sight of broadcaster Steve Stone in a slightly era-challenged navy blue Austin Powers costume and full wig was alone worth the cost of admission.

Despite the tremendous increase in marketing revenue the traditional form of team income remained strong, Between 1970 and 1990, Wrigley Field's ticket prices rose more or less with inflation, but the reclassification of seat types meant that more revenue was coming in overall. In the same period, the number of tickets held for day-of-game sale dropped, and general admission seating disappeared altogether.

In 1970, all box seats cost $3.50, grandstand tickets were $1.75 for adults and $1 for kids, and all bleacher seats were a buck. By 1976, box seat prices were $4.50, but there was a new category of seats, reserved grandstand (the first dozen or so rows behind the boxes) that went for $3.50, and regular grandstands were $2.50 for adults and half that for kids. Seats in the bleachers went up to $1.25. Between 1977 and 1980, box-seat tickets increased fifty cents every year. In 1983, after the Tribune Company had bought the club, bleachers had gone up to $3, but more important, the team had divided box seats into "club" and "field" sections that opened up the possibility of differential pricing. By 1987, all chairs were reserved, even the $4 bleachers and the seats in the farthest corners of the lower deck, which, like all other lower grandstand reserved tickets, cost $6; the cheapest place in the park was the upper deck, where the under-fourteens could sit for $3.50. In 1987, boxes were listed at $10.50. While that wasn't much above the 1970 rate when corrected for inflation, the club's ticketing philosophy had clearly changed. Wrigley's vision of seats available for anyone wanting to walk up had been replaced by a much more regulated—and, soon enough, heavily computerized—system. And around this time, price increases, like the cost of college, regularly began to outstrip inflation.

The Cubs rolled out new ticket prices for 1990, apparently believing that fans would cut them slack since the team had just won an NL East title—though they still never spent all that much money on free agents to keep the quality of the team up. Field boxes rose to $13, then $15 the following year, while bleachers went to $6 by 1991. In the mid-1990s, the Cubs discontinued their partial season-ticket package—usually covering forty or so weekend and night games a year—and offered only full-season packages. Almost imperceptibly, lower-middle-class fans were being priced out of the park.

It was the same squeeze in the park as was being seen outside it. The gentrification of Wrigleyville continued through the 1990s, as new generations of young people came into the area knowing little of the area's history. All they knew was that this was a fun neighborhood. And Wrigleyville is fun, especially if you're young. It is a far younger area, on average, than it has ever been—as late as 1970, 15 percent of Lake View's residents were over sixty-five; thirty years later it was about half that, with nearly 70 percent of the neighborhood's population between twenty and forty-four. According to the 2010 census, 41 percent of the area's population was between the ages of twenty-five and thirty-four. Population totals between 1980 and 2010 stabilized around ninety-five thousand, with a few more residences built each year.

Some residents of Lake View are resentful of what has happened to the neighborhood. Many locals despise the noise and traffic from Wrigley Field and are quick to tell stories of drunken fans urinating in local yards. Yet while anything that goes on in the ballpark or its immediate surroundings is the Cubs' responsibility—and the team must shoulder much of the blame for postgame shenanigans involving overserved fans—it's hardly true that all of the problems in the neighborhood come from baseball patrons. Every Friday and Saturday night, funseekers travel from around the city and the surrounding suburbs to Wrigleyville not to see a game but to eat, drink, dance, hear live music, shop, or just hang around.

Moving into Wrigleyville in 2014 and complaining about crowds and noise is like buying a house near an airport and whining about all those noisy planes. The anger of aggrieved Lake View citizens would perhaps be palatable if they hadn't chosen to live there, and we might all have more sympathy if property values there hadn't soared. Some community leaders who fought the installation of lights in the 1980s still feel betrayed by the Tribune Company. Others feel that promises made by the city about the future of the neighborhood have not been kept. And this resentment, which is not totally causeless, has played itself out in some increasingly strange ways. The saga of the lights had ended, but the battle of the rooftops was looming in the future.

HERE COME THE ALL-STARS

Ticket prices weren't the only thing to change after the 1989 season. With the All-Star Game coming to Wrigley in 1990, Major League Baseball conveyed to the Cubs the need to upgrade the visitors' clubhouses, which had not been significantly updated since the 1930s. The club, therefore, spent $6 million on improvements. Bruce Levine wrote in the July 10, 1990, *Sun-Times* that the new quarters included "state of the art clothing stalls and carpeting. Moreover, mirrored pillars give the appearance of more room." It was still a small clubhouse, though.

At the same time, the Cubs reroofed Wrigley Field and installed new gutters at a cost of $800,000. The organization also installed a new phone system, built new washrooms in the left- and right-field corners, opened a new restaurant (the Sheffield Grill) under the right-field lower deck, and remodeled the Stadium Club, where promotions and press conferences were held. Fans could also rent out the club for weddings and other occasions.

The 1990 All-Star Game was held at Wrigley Field on Tuesday, July 10. Of the 38,710 seats, fewer than eight thousand were made available to the general public. Around eighteen thousand went to Cubs season-ticket holders (who weren't guaranteed their regular season seats) with another twelve thousand allotted for purchase by Major League Baseball, which had club officials, sponsors, and celebrities to stroke.

Of course, if you were Michael Jordan, you could call the Cubs a week before the game and secure a couple of tickets. Joel Bierig, in the July 10, 1990, *Sun-Times*, noted that recently elected Mayor Richard Daley received fifty tickets; Governor Jim Thompson was on hand, and football coach Mike Ditka got seats, too. Former broadcaster Jack Brickhouse and his wife, Pat, got in, as did DePaul University basketball coach Joey Meyer.

Following a long rain delay, the American League won 2–0

on a two-run double by Texas's Julio Franco. The official attendance was 39,071, with many others enjoying the game from rooftops.

The All-Star Game was arguably the best thing to happen in Wrigley all season, as the Cubs limped to a 77–85 finish.

DAWSON'S FREAK

The next year was startlingly the same. By July 23, 1991, the Cubs were well out of the race already as they hosted the not-much-more-viable Cincinnati Reds.

The home plate umpire that night was "Country" Joe West, who may be the least popular arbiter in the game; many players find him combative, arrogant, and arbitrary. Andre Dawson, who didn't often take on umpires, had heard just about enough of West that night, and his frustration boiled over when West called him out on strikes in the seventh, with the Cubs up 5–2. Dawson questioned the call longer than most umpires like, and West simply waved the star outfielder away. This enraged Dawson, who bumped West, then tossed his bat. West ejected him and, shortly after, Cubs manager Jim Essian. Dawson, shoved into the dugout by teammate George Bell and umpire Eric Gregg, began hurling bats onto the field.

The crowd of 34,458 went nuts. West began counting the bats, noting the amount that Dawson would be fined, and the outfielder angrily threw more of them until fifteen lay near the third-base coaching box. In support of Dawson, bleacher fans began tossing full and empty beer cups, scorecards, hats, and anything else at hand onto the field. The antics delayed the game for around fifteen minutes.

In the bottom of the eighth, Reds reliever Rob Dibble allowed two runs, and the Cubs stretched their lead to 7–4. When Cub Doug Dascenzo then bunted, Dibble—in West's opinion—threw the ball directly at Dascenzo as he ran toward first. Dibble, ejected for intentionally attempting to injure another player, claimed innocence. Dawson was suspended, but for only one game.

THE WALK OF FAME

When the present doesn't look so great, it's a good time to focus on the heroes of yesteryear. The Cubs, lacking an official Hall of Fame despite the abortive 1937 attempt, opened a Walk of Fame in 1992. Each honoree had his name etched in a stone placed into the sidewalk near Wrigley Field's Clark and Addison entrance. The inaugural class comprised Ernie Banks, Fergie Jenkins, Ron Santo, and Billy Williams. Fans also eventually elected players Cap Anson, Glenn Beckert, Bill Buckner, Phil Cavarretta, Andre Dawson, Stan Hack, Gabby Hartnett, Rogers Hornsby, Don Kessinger, Andy Pafko, Rick Reuschel, Ryne Sandberg, Hank Sauer, Sammy Sosa, Rick Sutcliffe, and Hack Wilson; broadcasters Lou Boudreau, Jack Brickhouse, and Harry Caray; public address announcer Pat Pieper; and longtime clubhouse man Yosh Kawano. After ten years, however, the Walk had not captured the fans' imagination, and the stones were beginning to deteriorate. The Cubs removed the stones and instead hung banners for each honoree in the concourse under the grandstands, starting April 5, 2002.

COMPLAINT OFFICE

The 1993 season was a marginal improvement over previous years, but the 1994 season was miserable for the Cubs, who lost their first dozen home games. After a particularly painful defeat on April 29, manager Tom Trebelhorn tried a novel public relations strategy: he held a "town meeting" for fans in front of the firehouse near the left-field corner, always a hotbed of game-day activity for kids playing ball (fig. 27), teens and adults hoping for batting-practice homers, and other fans looking for a glance of their heroes. After talking to the press, showering, and changing, Trebelhorn emerged from the ballpark, stood on a bench outside the firehouse, and answered questions from the throng of perhaps two hundred fans. The angry crowd, a fair portion of which was inebriated, simply yelled at first, but Trebelhorn eventually gained control. "OK, what do you want to know?" he shouted.

FIGURE 27. The game outside the game; a young man swings the bat outside of the left-field corner in 1999. (Credit: Andrea Giafaglione)

Trebelhorn was unusually frank with the fans about his hitters, one of whom, he said, was a "dumb****" for not moving a man over. He was cheered by the fans at the end of the thirty-minute meeting then went into the firehouse to have some broiled chicken. Few associated with the team were happy with Trebelhorn's meeting. Players don't enjoy being publicly aired out by their manager, and Trebelhorn also lost the confidence of the front office. The Cubs hired Jim Riggleman to manage in 1995. Asked if he'd be holding any town meetings, an annoyed Riggleman shook his head from side to side.

Riggleman did have better results, for in 1995 the Cubs were at least in a race for a wild-card spot till nearly the end of the season. But there were still plenty of angry fans. On September 28, Randy Myers allowed a two-run pinch-homer to Houston's James Mouton in the eighth, giving the Astros a 9–7 lead. As the ball sailed over the left-field wall, James Murray, a twenty-seven-year-old bond trader, leapt over the brick fence down the first-base line and ran toward the mound. With the smallest crowd of the season (14,075) on hand (it was a weekday), security had been thinned out. But Myers, a survivalist, hunter, and a student of martial arts, saw Murray coming and dropped him with a hard forearm, then pinned him to the ground until security officers hauled the intruder off to the Town Hall police station.

BUSH LEAGUE

After the brief brush with contention in 1995, the years 1996 and 1997 saw two more terrible teams. In 1997, the Cubs did make a dramatic improvement to the park's beauty, however, replacing the AstroTurf tarp covering the center-field bleachers with green juniper bushes. The addition of plants was clearly in harmony with P. K. Wrigley's early attempts to plant Chinese elms near the scoreboard. Reports that another kind of green—marijuana—had surreptitiously been planted in the juniper were nothing but smoke.

GOODBYE, HARRY

Perhaps unable to take any more mediocrity afield, legendary Cubs broadcaster Harry Caray died on February 18, 1998. His age was given as eighty-four, but he was always coy about when he was born—many thought he was much older. Fans in Chicago and all over the baseball world mourned Caray's passing. Harold Carabina had been with the Cubs since 1982 and before that had spent thirty-seven years broadcasting the Cardinals, Athletics, and White Sox. A native of Saint Louis, he gained his greatest national fame with the Cubs, describing the action on WGN, which beamed the club all over the nation and even into Central America. Sadly, Chip Caray, Harry's grandson (son of Skip, excellent broadcaster of the Atlanta Braves), who had been slated to join the Cubs' broadcast team in 1998 and call games with his granddad, didn't get the chance.

Harry Caray is now memorialized at Wrigley by a large granite-based statue that was dedicated on August 12, 1999. The statue, twice vandalized by "fans" and once damaged by an equipment truck, was originally placed outside the right-field corner but was relocated to the center-field bleacher entrance in 2010.

With the beloved broadcaster gone, the homespun tradition of him leading the communal "Take Me Out to the Ballgame" sing-along after the top of the seventh inning was gone as well. But the team's marketing department came up with a way to fill the Harry-sized gap. Starting in 1998, the seventh-inning break featured "guest conductors" leading the crowd in singing. These guests are often local sports heroes but have also been celebrities in town to plug a book, a TV show, or a new CD. For several years, it seemed that the Cubs invited everyone who was starring on a television show on WGN-TV's WB or CW networks. As a result, renowned baseball figures N'Sync, Cuba Gooding Jr., Jane Seymour, and Mel Gibson—and these aren't even the most embarrassing ones—took often hideous turns in the television booth trying to remember the words and tune to "Take Me Out to the Ballgame," a song some of them had never heard. Even worse, the Cubs have adopted the dangerous idea of allowing celebrities from lesser sports—like basketball announcer Dick Vitale, hockey player Patrick Sharp, and football player Kordell Stewart—to claim airtime on their broadcasts by serving as guest conductors. Asking Dennis Miller, Danica Patrick, Ozzy Osbourne, Jesse Ventura, Kellie Pickler, or, worst of all, George Will to visit the booth is the kind of decision that marketing people may love, but it cheapens the Wrigley experience.

Harry Caray, at least, could claim to talk like a fan, think like a fan, and sing like a fan. Bellowing out "Ballgame" with him was a pleasant, local tradition that for Chicagoans had real meaning.

THE YOUNG, THE OLD, AND THE VERY STRONG

And yet, 1998 turned out to be a pretty good year. The Cubs asked twenty-year-old right-handed flamethrower Kerry Wood to take the ball on Wednesday, May 6, 1998, against the first-place Houston Astros. Despite dark skies, 15,758 flocked to Wrigley Field. Wood, a former first-round draft pick, began this, his fifth big-league start, with a statement, fanning the first three Houston batters on just fourteen pitches in the first inning. Houston's Shane Reynolds answered by striking out the side in the home half.

Houston's Ricky Gutierrez led off the third with an infield hit—the only safety the Astros collected all day. Other than that, the Astros rarely put the ball in play and in fact rarely even got the bat on the ball. Wood threw 122 pitches, only thirty of which were hit at all. As the game went on, Wood mixed in his hard, sharp breaking ball, and the strikeouts piled up. He whiffed five in a row in the fourth and fifth, then all three men in the seventh. Wood had struck out fifteen through seven innings and hadn't allowed a walk, much less a run. "I wasn't really worried about the strikeouts," Wood said later. "I knew it was getting up there. It was just one of those days where everything you throw is crossing the plate. It just felt like I was playing catch."

Rain began falling in the seventh inning, making it even

harder to see a spinning, speeding baseball. Some Astros later asserted that home plate umpire Jerry Meals was overly generous with his strike-zone calls, and Shane Reynolds's ten strikeouts in his eight innings lend some credence to the argument. But Wood was simply too much. He fanned Dave Clark, Ricky Gutierrez, and Brad Ausmus in the eighth to make it eighteen strikeouts.

Astros pinch hitter Billy Spiers led off the ninth and whiffed at a curve for the nineteenth strikeout, one short of the nine-inning major league record. Craig Biggio spoiled the fun with a groundout, but Wood huffed and puffed and got Derek Bell to wave at three breaking balls. In the 2–0 triumph, Wood threw a twenty-strikeout, no-walk one-hit shutout, something nobody had ever done. One hit batter and one infield single kept Wood from perfection. "I couldn't imagine ever doing this," Wood said later. "It's going to be special to strike out that many, regardless of who has done it. It hasn't settled in, and I'm still in awe a little bit."

In the clubhouse following the final out, Cubs first baseman Mark Grace held court. "That's without a doubt the best performance I've ever seen," he noted. After a short pause, he pointed to the assembled media and added, "And it's the best performance *you've* ever seen." In the wake of this dominating performance, Kerry Wood became Kid K, a new hero. Entrepreneurs did big business in "We've Got Wood!" T-shirts for several years.

Wood's success seemed to fuel the team as a whole, which went on to capture the National League wild-card slot. The later part of the season was marred only by the death of another Cubs broadcaster, Jack Brickhouse, on August 6. Brickhouse had been the Cubs' telecaster from 1947 through 1981, leaving the business before the advent of cable television; still, his genial, avuncular manner provided the soundtrack to many a Chicago summer, and he was *the* voice for a generation of Cubs fans. His trademark "Hey, Hey!" home-run call is preserved in red letters on Wrigley Field's yellow foul poles.

Kerry Wood aside, the big Cubs headlines in 1998 went to

outfielder Sammy Sosa, who that year was locked in a chase with Mark McGwire to break Roger Maris's single-season home-run record. This brought the Wrigley Field ball hawks—and the greed inherent in souvenir collecting—into the spotlight. For many years grown men have gathered outside of Wrigley Field on Waveland and Sheffield Avenues to await home-run balls flying from the park, both during batting practice and games. Dave Davison, Moe Mullins, and Rich Buhrke are legendary among the Cubs' ball hawk contingent.

By September 13, 1998, Sosa had already tied Maris's record, but so had McGwire, who had also hit one more to reach sixty-two homers on the year. Expectations ran high that Sosa could do it, too. At the game against the Brewers that day, a huge crowd of souvenir hunters, including mothers with babies in strollers, roved around Waveland Avenue, jockeying for position. Sosa hit his sixty-second homer in the ninth inning of the Cubs' eventual 11–10, ten-inning victory over the visiting Brewers—and when he did so, hell broke loose. Strollers were shoved aside, kids elbowed, and bystanders knocked down as collectors and glory hounds piled up to get the ball. Moe Mullins claimed he had the ball but that it was pried from his hands. Many locals supported Mullins's claim.

The fateful ball wound up in the mitts of Brendan Cunningham, a suburban mortgage broker not regularly at the park. Cunningham, clutching his prize, was chased down Kenmore Avenue by members of the press, other fans, and angry allies of Mullins, and he finally needed a police escort to get home. Cunningham immediately announced plans to sell the ball. Mullins, injured in the pileup, sued Cunningham. The whole business dragged on until both parties agreed to simply give Sosa the baseball. McGwire eventually won the home-run title with seventy.

CAPGATE

Given their proximity to the field, Wrigley Field fans are usually extremely well behaved—well, except when Sammy Sosa is breaking home-run records. But during a Dodgers-Cubs night game on May 16, 2000, an ill-advised prank put black eyes on the fan base (literally) as well as on Major League Baseball (figuratively). A full house of 38,860 watched as the two clubs battled down to the wire. During the game, some members of the crowd had thrown beer toward the Dodgers bullpen. In the last of the ninth, a fan, Josh Pulliam, ran down to the wall separating the bullpen from fans, punched reserve catcher Chad Kreuter in the back of the head, and swiped his cap. The aggrieved Kreuter leapt into the stands in response. More players surged into the crowd, some more enthusiastically than others, and fought with fans as security personnel rushed to the scene.

It was one of the ugliest imbroglios seen at the park. Security tossed several fans out, and Frank Robinson, MLB's vice president for baseball operations, later meted out nineteen suspensions for Dodgers players and coaches totaling some sixty games, though many were appealed and overturned. Kreuter, who served an eight-game suspension and paid a $5,000 fine, was unrepentant. "The guy that hit me, I want to serve notice that I'm coming after him. I'll make him accountable, and I will definitely seek him out to see that he is accountable for his actions." Josh Pulliam—who worked for a Tribune Company subsidiary at the time and is now a political lobbyist—went into hiding for a time, and Kreuter eventually chose not to press charges. One fan hurt in the melee, Ronald Camacho, sued the Cubs for detaining and then ejecting him without justification and won a $475,000 judgment. Camacho also collected $300,000 from the Dodgers for his injuries.

TEAR THE ROOF OFF

As far back as Wrigley Field has existed, fans have gathered on rooftops (illegally, in earlier years) to watch Cubs games—usually on lawn chairs with a sandwich and a beer. But in the 1990s, it became big business. Some building owners began charging increasingly large sums to allow fans to sit on the roofs of condos and apartments on Waveland and Sheffield. These entrepreneurs built tiered stands—with stadium seating and bleachers—on the rooftops, installed barbecue grills, obtained liquor licenses, and set up shop. Prices for a seat can run well into the three figures.

The Cubs did not enjoy this development, feeling—perhaps correctly—that their product was being stolen. Of course, the Cubs have long benefited from the "neighborhood" feel of the park, and it's arguable that at least some people in the neighborhood deserve to make ancillary profits. The tension between the club and the rooftop owners was about to lead to a major conflict that became entangled with the club's plans for expansion of its facility.

On June 18, 2001, the Cubs announced plans to alter Wrigley Field in three significant ways:

- To convert the parking lot and car wash between Clark Street and Wrigley into a multilevel complex with team offices, stores, and parking.
- To build a new stadium club and restaurant below the box seats and install new high-priced seating at field level near home plate.
- To build new outfield bleachers above and out from the current seats.

All three plans had detractors, but the real stink arose over the new bleacher seats—twenty-six hundred of them—which would be constructed on poles that would jut out onto the sidewalks on Waveland and Sheffield. Not coincidentally, these seats would have blocked the views from the rooftops.

Initial resistance to the plan focused on the poles. Some opponents said that the new overhang would create places for homeless people to stay; some said that more bleacher fans would mean more urination in their front yards; some simply felt that the new seats would be ugly. Others just didn't want the Cubs to get their way about anything.

Alderman Bernie Hansen, an initial supporter of the plan, said that the Cubs' ideas rated an A–, telling the Associated Press, "The calls I've been getting have been very much in favor of it. There will always be the naysayers . . . but they really don't speak for the majority of the community." Soon, however, Hansen began hearing more noise, and petitions began to circulate.

The situation became more complicated after it was revealed in August 2001 that the Cubs did not in fact own the land under the parking lot on which they wished to build the new office structure. The Cubs had paid $150,000 to buy that parcel in 1982 from the Chicago, Milwaukee, Saint Paul, and Pacific Railroad, which was going bankrupt, but the city announced that the land did not ever belong to the railroad and therefore should not have been sold. It was, in fact, a part of Seminary Street. The team could not build on this land now without an extra round of negotiation and wrangling, and worse yet, the city asked the Cubs—already paying property taxes on the ground—to pay back rent.

An observer at this point might ask why the city was trying to obstruct the plans of a major institution and employer like the Cubs, particularly in a time when cities usually bend over backward to accommodate their sports teams. In fact, Chicago itself in this era was abetting the Chicago Bears' desire to desecrate Soldier Field in the name of greater revenue through new luxury seating. And prior to that, the White Sox bullied the city and state into building them a new park in 1990. Yet now the Cubs could not win city approval to make changes to their own park with their own money. Why is that?

The answer comes down to two uniquely Chicagoan political figures: the alderman and the mayor. The alderman is like a ward leader, and he or she represents an area's residents and businesses—in this case, a number of people who didn't like the impact of Wrigley Field on the neighborhood in the first place, as well as the owners of the rooftop-view buildings themselves, who were trying to protect their profits. Some of these well-heeled building owners also made campaign contributions to their aldermen, and others, in order to be more clearly heard. For its part, the Cubs handpicked its own "citizen's group" to attempt to influence the alderman, but it was too late. And then there was the mayor.

The mayor was Richard M. Daley, and Richard M. Daley just didn't like the *Tribune*. Some of this was historical—Daley's father, Richard J. Daley, hadn't liked the *Tribune* when he had been mayor, either—and some of it was political: Daley was a Democrat, and the *Tribune* was a Republican outlet. As a result, Daley, a Sox fan at heart, had little reason to back any Cubs' expansion plans.

As part of the battle over the renovations and, by proxy, the rooftops, some neighborhood activists, aided and abetted by the city, wanted to have Wrigley Field declared a city landmark. If the park were a landmark, the Cubs would have to go through a municipal appeal process any time they wanted to alter it— greatly reducing the likelihood they would succeed or, at least, that they would succeed without making concessions.

The Cubs and their opponents soon found themselves making some strange arguments. On the one hand, the team was forced to run down its own facility in public—while continuing to market Wrigley Field's beauty—in order to argue against landmarking and make the case for renovations. Cubs executive vice president of business operations Mark McGuire told Fran Spielman in the September 5, 2001, *Sun-Times*, "Upon close scrutiny, there are areas of Wrigley Field that are neither historic nor very special." Neighborhood opponents to renovations, meanwhile, had to claim that the park is perfect as it is, while at the same time arguing that Wrigley was a nuisance to the area and that the Cubs were not good neighbors.

For its part, the city did not want the Cubs to change the ivy, the scoreboard, the marquee outside the main entrance at Clark and Addison, or the shape of the park. (The city did not seem to care about things like washrooms or concession stands.) Since the Cubs have little interest in altering the ivy, the scoreboard, or the marquee, the real question was what would happen to unspecified areas such as the bleachers, the areas underneath the stands, the grandstand seating, and the outside walls.

As these questions dragged on, late in 2001 the Cubs took what they felt was a provocative but necessary step: they put windscreens over the back fences in the bleachers. Perhaps it was an overreach. Nobody liked the green vinyl windscreens, an eyesore to those inside and outside of the ballpark. The rooftop owners, of course, fumed. Some of them claimed that their rights were infringed on by the Cubs' decision. (Apparently it is a right now to be able to steal a product and resell it.) But the city—now generally opposed to the Cubs, no matter the merits of their claims—listened to the rooftop owners. The screens came down. But the Cubs had made a point—they would act, even in an unpopular way, to protect their interests. Soon, the Cubs offered a compromise: they sheared five hundred seats from the original bleacher expansion plan, vowed to plant ivy on the outside of the new walls and on the poles, and set up a neighborhood watch program. That went nowhere.

Unfortunately, there were no "good guys" in this fight. For whom should an objective observer have rooted? The baseball club run by a union-busting corporation used to getting its own way? Neighborhood loudmouths fueled by delusions of grandeur and naked greed? Or a city government more interested in goring an ox than serving the public interest? This political knot wasn't going to get cut anytime soon.

SOME FANS

Not all the commotion was off the field. During the 1980s and 1990s, a handful of veteran fans, including "Bleacher Preacher" Jerry Pritikin, Ronnie "Woo Woo" Wickers, the Duchess, and Carmella Hartigan, carved out places in Cubs lore. Hartigan, who died at one hundred on December 21, 2002, was a favorite. She had thrown out a ceremonial first pitch in 1998 and collected her reward—a kiss from Sammy Sosa. She had often been

FIGURE 28. Left-field bleacher fans, including ninety-four-year-old Carmella Hartigan on the left, enjoy the middle of the seventh inning in 1996. (Credit: Andrea Giafaglione)

interviewed, talked with, and given babies to hold and kiss. In 2001, she had fallen in front of the Waveland Avenue firehouse, broken her hip, and needed hip replacement surgery. From that point, she hadn't often been in her seat, although her place in the back row of the bleachers was as good as reserved; Hartigan had been at the park for nearly every game when healthy (fig. 28).

Ronnie Wickers, in contrast, you didn't have to look for. An African American born in 1941, he came to his first Cubs game in his teens. He wanders around Wrigley Field in a Cubs uniform, constantly yelling "Cubs! Woo! Cubs! Woo!" He's always in the park—someone usually buys him a ticket—and there is no shortage of people who will reward his efforts with a beer. Like him or loathe him, Ronnie is as much a part of Wrigley Field as anyone. He sang "Take Me Out to the Ballgame" in 2001 and received much attention after being struck by a car four years later.

HIGHER AND HIGHER

Part of the drive to remodel Wrigley and to capture more of the revenue of the rooftops came on account of baseball's "new economics"—which is to say, in the wake of some critical rulings in the mid-1970s, players were more able to become free agents and sell their skills to the team willing to pay the most. Paying players what they're worth meant that ticket prices clearly had to rise. The Tribune Company saw this and took action. In 1994, the Cubs instituted seasonal pricing. Club and field boxes cost $19 for summer games and $15 in April, May, and September. Bleachers, up to $10 in the summer, were $6 otherwise.

During 1994, Major League Baseball owners—in an attempt to curb salaries—provoked a strike that crippled the sport and forced the cancellation of the World Series. (The Cubs, at 49–64, were probably just as happy to see the season end early, but no one else was.)

When the 1995 season opened after a delay, the Cubs—now in the new NL Central alongside the transplanted Milwaukee Brewers—in a show of good faith intended to help bring back fans, held ticket prices at prestrike levels through 1996. Attendance at Wrigley Field returned to prestrike levels more quickly than at many other ballparks despite Chicago's on-field ineptitude in both years.

But in 1997, though the team was coming off a 76–86 season, ticket prices rose again. Prime tickets for the best boxes were raised to $21, with lower-deck reserved at $14 and bleachers $12. Budget tickets—those for less-attended early and late-season contests—rose to $15, $8, and $6 respectively. The Cubs scheduled just seventeen budget-price games.

Sammy Sosa's record-breaking season was in 1998, and the Cubs made the playoffs. This allowed the club to raise prices again, which it did claiming that extra revenues were needed for higher payrolls. (While the Cubs have usually maintained high payrolls, this is often due to poor long-term contract decisions rather than good ones.) Club and field boxes now cost $25 for prime games, and terrace reserved seats were $16. Bleacher seats were hiked to $15 a shot, with family section tickets priced at $20. Even standing-room seats for the sxity-three prime games ran $8.

By 2001, the team priced club boxes at $30, field boxes at $28, and the bleachers $20 for prime games. Prices for the seventeen bargain games, now called "value dates," were about half of the regular prices. The cheapest seats were now in the upper-deck grandstand, running $10 for adults and $6 for kids (less on value dates). In 2002, the Cubs raised prices again, after an 88–74 finish. Infield club boxes now cost $36 each for prime games. No box seat in the park cost less than $26. Bleacher seat prices rose to $24 for prime games and $12 on value dates, and for the first time, there were no discounts for kids, breaking a tradition the Cubs had started in the 1930s.

The parade continued in 2003 as the Cubs split their games into three plans—prime (nineteen games), regular (fifty-four games), and value (eight games). The former prime prices were now the cost of regular games, while prices went even higher for selected contests. And the team scheduled half the value games than the previous year. The cheapest box seats in the park, in the upper deck, were a whopping $32 for prime dates, with bleachers a spectacular $30—$12 even on so-called value dates. The only tickets available at Wrigley Field, at any time, for less than $10 were upper-deck grandstand ($6) and senior citizen tickets ($5) on the eight value days.

And for their money between 1999 and 2002, fans got to watch the team go 287–361. The occasional on-field youth clinics (fig. 29), photo sessions, and little-league games did little to mollify the fans' unease.

WAR AND REMEMBRANCE

But even in the bad years, fans kept coming, especially to see longtime rivals. The Cubs-Cardinals rivalry is among the best in baseball, going back to the clubs' nip-and-tuck finishes in the

FIGURE 29. During the 1990s, Wrigley Field became host to a myriad of nongame revenue-generating events. Here, children enjoy a 1999 on-field clinic. At this time, the buildup of the rooftop clubs had not yet reached critical mass. (Credit: Andrea Giafaglione)

1930s and the inherent sparring between two geographically close clubs. For decades, fans of both clubs have traveled with their team to the "enemy" city. The friendly war has spawned hundreds of great stories, loads of good times on both sides, and at least one book. Saturday, June 22, 2002, however, was memorable for another reason.

That day, Cardinals pitcher Darryl Kile didn't show up as scheduled at Wrigley Field. None of his teammates had seen him, and calls to his cell phone went unanswered. Finally, hoping that they'd find nothing, law enforcement officials and hotel workers forced opened the door to his room at the Westin Hotel and saw Kile's body. He had died from an undiagnosed heart problem. The news quickly reached Wrigley Field. His teammates, stunned and saddened, informed the Cubs. Commissioner Bud Selig gave the clubs the okay not to play.

Not long after the game's scheduled start time of 2:20, Cubs catcher Joe Girardi informed the fans that there would be no game. With his Cubs teammates behind him, Girardi walked up to a hastily connected microphone and said, "We regret to inform you that because of a tragedy in the Cardinals family, the commissioner has canceled the game today. Thank you. Be respectful. You will find out eventually what has happened. I ask you to please say a prayer for the Saint Louis Cardinals family," Girardi concluded emotionally. It was the first sign of what many people in baseball already knew—that Girardi was a quiet but intense leader capable of shouldering such a burden. The fans were shocked; few, if any, knew what was happening. Some booed. A few applauded. Most, however, simply filed out of the park. Word quickly spread through the stands, and some fans left Wrigley in tears.

The following evening, when Kile had been scheduled to pitch, the Cubs and Cardinals played on ESPN's *Sunday Night Baseball*. Distracted and saddened, the Cardinals lost 8–3 in front of 37,647. The message board showed no between-innings commercials, and no music was played besides an unaccompanied version of "Take Me Out to the Ballgame." The left-field foul pole flag, usually sporting Ernie Banks's number 14, was removed, replaced instead by a Cubs flag at half-mast. Down the right-field line, Billy Williams's number 26 flag was supplanted by a Cardinals flag. The National League team flags surrounding Old Glory on the center-field scoreboard were absent. On the small electronic board in center field, Kile's number 57 was shown all game long and remained bright even after the game was over and the stadium lighting turned off.

In a year in which the Cubs finished 67–95, this was a sadly memorable moment. Another memorable event came later in June when a section of the ivy on the right-center-field wall had begun to wilt and die, eventually turning an ugly shade of brown. Early speculation had a White Sox fan pouring some sort of bleach on the ivy to kill it—the Sox had just been at Wrigley for an interleague series—but there was no hard evidence.

SNOW DAY 2003

After losing their 2003 home opener to snow on April 7, the Cubs hosted the Expos the next day in thirty-two-degree temperatures. The announced crowd of 29,138 was actually perhaps half that. Prior to the game, Ted Butterman's Cubs quintet, fixtures at Wrigley Field for many years, played Dixieland jazz. Steve Stone, returning to the WGN television booth following a two-year absence, emceed the pregame ceremonies. With the outfield soggy and snow resting in the outfield basket and in the still-bare ivy branches, seventy-two-year-old Ernie Banks, youthful in spirit, hobbled to the mound with Sammy Sosa. The two threw out simultaneous ceremonial first pitches. Wayne Messmer sang the Canadian and American national anthems, with some louts booing "O Canada" in response to some north-of-the-borderites doing the same to "The Star-Spangled Banner" at a recent hockey game. The Cubs won 6–1.

The Cubs made an interesting change to the bleachers in 2003. The very top of the center-field seating section, under the scoreboard, was coverted to a standing-room area. Seats from the last rows were removed to give fans some room to walk or look out the back fence toward the northeast. Probably the most popular part of the new bleacher section, however, was the freshly installed beer counter. Cubs management also installed two large electronic message boards into the left- and right-field upper decks. These boards give out-of-town scores, show animated pictures of the American flag during "The Star-Spangled Banner," and run ads between innings.

BROKER THAN BROKEN

The decision to hire Dusty Baker to manage in 2003 gave the organization a positive public relations shot. Baker had taken the

San Francisco Giants to the World Series the year before. Unfortunately, the rest of the public relations early that year was pretty bad.

In a bruising story published April 10, Greg Couch of the *Sun-Times* made clear what many already believed: the Cubs had been running their own brokering operation. An operation called Wrigley Field Premium, located a short distance from the ballpark, had been selling tickets, provided by the Cubs and never made available to the public, at highly inflated prices—such as the $1,500 being asked for the upcoming June series against the Yankees. While the Cubs had claimed that Premium was a separate entity, the company's president was found to be Mark McGuire, the Cubs' executive vice president of business.

The Cubs' defense was that brokers buy up tickets and resell them at outrageous rates all the time, so the club should be able to do it, too. That argument *seems* logical, but it depends on a fair market. In the case of Premium, the tickets were never made available to the public, or even to brokers, at face value. The Cubs had become scalpers. Moreover, by using a shell corporation to filter tickets to the public, the Cubs were able to keep some income out of baseball's revenue-sharing program, which was intended to keep a degree of parity among small- and large-market teams.

In November 2002, a local group, which included several rival ticket brokers, filed a class-action suit to force the Cubs to stop reselling through Wrigley Field Premium. The suit, which sought refunds for all customers who bought tickets through the service from April 2002 through mid-May 2003, claimed that the team was engaging in fraudulent business practice, filtering tickets to a shell corporation and revending them at higher prices.

The trial ended in August 2003, and on November 24 Judge Sophia Hall ruled in favor of the Cubs. She found nothing in Illinois law to prevent the Cubs from the practice of selling tickets at higher prices through the subsidiary corporation. In the judge's words, the plaintiffs did not "prove that the business relationship between them violates any law or violates custom or practice." Hall recommended that since the current laws concerning such relationships between parent and subsidiary businesses are obsolete, that state legislature take on the concept of making such transactions illegal. No such legislation has appeared.

Now that it was unnecessary for the Cubs to pretend that Wrigley Field Premium is a separate entity, it started sharing office space down the street from the park with the team's concessionaires.

RUN, DUSTY, RUN

The on-field news in 2003 was not all bad, however. Built around an impressive starting rotation including Kerry Wood and rookies Mark Prior and Carlos Zambrano, the Cubs moved into first place on April 15 and remained on top until late June. From that point, however, the Cubs began sinking, staggering into the All-Star break on a 6–13 skein, and near the end of July were in third, five and a half behind Houston and Saint Louis. A July 22 deal with Pittsburgh, however, brought over outfielder Kenny Lofton and third baseman Aramis Ramirez, and the newcomers could hit. A string of ten wins in fourteen games catapulted the Cubs into first again on August 15, and despite a short slump, they stayed in contention.

The Cardinals, tied with Houston for the NL Central lead and, two and a half games ahead of the Cubs, entered Wrigley Field on Labor Day, September 1, for a five-game set. Following a ridiculous four-hour-and-seventeen-minutes rain delay, Mark Prior shut down the Cardinals 7–0 in the opener. The next day, the two clubs split a day/night doubleheader. Sosa's two-run homer in the fifteenth won game 1 4–2, but the Cards won the nightcap 2–0, keeping Chicago in third, a game and a half behind. The second game turned on a line drive hit by the Cubs' Moises Alou with runners on base that umpire Justin Klemm ruled foul; Alou and Cubs reliever Antonio Alfonseca were ejected for arguing, further inflaming the crowd of 39,290.

With the season hanging in the balance on September 3, the Cubs fell behind the Cardinals 6–0 in the sixth but came back. Down 7–6 in the eighth, Chicago tied the game on Mark Grudzielanek's triple, and Alou's RBI single proved the winner in a dramatic 8–7 triumph. The win knocked the Cards into second, bringing Chicago within a game of Houston's division lead.

On September 4, the Cubs took the fourth of five games, coming back from 2–0 and 5–3 deficits, at various points of the game, to win 7–6, pulling a half-game behind the Astros. Both Chicago and Houston continued to play well for the next three weeks. After taking two of three at Cincinnati, the Cubs returned home September 26 still tied for the division lead. That day, the Cubs were rained out, but Milwaukee pasted the Astros 12–5 to put the idle Chicagoans ahead by a half-game.

With the Astros now in second, the Cubs' destiny was in their own hands. On September 27, a murky Saturday, 40,121 frenzied fans jammed Wrigley Field for a makeup doubleheader. Mark Prior, who in a space of just a few months had become the National League's most exciting pitcher, led the Cubs over the Pirates 4–2 in the first game. In game 2 the Cubs jumped out to a 1–0 lead on Sosa's first-inning homer, his fortieth of the season. In the last of the second, Chicago routed Ryan Vogelsong from the mound, scoring five times to put the game away. As the crowd grew ever more celebratory, the scoreboard posted the inning-by-inning results in Houston, where the Brewers were winning. Finally the Astros succumbed, giving the Cubs a clinch for a tie. An hour or so later, when the Cubs took the title outright with their 7–2 win, the sun suddenly came out, bathing the fans and the celebrating Cubs in brilliant twilight.

Fans poured from Wrigley Field and into the streets, joining the many thousands in local bars or milling around Clark and Addison. Television crews filmed the spectacle as the police were forced to shut down automobile traffic for blocks around. The celebration went long into the night in Wrigleyville; the team had clinched its first division title since 1989.

The following afternoon, on the season's last day, the Cubs in a pregame ceremony retired Ron Santo's uniform, number 10, running a flag up the left-field pole to make it official. Santo, about to undergo a cancer operation, had lost both legs to diabetes. He said that the National Baseball Hall of Fame, which he was not in, couldn't possibly mean as much to him as this. Only two Cubs—Ernie Banks and Billy Williams—had been so honored previously.

CURSES? FOILED AGAIN!

The revelry continued as the Cubs defeated the Atlanta Braves in a dramatic five-game Division Series and moved to the Championship Series against the surprising Florida Marlins. Chicago blew its home-field advantage, however, dropping game 1 by a score of 9–8 in eleven innings after squandering a 4–0 first-inning advantage. From that point, though, the Cubs started to blow through the Marlins, winning 12–3 in game 2 behind Mark Prior and then, in Florida, games three and four, 5–4 and 8–3, respectively. Chicago could have won the series in Florida, but the Marlins stayed alive on Josh Beckett's 4–0 shutout. Cubs fans weren't worried—they had Prior and Wood on tap for the final two at Wrigley. On October 14, 39,577 rooters squeezed into Wrigley Field for game 6. (Somehow Ronnie "Woo Woo" Wickers got in, too. Where was "One-Eyed" Connolly?) Scoring once in the first, sixth, and seventh, Chicago led 3–0.

But with one out in the eighth and Marlins center-fielder Juan Pierre on second, disaster struck. Luis Castillo lofted a fly ball to left field that veered toward the wall in foul territory. Wrigley Field's unique design, which allows very little foul territory down the lines, worked against the club in this instance; Moises Alou ran toward the wall, leapt for the ball, but couldn't get it. Several fans had instinctively reached for the ball. Alou angrily argued fan interference, but the umpires weren't buying.

And the roof fell in. Prior walked Castillo, and Pierre went to third on the rattled pitcher's wild ball four. Ivan "Pudge"

THE EMPIRE OF THE TRIBUNE

Rodriguez singled in a run to make it 3–1. The Cubs bullpen began heating up and restless fans worried. Miguel Cabrera then momentarily calmed the fans by hitting a chopper to short. But Alex Gonzalez muffed the ball, loading the bases, and former Cub Derrek Lee's double to left on the first pitch tied the game. Cubs reliever Kyle Farnsworth didn't help: Two intentional walks and a sac fly later, the Marlins were up 4–3. Mike Mordecai then ripped a three-run double to left-center. By the time the twelve-batter inning had ended, the Cubs were down 8–3—and that's how the game ended.

Anger centered on the fan who had reached for the foul ball in the eighth inning, Steve Bartman. By the ninth inning, Bartman was forced to vacate his seat because of threats to his safety. Over the next few days, the *Sun-Times* irresponsibly published his name, place of employment, phone number, and even his address, which furthered the frenzy.

The Cubs themselves issued the following statement: "Games are decided by what happens on the playing field—not in the stands. It is inaccurate and unfair to suggest that an individual fan is responsible for the events that transpired in Game 6."

The following night, almost as an anticlimax, the Cubs blew another lead and lost to the Marlins 9–6, ending their season. Chicago players and fans went home for the winter licking their freshly salted wounds. Poor Steve Bartman was never the same.

LET'S MAKE A DEAL

In the off-season, the long-simmering renovation saga took some additional turns. It had become obvious that the Cubs could not alter their park until the City Council had weighed in on the landmark status issue. On January 27, 2004, a council committee granted Wrigley Field limited landmark status, meaning that certain areas could not be altered without city permission. Those areas were the park's four outside walls, the roof, the marquee sign at Clark and Addison, the center-field scoreboard, the grandstands, the brick wall and ivy surrounding the playing field, and the bleachers. Amazingly, this did not scotch the team's bleacher expansion plan. Alderman Tom Tunney, who had succeeded Bernie Hansen, said that any such expansion would be taken up separately by the City Council.

The Cubs had opposed landmark designation, but they did not come away empty-handed this off-season, as the city also took up the question of whether the Cubs could add night games starting in 2004. After the Cubs had dickered with the mayor's office for several months, the two sides announced on March 6 that the previous limit of eighteen night games would be raised. The team held twenty-seven night tilts in 2006 and twenty-eight the following season. The city insisted that in exchange the Cubs contribute to a fund that would address neighborhood concerns about sanitation, parking, and traffic congestion. Money was also set aside by the team to fund a study of an Addison Street off-ramp for Lake Shore Drive. (As of 2013, the off-ramp remains on the drawing board.) Only after the deal was completed did it become known that the Cubs would be contributing only slightly more than $83,000 a year toward the fund. Some found this piddling.

Next on the team's docket was taking care of the business with the owners of rooftop clubs, most of which by now had banded together as the Wrigleyville Rooftop Owners Association. Having failed at negotiations, threats, and legal action, Cubs ownership took a new tack: "Keep your friends close and your enemies closer," as the saying goes. On March 20, 2004, the Cubs announced a twenty-year agreement with the association to share revenues for that season and, presumably, the near future. The treaty allowed the rooftop businesses to remain in operation with the Cubs' blessing, in exchange for which they would pay 17 percent of their gross revenues to the team.

One rooftop business, however, Skybox—which sat on a three-story building down the left-field line—held out, with attorney

Chris Gair stating that the company would "never pay anything" to the Cubs. The other rooftop owners were incensed at the possibility that Skybox could hold out successfully. The Cubs weren't too happy either, and as the season began, they hired engineers to devise ways to block Skybox's building's view of the field. Alderman Tunney criticized the Cubs for this, and the two sides seemed headed for another court battle. On April 8, however, U.S. District Judge James Holderman brokered a closed-door agreement that brought the errant rooftoppers into the fold.

After all that, the Cubs would receive around $2 million per year from the rooftops, while the clubs could now operate freely, and fans that want to sit on an apartment building roof to watch a baseball game can do so. Money's not the main thing, as they say—it's the only thing.

Baseball at Wrigley Field, even more than ever, was business. Big business.

TIX TALK

Despite the heartbreak of the 2003 season, tickets for 2004 went quickly. By Opening Day, almost every seat had already been vended—some of them by Wrigley Field Premium. Even the regular tickets were more expensive, though, as prices ballooned 17.5 percent, the third highest increase in the major leagues. Bleacher seats (by now no longer reserved) topped out at an amazing $35 for "prime" dates, while for the same dates all boxes were at least $36. Seniors were now allowed half-price terrace reserved tickets for all Wednesday games, but all children above the age of two were required to have a full-price ticket. The 2004 *Team Marketing Report*'s "Fan Cost Index" noted that the Cubs' ticket prices ranked behind only those of the Boston Red Sox.

Back in the 1970s and 1980s when new stadiums had fifty thousand seats, a seat at Wrigley was a relatively rare commodity and therefore pricey. But that trend reversed, and by 2012 nine major league parks had seating capacities smaller than Wrigley's,

and in five more, capacities were less than a thousand larger. By the early 2000s, Cubs ticket prices were hardly justified by the club's on-again, off-again performance.

And still it wasn't enough. To fit in more customers, the Cubs decided for 2004 to cut down their already bite-sized foul territory behind home plate and install four new rows of seats. This required tearing down the brick wall behind the plate, in place since the late 1930s. As required by the landmark status decree, the construction team used the old brick to rebuild the wall when the work was done. The 213 new seats were sold in a preseason lottery, with some, of course, held back for visiting celebrities and friends of the Tribune Company.

The park's changes that year weren't limited to new seats. Building on the "success" of the upper-deck message boards, the team replaced the upper-deck auxiliary scoreboards down the left-field and right-field lines with new LED boards, which convey the score of the game less efficiently but have the distinct financial advantage of displaying rotating advertisements. In addition, the center-field message board was extended the full length of the scoreboard, allowing for the same rotating advertising shown on the auxiliary boards.

THE WALLS CAME DOWN

Between the seating and the signs, work was being done on the park—but not the right kind. During summer 2004, perhaps the Cubs' worst nightmare came to pass as chunks of cement began falling from both the interior and exterior of Wrigley Field. On June 9, a chunk of concrete the size of a brick was discovered outside the park. A month later, another hunk, this one half a foot long, fell in the concourse and nearly hit a five-year-old boy. Five days after that, a worker at the park found a third piece of concrete, again around six inches in length, that had fallen from the inside walls. The Cubs antilandmark contention that the park was crumbling seemed to have some merit.

Prodded by the city's Buildings Department, the Cubs had inspections conducted and, with the team out of town, installed strong netting under the entire upper-deck seating bowl. It certainly wasn't pretty, but the nets would catch anything else that fell. The team was allowed to proceed with its next scheduled home game, on July 30.

While the falling debris injured nobody, the story raised hackles among those who felt that ninety-year-old Wrigley Field had outlived its usefulness. How long should any park be expected to stand? Those who want to junk Wrigley Field argue that the old ballpark is cursing the team, which doesn't explain the division titles won in 1984, 1989, 2003, 2007, or 2008. Some writers complain that the park is ugly or smells bad—this is clearly a question of taste. Wrigley has stood for decades, but it has always required extensive structural maintenance. When management doesn't make that a priority, the place suffers. But it doesn't have to.

The Tribune was not entirely uninterested in structural work—witness the long-simmering bleachers renovation, which finally got under way after further negotiation following the 2004 season. Those negotiations had turned not just on Mayor Daley's animosity toward the Tribune Company but on some reasonable arguments. First, in order to add eighteen hundred bleacher seats, part of the original outside stadium wall would have to be reconstructed. This required waiving landmark restrictions, though the Cubs agreed to use as many of the original bricks as possible. In addition, the bleachers would overhang the street, requiring posts in the sidewalk, making it less usable and creating a shaded area in which some feared homeless people could squat—though the police and Wrigley security weren't likely to allow this. In the final design, the overhang was redesigned so that it did not jut out as much as originally proposed.

In January 2005, Alderman Tom Tunney threw his support behind the plan, and Daley soon acquiesced after extracting fur-

ther compromises from the team, which included supplying trolleys to take fans to and from Michigan Avenue hotels as well as to some train stops. The Cubs and the city agreed to the plan in March 2005, and the landmarks commission and building commission followed soon after.

In the process of settling all the issues on the table, the Cubs also paid the city a figure (reported by some as $3.1 million and others as $2.1 million) to once again buy the long-disputed small strip of land west of the ballpark. The Cubs had also hoped to win approval, finally, for a new building on this site, but this triangle-shaped construction, slated for team offices, parking, a Hall of Fame, and a souvenir shop, among other things, was delayed until the end of the 2006 campaign. The Tribune Company, suffering severe cash flow problems in the wake of business downturns and the cost of the bleacher project, could not commit the $30 million necessary for the new structure. When asked if the Cubs would consider asking for city or state money, Mike Lufrano, the Cubs' vice president for community relations, demurred. "That's not something we've ever done. . . . Everything at Wrigley Field has always been privately funded." Whether the Cubs had any chance of convincing the city, during its negotiations, to kick in cash is a question that will never be answered.

Work began on the bleachers as soon as the Cubs left the field after their final 2005 home game. Every bleacher seat was torn out so that the rows and columns of the structure could be completely resized. By late December, the new metal foundations had been laid, and in January 2006, workers began pouring concrete for the new seating.

The extra rows eliminated the back aisle from the left to right bleachers. Many longtime bleacher fans were dismayed by this, as it made the outfield seating feel even more claustrophobic than it had been. In addition, there were no longer standing-room bleacher tickets—there was no standing room. The left-field and high center-field sections remained general admission, while the right-field seats would henceforth be entirely reserved. The Cubs moved the family section from the left-field bleachers to a section of box seats down the left-field line. As stipulated by the Americans with Disabilities Act, the project did add wheelchair seating as well as an elevator from street level. A nice surprise was the installation of a chain-link door in the outside wall near the right-field line, which allowed fans to look into a portion of the park at all times. It is similar to the one installed earlier at San Francisco's AT&T Park.

One major element of the renovation was a hundred-seat restaurant/private club built in the bottom portion of what had previously served as the hitting background. The club's dark-tinted windows allowed restaurant patrons to view the field without being watched and also allowed batters to see the baseball coming out of the pitcher's hand. Four rows of juniper berry bushes remained, above the center-field home-run basket.

SHOW ME THE MONEY

The Cubs, admirably, financed the refurbishing themselves, at a cost that was said to range toward $50 million. In addition, they paid the city to install a stop light at Clark and Waveland for a measly $300,000, though this work was pushed back and now seems to be part of the latest round of renovations. But the Cubs were going to get that money back—whether in ticket sales, concessions, or some other fashion.

In January 2006, the Cubs again combined marketing savvy and a strange bout of tone deafness to team tradition by announcing that the "new" outfield section would officially be named the "Bud Light Bleachers." Everyone in baseball knew that naming rights would be sold for portions of Wrigley Field; but did the Cubs really have to name the new bleachers after the brewery whose money built the team's chief rival, the Saint Louis Cardinals? It had been hard enough for longtime Cubs fans to watch Harry Caray's "Cub Fan, Bud Man" ads in the 1980s—now their bleachers were associated with bad memories of dramatic losses to Saint Louis. And the ugly new sign over the bleacher entrance ensured that no one would forget the name.

BEYOND BASEBALL

Any Major League Baseball stadium is guaranteed only eighty-one events a year. The Cubs, like other franchises, started looking for ways to bring in revenue on off days with nonbaseball events. Not since vaudeville days had Wrigley Field hosted any sort of musical entertainment, but that changed in 2005, when a bunch of Parrotheads invaded the National League's oldest field. Singer Jimmy Buffett, always a Cub fan—he had sung "The Star-Spangled Banner" prior to game 1 of the 1984 NL Championship Series—became the first modern entertainer to perform a separate-admission concert (meaning: musical entertainment not part of a ballgame) at Wrigley Field. He and his band did two shows on Labor Day weekend, and his fans, the aforementioned Parrotheads, packed the ballpark.

While many in the neighborhood worried about the potential effect of thirty-five thousand people drinking and listening to music in the park, the Buffett fan base was actually quieter and more mellow than those in attendance at most baseball gatherings. The financial and, to some, aesthetic success of the Buffett endeavor smoothed the way to more concerts, all blockbusters. In 2007, the Police performed at Wrigley as part of their unlikely reunion tour, and in 2009 Elton John and Billy Joel coheadlined a pair of shows, and Rascal Flatts performed as well.

Other sports had been played in Wrigley in the past—the Bears, of course, were there until 1970, and the North American Soccer League's Chicago Sting played there for several seasons. The park also hosted the very occasional charity event in the 1980s. But in recent years, Wrigley Field has seen other uses far more frequently, straining the facility but increasing the bottom line. Film and television producers have used Wrigley as either a backdrop or a location, and the gates have been thrown open for a dizzying number of private corporate events.

Some of these other events were even baseball games. The Road to Wrigley Series allowed Cubs minor-league affiliates to play in the big-league park in 2008, 2009, and 2010. Two of those games featured the Peoria Chiefs, then a Cubs Class-A team, while the other featured the Triple-A Iowa Cubs. A program called RBI (Reviving Baseball in Inner Cities), designed to encourage disadvantaged youth to play the game, has also held games at Wrigley. Beginning in 2008, athletic wear company Under Armour (an advertising partner of the Cubs) and the Baseball Factory, an organization that holds tryout camps and provides instruction, have cosponsored the Under Armour All-America Game—featuring top high-school players—at Wrigley Field. While the games have been televised on the MLB Network, publicity for them has lagged and attendance has been low.

TRIALS OF THE *TRIBUNE*

The Cubs announced in February 2007 that, for the first time, they would sell advertising on the outfield wall. Under Armour—whose spokesmen included new Cubs outfielder Alfonso Soriano, signed to a $136 million deal that off-season, allegedly more on account of the marketing department and Tribune leadership than on account of GM Jim Hendry and his baseball operations team—bought space on two of the five metal doors embedded in the ivy-covered walls. Jay Blunk, the team's director of sales and marketing, asserted in an MLB.com story, "The Cubs have an impeccable track record of tastefully adding signage. No question, there's been a change in the culture here. It's an aggressive culture."

The oft-repeated line that new revenue streams allow the team to "compete" has generated plenty of cash for the team but few wins on the field. The Soriano contract, reviled by most baseball analysts at the time for its length and its amount, is a great example of a marketing-driven decision that hampered the ballclub on and off the field for years.

Tribune management was about to get a real shock, however. The core business of the company, the newspaper, was coughing and sputtering and nearly breaking down under the pressures of the Internet age. Former cash cows like classified advertising had been taken out to slaughter. Large print media companies like the Tribune found themselves in hot water.

The company announced, on April 2, 2007, its intention to sell the *Chicago Tribune*, *Los Angeles Times*, and most of its other assets—including Wrigley Field, the Cubs, and its 25 percent of Comcast SportsNet, the team's cable home—to Sam Zell for $8.2 billion. Twenty months later, the Tribune Company filed for bankruptcy, citing some $13 billion in debt.

Once Zell bought the Cubs, he made few changes, keeping management in place while he considered what to do with the franchise—which he repeatedly said that he didn't care much about in the first place. He did consider selling naming rights to Wrigley Field, but the quick negative reaction likely scared off any potential suitors, and Zell backed off. In any event, the "Wrigley Field" signs at the bleacher and home plate entrances are landmarked; even if a company bought naming rights, it would not be able to touch them.

BANKING IT WITH BANKS

Late in the 2007 season, the Cubs brought in some more cash through a program in which fans could buy bricks with engraved messages for $175. The bricks were then laid into the sidewalk on Addison Street outside Wrigley Field. Marketing efforts encouraged fans to create a permanent memory as part of their Cub fandom, and the immediate reaction was positive; fans lined up for the opportunity. Unfortunately, "permanent" doesn't mean permanent. Before the 2009 campaign, the Cubs uprooted and moved many of the bricks—without telling anyone in advance—to make room for outside seating at the new Captain Morgan Club. The contracts that fans had signed when they bought the bricks gave the team this right. Many fans did not know where their bricks had gone or that they had even been relocated (most of them were reinstalled close to the Ernie Banks statue near the facade), and the episode brought on a torrent of criticism.

Speaking of Ernie Banks, the Cubs installed that statue of him on Opening Day 2008, March 31—a festive occasion despite the cold and rain. The cast-iron statue, designed by Lou Cella of north suburban Highwood, featured Banks in his memorable erect batting stance, ready to unleash a powerful swing. It received good marks, and replicas were made available for fans to purchase. Some members of the press wondered why this hadn't been done many years before and whether the grounds would see more such statues. Unfortunately, nobody bothered to proofread the statue: Banks's trademark phrase read "LETS PLAY TWO." While an apostrophe was quickly chiseled in, the spacing never looked right.

NEW KID IN TOWN

Soon there would be more than an apostrophe missing at Wrigley Field. The letters *T*, *r*, *i*, *b*, *u*, *n*, and *e* were about to depart as well. Not more than a year after purchasing the franchise, Sam Zell made the decision to spin off the Cubs and sell Wrigley Field as well. His stewardship of the Tribune was getting nothing but bad notices, and few fans were unhappy that he was selling.

After a lengthy bidding process, Tom Ricketts, point man for his family fortune (patriarch Joe Ricketts founded Ameritrade) and for a group including his two brothers, a sister, and his parents, submitted a winning $900 million package for the team, Wrigley Field, and the Tribune's stake in Comcast. (The Cubs themselves were valued by *Forbes* at $642 million.) Tom Ricketts was introduced at that winter's Cubs Convention—an annual fan gathering, first held in January 1985, that has since become the model of pro sports off-season celebrations—to rapturous applause. The family took over the team on October 27, though the Tribune retained a 5 percent stake in the club.

It was time to build another new tradition. Dallas Green wasn't available this time—and Cubs fans could only hope that the new owners would make the Tribune's stewardship a pale memory in short order.

10

THE CUBS WAY, 2009 AND BEYOND

THE FAMILY BUSINESS

Tom Ricketts, who was born in 1963, met his wife in the bleachers at Wrigley Field. And some time after he attended the University of Chicago, Ricketts and his brother shared an apartment at Addison and Sheffield. Baseball was not in his blood, exactly, but after the decades of corporate ownership, it seemed a good sign that an identifiable family was in charge of the team, one with a local connection.

Everyone in the Ricketts family is a Republican except Tom's sister Laura, who has worked for Democratic political candidates and is an out lesbian who serves on the board of the civil rights organization Lambda Legal. She is the first openly gay person to be involved in the ownership of a major-league team. While this opened up the possibility of new kinds of marketing aimed at the gay and lesbian community, the family's overall political position was going to be a significant factor as it began the daunting task of rebuilding the Cubs once more. As would any team owner, Tom Ricketts often advocated for unpopular things—public money, salary dumps, trades of established players—while attempting to remain sensitive to the Cubs' role in the community.

WINTER CLASSIC

Even before the Rickettses formally took over, some innovations were already being seen at Wrigley, starting with the icing over of the field. When Cubs president John McDonough had left in

2007 to run the National Hockey League's (NHL) Chicago Black-hawks, anyone familiar with Chicago's current sports scene could have predicted that hockey's profile in the city would rise. Mc-Donough is a marketer and promoter par excellence, although some feel that his approach can detract from whatever product is being presented. Creator of the Cubs Convention and the not-so-successful Guest Conductor program in the middle of the seventh inning, McDonough soon worked his magic on the Hawks.

One bit of fairy dust he brought to the formerly moribund NHL franchise was using his connections to arrange having the Winter Classic—the league's annual New Year's Day outdoor showcase—played at Wrigley Field. On January 1, 2009, after weeks of intense and ridiculously complicated preparation involving ice-generating trucks, the laying down of an aluminum and plywood base, construction of on-field walkways, camera installation, and back and forth between the players' association and the league concerning ice and clubhouse conditions, the Blackhawks and Detroit Red Wings faced off before a capacity crowd of 40,818.

The rink stretched from third base to first base, awarding fans in the upper deck the best view. For once, box seats were among the least interesting seats in the park. Detroit defeated Chicago 6–4. Following the game, the rink was left open for public skating, with proceeds from admission going to Cubs Care, the team's charitable arm.

Not only did the event lend glitter to the NHL and to Wrigley Field, it but also generated significant capital. The press, NHL personnel, and fans partying at bars and restaurants spent millions of dollars in the city. Even when the Cubs weren't on the field, Wrigley Field was still a money machine.

In the aftermath of the Winter Classic, the Cubs opened a public skating rink northwest of Wrigley Field in December 2009, charging $10 per adult and $6 per child. The rink operated until 10:00 P.M. on weekdays and 11:00 P.M. on weekends during the winter months.

Building the rink required using space in the parking lot otherwise occupied during the baseball season. In addition, workers ripped down a building, on Clark Street north of Addison, which in the 1970s and 1980s had housed Yum Yum Donuts (and more recently the Cubs media relations department). Few, if any, disputed the team's decision to tear down the outmoded eyesore.

While the Rink at Wrigley may not be the best skating facility in the city—and unlike Park District rinks, it isn't free—it doesn't claim to be. The rink is a good neighborhood spot, and its location right next to Wrigley Field makes it very appealing for families and to baseball fans pining for spring.

SIGNS OF THE TIMES

Other changes were in the works at Wrigley, more permanent than the Winter Classic rink. Prior to the 2009 season, the Cubs replaced the Friendly Confines Café with the Captain Morgan Club, sponsored by the rum company of that name and run by the Harry Caray Restaurant Group, in time for the April 13 home opener. The new hangout, open to ticket holders as well as the general public, included indoor and outdoor seating, typical bar food, and a full bar. Once, talk of hard liquor at Wrigley Field would have been greeted with a scoff, but the team has been selling tequila drinks since the 1990s. The debut of the Captain Morgan Club only solidified liquor's presence at the old ballpark.

Whereas liquor might have once caused public outrage, by early 2010 the offender of public morals was advertising. Ever intent on generating more revenue, the Cubs pushed some folks' boundaries of taste and credulity by announcing its intention to place a large sign for Toyota automobiles high over the left-field bleachers.

New Cubs marketing vice president Wally Hayward was quoted in the March 17, 2010, *Sun-Times*: "We are at a big competitive disadvantage if we cannot generate incremental sponsorship revenue in a tasteful manner that helps preserve Wrigley Field.

We're not looking to add a whole wall of signage out there like other stadiums across the country." In this case, "tasteful" meant a 360-square-foot sign, featuring the Toyota name and logo, poking more than thirty feet above bleacher level (nearly sixty feet in the air) and lighting up at night.

The sign was positioned carefully so as not to interfere with the view of any Cub-partnered rooftops that have private clubs. It was positioned, however, to block TV cameras' view of the building on Waveland that does not feature a rooftop club but instead hosts an advertisement, for which the Cubs get no profit, for a gambling casino. Toyota paid the Cubs some $2.5 million over a three-year period for the exposure.

Alderman Tom Tunney initially came out against the sign, feeling it was out of character with the neighborhood. Eventually, Tunney, who receives campaign contributions from rooftop owners and, as a small business owner himself, has to constantly balance community standards against commerce, began to hedge his bets. "I'm not commenting on whether I'm for or against the sign. I'm worried about making sure that process is followed correctly," he said. After some opposition from fans—and Tom Gramatis, who had just paid more than $8 million to buy the building with the casino ad—Chicago's landmarks commission, building committee, and city council backed the Cubs' plan. On June 9, workers strapped the sign to the back of the left-field bleacher wall, only technically honoring the rules against changing the wall structure (a move prohibited by Wrigley's landmark status).

On June 11, *Chicago Tribune* architecture critic Blair Kamin wrote, "The new Toyota sign at Wrigley Field is uglier than expected. The controversial sign, which the Cubs hastily erected after receiving City Council approval Wednesday, is a wart on the face of baseball's grand dame—a highly visible intrusion of advertising into a ballpark that fans prize precisely because it provides relief from ad clutter." Kamin was not alone in his opinion.

Nor was the Toyota sign the only new advertising icon in the area. In spring 2010, workmen installed a giant yellow object northwest of the park on Cubs property. This thing was called "the noodle" and it came from Kraft Foods, which was advertising its boxed macaroni and cheese. The silly but eye-catching campaign continued through the season and was brought back in 2012, with the large piece of artificial pasta now sitting at the northwest corner of Clark and Addison (in front of the Cubs' sanctioned souvenir shop), sprinkled with pieces of metal meant to simulate bits of bacon. And to make things better—or worse, depending on your taste—every few minutes the sculpture emits the scent of frying pork belly.

This smell couldn't mask what was happening on the field, however. Despite some solid improvements in the physical environment in 2010—a new weight room for the athletes and improved rest rooms on the concourse level—the team, after playoff appearances in 2007 and 2008, was continuing another long slide to the basement, finishing 75–87.

Focusing on past glories rather than the present may have been behind another physical change that year: the installation on September 7 of a statue near the Captain Morgan Club on Addison honoring Billy Williams, who after his playing career has been a Cubs coach and special adviser for decades. Although the Hall of Fame outfielder never enjoyed the same adoration as Ernie Banks or Ron Santo, Cubs fans revere the soft-spoken Williams for his consistency, workmanlike attitude, and frequent bursts of greatness. Williams played 1,117 consecutive games from 1963 through 1970—a National League record until 1983. He made six All-Star squads and twice finished second in NL Most Valuable Player voting. The Cubs retired his number 26 in 1987, the year he entered the Hall of Fame.

NEW OWNER ON THE BLOCK

Concurrent with the Toyota sign developments, the Ricketts family revealed in May 2010 that the Cubs had made a capital investment in a rooftop club at 3621 North Sheffield, past the park's right-field wall. This went far beyond the 2004 deal, in which the Cubs were continuing to receive 17 percent of all rooftop revenues; now, the Cubs were active partners with one of their former enemies.

The complexity of the situation became apparent in the next month, when the Cubs filed a lawsuit (which is still pending) against the owners of the 3621 club, to collect some $211,000 owed to them from the 2009 season. The owners of the club, Dean Bravos and Lee Gramatis—the latter involved in sports bars and Wrigley rooftops for years—claimed penury and had shut down for 2010. (*Tom* Gramatis, proprietor of several rooftop clubs, was the lone holdout in the original rooftop deal and was the loser in the "Toyota sign" controversy.)

The relationship between the team and the neighborhood had changed significantly since 2004. In addition to buying into 3621 North Sheffield, the Cubs have also received permission from the city to close down the streets beyond the left-field and right-field walls on game days. This decision costs the city money and personnel. The Cubs can legitimately be said to be taking over the neighborhood—while the city subsidizes the safety and order of the enterprise. One positive is that the Cubs put a free bicycle-parking structure in place in the parking lot bordering Waveland Avenue.

Another related development took place on November 18, 2010, as the Ricketts family closed a deal to buy the land on West Clark Street north of Addison. The owners—the McDonald's corporation—had been operating a restaurant on the site for more than two decades, doing roaring business. While the family bought the land, McDonald's continues to run its fast-food outlet and, as part of the deal, must be included in any future site changes. Within a year of the deal, the Cubs built a souvenir shop on the northwest corner of Clark and Addison, hoping to get a larger piece of the outside-the-park cap/jersey/tchotchke business heretofore dominated by other entrepreneurs.

Two days after closing the real estate deal, the Cubs made some money by hosting a football game, the first held at Wrigley since the Bears decamped in 1970. Northwestern University and the University of Illinois met in a Big Ten matchup on November 20—the first time they had smashed helmets at Wrigley (then called Cubs Park) since 1923.

The marketing opportunities seemed almost too good to be true; who wouldn't want to capitalize on an intense regional matchup, televised nationally on ESPN U, involving young people with appetites for alcohol? Temporarily repainting the front-entrance marquee purple, Northwestern's color, was perhaps not the best artistic decision, however.

Northwestern groundskeeper Randy Stoneberger and his Cubs counterpart, Roger Baird, collaborated in the early fall to set up the playing surface, laying out the field with one end zone in the right-field corner and the other near the Cubs' dugout. (When the Bears roared at Wrigley, the field stretched from the first-base dugout to left field, with temporary stands installed in center and right fields.) There was just one problem, which anyone familiar with the field from the Bears days would recall: there was no way to configure the field so that it would be regulation size. Back in the day, the league had given Bears owner/coach George Halas special dispensation to have end zones some two yards shorter than those in other stadiums. But the rules of the National Collegiate Athletic Association (NCAA) read that areas surrounding the end zones must be twelve feet long "except in stadiums where total field surface does not permit. In these stadiums, the limit lines shall not be less than six feet from the sidelines and end lines." Wrigley's dimensions did not present nearly enough space to meet this requirement, and the installation of special purple padding on the right-field wall apparently did not sway the NCAA. One goalpost actually had to be placed in the home-run basket attached to the right-field wall, and in one area the padded wall ran into the border of the end zone.

Oddly, this became an issue only a couple of days before kick-off. On Friday, November 19, the NCAA and both universities' athletic departments announced that the offensive team would be pointed toward the west end zone (near the Cubs dugout) *on every possession*. Cubs president Crane Kenney, quickly attempting to wipe any egg from his face, stated that all the relevant Big Ten, Northwestern, and University of Illinois officials had walked through the field several times and had not previously voiced any complaints. Clearly, the late decision to have the players make this unusual shift lends support to his claim.

While the NCAA's decision may have increased safety, having the game move in only one direction looked foolish. Despite the income gained by all parties, it will take some sort of adjustment for the NCAA to allow more college football at Wrigley Field.

GOODBYE, RON

Wrigley Field had now hosted hockey and football, as well as concerts. The Dave Matthews Band played in 2010, and Paul McCartney held two rapturously received shows the following year. Each show required City Council approval. The concerts ramped up in 2012; Roger Waters performed *The Wall* on June 8, and the next night country superstar Alan Jackson took the stage. Bruce Springsteen's two shows that Labor Day weekend received rave reviews. Wrigley Field's grounds crew deserves much credit for keeping the field itself in great shape despite the increase in non-baseball activity.

But Wrigley Field is still defined by its baseball legends, one of whom, longtime third baseman and broadcaster Ron Santo, died on December 3, 2010, from complications of diabetes and bladder cancer. He was seventy. Given Santo's longtime health issues, his death was not unexpected, but it still resulted in an outpouring of love and grief from local fans. A week later, a mass was held for a capacity gathering at Holy Name Cathedral. He was cremated and his ashes spread over Wrigley Field.

The Cubs officially commemorated Santo on August 10, 2011,

unveiling a statue of the nine-time All-Star and six-time Gold Glover in action. The statue, similar in style to those of Harry Caray, Ernie Banks, and Billy Williams, was placed near the right-field corner entrance. Harry Caray's statue was moved to the bleacher entrance. Pat Hughes, Santo's broadcast partner for fifteen seasons, took part in the ceremony along with Williams, Banks, and Fergie Jenkins. WGN radio and the Cubs hired Keith Moreland, a popular member of the 1984 squad, as Santo's permanent radio replacement in early 2011.

Santo had become a perennial near-miss in the Hall of Fame voting. The Veterans Committee finally got around to enshrining him, a more than deserving candidate, in December 2011. It was almost as if the committee wanted to deny him the spot until he had died. It was a bittersweet moment for many a Cubs fan.

CAN'T ANYBODY HERE PLAY THIS GAME?

Ron Santo was not the only person to leave the ballpark after 2010. Attendance overall had fallen each year since 2008, and by the end of the miserable 2012 campaign turnstile spins had dropped by more than five thousand per game from five years earlier. Worse yet, season-ticket holders were staying away even after having bought tickets; the amount of empty seats embarrassed the franchise.

Once it was clear that the 2011 season was lost, Tom Ricketts, who had been evaluating personnel and operations, cleaned house. General Manager Jim Hendry and manager Mike Quade were relieved of their duties, and over the next year other longtime employees either resigned or were cashiered. Hendry had gone all in on the 2007 and 2008 teams, but neither team had survived the first round of the playoffs. As those players declined or were traded, Hendry seemed to struggle to define a rebuilding plan.

Also gone following the conclusion of the 2011 campaign was the Cubs' sixty-one-year relationship with Old Style beer, a ballpark staple and WGN radio sponsor. No more would the phrase "pure brewed . . . from God's Country" be heard on Cubs broadcasts. The Cubs, while continuing to sell Old Style, added higher-octane craft brews to their menu, beers that command higher prices than more common domestics.

Brought in to fix the on-field mess and create a new long-term plan was Theo Epstein, the former wunderkind responsible—some said—for the success in recent years of the Boston Red Sox, although the job he inherited in Chicago was far more difficult. When Epstein took over in Boston, the team already had a significant talent base. Epstein, hired as president of baseball operations, with Jed Hoyer as general manager, has generally kept quiet on ballpark issues, leaving the lobbying to Tom Ricketts. Epstein has enough problems on the field.

A BIG BOARD

The physical redevelopment of the stadium continued, with significant changes to the right-field bleachers for 2012, including an elevated patio (with tables and a beer stand) in the "s-curve" section and, underneath it, a new LED scoreboard atop the right-field wall. The patio section is available for groups of fifty, one hundred, or a hundred and fifty only, with each entrant paying an all-inclusive food and beverage fee. These new features required elevating the bleachers in order to ensure that fans could still see the field.

The seven-foot-tall, seventy-five-foot-wide scoreboard caused some problems early in the season for opposing pitchers warming up in their bullpen; the lights of the board made it hard for them to see return throws from their catchers. Adjustments to the lighting were made. In a nice nod to the past, the typography used on the board, and some of the graphics, were similar to those designed by former P. K. Wrigley employee Otis Shepard.

New ads appeared on the metal doors in the outfield, including one from the Target department store chain, while Audi ponied up to sponsor a fourteen-person suite down the right-field line. Out of the usual lines of sight, a second batting-cage area was installed under the left-field bleachers, augmenting the one below the right-field bleachers. The Cubs also moved their corporate offices to the building at Clark and Waveland that had previously housed the concession headquarters and Wrigley Field Premium. While the offices inside the ballpark are now meant to be empty, at least one adjunct member of the Cubs game-day entertainment staff set up shop in a vacated space, hoping not to be noticed.

NOT SO SUPER

These changes were significant, but the Rickettses' biggest push to transform Wrigley was yet to come. Early in the 2012 season, the Cubs asked for $300 million in public funds to fund a significant sprucing-up project. The Ricketts family hoped the City Council would agree to spend $150 million of city amusement taxes on a park renovation and issue another $150 million in bonds to cover the rest of the expenses. The Cubs also asked the city to relax Wrigley Field's landmark status, presumably to allow the team to explore installing a huge electronic scoreboard.

Spending three hundred million bucks on the Cubs wasn't going to be an easy sell either in the city or with the state, which has serious budget problems.

Then, unfortunately, Joe Ricketts—family patriarch and outspoken conservative—made the process even more complicated when his political interests antagonized Mayor Rahm Emanuel. During the 2012 election campaign, Ricketts became associated with a proposal to use his Super Political Action Committee to carry out attack ads against President Barack Obama—whom Emanuel had served as White House chief of staff from 2008 to 2010. Ricketts Sr. denied that he had endorsed the plan or even had anything to do with it, but Emanuel used the ill-timed revelation to put the already thorny issue of Wrigley Field refurbishment on the back burner.

The idea behind asking for public money in the first place, said the Ricketts family, was to allow them to spend their money on free agents and organizational infrastructure, rather than park repairs and upkeep. The Rickettses are wealthy but not unlimitedly so, so there is a certain logic here; nevertheless, it sits oddly alongside Republican Party tenets of personal self-sufficiency and low government spending. The Cubs, after all, are a private business, of the sort that, it is said, want nothing from government and expect to be left alone. The Rickettses' logic becomes all the shakier when the family that doesn't want to pay for its business's upkeep does manage to fund a Super Political Action Committee.

This is not to say that the city, the state, and the team couldn't make a deal that would benefit all parties. Perhaps the state should propose that fans be awarded voting and earning shares of the team in exchange for spending tax dollars on a private corporation's needs. Perhaps the Cubs could institute a free ticket program for local children. Maybe residents of Chicago, or Illinois in general, should get reductions on their ticket prices. Fair's fair, after all.

Of course, the Cubs have attempted over the last few years to show tangibly their appreciation for the neighborhood and concern for public well-being. The open gate in the right-field bleacher wall is one such thing; the public bike park and the Rink at Wrigley are others. The team does help promote some local businesses, and every fall the Cubs thank area residents with an invitation-only postseason event at which fans get to, among other things, play catch in the outfield. CubsCare, the franchise's charity arm, has done much good work in the greater Chicago community. But these are gestures, not multimillion-dollar commitments.

FUTBOL

The battle over the next round of renovations to Wrigley Field was only beginning. In the meantime, new nonbaseball events and promotions continued to be developed. One of these, on

FIGURE 30. Wrigley Field shown converted for the 2012 Friendly at the Confines soccer match. The dirt infield has been temporarily covered with sod. (Credit: Wikipedia Commons)

Sunday, June 22, 2012, was an exhibition game (or "friendly") between two touring squads from European Leagues: Italian club AS Roma and Zaglebie Lubin, from Poland. The park hadn't hosted a soccer game since the Chicago Sting had taken the field from 1978 through 1984—one of five locations they played at over fifteen years.

As had been the case when "Der Sting" played at Wrigley, officials set the goal nets for the 2012 Friendly at the Confines soccer match parallel to the right-field wall and the third-base dugout (fig. 30). This gave left-field bleacher fans and those down the right-field line the best full view of the pitch. One new wrinkle, however, was the conversion of the infield dirt to full grass, a privilege not afforded the Sting. More than twenty-two thousand attended the game, which ended in Roma's easy 4–0 victory. Fans had a good time, but reviews of the pitch were mediocre. Jack McCarthy of the June 23 *Tribune* quoted Roma's goalie, Maarten Stekelenburg, as saying, "I've played on better fields."

LIGHT UP THE NIGHT

Concerts, soccer matches, and corporate events aside, the Cubs also hope to increase evening activity at Wrigley in the traditional way: night games. With the current cap of thirty per season scheduled to run out in 2016, the team let it be known that they would love to play more contests after dark.

In August 2012, the Lake View Citizens Council (LVCC) offered the Cubs a deal. The LVCC, which has the ears of city hall through its association with Alderman Tunney, proposed that the Cubs be allowed to schedule up to thirty-three night games per year as well as four "event nights," which could be expanded to six if the Cubs forfeited two night games. In addition, the LVCC would recommend that the City Council could forgo approving each concert. The only thing the Cubs would have to do is kick in some $200,000 a year—or $75,000 per event night—to a fund for neighborhood improvements. That's not even half a season's pay for a rookie middle reliever.

The roll call of concerts continued in 2013, as Pearl Jam and Jason Aldean headlined shows in July. The Pearl Jam show, which also featured Ernie Banks, suffered a rain delay, and with Alderman Tunney's permission ran till 2 A.M.

While most night games wrap up around ten o'clock or so, the 2012 Cubs—not otherwise a distinguished squad—did set a record in this regard on September 17. That night's 7:05 start between the Cubs and Pirates was delayed by rain. And more rain. And more rain. With the Pirates in the race for a wild-card playoff spot and no available off days left in the season, the game had to be played. So clubs, umpires, broadcasters, writers, and thousands of fans waited it out. The first pitch came at 10:42 P.M., the latest first pitch ever at the park. By the time the Pirates wrapped up a 3–0 win at 1:28 A.M. on September 18, only a few hundred fans were left in the stands for the latest *finish* ever at Wrigley. According to Paul Sullivan in the *Tribune* later that day, even Ronnie Wickers couldn't be bothered to utter a single "Cubs! Woo!"

SOMEONE KEEPS MOVING MY CHAIR

After the team staggered to a 61–101 finish—and after President Obama was handily reelected—the Cubs renovation plans came front and center once more in the off-season. And this time the public discussion really took off.

The club announced plans to reconfigure the box seats around home plate. The team petitioned the city's landmark commission to move the brick wall three feet toward home plate in order to wedge in fifty-six new chairs. At around $200 per game on a season ticket plan, just one of these seats generates more than $16,000 of revenue. On a perhaps related note, the team announced in October that bleacher tickets would cost less in 2013, but this drop was countered by expected gains from a reallocation of games played under the five season-ticket plans (Marquee, Platinum, Gold, Silver, and Bronze).

Moving the wall will shrink Wrigley's foul territory yet again, making it the smallest in the major leagues. But the move has an ancillary benefit, as the new configuration will allow for seats near the third-base dugout that can be moved to make way for a larger field when football teams wish to ply their trade at Wrigley. Having the Northwestern Wildcats, Notre Dame Fighting Irish, or other Midwest-identified team play a contest at Clark and Addison would raise capital as well as reinforce awareness of Wrigley as a multisport facility—the exact opposite of the tack the Tribune Company took in the 1980s to protect the aging ballpark.

The Cubs also announced their desire to bring back the Friday 3:05 starts that had been scheduled during the 1980s. Those starts brought in businesspeople and young singles looking to begin their weekends early and added some novelty to the schedule. It seems likely that the Ricketts family is motivated not by a love of all things eighties (Rubik's Cubes? *Thriller*?) but by their feeling that the fewer 1:20 starts they put on the calendar, the better. This and other changes were part of a long-term plan the club forged ahead with in 2013.

OBSCENE PROFITS?

Frustrated by an inability to get immediate approval for either their newest night game concept or a ballpark renovation initiative, the Cubs opened 2013 with veiled threats to build a new palace in suburban Rosemont, a move that locals greeted mostly with guffaws.

The team has consistently tied the need for more night games to its stated desire to fix Wrigley Field's infrastructure. But moaning about the park's poor condition hardly rings true; Ricketts and company have been free to fix Wrigley's facilities, flooring, walls, bathrooms, and girders at any time. Their refusal to do so until getting reassurance of increased ad revenue through new signage and extra night contests belies the fact that the franchise continues to be not just profitable, but—if such a thing exists—obscenely so.

Forbes, certainly no bastion of wild-eyed liberalism, rated the Cubs as baseball's most profitable franchise in its March 27, 2013, issue, also noting that once the team's current broadcast deals expire following the 2014 season, they will—either through new negotiations with a cable provider or, as rumored, the creation of a new team-run television network—earn even more than the $32.1 million operating income realized in 2012.

This fact, and the club's tepid rebuilding program, continued to keep Cubs a loser in the public relations battle, as attendance remained low during the early portion of 2013 while another patchwork club stumbled out of the gate.

MOVING TOWARD A SOLUTION

On April 15, the Cubs and City Hall announced that they had agreed, in principle, on a deal in which the club would spend some $300 million to improve Wrigley Field in exchange for the right to slate more night games, erect extra advertising signage, and create a $200 million plaza including a hotel/conference center, team offices, and a parking garage, all just north of Addison on Clark Street. One of the planned "improvements" is a Jumbotron-type scoreboard, which will display copious amounts of advertising. Whether this is actually an improvement is up to the individual customer. Another improvement that the club petitioned is the right to construct elevators at two locations outside of the stadium, one in the left-field corner and one near the right, possibly as ingress and egress sites for bleacher fans.

The Cubs also insisted on permission to sell advertising on the new buildings at Clark and Addison. While everyday entrepreneurs in Chicago are forced to pay fees to the city for each sign, awning, and entrance on their businesses, the Cubs will have free rein to vend out all available space on their properties, raising a strong possibility that the corner will begin to look more like Times Square than a residential area that happens to have a ballpark.

In addition, the Cubs—now allowed only to sell beer through the seventh inning during night games—petitioned to sell beer until the end of the seventh or 10:30 P.M., whichever is latest. At $8 per beer, even an extra five hundred beer sales per game for five night games would gross an additional $20,000.

Early in June, Chicago mayor Rahm Emanuel announced that the team, stuck on "just" thirty night games since 2004, could schedule thirty-five evening contests for 2014 and as many as forty-six for 2015. In addition, the team was also granted immediate permission to move six 1:20 or 12:05 games to 3:05. The city got a few bones in exchange, including approval of rainout re-scheduling dates, a limiting of Friday and Saturday night games to two per season, and the right to revoke some night games if the club were to schedule "too many" concerts. Still unsettled were details on the Cubs' desire to shut down streets around the park for festivals.

The main physical expansion, however, still required formal permission.

THE DIFFERENCE IS . . .

This proposed series of changes stood to make Wrigley, perhaps for the first time, unrecognizable to someone time traveling from 1914. It's not just about new scoreboards and an office building and hotel; everything is going to be different.

The current Captain Morgan club, near the right-field corner on Addison, is set to be expanded to a multistory restaurant and bar. The build-out will also provide some space for a new visitors' clubhouse. In addition, the Cubs want to convert the space between Clark Street and the ballpark—now used for parking and the Rink at Wrigley—to a plaza that could be used for various food or memorabilia markets in the spring, summer, and fall, as well as the rink in the winter. The plaza will contain large video boards and fifty-foot-tall obelisks with LED advertising.

The ballpark itself will also be altered. The Cubs intend to build new clubhouses, install batting cages under the grandstands, enlarge the luxury boxes, and expand the current outdoor upper-deck seating and concessions area, now located behind the press box, over the entire Clark and Addison marquee. (Plans to return the marquee to its 1930s look—including windows, terra cotta, and wrought iron—drew some applause from observers.)

The team also wants a standing deck in foul territory past the left-field wall, a ribbon board above the batter's eye that will present rotating advertisements (in addition to those shown on the Jumbotron and the board in right field), and a party deck in the middle of what are now the upper-tier center-field bleachers.

Wrigley's already small foul territory will shrink as well when the club adds new front-row seating in back of home plate and down both base lines.

TUNNEY COMES OUT SWINGING

Just prior to the city's scheduled hearings on the expansion in late June, Forty-Fourth Ward alderman Tom Tunney weighed in. On June 27, Tunney—as always, forced to walk a tightrope between the neighborhood at large and the rooftop owners, whose views aren't necessarily held by most area residents—informed the Cubs that he would not support the overall plan without a one-third reduction in the size of the planned Jumbotron. The alderman also objected to a proposed one thousand-square-foot right-field advertising sign, averring that it should be 35 percent smaller. Both scoreboard and ad sign would block the views of rooftop club owners.

Tunney also objected to certain parts of the proposed hotel, which the Cubs hoped to build on the land currently hosting a McDonald's. The alderman stated that the new structure and its proposed outdoor party deck would bother residents of Patterson Street, a small thoroughfare a block north of Addison. In addition, Tunney argued against the Cubs' desire for a bridge spanning Clark Street just north of Addison. The bridge would connect the hotel to a multistory office building to be built between the ballpark and Clark Street just south of Waveland. That building, featuring a large clock tower, would contain team offices, shops, and, perhaps, other rentable office space. One nice touch has the Cubs proposing to show movies for neighborhood residents on a video board attached to a side of the office building.

The concept of an open bridge raised some legitimate what-ifs. Would a drunken bridge-walker drop or throw something onto the street below? Could someone fall off? With alcohol involved, those possibilities are more than remote.

In response, Cubs management held to its earlier claim that the entire plan would fall apart if the club were required to make any further concessions. But eventually, the club agreed to shear the proposed right-field billboard to 650 square feet and to build a Jumbotron of "only" fifty-seven hundred square feet, giving Tunney a small victory. Once the Cubs gave a bit on these elements, the city's Commission on Chicago Landmarks approved their construction.

Then, on July 19, the Cubs announced that the Chicago Plan Commission had signed off on the $500 million renovation project. The deal came down thus. First, the Cubs agreed to consider enclosing the bridge across Clark Street. Alderman Tunney then dropped his objection to the bridge's construction. Second, the entrance to the hotel, while still on Patterson, would be moved closer to Clark Street. Tunney and the Cubs agreed to table the issue of the hotel's proposed outdoor deck. Nobody questioned whether the Cubs should be able to advertise on any parts of the property they wish. In addition, nobody bothered to ask why a previous landmarks commission agreement, which guaranteed the "uninterrupted sweep of the bleachers," could be simply ignored in favor of new advertising boards.

On July 24, the City Council approved the overall plan, while holding several items open for further debate, including new streetlights and how to locate the entry for the proposed hotel properly. Perhaps the most important unresolved argument is the relationship between the rooftop club owners and the Cubs. The team very much wants to keep the rooftop owners from suing over the breaking of their previous agreement. One idea to mollify the rooftop owners is to extend the right-field wall farther onto Sheffield Avenue, which would allow the installation of the new advertising board in a location that would less affect the views from the right-field rooftops. The Cubs would require the rooftop club owners to promise not to sue the team if such a move were undertaken. And even if the two sides agree on this, it is not obvious that the ballpark's profile could or should be extended in that way.

Beginning sometime soon, the entire corner of Clark and

Addison will be transformed into something dramatically different. While this frightens some neighborhood residents, it is hardly a new idea. From the seminary to the coal company to Weeghman Park, the Yum Yum Donuts Shop, the McDonald's, the skating rink, and the endless procession of new bars and restaurants in the area, Clark and Addison has rarely been stagnant.

NOTHING EVER ENDS

When all is said and done, what ultimately remains is Wrigley Field itself—an oasis of purity, its supporters say, in the increasingly polluted world of sports. Wrigley's essence—the ivy, clean sight lines, mammoth scoreboard, grass field, bullpen mounds, center-field hitting background, intimate seating, neighborhood high-rises, gorgeous blue Lake Michigan looming east of the park, and trains rumbling by—might as well as have escaped from a fairy tale, they say.

But the reality is quite different. Wrigley Field is, in economic terms, thoroughly modern, as it always has been, trading on nostalgia while making plenty of room for current business practices. Wrigley Field, for many years unburdened by signage, now sports advertising on the outfield walls and all over its message boards. There are no fairytale entries in the ledgers—only red marks.

The real difference is in ticketing policy. The team has shifted from serving a democratic customer base to serving a higher-income, largely white, business-driven clientele, with only a few refunded tickets available for general admission on the day of the game. This strategy is a conscious repudiation of a ticketing philosophy the Cubs had held for more than sixty years. Were they still alive, William and P. K. Wrigley, who owned the team from 1920 through 1977, would probably be aghast to see their philosophies, which helped build a fanatical customer base, discarded like gum wrappers. Then again, they'd probably recover fairly quickly when presented with the balance sheets.

It is also no longer heaven to play at Wrigley Field, especially if you're on the opposing team. A July 2, 2003, *Sports Illustrated* poll of more than five hundred major league players named Wrigley Field the game's worst playing surface and Wrigley Field's visitors' clubhouse the second worst in the majors.

And yet . . . with plenty of reasons to be cynical, why are even the most hard-bitten baseball bugs in love with Wrigley Field? Why do sober adults dissolve into childlike paroxysms of ecstasy when entering the park? Why do we feel that such a place stands for the past?

One reason could be that the park has been open longer than most current fans have been alive. Most of the important changes to Wrigley, the ones that made the park look like it does today, don't threaten fans' emotional ownership of the park because those changes occurred more than seventy years ago. There may not be anyone alive who remembers how the place looked in the early and middle 1920s, with only one deck. Few if any fans can recall what the park looked like prior to the ivy being planted. Most fans don't even remember what Wrigley was like before the luxury boxes or television monitors were installed. It's already been twenty-five years since lights were strapped to the roof of the upper deck.

Gradual, rather than radical, change has been the rule during the park's long life. It was constructed in 1914. The upper decks were added in 1927 and 1928. The ivy and the iconic scoreboard followed in 1937. Gradually, wooden seats were added, removed, reconfigured, moved, curved in toward the field, and eventually replaced with plastic chairs, which were soon fitted with cup holders bearing advertising slogans. The basket was added to the outfield wall in 1970. The outfield catwalks were converted for seating in the 1980s. A press box was added to the upper deck in 1989, with luxury boxes constructed in the old press box space. The process of latching the light towers to the park was completed in 1988.

It's only by looking closely at the park and its history that one can see the nature of the changes at Wrigley Field and how those changes have served to build an image of constancy and steadfastness against the encroachment of modernity. It's taken a lot of money and a lot of time to make Wrigley look so unpretentious—or, to paraphrase Dolly Parton, "I had to get mighty rich to be able to sing like I was poor."

And rich the Cubs' owners and players have become from Wrigley Field. Bleacher seats—literally slats without seat backs—ballooned in price from $2 to $30 in just two decades. By 2012, single-game ticket prices had become subject to a complex algorithm that factored in probable scarcity, time of year, and game designation. In some cases, the Budweiser Bleacher patio tickets cost $120. Corporate luxury boxes, constructed directly in the sight lines of seats in the rear of the lower grandstand, block the view of fly balls. Season ticket plans have been gradually rewritten to be affordable only to the wealthiest of patrons. All of this went down as the gap increased between rich and poor in America.

And the Cubs' financial aspirations have rubbed off on the neighborhood. The advent of cable television made Wrigley Field a destination spot for visitors from all over the world. Ticket resale agencies have opened up around the park, including the one owned by the Cubs themselves, and on the web. Some of these sites, primarily StubHub, allow fans to post unused tickets and resell them, which at least makes some sense. In addition, fans do have the opportunity to buy cheaper tickets if they don't mind going to less important games or those played on weekdays.

The rooftops of surrounding apartment buildings, used long ago by the building residents to catch some sun while watching the game from a distant perch, have now become private clubs where the rich few pay to sit in specially constructed bleachers. The wealthy proprietors of such clubs garnered enough favor with local politicians that, incredibly, they became players in negotiations over Wrigley Field itself.

Some neighborhood residents and community groups, whose property values have expanded because of the development and the housing scarcity resulting from Wrigley Field's popularity, complain about their gift horse, looking for concessions from the Cubs rather than thanking their lucky stars that they live in such a desirable area.

Lake View once was working class, a neighborhood of small houses, three-flats, factories, a few bars, and a big ballpark that people came to when they had free time. When the Cubs were good, the fans came; when they weren't, the fans didn't come nearly so often. At times, the area was seedy. But even when the club wasn't good, the park was at least clean, safe, and—aside from some sections full of gamblers—family oriented, so generations of Cubs fans were raised on the idea of fun at the ballpark rather than on the expectation of watching a winning team. It was an inexpensive place to spend an afternoon and watch baseball, and the combination of sunshine, baseball, green grass, and fun was unmatched, even at Comiskey on the South Side.

But now Wrigley Field is an industry unto itself. It is no longer inexpensive. Baseball often seems to be the last thing on the mind of many of the park's patrons. In fact, the Cubs seem to thrill in making baseball a momentary distraction from their true, if unstated, purpose: milking fans out of as much money as possible. Even with all their capital, the Cubs have been unable to put together a consistently winning club. North Side fans and players remain lovable losers as their owners sit pretty.

Despite the encroachment of advertising into the park, beyond the flashing lights and loud piped-in music (of which there is still less than at almost any other sports arena), beyond the greed and stress inherent in today's professional sports landscape, being at Wrigley Field is still a great experience. It has green grass. It has good sight lines. It has plenty of different kinds of food and beverages. It still has Gary Pressy at the organ. And it has baseball, still the greatest game of them all.

Fans still come to revel in Wrigley Field's atmosphere. It's a living wonderland for baseball fans, one that is so grand—surely larger than the team that it houses—that it has become shrouded in myth and legend. Most of Wrigley Field's patrons seem to like to feel that they've stepped into baseball's past. The truth is, however, that if the sport is to again capture America's imagination, the particular retro-styled charm of Wrigley Field may be baseball's future. It is uncertain, however, whether the Cubs, the city of Chicago, and the residents of Lake View can hold together the magic of Wrigley Field long enough to save the game.

ACKNOWLEDGMENTS

This book benefited from the wisdom of many friends and colleagues. George Castle remains one of the best baseball beat writers around. He provided entertaining and edifying stories to the first edition of this book. In addition, he did research, conducted interviews, shared ideas, and lent me articles and photos that taught me about Lake View and the fans in the right-field bleachers during the 1970s. Thank you, George, again. Someday we'll see that ticker-tape parade.

Raymond D. Kush wrote, in the mid-1970s, the first serious work about the construction of Wrigley Field. This piece, published in the 1981 issue of the Society for American Baseball Research (SABR)'s *Baseball Research Journal* (vol. 10), paved the way for much ensuing Wrigley Field research. Meeting Ray, and sharing in his knowledge, was a pleasure, and he selflessly provided notes, edits, and reminiscences.

Unofficial but indispensable Cubs historian Ed Hartig lent me his well-researched Wrigley Field chronology back in 2003. This information helped me verify dates and pointed me in some new directions. Ed also gave feedback that allowed me to present a more accurate work.

I am lucky to have good friends. Gary Gillette is always more than generous with his time, feedback, ideas, and friendship. For his good nature, wisdom about baseball, the pizzas he and Vicki Gillette make, and the kindnesses of their kids Kamil and Karolina, I will be forever grateful. Thanks, guys.

Pete Palmer was, as always, very helpful. I thank him. Mark Caro, "Disco Dan" Epstein, Cecilia Garibay, Thom Henninger, Frank Kras, John Shea II, and Tom Shea—irreplaceable every one—read chapters and contributed valuable feedback. Several of these people have written tremendous books of their own, which I urge you to check out.

The Hungerdungers—the aforementioned Mr. Caro, Pat Byrnes, Lou Carlozo, Jon Eig, Jim Powers, and Bardball.com's James Finn Garner—provided the type of fellowship and feedback that only fellow scriveners can.

Society for American Baseball Research members Reed Howard, Bob McConnell, Peggy Gripshover, Dave Smith, David Vincent, and Stew Thornley shared information and research. I advise anyone who enjoys this book to learn more about this great organization. Of all the SABR members who helped, perhaps my greatest appreciation goes to Walt Wilson, who sent several generous letters including corrections, clippings, and elaborations on both small and large points. Walt and so many others like him make SABR truly special.

Thanks also to Sharon Pannozzo, Chuck Wasserstrom, and Samantha Newby, all formerly of the Chicago Cubs' media relations department.

The staff of the Chicago Public Library was helpful. Gloria Price made the archives of the Lake View Historical Society available to me. I also benefited from the resources of the mighty Mid-Continent Public Library, the Saint Louis Public Library, the Library of Congress in Washington, DC, Loyola University Chicago Cudahy Library, the Saint Paul Public Library, and the late, lamented *Sporting News* Research Center in St. Louis, where I was helped by Steve Gietschier and Jim Maier.

Karen Chasteen of the Richmond County School District in Richmond, Indiana, contributed information about Charles Weeghman. Denise Young of the William Wrigley Company deserves thanks for sharing articles from the company's files.

Andie Giafaglione has taken many wonderful photos of Wrigley Field, some of which are included in this book. Thanks, AG.

John Horne of the National Baseball Hall of Fame and Museum made acquiring photos an easy and enjoyable process. I appreciate his assistance.

The awesome Ronna Zack supplied me with architectural plats of several Wrigleyville streets from various eras ranging back to 1894, for which I am very grateful.

Thanks also to Dennis McClendon of Chicago CartoGraphics for his map of Wrigleyville.

Thanks also to George Castle's interviewees: the late Martin "Red" Mottlow, the late Carmella Hartigan, and, above all, the late E. R. "Salty" Saltwell, who might have known more about Wrigley Field than anyone.

Timothy Mennel of the University of Chicago Press edited this updated manuscript and shepherded me through the contract process. He was ably assisted throughout by Russ Damian. Yvonne Zipter was everything one could ask for—and more—in a manuscript editor. I am grateful to be associated with the University of Chicago and thank Tim, Russ, Yvonne, the University, Lauren Salas, Ellen Gibson, and the Press's sales and marketing staff for their belief in this book.

Christina Kahrl, Don McKeon, and Julie Kimmel midwifed the original edition of this book for Potomac Books in 2004. I thank them.

I appreciate my family and friends' encouragement of my work. My mother, Marion Light, fed my baseball fanaticism; she even accompanied my brothers and me to the thoroughly out-of-control Opening Day 1977 at Wrigley Field. My dad, John Shea II, took his three sons to their first game and taught me about baseball. My brothers John III and Tom have shared with me countless baseball experiences, many of them at Clark and Addison.

Many people in the game have shown generosity with their time and knowledge. I'd like especially to thank Pat Hughes, Bart Johnson, Bill Harford, Grover "Deacon" Jones, Ferguson Jenkins, and Jeff Huson, who allowed me to "shadow" him for a few days many years ago in a true act of kindness.

I have had great times at the ballpark with Sheila Spica, Toby Dye and Kitty Knecht, Carlos Orellana, Gary Pressy, Jack O'Regan, Gary Skoog, Steve Leventhal, Phil Meyers, John Thorn, Cecilia

Tan, Kevin Cuddihy, Anthony Salazar, Tara Krieger, Cheryl Raye-Stout, John Andersen, Gord Fitzgerald, Bob Purse, Joe Stillwell and the other guys from STATS, and Agustin, Adrian, Christina, Liz, Marco Antonio, and Carolina Margaret Garibay. (Soon, Ava, soon.)

A toast, also, to absent baseball friends and colleagues: Greg Spira, Larry Epke, Wilbur "Moose" Johnson, Larry Gross, Curt Motton, Lenny Yochim, Carolina Garibay Luna, Harry Caray, and Ron Santo. I miss all of you.

My biggest thanks, however, are due to Cecilia Garibay. Our second date, in 1982, was at Wrigley Field. I spent most of the game watching her.

BIBLIOGRAPHY

Note: Citations for newspapers and all other periodicals appear in the text.

Angle, Paul. *The Memoir of a Modest Man*. Skokie, IL: Rand McNally, 1975.

Banks, Ernie, with Jim Enright. *Mr. Cub*. Chicago: Follett, 1971.

Benson, Michael. *Ballparks of North America*. Jefferson, NC: McFarland and Company, 1989.

Brown, Warren. *The Chicago Cubs*. New York: G. P. Putnam's Sons, 1946.

Browne, Lois. *The Girls of Summer*. Toronto: HarperCollins, 1992.

Castle, George. *The Million-to-One Team*. Dallas: Taylor, 2000.

Chieger, Bob. *The Cubbies*. New York: Simon and Schuster, 1987.

Claerbaut, David. *Durocher's Cubs*. Dallas: Taylor, 2000.

Clark, Steven Bedell. *The Lakeview Saga, 1837–1985*. Chicago: Lake View Trust and Savings Bank, 1985.

Duis, Perry. *Challenging Chicago*. Champaign: University of Illinois Press, 1998.

Enright, Jim. *Chicago Cubs*. New York: Macmillan/McGraw-Hill, 1975.

Gershman, Michael. *Diamonds*. New York: Houghton Mifflin, 1999.

Gifford, Barry. *The Neighborhood of Baseball*. New York: Dutton, 1981.

Gold, Eddie, and Art Ahrens. *Day by Day in Chicago Cubs History*. Champaign, IL: Human Kinetics, 1982.

Golenbock, Peter. *Wrigleyville*. New York: Macmillan, 2007.

Green, Stephen, and Mark Jacob. *Wrigley Field*. New York: McGraw-Hill, 1982.

Hageman, Bill. *Baseball between the Wars*. New York: McGraw-Hill, 1981.

Hartel, William. *A Day at the Park*. Coal Valley, IL: Quality Sports, 1995.

Holtzman, Jerome. *The Jerome Holtzman Baseball Reader*. Chicago: Triumph Books, 1993.

Ibach, Bob, Ned Colletti, and Stephen Green. *Cub Fan Mania*. New York: Leisure Press, 1983.

Jenkins, Ferguson, with George Vass, *Like Nobody Else*. Washington, DC: Henry Regnery, 1973.

Kruse, Karen. *A Chicago Firehouse*. Chicago: Arcadia, 2001.

Langford, Jim. *The Game Is Never Over*. South Bend, IN: Hardwood Press, 1982.

Levitt, Daniel. *The Battle That Forged Modern Baseball*. Lanham, MD: Ivan R. Dee, 2012.

Lowry, Philip. *Green Cathedrals*. New York: Walker and Company, 2006.

Okkonen, Mark, and the Society for American Baseball Research (SABR). *The Federal League of 1914–15*. Cleveland: SABR, 1989.

Pacyga, Dominic, and Ellen Skerrett. *Chicago, City of Neighborhoods*. Chicago: Loyola University Press, 1986.

Pietrusza, David. *Judge and Jury*. Dallas: Taylor, 1998.

———. *Major Leagues*. Jefferson, NC: McFarland and Company, 1991.

Santo, Ron, with Randy Minkoff. *For Love of Ivy*. Chicago: Bonus Books, 1993.

Society for American Baseball Research (SABR). *Baseball Research Journal, 1979*. Cooperstown, NY: SABR, 1979.

———. *Baseball Research Journal, 1981*. Cooperstown, NY: SABR, 1981.

———. *The National Pastime, Spring 1985*. Cooperstown, NY: SABR, 1985.

Sporting News. *Take Me Out to the Ball Park*. Saint Louis: Sporting News, 1987.

Talley, Rick. *The Cubs of '69*. New York: McGraw-Hill, 1990.

Theodore, John. *Baseball's Natural*. Carbondale: Southern Illinois University Press, 2002.

Veeck, Bill, with Ed Linn. *Veeck—as in Wreck*. New York: G. P. Putnam's Sons, 1962.

Wheeler, Lonnie. *Bleachers*. New York: Contemporary Books, 1989.

Wilbert, Warren. *A Cunning Kind of Play*. Jefferson, NC: McFarland and Company, 2002.

Wood, Bob. *Dodger Dogs to Fenway Franks*. New York: McGraw-Hill, 1988.

INDEX

NOTE: Page numbers followed by *f* indicate a figure.